TINY GIANTS

nate powell

Soft Skull Press
71 Bond St
Brooklyn NY 11217
www.softskull.com

Printed in Canada

Distributed to the booktrade by Publishers Group West
www.pgw.com | 1 800 788 3123

design by Charles Orr

ISBN 1-887128-56-5

Contents

Introduction

If you're picking up this book, chances are you've already seen Nate's stories and art in *Walkie Talkie*. If not, you should be. I was first shown Nate's stuff by Top Shelf publisher Chris Staros, who said something to the effect that Nate was "one of the best-kept secrets in comics." Now, I've heard crap like that before, and I totally disagree with Chris. What secret? Diana Schutz over at Dark Horse also knew of Nate's stuff, and raved.

But don't JUST take our words for it.

Tiny Giants collects Nate's earlier work, and when I look at Nate's story and art, I get the same spacious, bold feeling of design and blacks I felt in the first fifty *Cerebus*es. And his faces and figures recall early Wrightson and . . . well, the name and influence game gets pretty silly after that. Nate is simply Nate. His own voice, an uncommonly strong one for his age. His stories present the same dreamy quality set against stark, barren reality that Nate himself possessed when I met him for the first time. Charming. Unsettling. Insightful and deceptively quirky—just like Nate. I could go on and on about why you should give this book a try, but just read, soak up, enjoy, discover . . .

. . . for yourself.

Sam Kieth

Author's Note

oh my, these stories certainly aren't true. mostly, that is. people and places and what we said all switched up but in there somewhere. we can't help but to speak in code, fumbling with each other's own stories, maybe steeped in reference but looking to verbalize "yes! i know what you mean! i remember exactly what it's like!" naturally there's a good deal of arrogance in that embrace.

as creators and artists and narrators and advocates, it's important to mind how we translate our inspirations—how we incorporate the people around us into our document of human experience. my stories speak from a limited perspective and it is crucial to accept and deal with the limitations of subjective personal narrative.

all likenesses in my stories are homages. representation is done lovingly but with an awareness of potential misunderstanding and discomfort.

the stories in this book are from late 1998 to early 2003, and they function as a body of work to document efforts to develop a consistent and responsible voice, as well as to search for better ways to stitch together a hundred vignettes with solid and more relevant content. there is much failure from which to grow and learn.

this is not a complete collection, and does not include any collaborations with author and long-time friend Emily Heiple. a very sincere thanks to her for inspirations and challenges, for helping shape each other to better write our own lives as we go. very much love and gratitude go to Mara Golubovich, Art Middleton, and everyone in providence who works up a sweat for what they love, Mike Lierly, Nate Wilson, and all in the Soophie family. All aforementioned are material collaborators and the very best of spirits.

as usual, i feel like i'm going to explode.

love, nate powell[*]
providence, rhode island
spring 2003

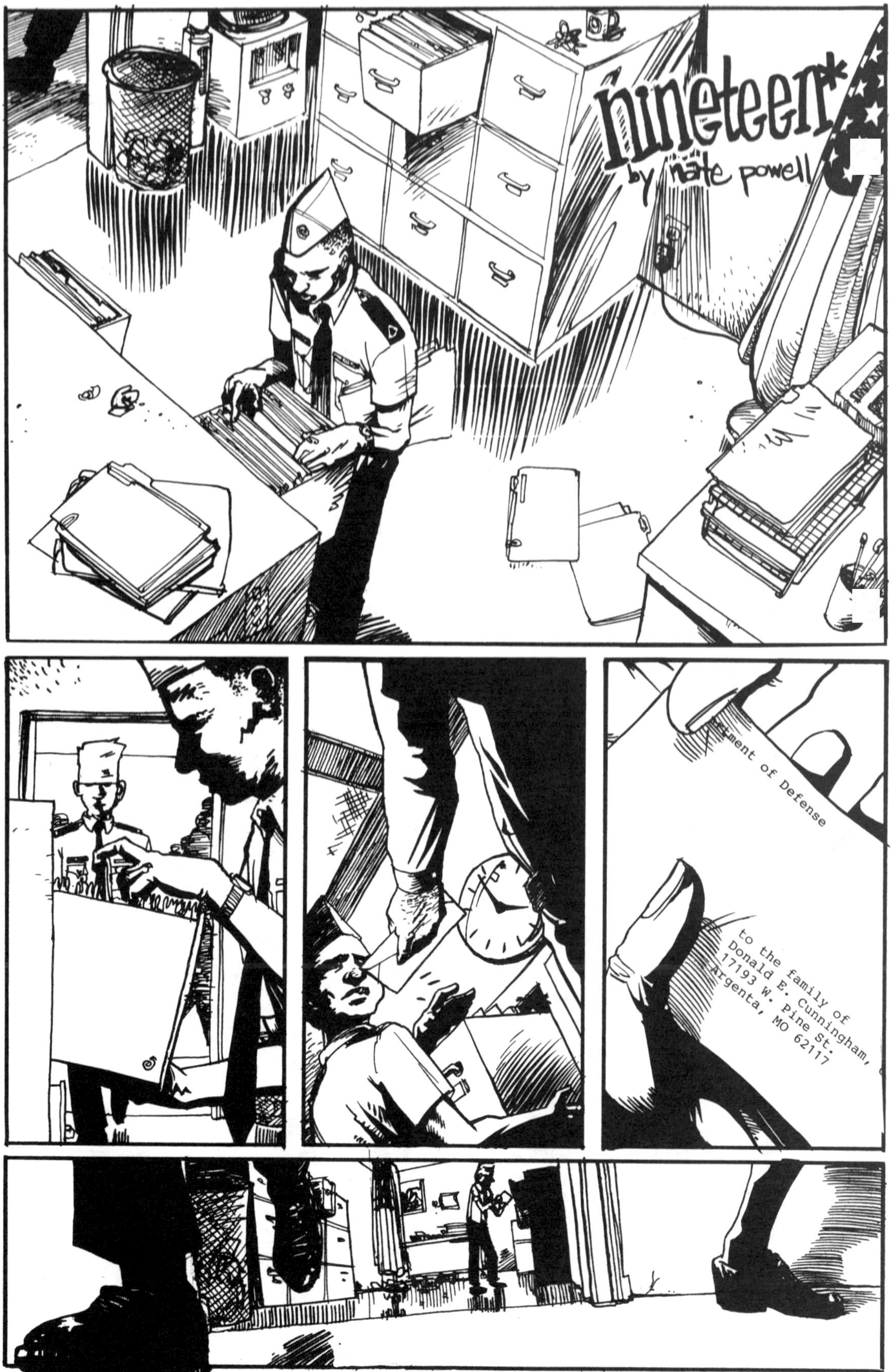

nineteen*
by nate powell
tment of Defense
to the family of
Donald E. Cunningham,
17193 W. Pine St.
Argenta, MO 62117

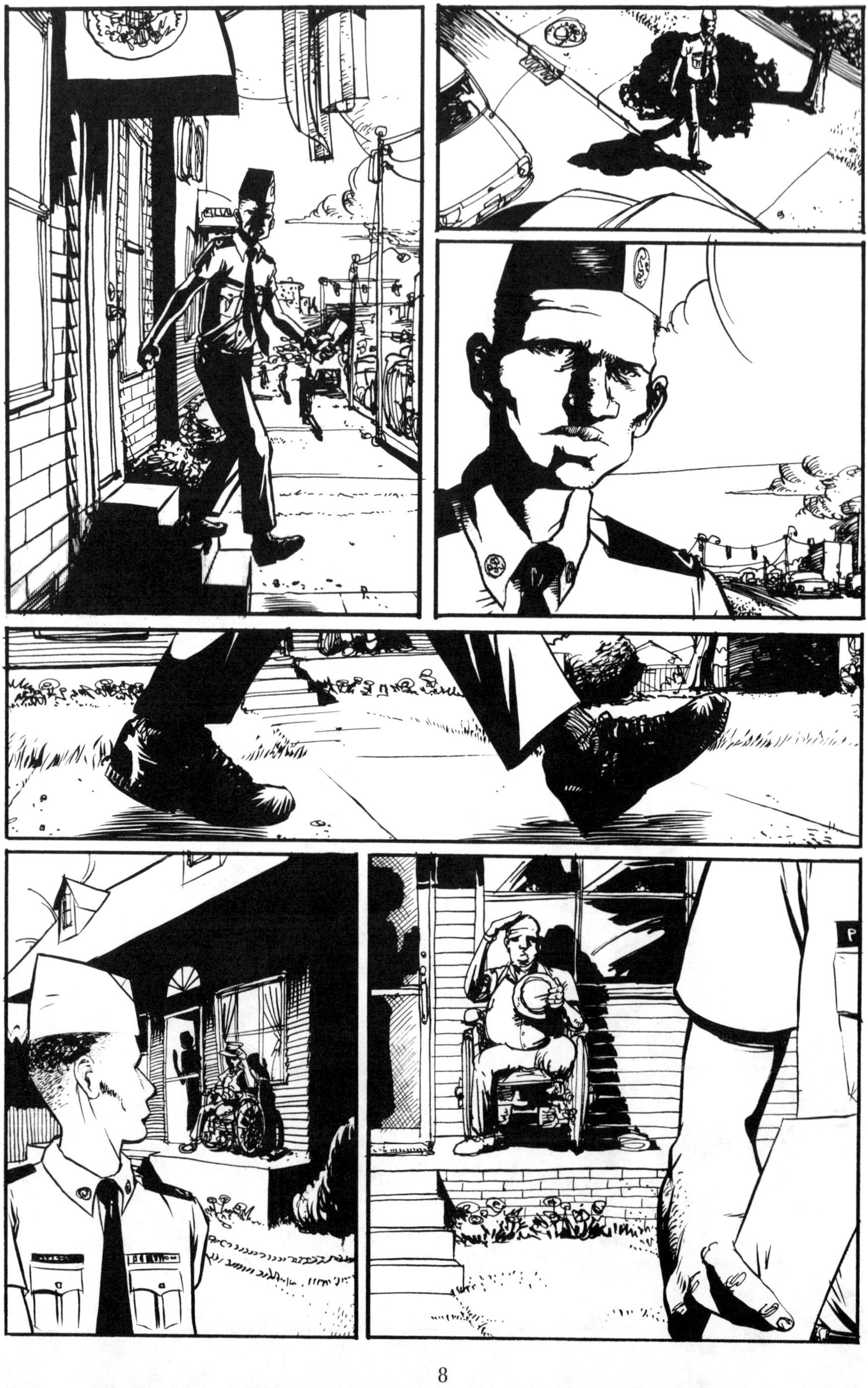

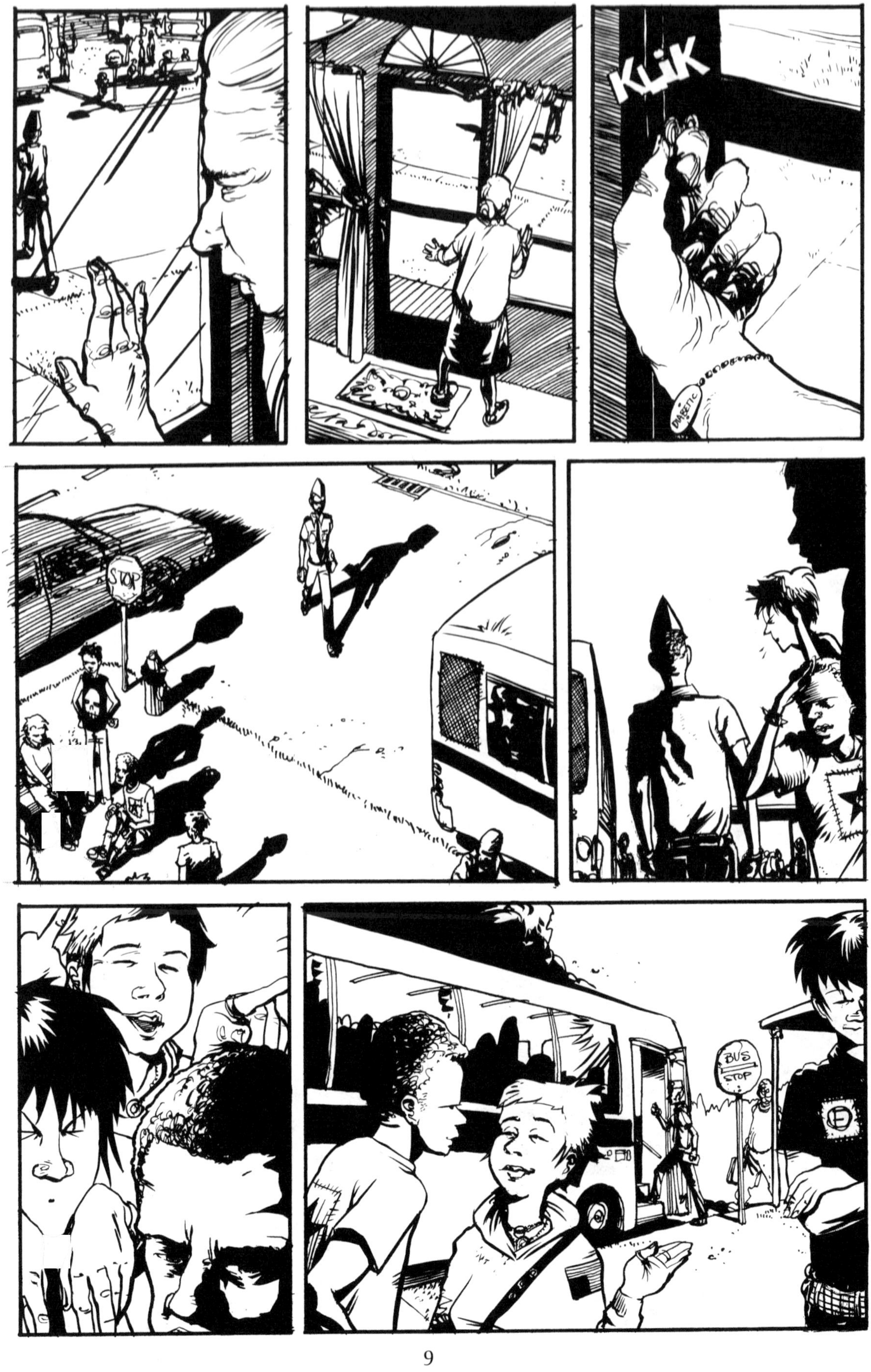
KLiK
DIABETIC
STOP
BUS
STOP

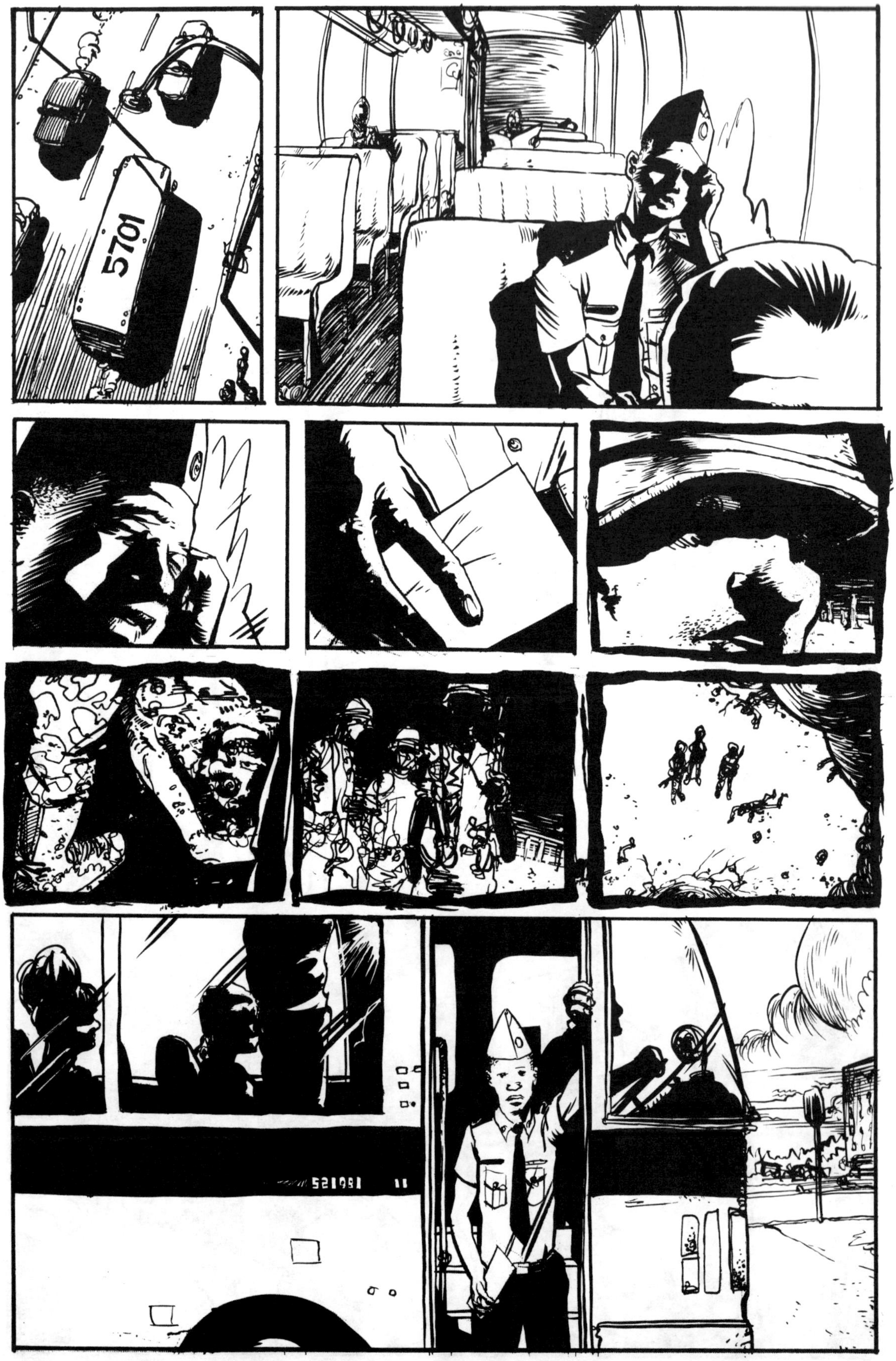
5701
521981

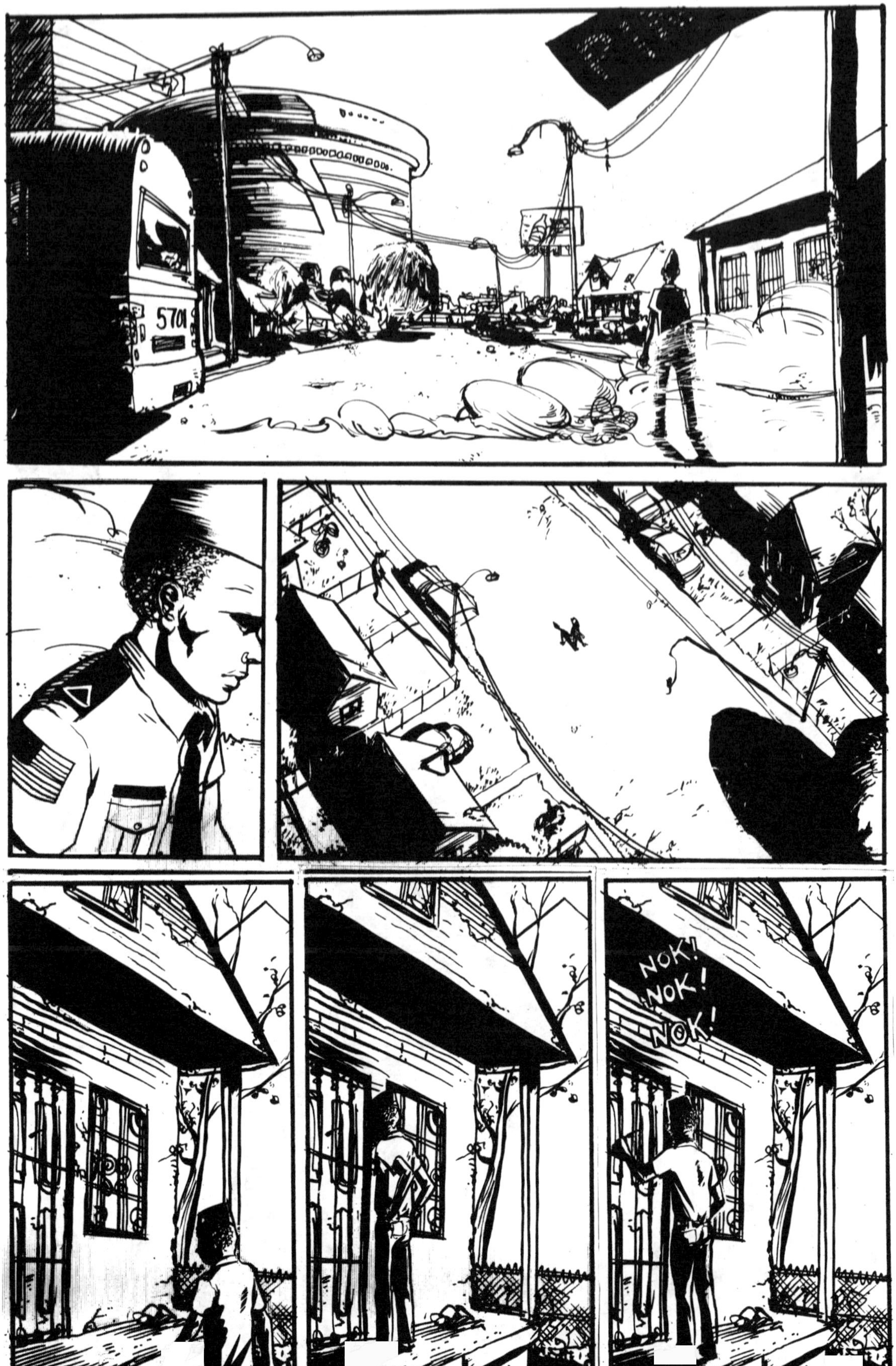
NOK!
NOK!
NOK!

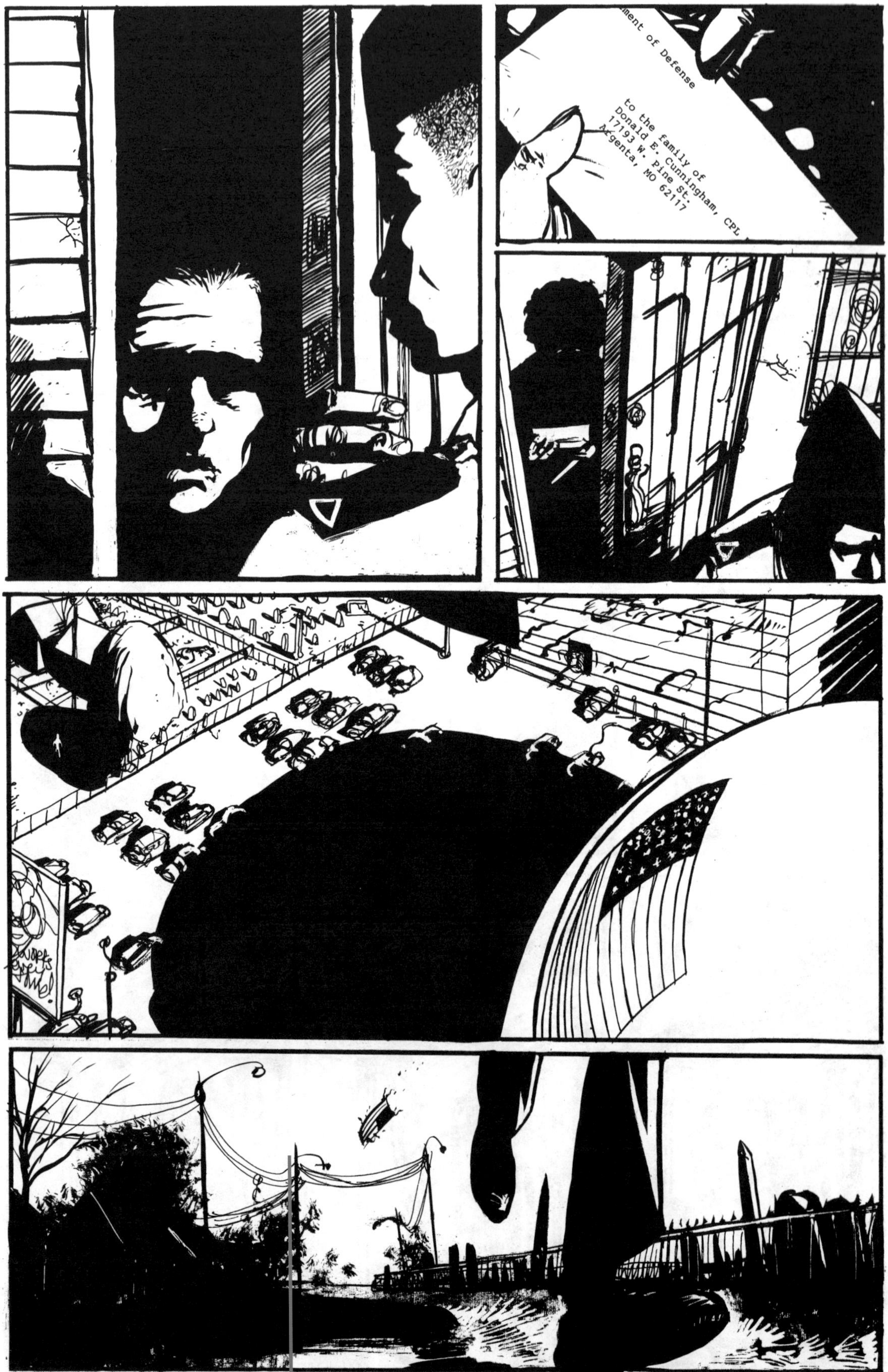
ment of Defense
to the family of
Donald E. Cunningham, CPL
17193 W. Pine St.
Argenta, MO 62117

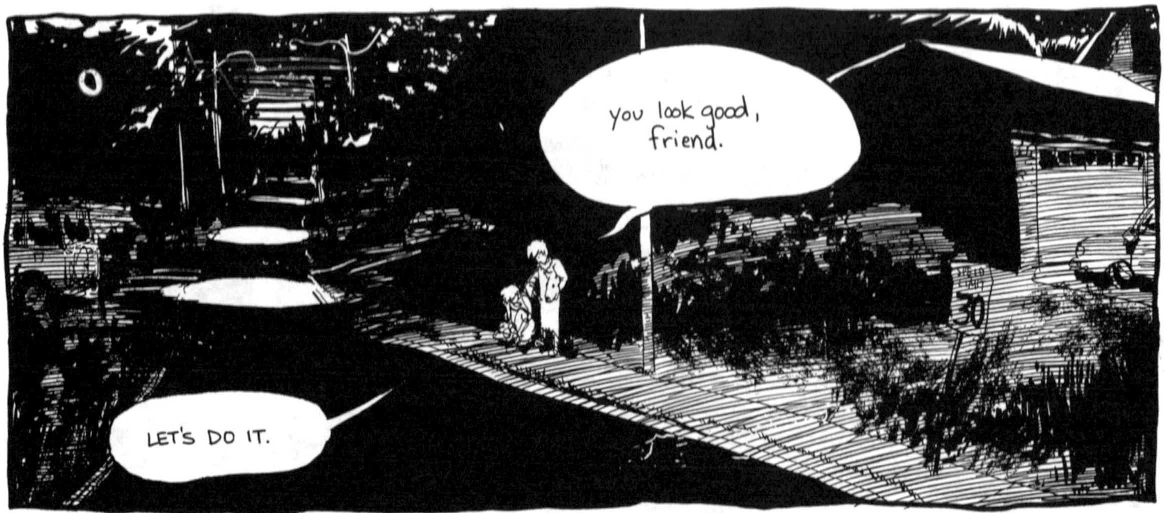
you look good, friend.
LET'S DO IT.

INVISIBILITIES

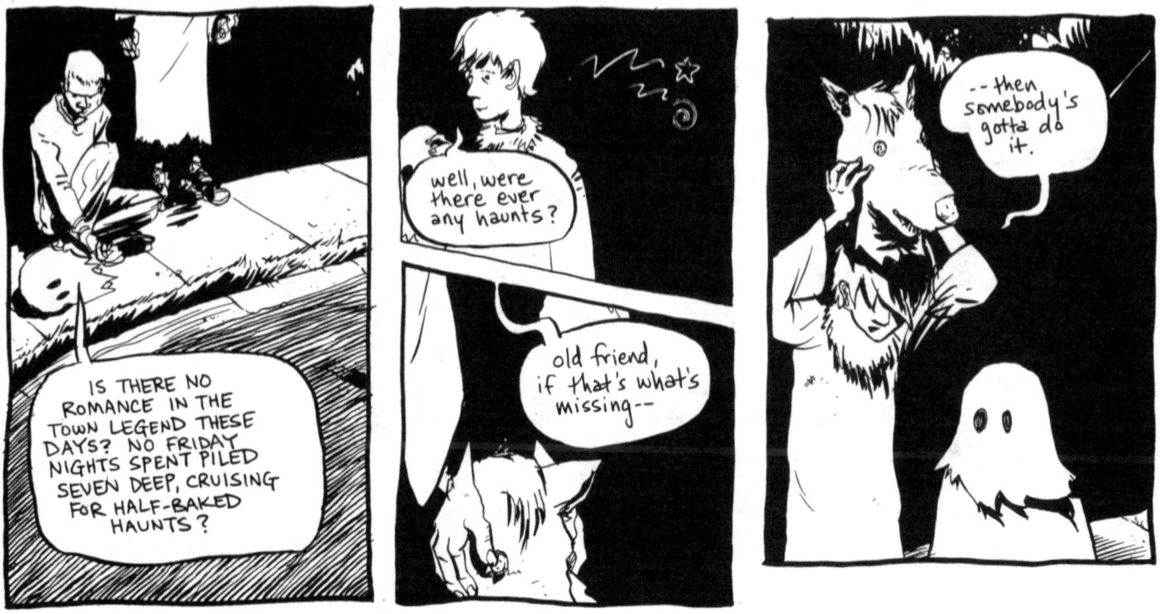
IS THERE NO ROMANCE IN THE TOWN LEGEND THESE DAYS? NO FRIDAY NIGHTS SPENT PILED SEVEN DEEP, CRUISING FOR HALF-BAKED HAUNTS?
well, were there ever any haunts?
old friend, if that's what's missing--
--then somebody's gotta do it.

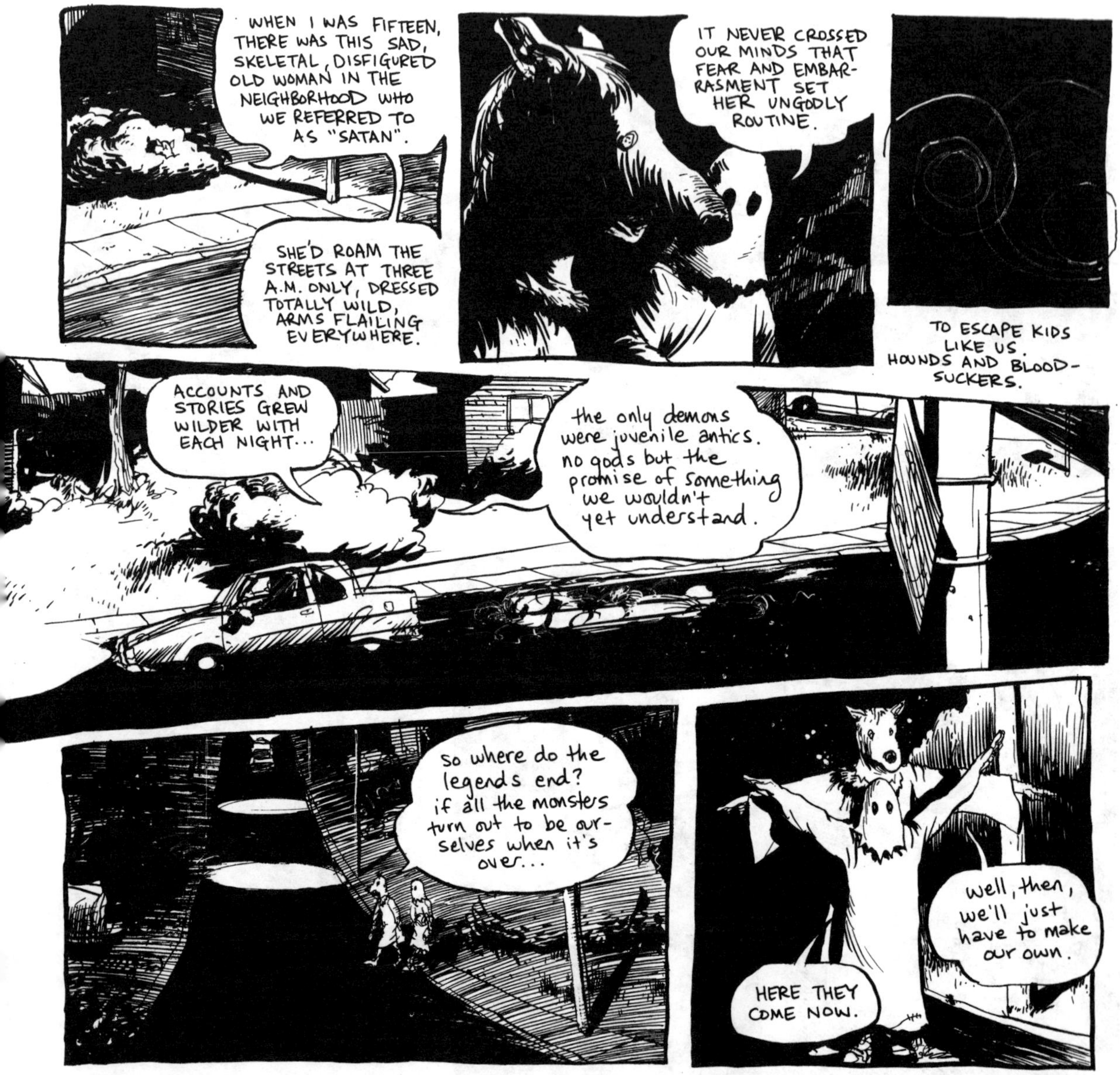
WHEN I WAS FIFTEEN, THERE WAS THIS SAD, SKELETAL, DISFIGURED OLD WOMAN IN THE NEIGHBORHOOD WHO WE REFERRED TO AS "SATAN".
SHE'D ROAM THE STREETS AT THREE A.M. ONLY, DRESSED TOTALLY WILD, ARMS FLAILING EVERYWHERE.
IT NEVER CROSSED OUR MINDS THAT FEAR AND EMBARRASMENT SET HER UNGODLY ROUTINE.
TO ESCAPE KIDS LIKE US. HOUNDS AND BLOOD-SUCKERS.
ACCOUNTS AND STORIES GREW WILDER WITH EACH NIGHT...
the only demons were juvenile antics. no gods but the promise of something we wouldn't yet understand.
so where do the legends end? if all the monsters turn out to be ourselves when it's over...
well, then, we'll just have to make our own.
HERE THEY COME NOW.

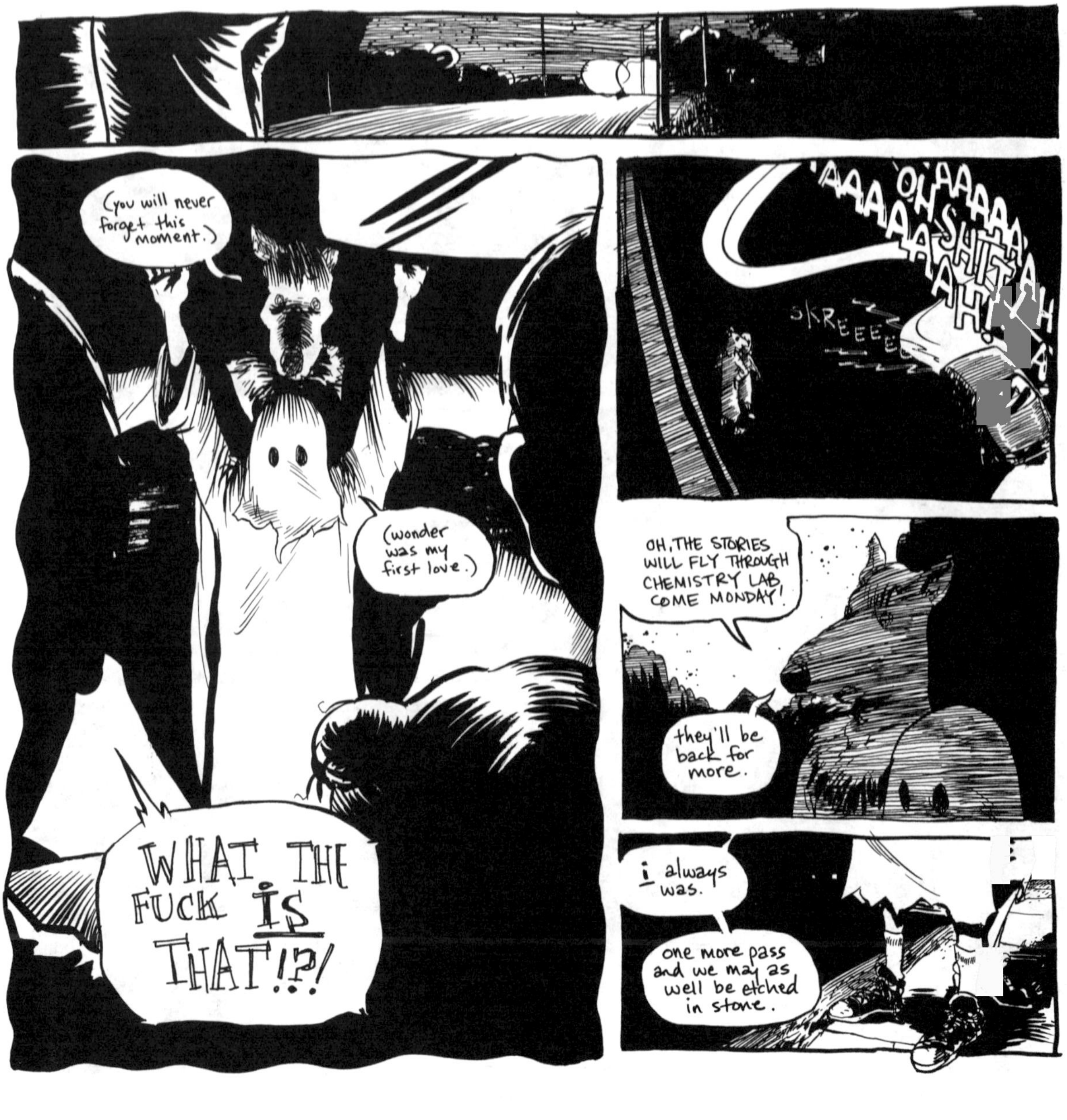
(you will never forget this moment.)
(wonder was my first love.)
WHAT THE FUCK IS THAT!?!
OH SHIT
SKREEEEE
OH, THE STORIES WILL FLY THROUGH CHEMISTRY LAB COME MONDAY!
they'll be back for more.
i always was.
one more pass and we may as well be etched in stone.

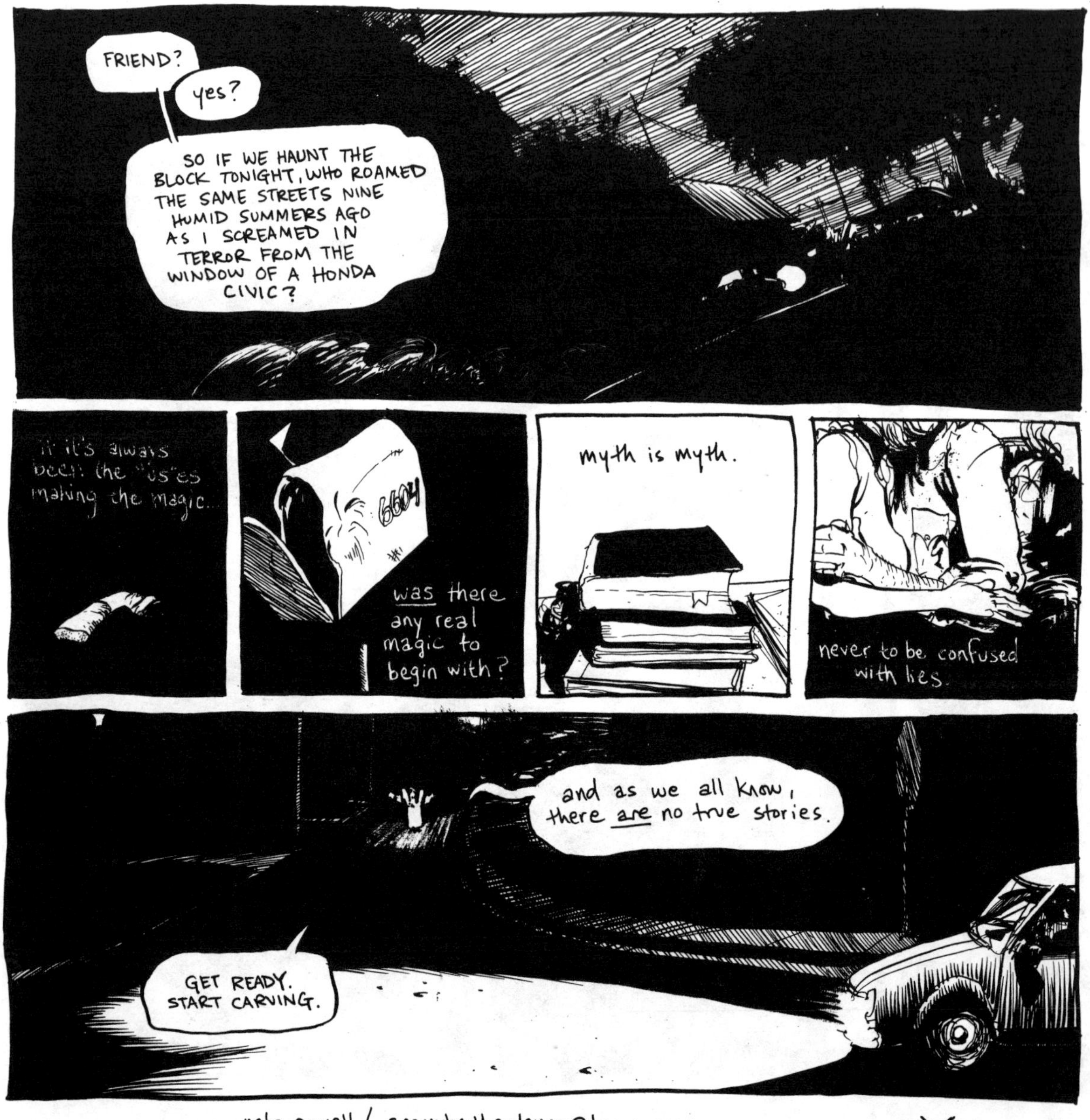
FRIEND?
yes?
SO IF WE HAUNT THE BLOCK TONIGHT, WHO ROAMED THE SAME STREETS NINE HUMID SUMMERS AGO AS I SCREAMED IN TERROR FROM THE WINDOW OF A HONDA CIVIC?
if it's always been the "us"es making the magic...
6604
was there any real magic to begin with?
myth is myth.
never to be confused with lies.
and as we all know, there are no true stories.
GET READY. START CARVING.

nate powell / seemybrotherdance@lycos.com

X 7-02

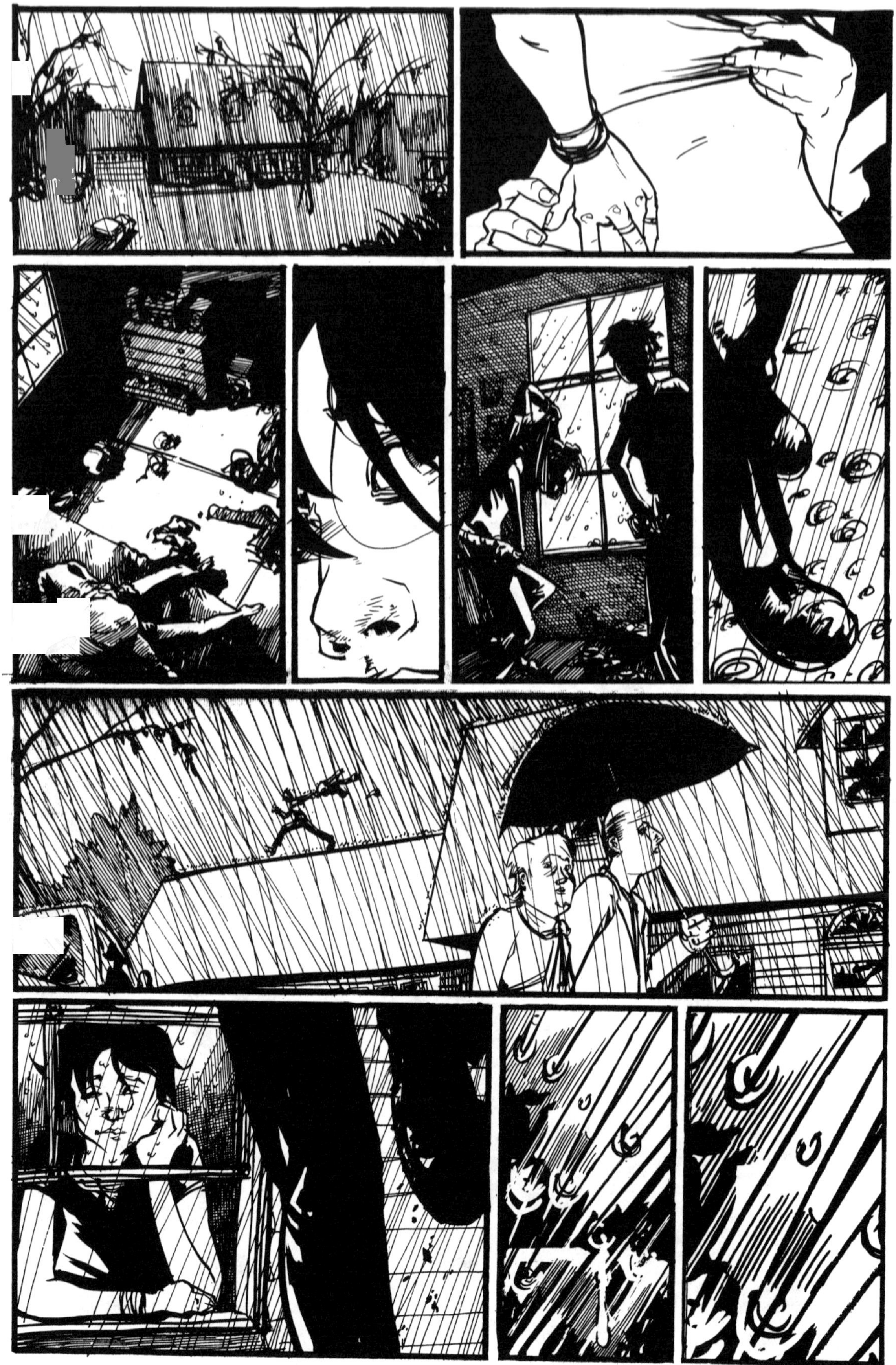

"UNDER YOUR CONTROL"
NATE POWELL 2/00.

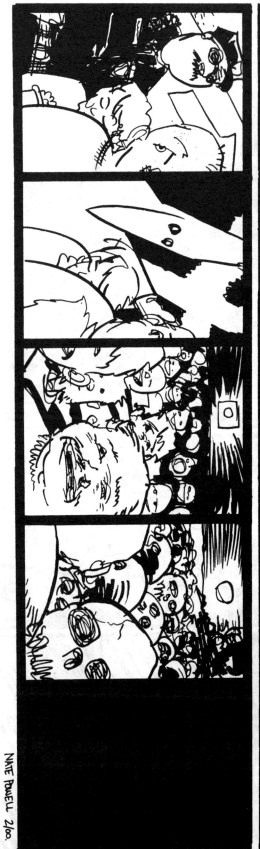

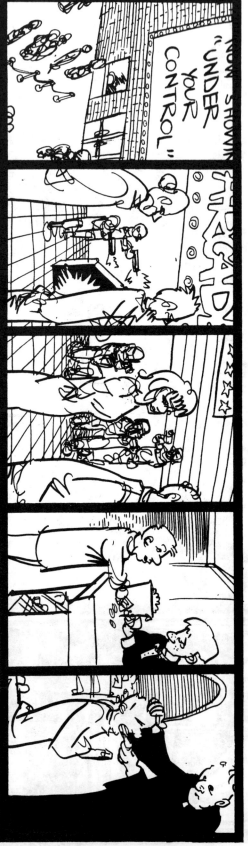

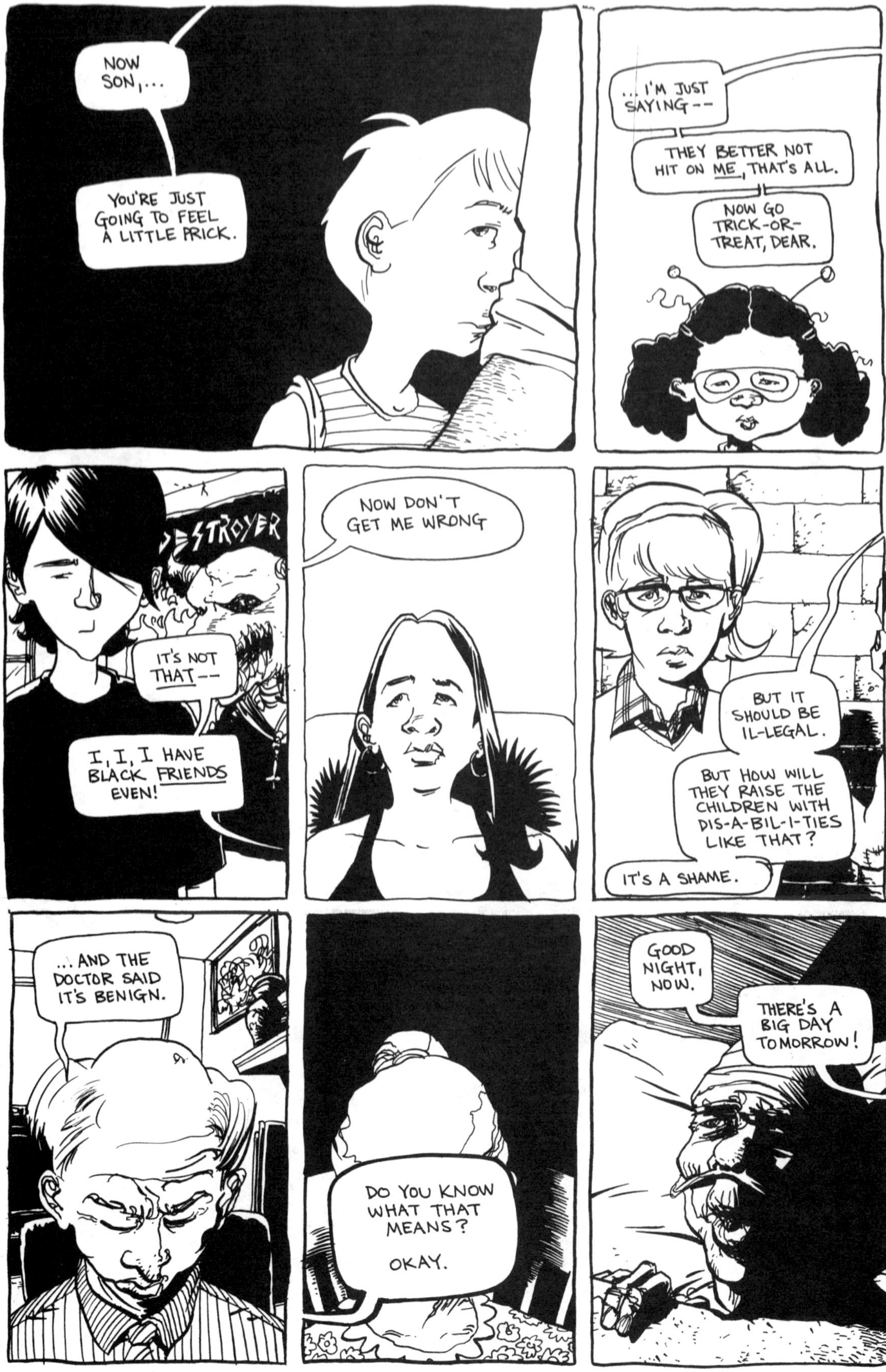
NOW SON, ...
YOU'RE JUST GOING TO FEEL A LITTLE PRICK.
... I'M JUST SAYING --
THEY BETTER NOT HIT ON ME, THAT'S ALL.
NOW GO TRICK-OR-TREAT, DEAR.
DESTROYER
IT'S NOT THAT --
I, I, I HAVE BLACK FRIENDS EVEN!
NOW DON'T GET ME WRONG
BUT IT SHOULD BE IL-LEGAL.
BUT HOW WILL THEY RAISE THE CHILDREN WITH DIS-A-BIL-I-TIES LIKE THAT?
IT'S A SHAME.
... AND THE DOCTOR SAID IT'S BENIGN.
DO YOU KNOW WHAT THAT MEANS?
OKAY.
GOOD NIGHT, NOW.
THERE'S A BIG DAY TOMORROW!

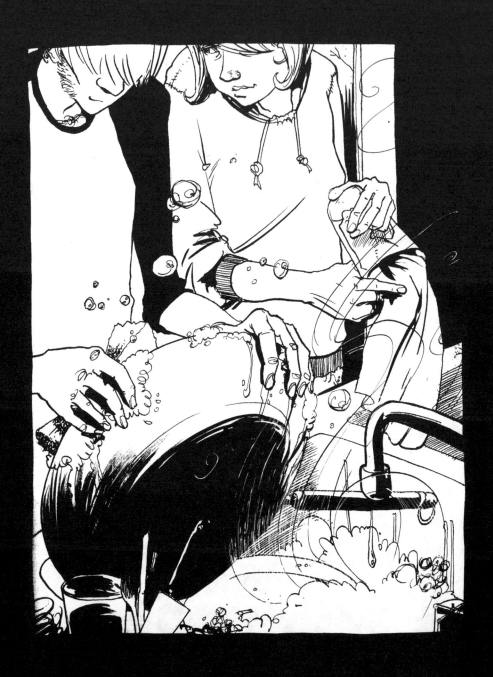

Satellite worlds

PART ONE OF TWO

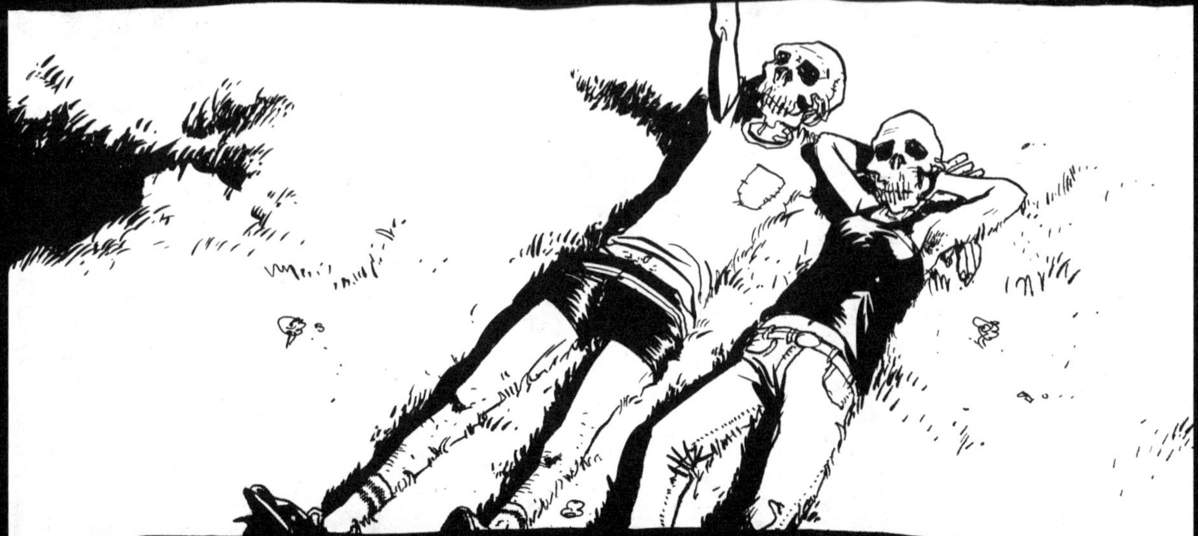

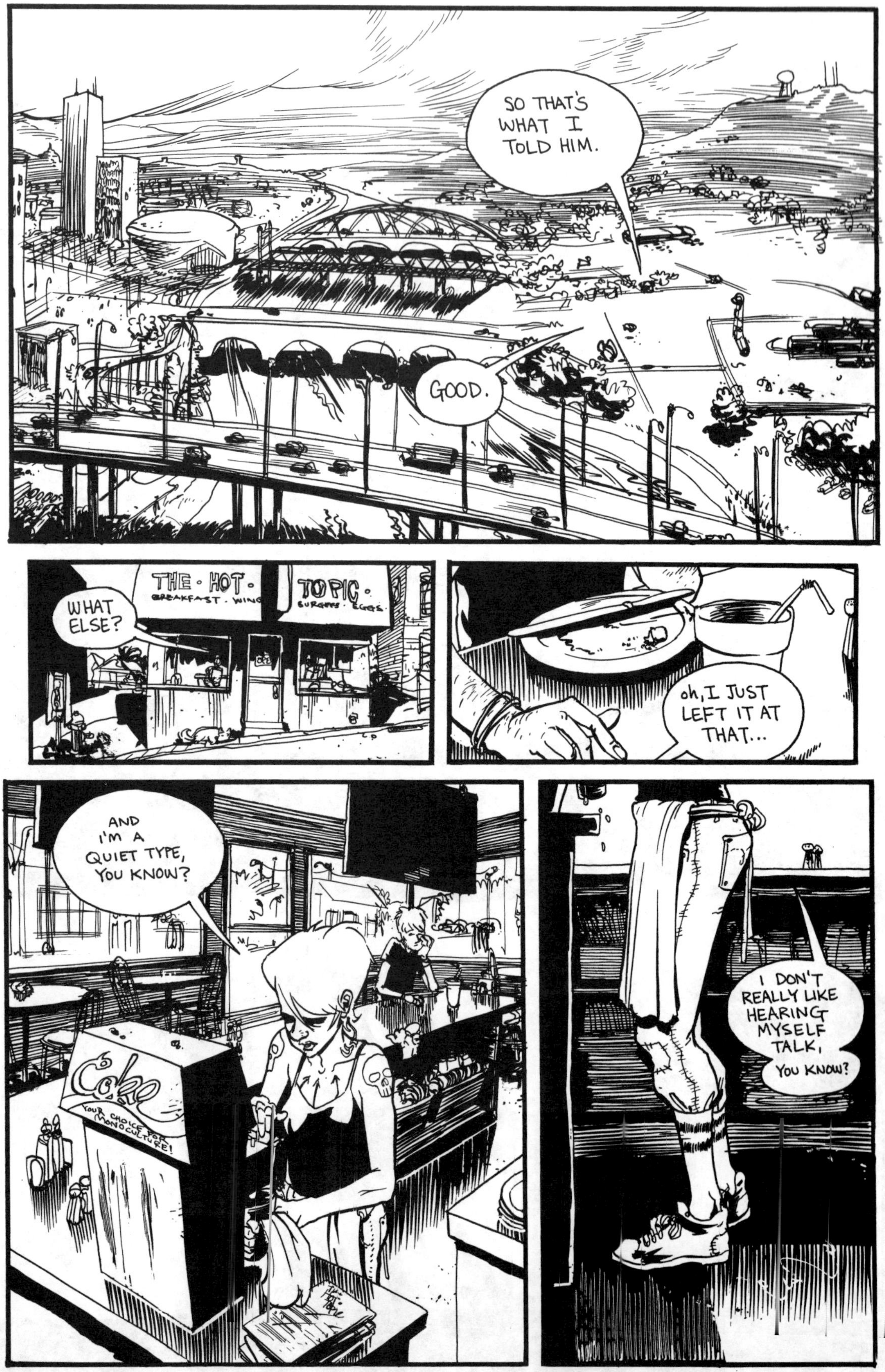
SO THAT'S WHAT I TOLD HIM.
GOOD.
THE HOT TOPIC
BREAKFAST WING
BURGERS EGGS
WHAT ELSE?
oh, I JUST LEFT IT AT THAT...
AND I'M A QUIET TYPE, YOU KNOW?
Coke
YOUR CHOICE FOR MONOCULTURE!
I DON'T REALLY LIKE HEARING MYSELF TALK,
YOU KNOW?

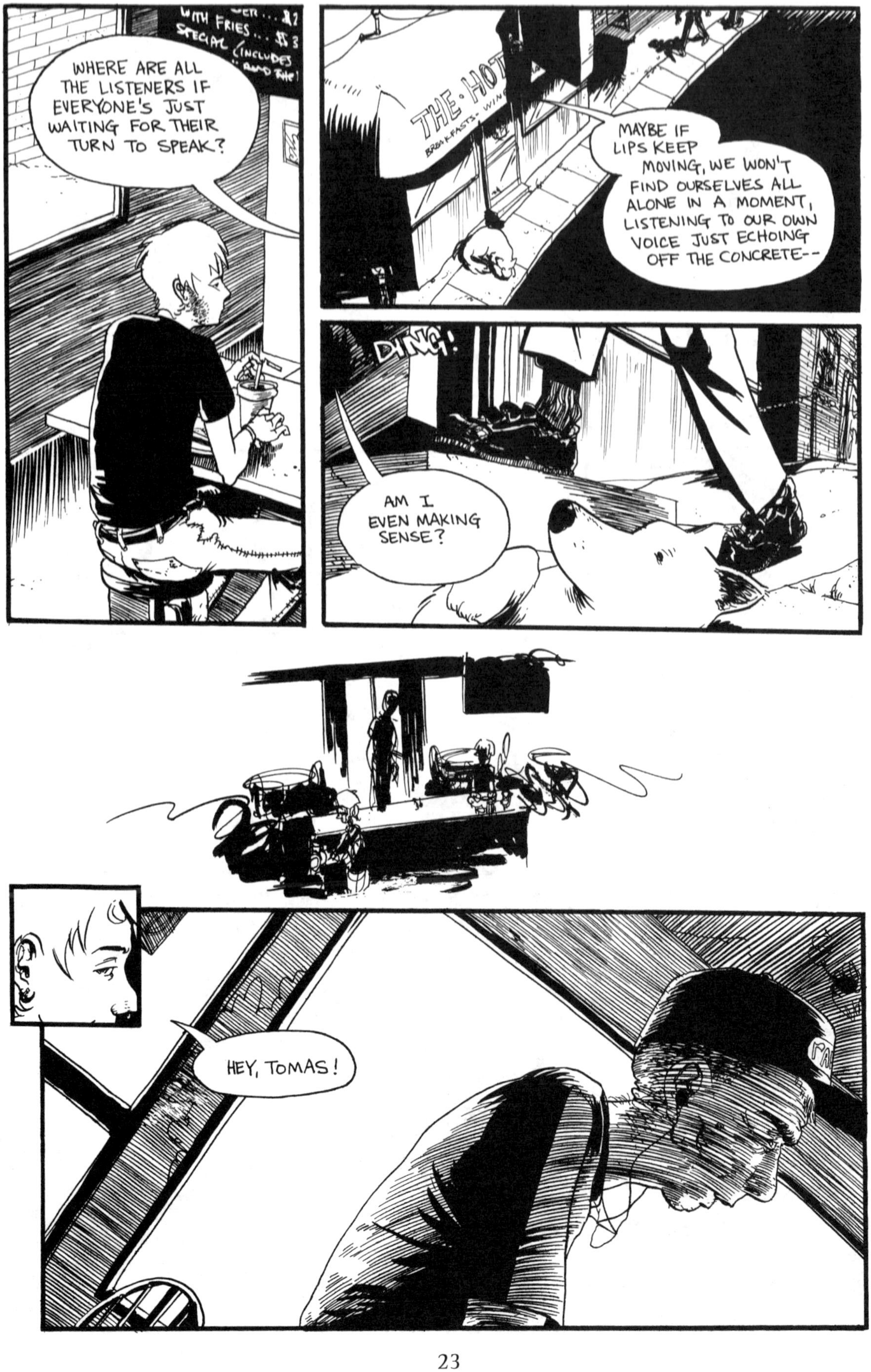
WHERE ARE ALL THE LISTENERS IF EVERYONE'S JUST WAITING FOR THEIR TURN TO SPEAK?
MAYBE IF LIPS KEEP MOVING, WE WON'T FIND OURSELVES ALL ALONE IN A MOMENT, LISTENING TO OUR OWN VOICE JUST ECHOING OFF THE CONCRETE--
DING!
AM I EVEN MAKING SENSE?
HEY, TOMAS!

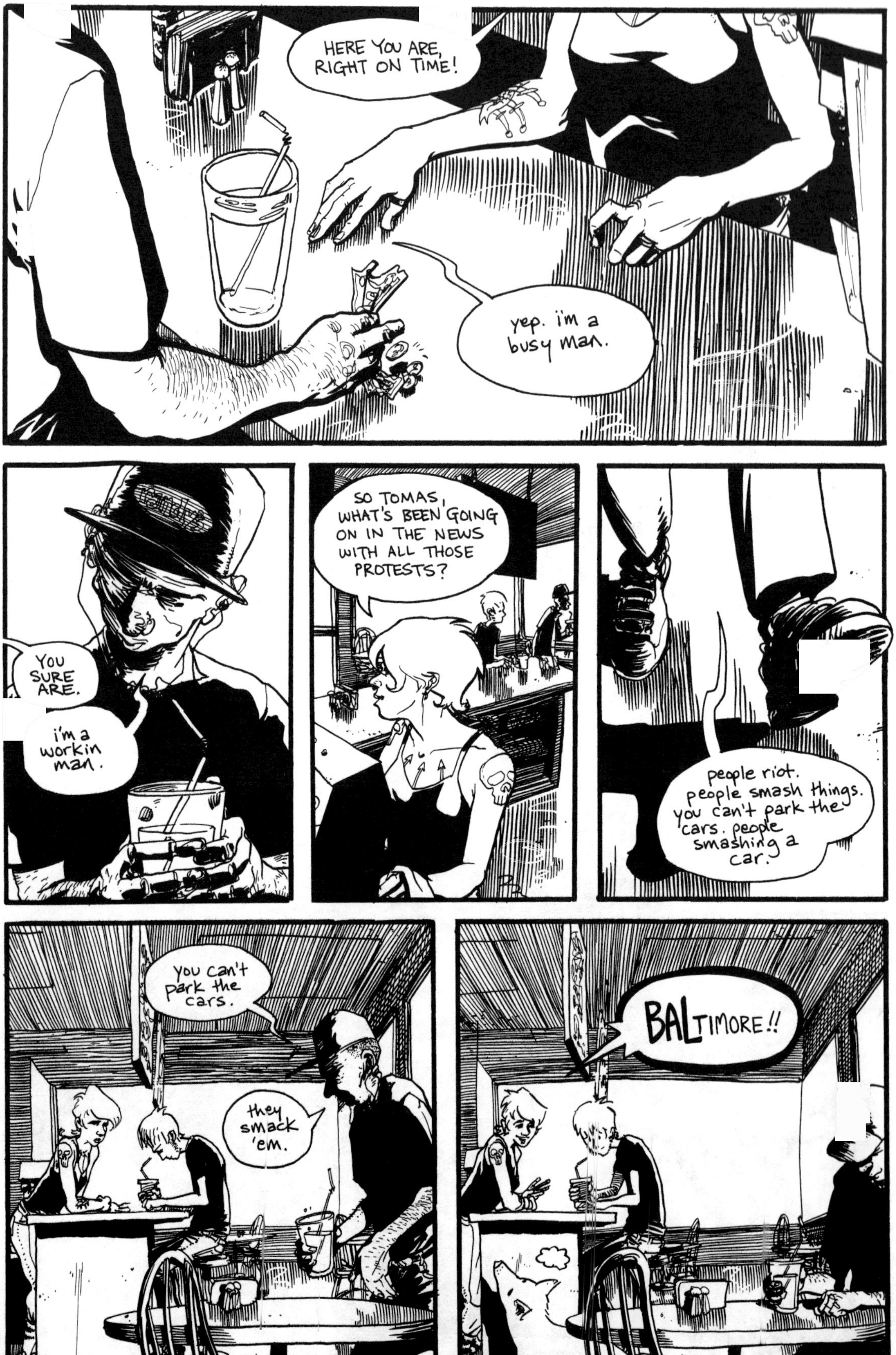
HERE YOU ARE, RIGHT ON TIME!
yep. i'm a busy man.
YOU SURE ARE.
i'm a workin man.
SO TOMAS, WHAT'S BEEN GOING ON IN THE NEWS WITH ALL THOSE PROTESTS?
people riot. people smash things. you can't park the cars. people smashing a car.
you can't park the cars.
they smack 'em.
BALTIMORE!!

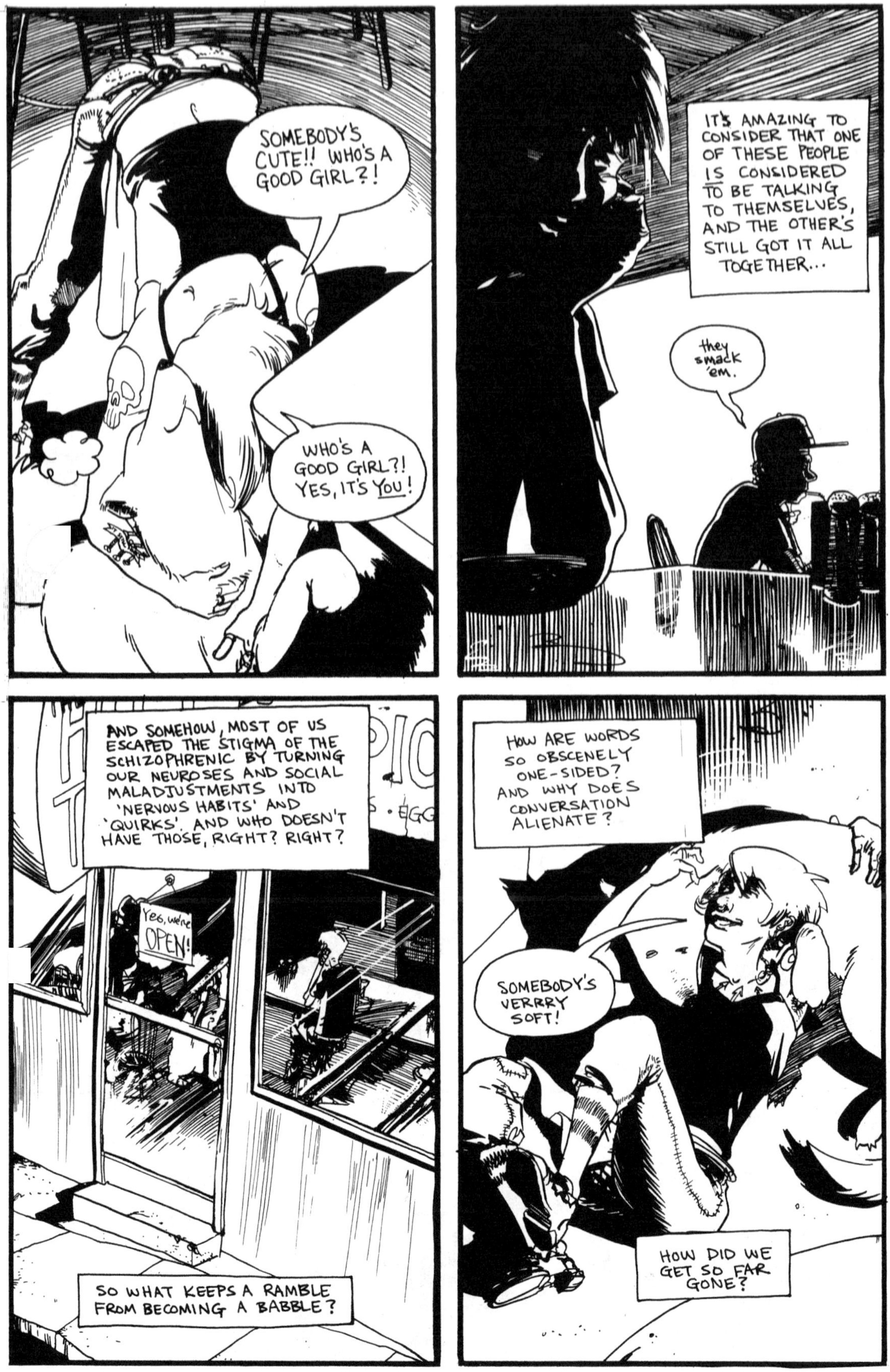
SOMEBODY'S CUTE!! WHO'S A GOOD GIRL?!
WHO'S A GOOD GIRL?! YES, IT'S YOU!
IT'S AMAZING TO CONSIDER THAT ONE OF THESE PEOPLE IS CONSIDERED TO BE TALKING TO THEMSELVES, AND THE OTHER'S STILL GOT IT ALL TOGETHER...
they smack 'em.
AND SOMEHOW, MOST OF US ESCAPED THE STIGMA OF THE SCHIZOPHRENIC BY TURNING OUR NEUROSES AND SOCIAL MALADJUSTMENTS INTO 'NERVOUS HABITS' AND 'QUIRKS'. AND WHO DOESN'T HAVE THOSE, RIGHT? RIGHT?
Yes, we're OPEN!
SO WHAT KEEPS A RAMBLE FROM BECOMING A BABBLE?
HOW ARE WORDS SO OBSCENELY ONE-SIDED? AND WHY DOES CONVERSATION ALIENATE?
SOMEBODY'S VERRRY SOFT!
HOW DID WE GET SO FAR GONE?

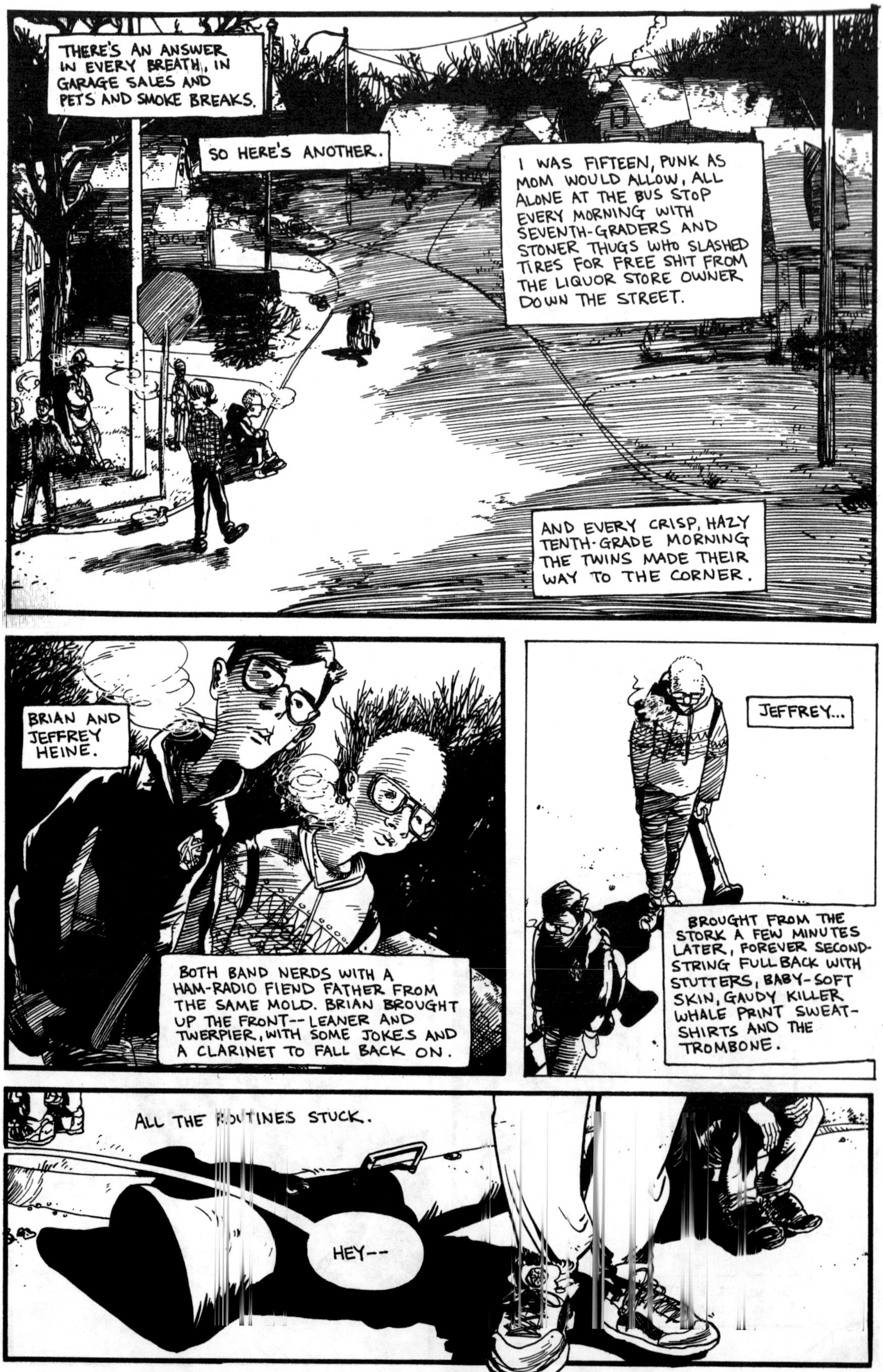
THERE'S AN ANSWER IN EVERY BREATH, IN GARAGE SALES AND PETS AND SMOKE BREAKS.
SO HERE'S ANOTHER.
I WAS FIFTEEN, PUNK AS MOM WOULD ALLOW, ALL ALONE AT THE BUS STOP EVERY MORNING WITH SEVENTH-GRADERS AND STONER THUGS WHO SLASHED TIRES FOR FREE SHIT FROM THE LIQUOR STORE OWNER DOWN THE STREET.
AND EVERY CRISP, HAZY TENTH-GRADE MORNING THE TWINS MADE THEIR WAY TO THE CORNER.
BRIAN AND JEFFREY HEINE.
BOTH BAND NERDS WITH A HAM-RADIO FIEND FATHER FROM THE SAME MOLD. BRIAN BROUGHT UP THE FRONT-- LEANER AND TWERPIER, WITH SOME JOKES AND A CLARINET TO FALL BACK ON.
JEFFREY...
BROUGHT FROM THE STORK A FEW MINUTES LATER, FOREVER SECOND-STRING FULLBACK WITH STUTTERS, BABY-SOFT SKIN, GAUDY KILLER WHALE PRINT SWEAT-SHIRTS AND THE TROMBONE.
ALL THE ROUTINES STUCK.
HEY--

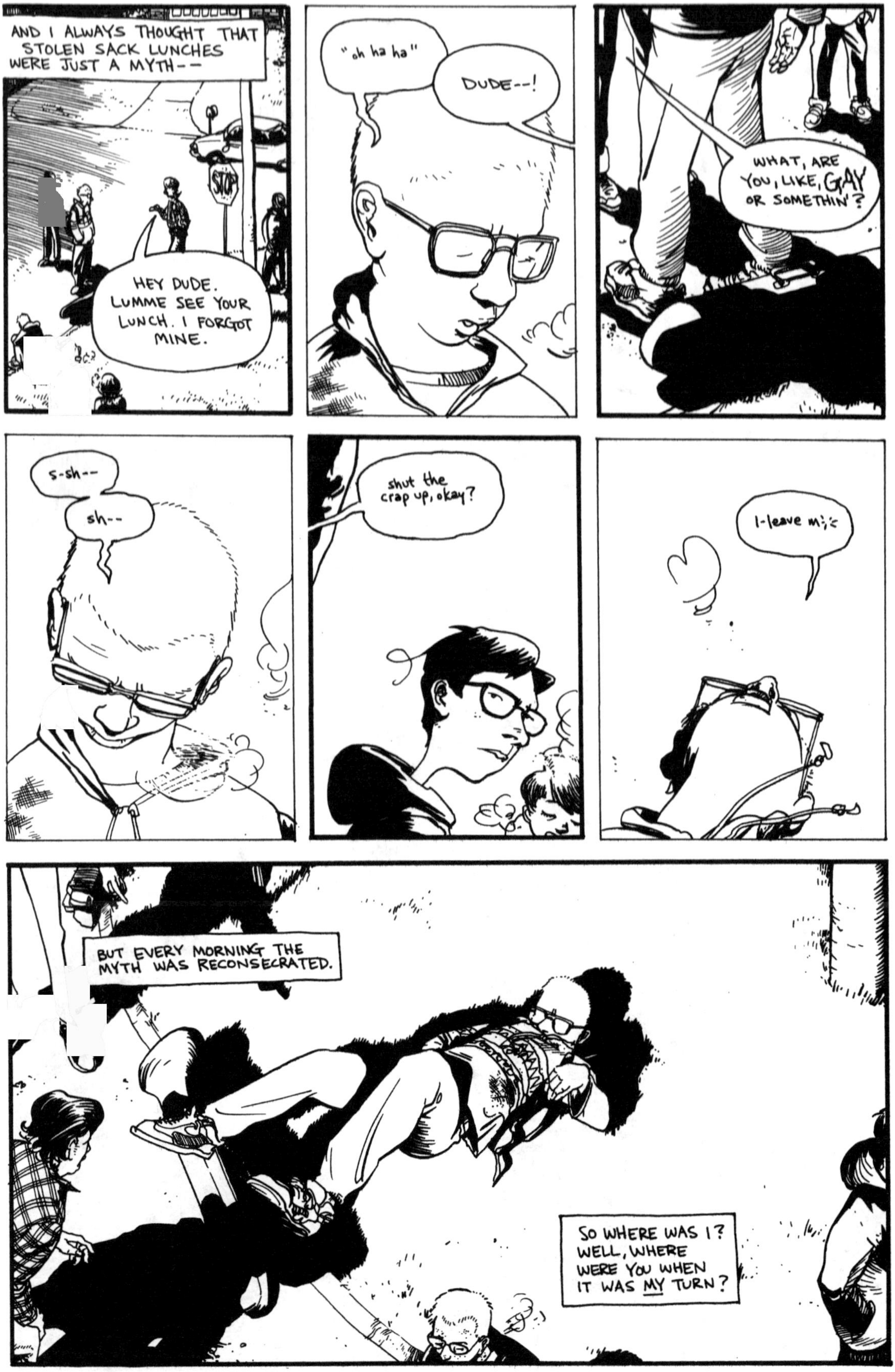
AND I ALWAYS THOUGHT THAT STOLEN SACK LUNCHES WERE JUST A MYTH--
STOP
HEY DUDE. LUMME SEE YOUR LUNCH. I FORGOT MINE.
"oh ha ha"
DUDE--!
WHAT, ARE YOU, LIKE, GAY OR SOMETHIN'?
s-sh--
sh--
shut the crap up, okay?
l-leave m;:
BUT EVERY MORNING THE MYTH WAS RECONSECRATED.
SO WHERE WAS I? WELL, WHERE WERE YOU WHEN IT WAS MY TURN?

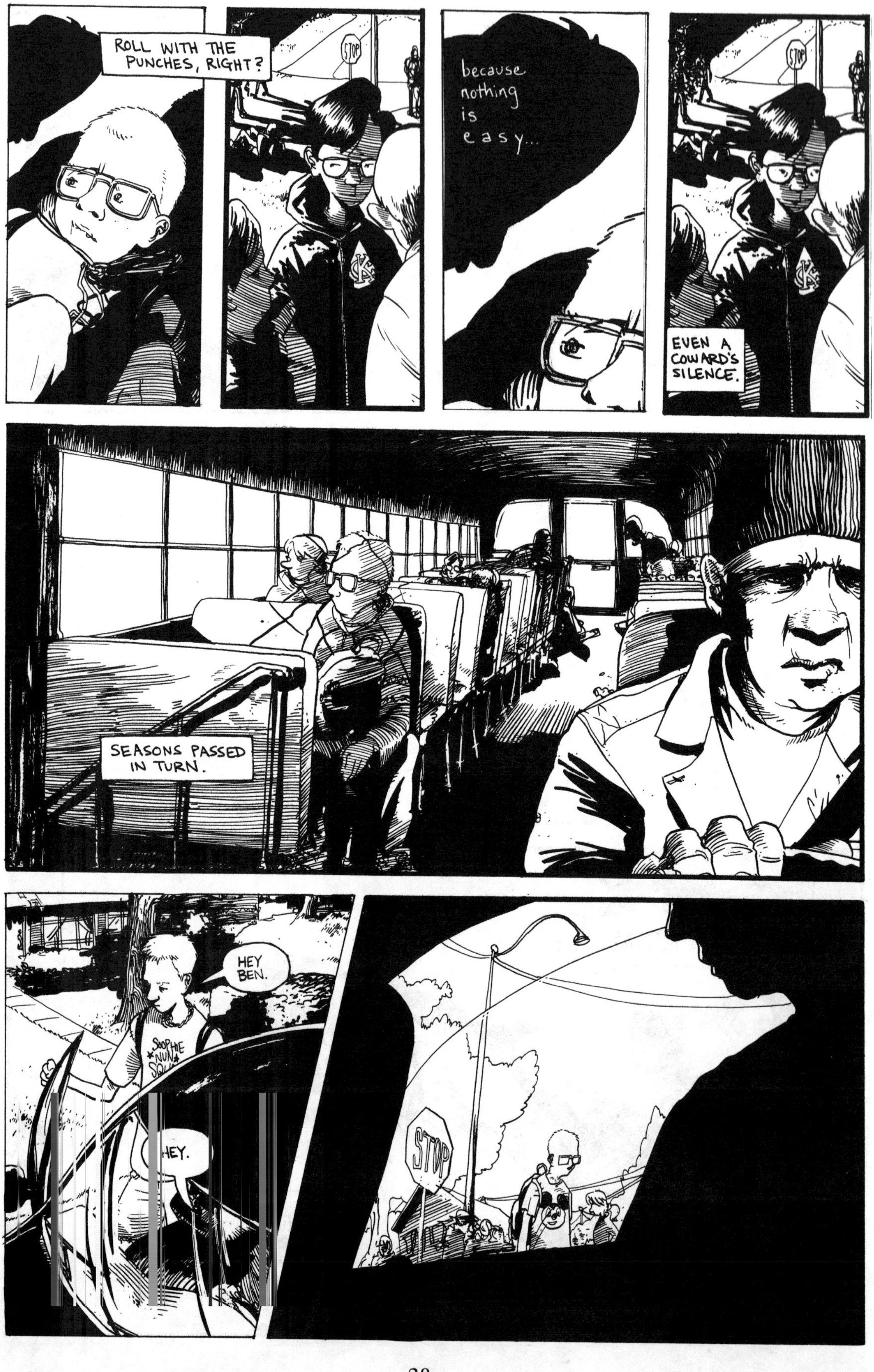
ROLL WITH THE PUNCHES, RIGHT?
STOP
because nothing is easy...
STOP
EVEN A COWARD'S SILENCE.
SEASONS PASSED IN TURN.
HEY BEN.
HEY.
STOP

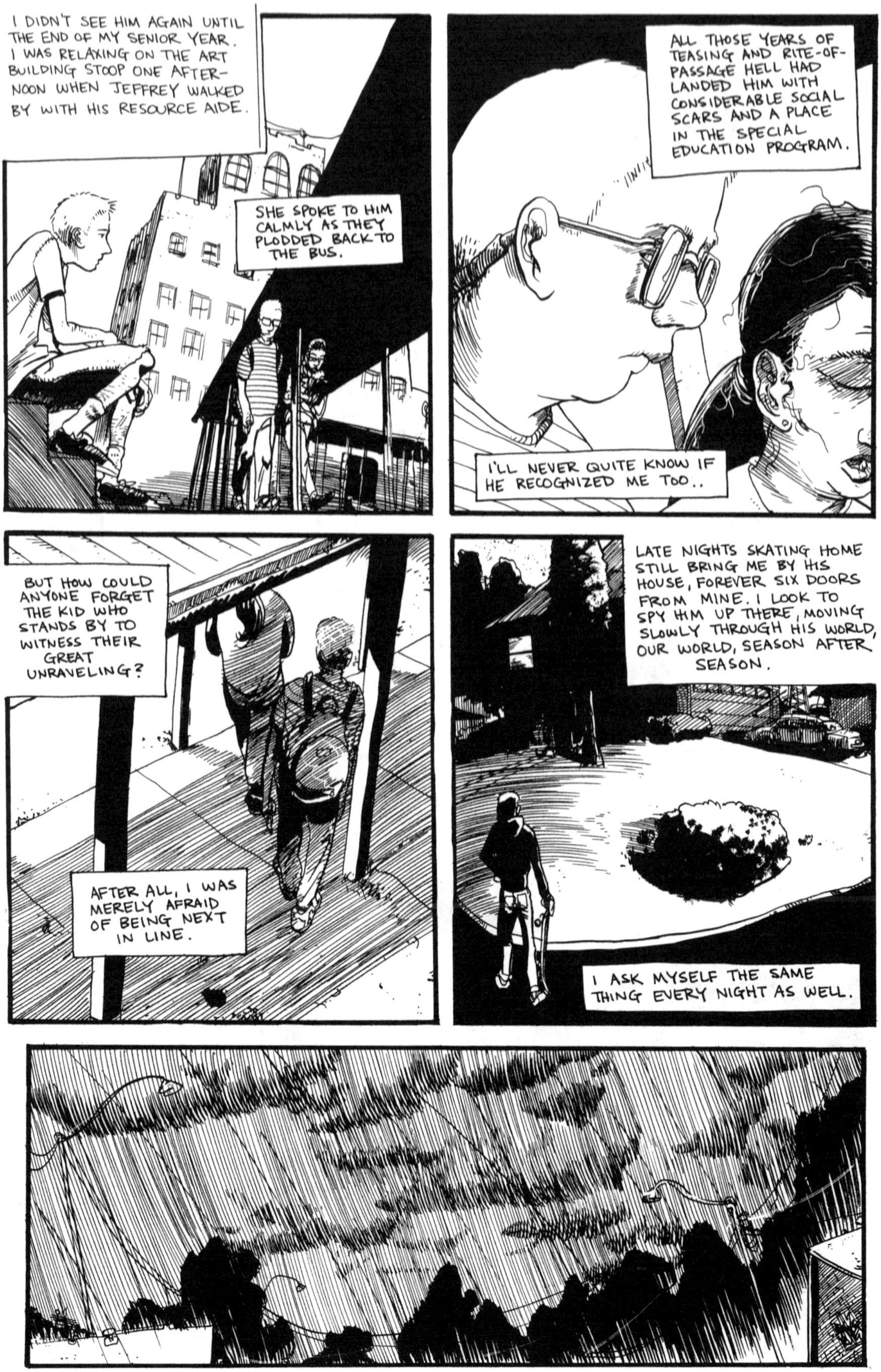
I DIDN'T SEE HIM AGAIN UNTIL THE END OF MY SENIOR YEAR. I WAS RELAXING ON THE ART BUILDING STOOP ONE AFTER-NOON WHEN JEFFREY WALKED BY WITH HIS RESOURCE AIDE.
SHE SPOKE TO HIM CALMLY AS THEY PLODDED BACK TO THE BUS.
ALL THOSE YEARS OF TEASING AND RITE-OF-PASSAGE HELL HAD LANDED HIM WITH CONSIDERABLE SOCIAL SCARS AND A PLACE IN THE SPECIAL EDUCATION PROGRAM.
I'LL NEVER QUITE KNOW IF HE RECOGNIZED ME TOO..
BUT HOW COULD ANYONE FORGET THE KID WHO STANDS BY TO WITNESS THEIR GREAT UNRAVELING?
AFTER ALL, I WAS MERELY AFRAID OF BEING NEXT IN LINE.
LATE NIGHTS SKATING HOME STILL BRING ME BY HIS HOUSE, FOREVER SIX DOORS FROM MINE. I LOOK TO SPY HIM UP THERE, MOVING SLOWLY THROUGH HIS WORLD, OUR WORLD, SEASON AFTER SEASON.
I ASK MYSELF THE SAME THING EVERY NIGHT AS WELL.

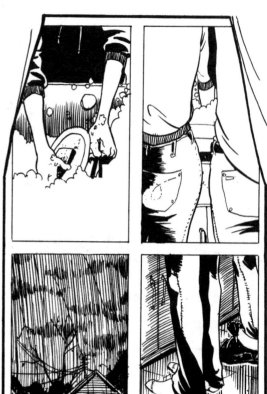

C'MON...

..LET'S GO SEE IF HE'S FEELING ANY BETTER.

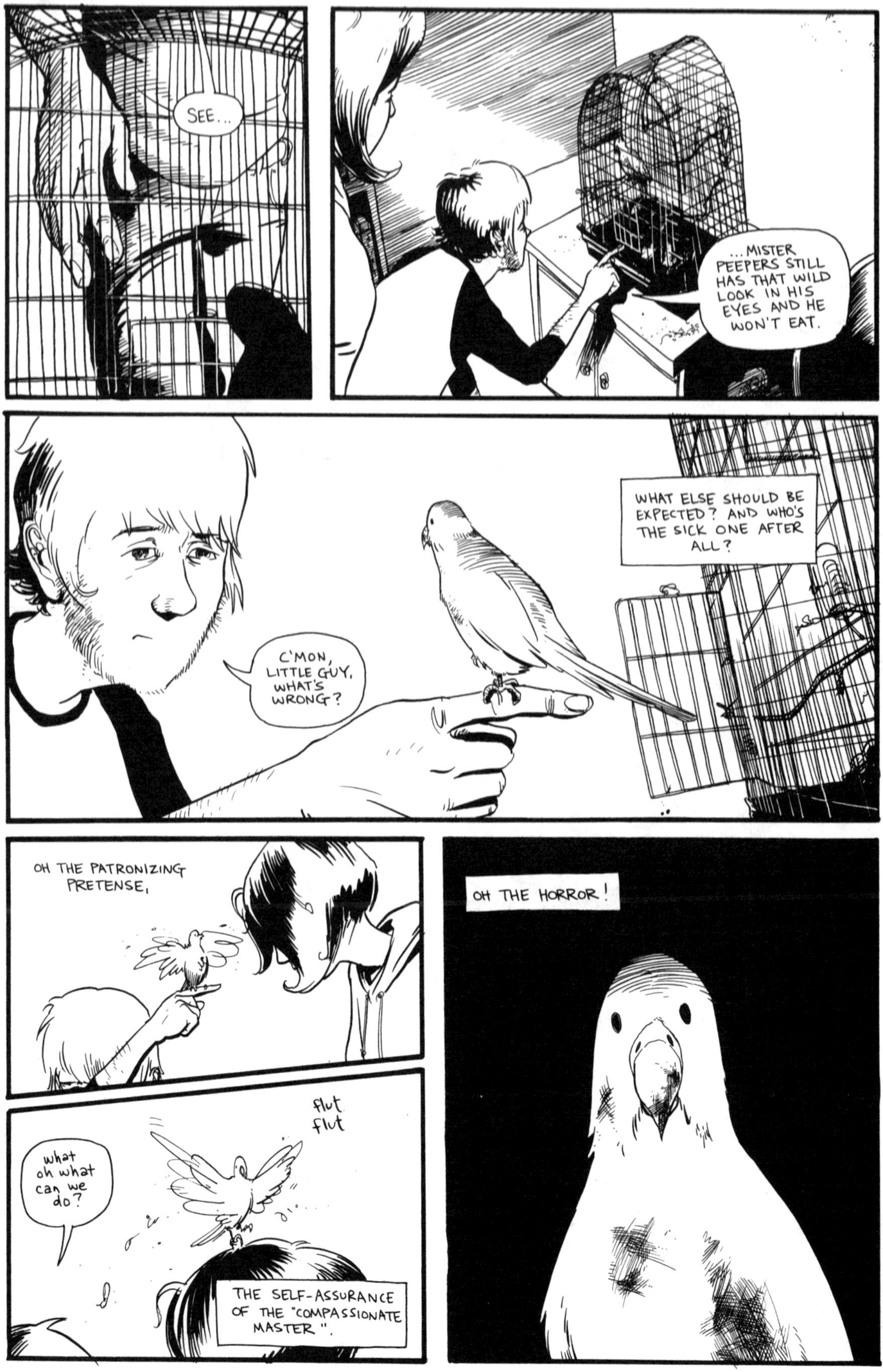
SEE...
...MISTER PEEPERS STILL HAS THAT WILD LOOK IN HIS EYES AND HE WON'T EAT.
WHAT ELSE SHOULD BE EXPECTED? AND WHO'S THE SICK ONE AFTER ALL?
C'MON, LITTLE GUY, WHAT'S WRONG?
OH THE PATRONIZING PRETENSE,
flut flut
what oh what can we do?
THE SELF-ASSURANCE OF THE "COMPASSIONATE MASTER".
OH THE HORROR!

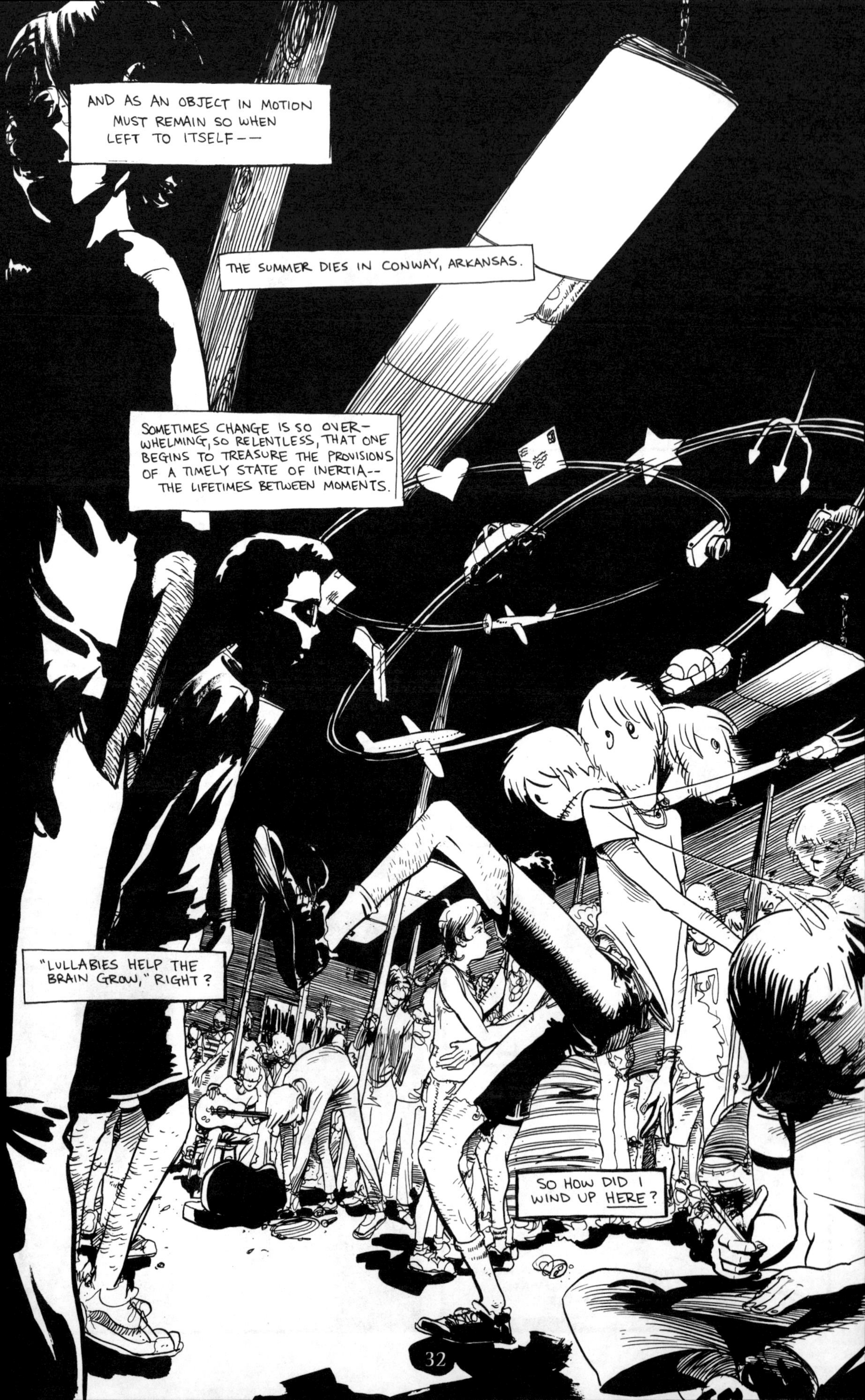
AND AS AN OBJECT IN MOTION MUST REMAIN SO WHEN LEFT TO ITSELF--
THE SUMMER DIES IN CONWAY, ARKANSAS.
SOMETIMES CHANGE IS SO OVERWHELMING, SO RELENTLESS, THAT ONE BEGINS TO TREASURE THE PROVISIONS OF A TIMELY STATE OF INERTIA-- THE LIFETIMES BETWEEN MOMENTS.
"LULLABIES HELP THE BRAIN GROW," RIGHT?
SO HOW DID I WIND UP HERE?

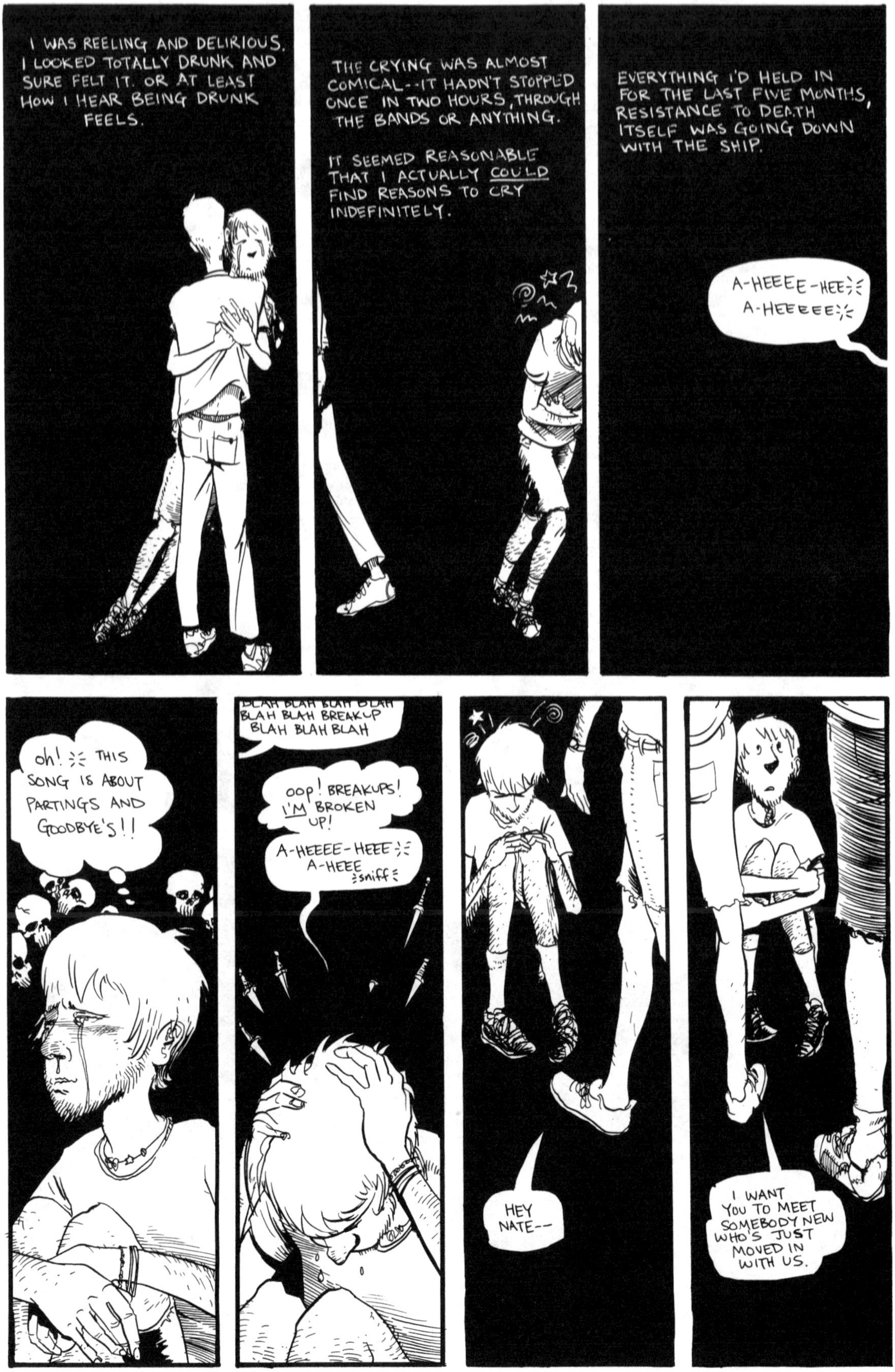

I WAS REELING AND DELIRIOUS. I LOOKED TOTALLY DRUNK AND SURE FELT IT. OR AT LEAST HOW I HEAR BEING DRUNK FEELS.
THE CRYING WAS ALMOST COMICAL--IT HADN'T STOPPED ONCE IN TWO HOURS, THROUGH THE BANDS OR ANYTHING.
IT SEEMED REASONABLE THAT I ACTUALLY COULD FIND REASONS TO CRY INDEFINITELY.
EVERYTHING I'D HELD IN FOR THE LAST FIVE MONTHS, RESISTANCE TO DEATH ITSELF WAS GOING DOWN WITH THE SHIP.
A-HEEEE-HEE A-HEEEEEE
oh! THIS SONG IS ABOUT PARTINGS AND GOODBYE'S!!
BLAH BLAH BLAH BLAH BLAH BLAH BREAKUP BLAH BLAH BLAH
oop! BREAKUPS! I'M BROKEN UP!
A-HEEEE-HEEE A-HEEE sniff
HEY NATE--
I WANT YOU TO MEET SOMEBODY NEW WHO'S JUST MOVED IN WITH US.

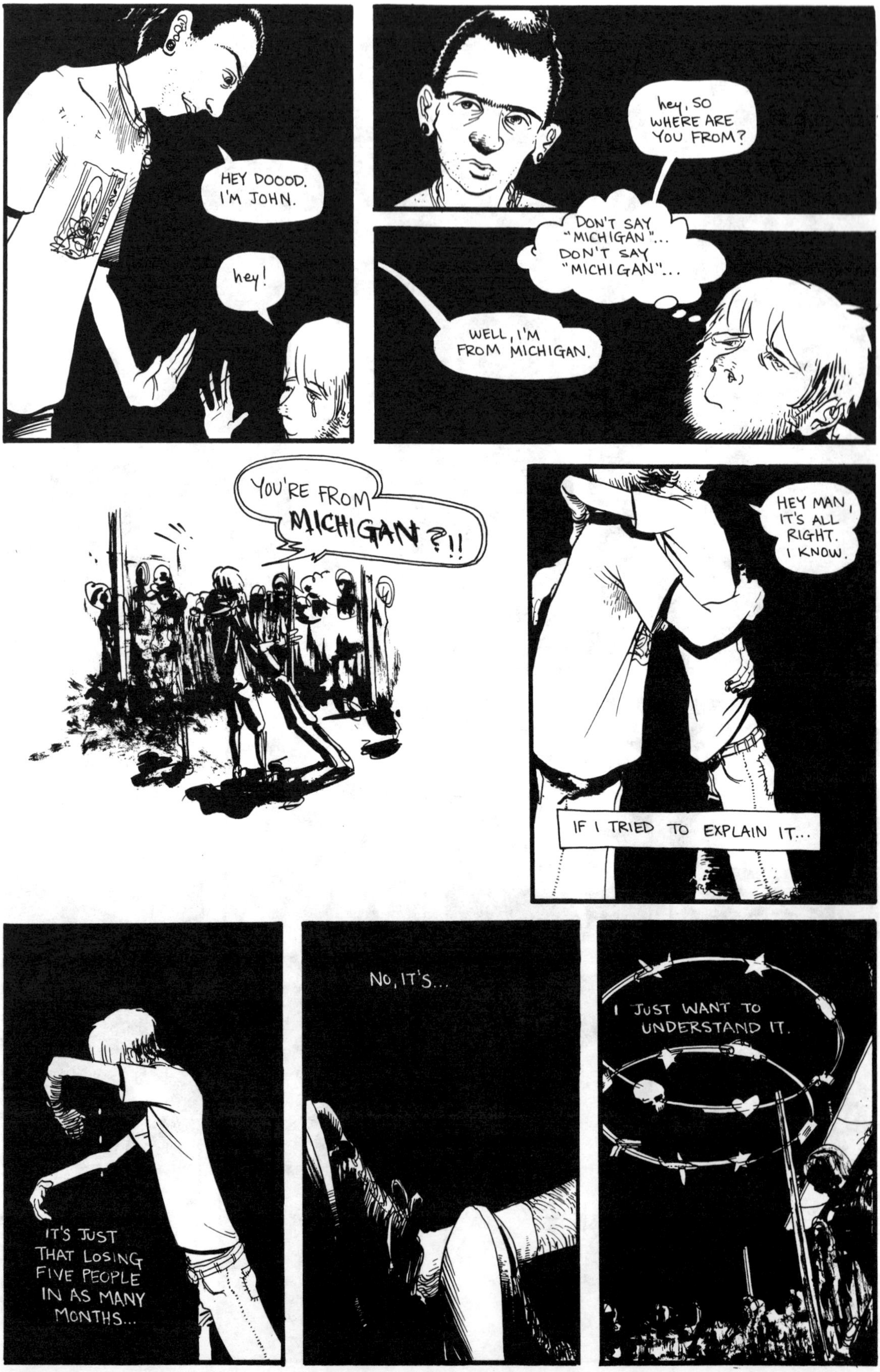
HEY DOOOD. I'M JOHN.
hey!
hey, SO WHERE ARE YOU FROM?
DON'T SAY "MICHIGAN"... DON'T SAY "MICHIGAN"...
WELL, I'M FROM MICHIGAN.
YOU'RE FROM MICHIGAN ?!!
HEY MAN, IT'S ALL RIGHT. I KNOW.
IF I TRIED TO EXPLAIN IT...
IT'S JUST THAT LOSING FIVE PEOPLE IN AS MANY MONTHS...
NO, IT'S...
I JUST WANT TO UNDERSTAND IT.

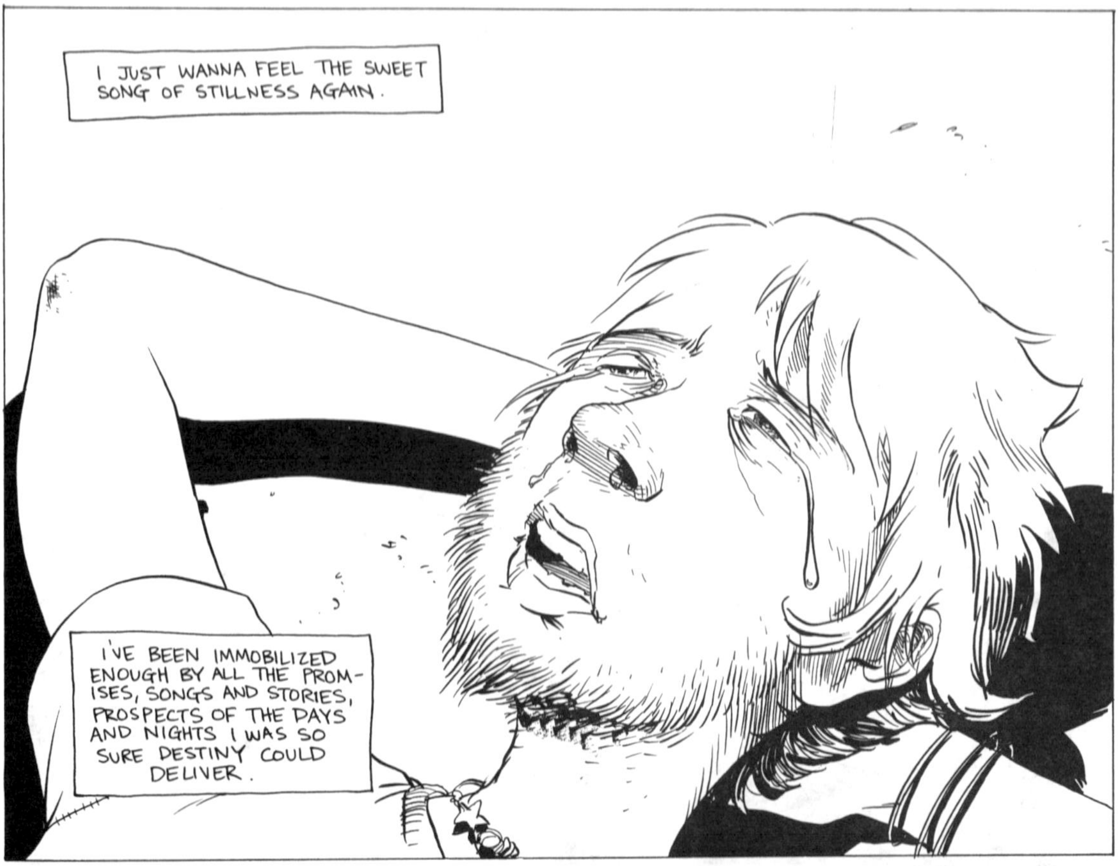
I JUST WANNA FEEL THE SWEET SONG OF STILLNESS AGAIN.
I'VE BEEN IMMOBILIZED ENOUGH BY ALL THE PROMISES, SONGS AND STORIES, PROSPECTS OF THE DAYS AND NIGHTS I WAS SO SURE DESTINY COULD DELIVER.

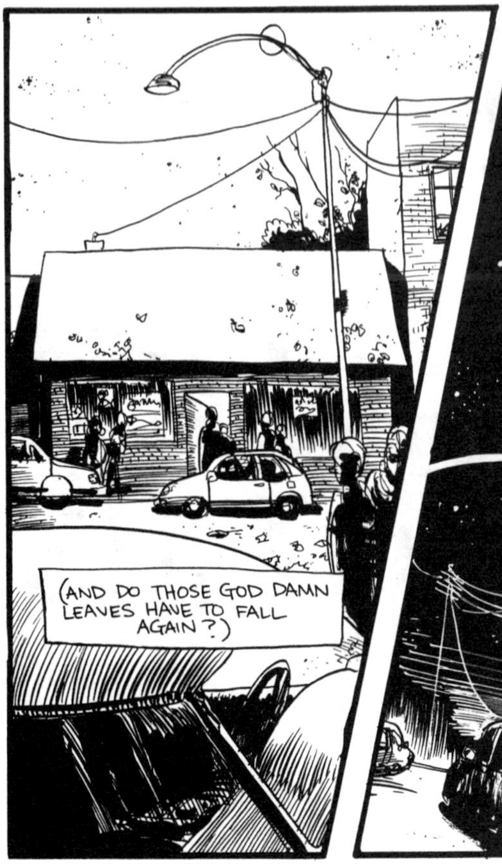
(AND DO THOSE GOD DAMN LEAVES HAVE TO FALL AGAIN?)

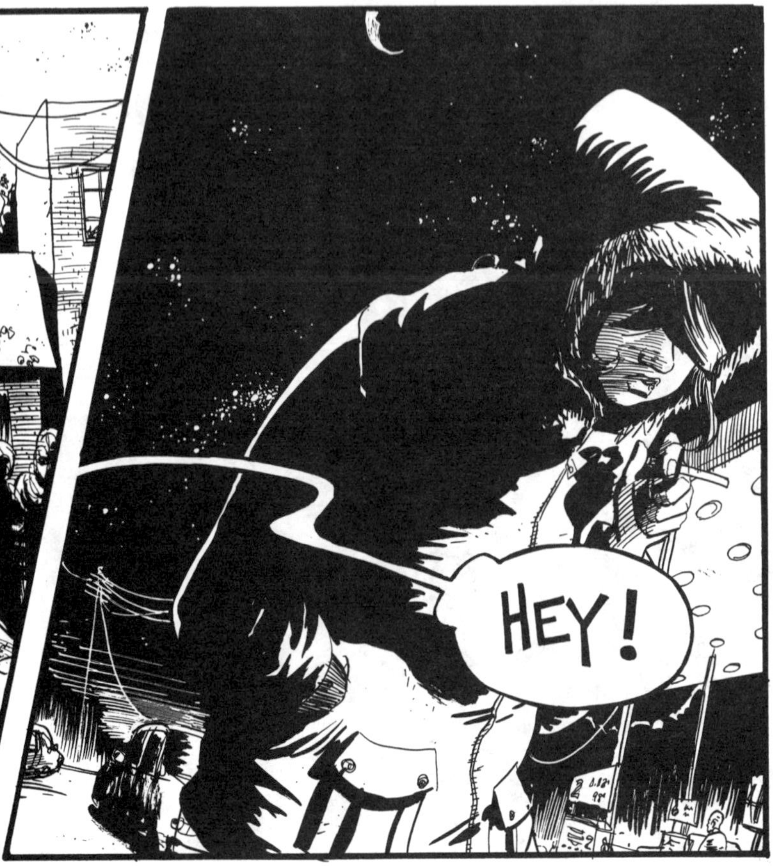
HEY!

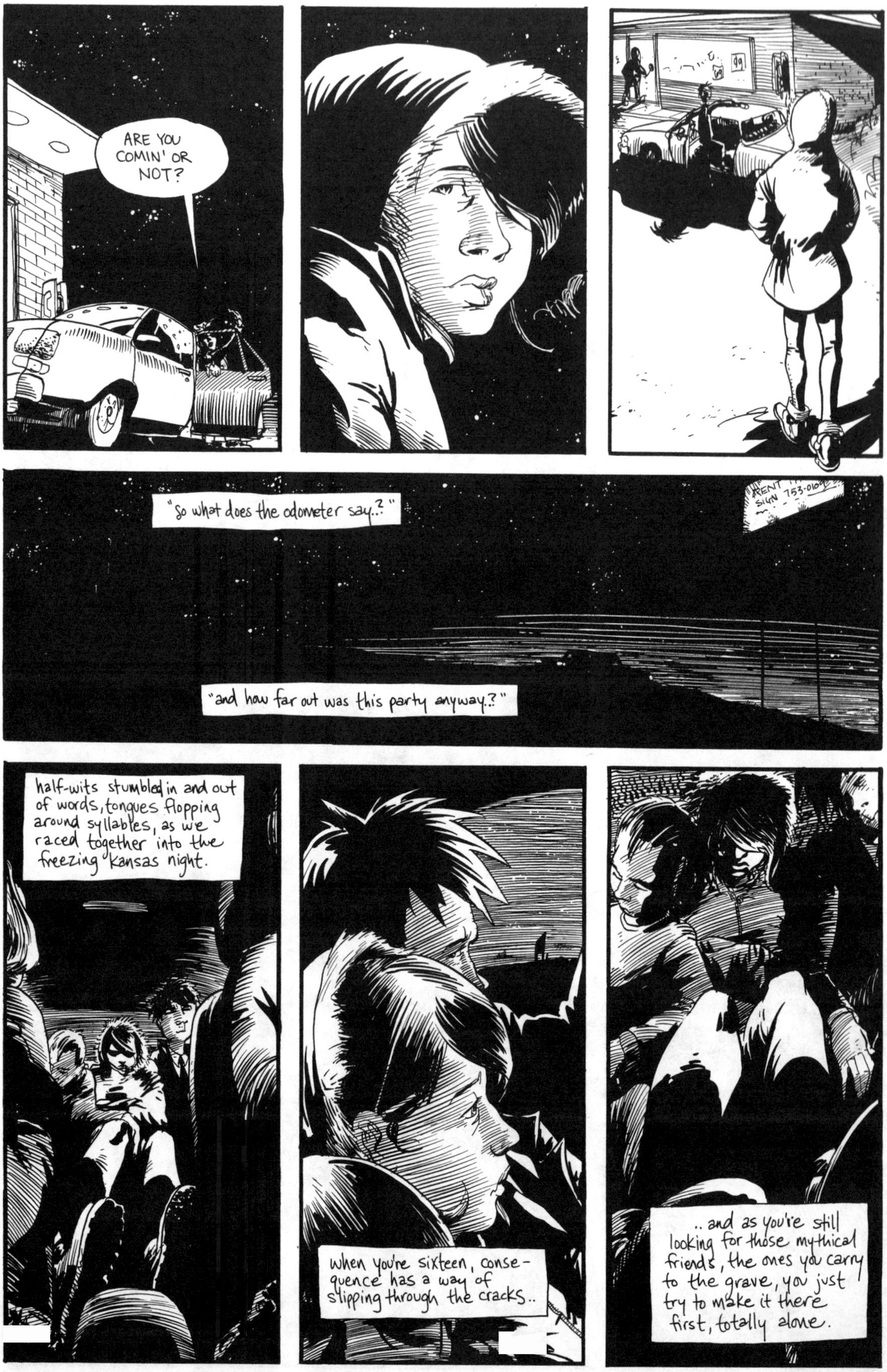
ARE YOU COMIN' OR NOT?
"so what does the odometer say..?"
"and how far out was this party anyway..?"
half-wits stumbled in and out of words, tongues flopping around syllables, as we raced together into the freezing kansas night.
when you're sixteen, consequence has a way of slipping through the cracks..
.. and as you're still looking for those mythical friends, the ones you carry to the grave, you just try to make it there first, totally alone.

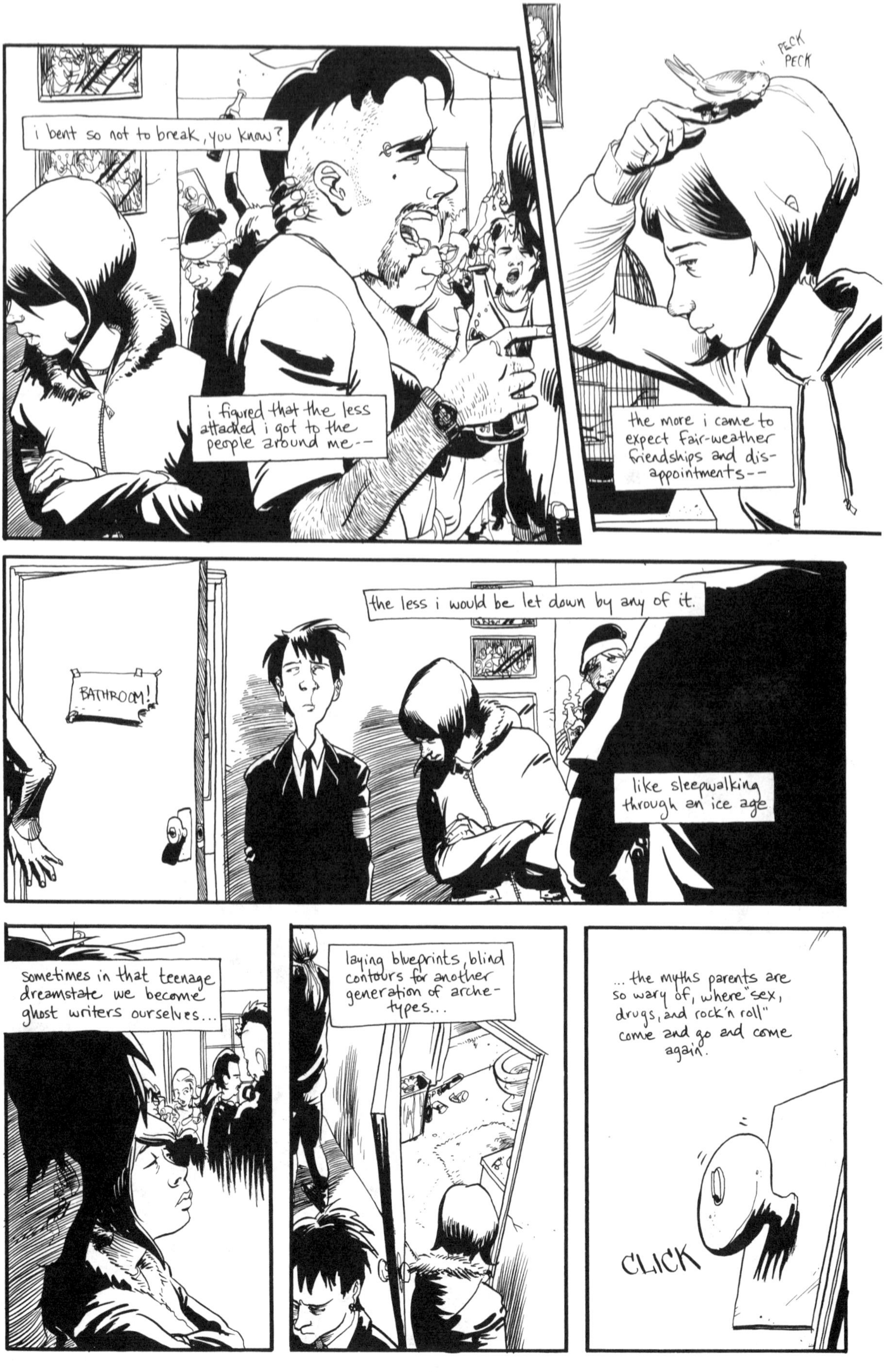
i bent so not to break, you know?
i figured that the less attached i got to the people around me--
PECK PECK
the more i came to expect fair-weather friendships and disappointments--
the less i would be let down by any of it.
BATHROOM!
like sleepwalking through an ice age
sometimes in that teenage dreamstate we become ghost writers ourselves...
laying blueprints, blind contours for another generation of archetypes...
... the myths parents are so wary of, where "sex, drugs, and rock'n roll" come and go and come again.
CLICK

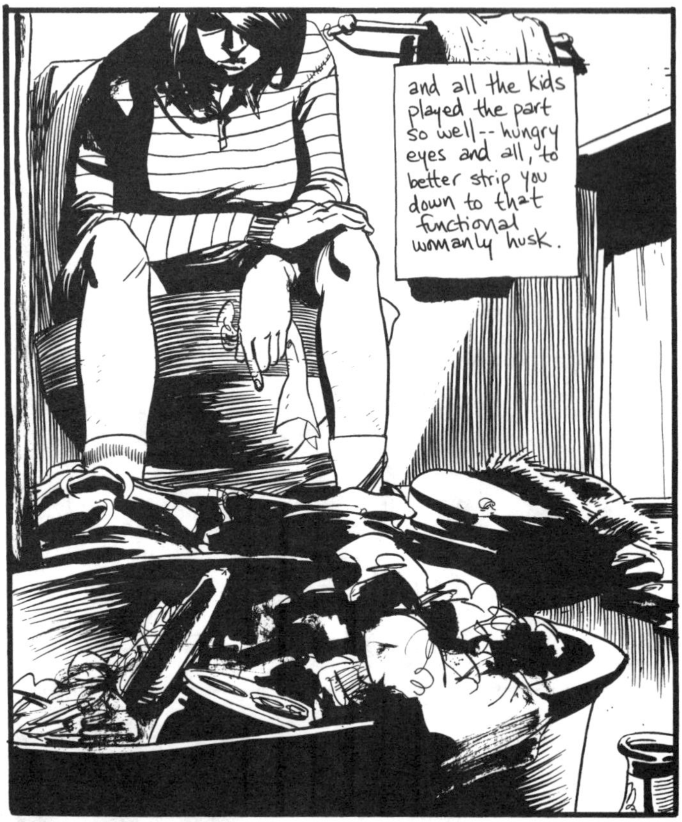
and all the kids played the part so well-- hungry eyes and all, to better strip you down to that functional womanly husk.

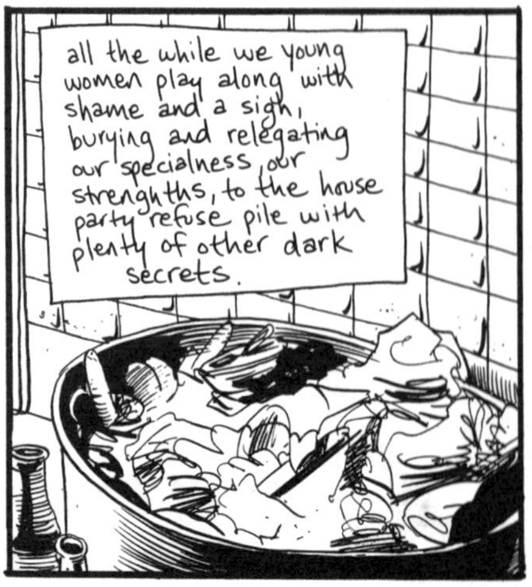
all the while we young women play along with shame and a sigh, burying and relegating our specialness, our strenghths, to the house party refuse pile with plenty of other dark secrets.

and as those boys around me _did_ make me feel objectified, i gradually assumed that the surest way to be appreciated or noticed was with that goddamn husk.

at the time, sleepwalking was simply survival.

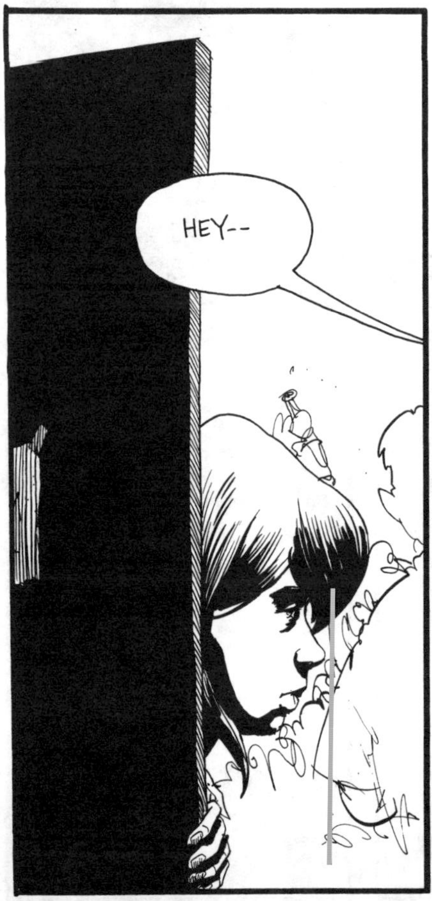
HEY--

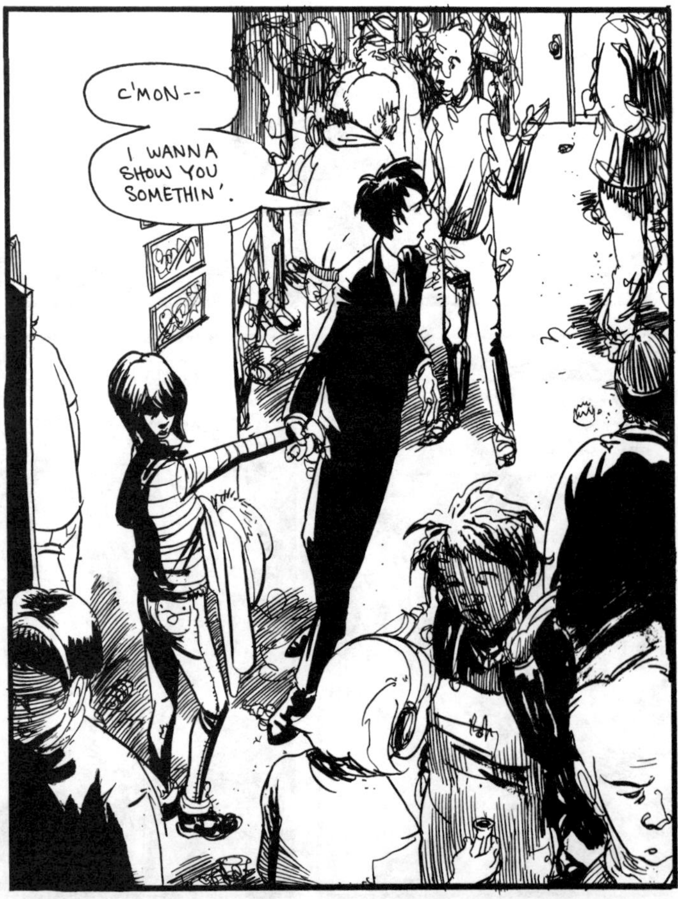
C'MON--
I WANNA SHOW YOU SOMETHIN'.

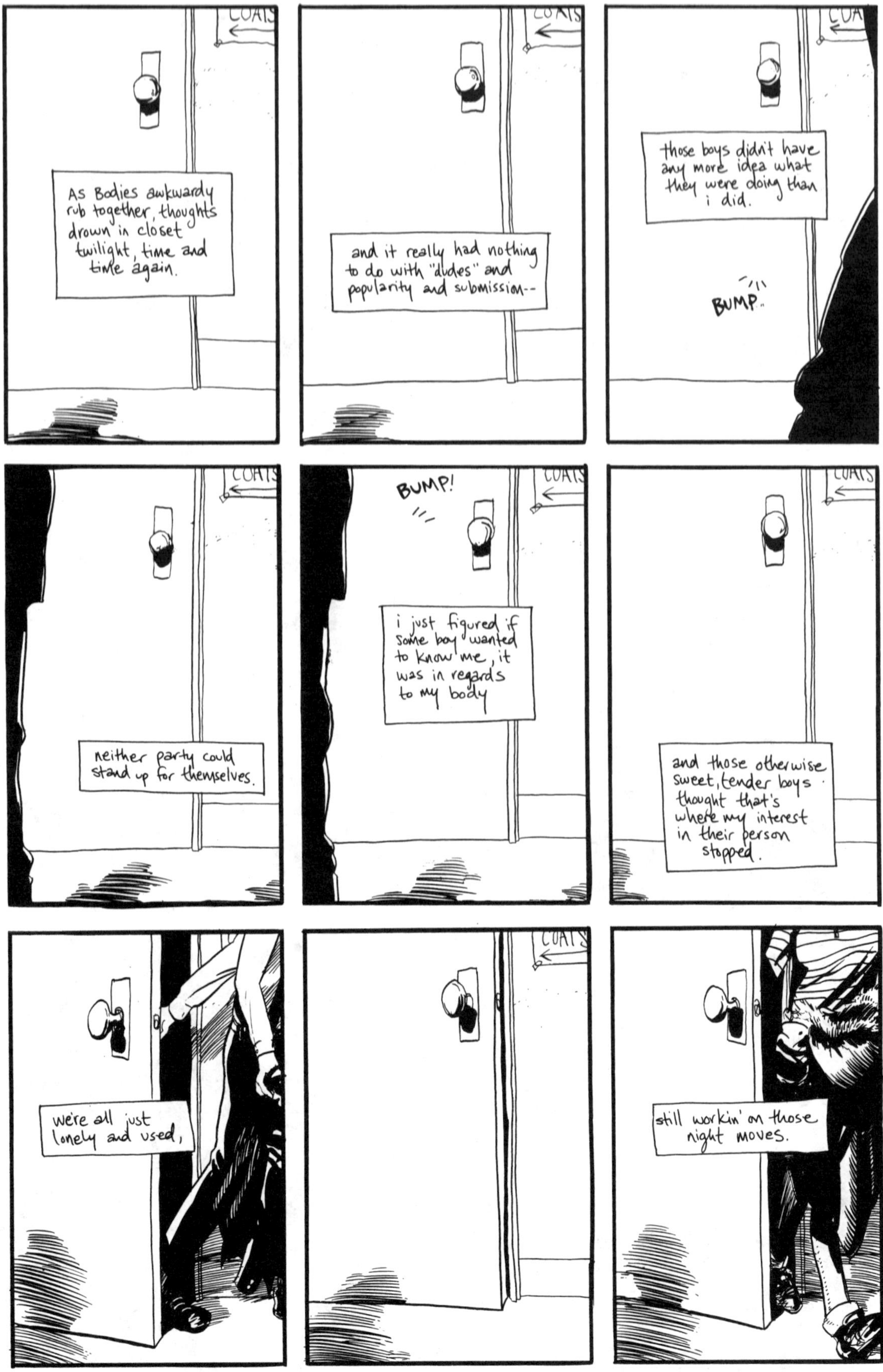
COATS
As Bodies awkwardy rub together, thoughts drown in closet twilight, time and time again.
COATS
and it really had nothing to do with "dudes" and popularity and submission--
COATS
those boys didn't have any more idea what they were doing than i did.
BUMP..
COATS
neither party could stand up for themselves.
BUMP!
COATS
i just figured if some boy wanted to know me, it was in regards to my body
COATS
and those otherwise sweet, tender boys thought that's where my interest in their person stopped.
we're all just lonely and used,
COATS
still workin' on those night moves.

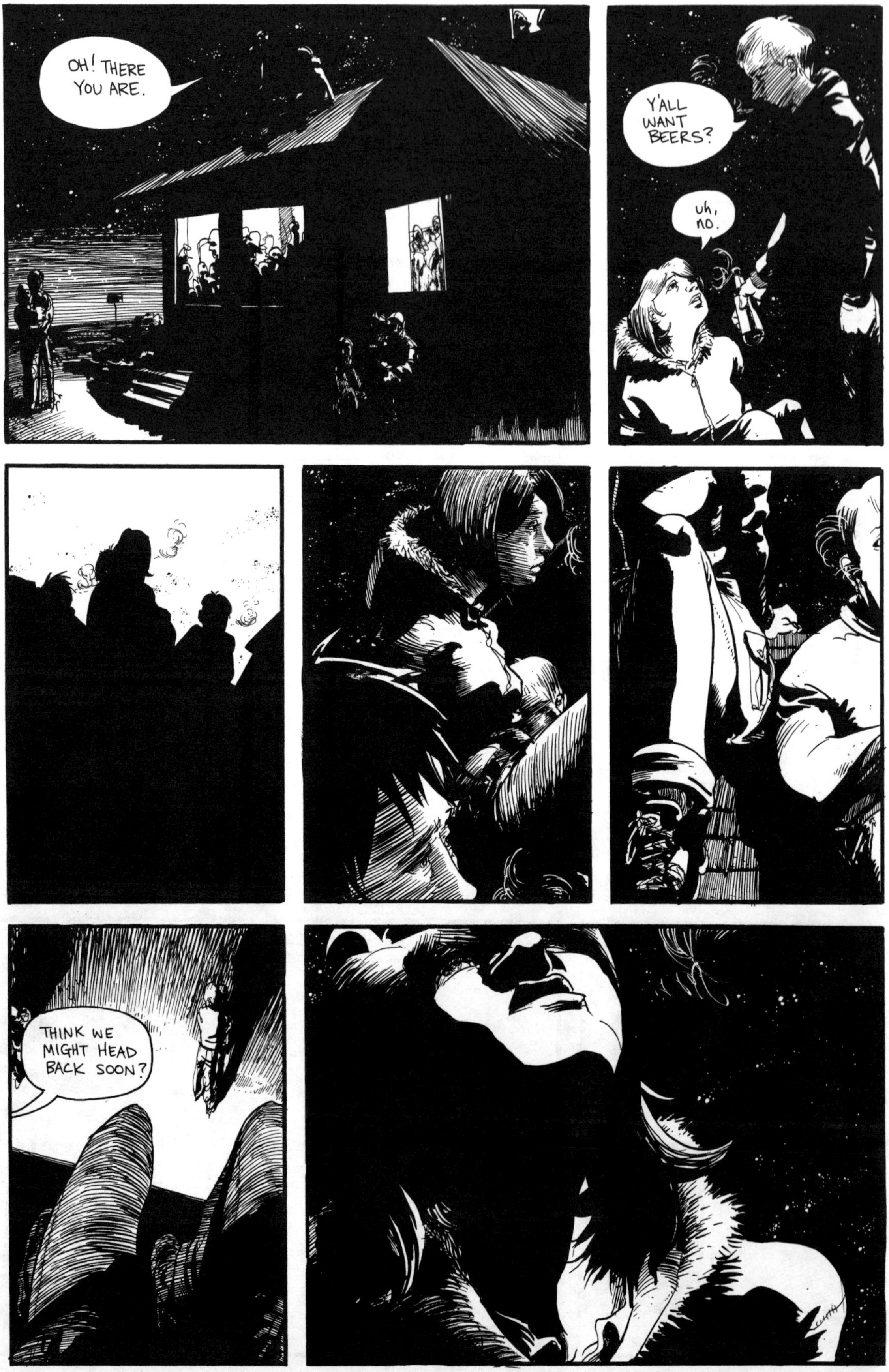
OH! THERE YOU ARE.
Y'ALL WANT BEERS?
uh, no.
THINK WE MIGHT HEAD BACK SOON?

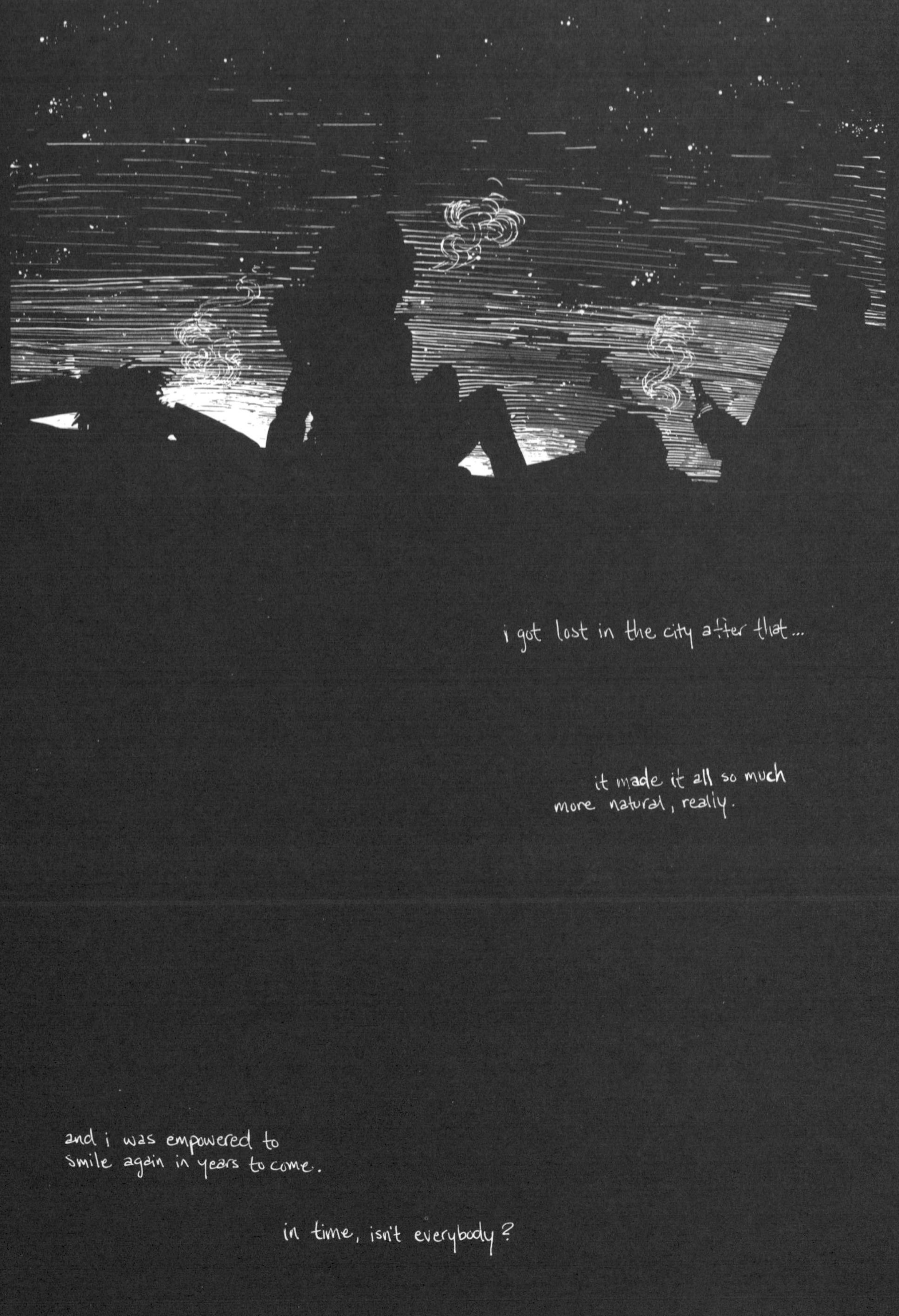
i got lost in the city after that...
it made it all so much more natural, really.
and i was empowered to smile again in years to come.
in time, isn't everybody?

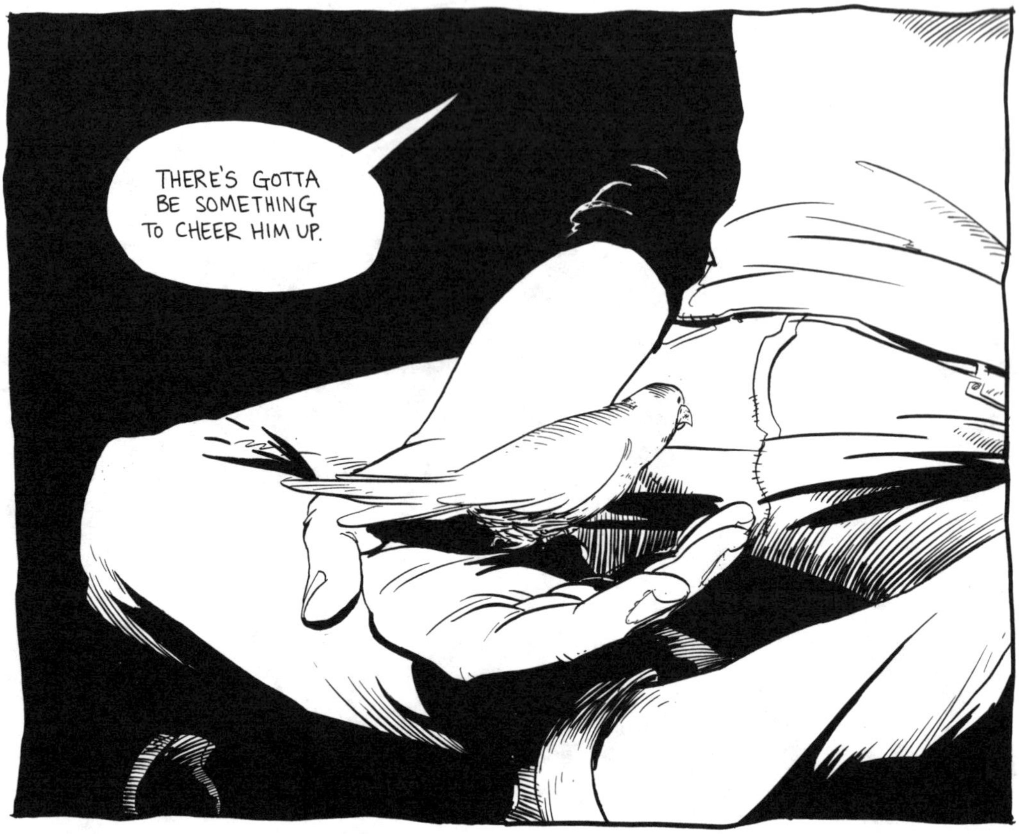
THERE'S GOTTA BE SOMETHING TO CHEER HIM UP.

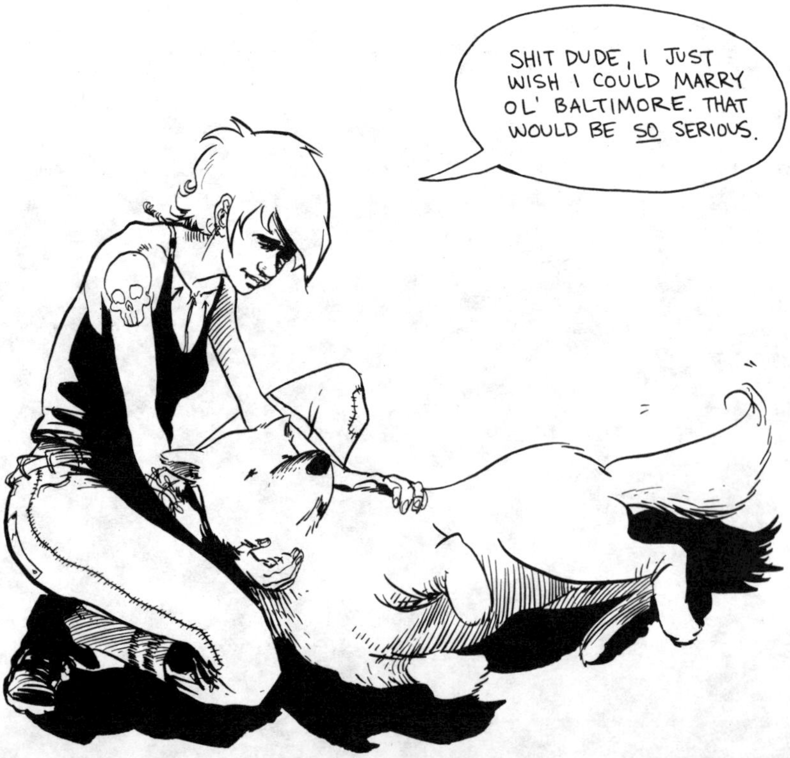
SHIT DUDE, I JUST WISH I COULD MARRY OL' BALTIMORE. THAT WOULD BE SO SERIOUS.

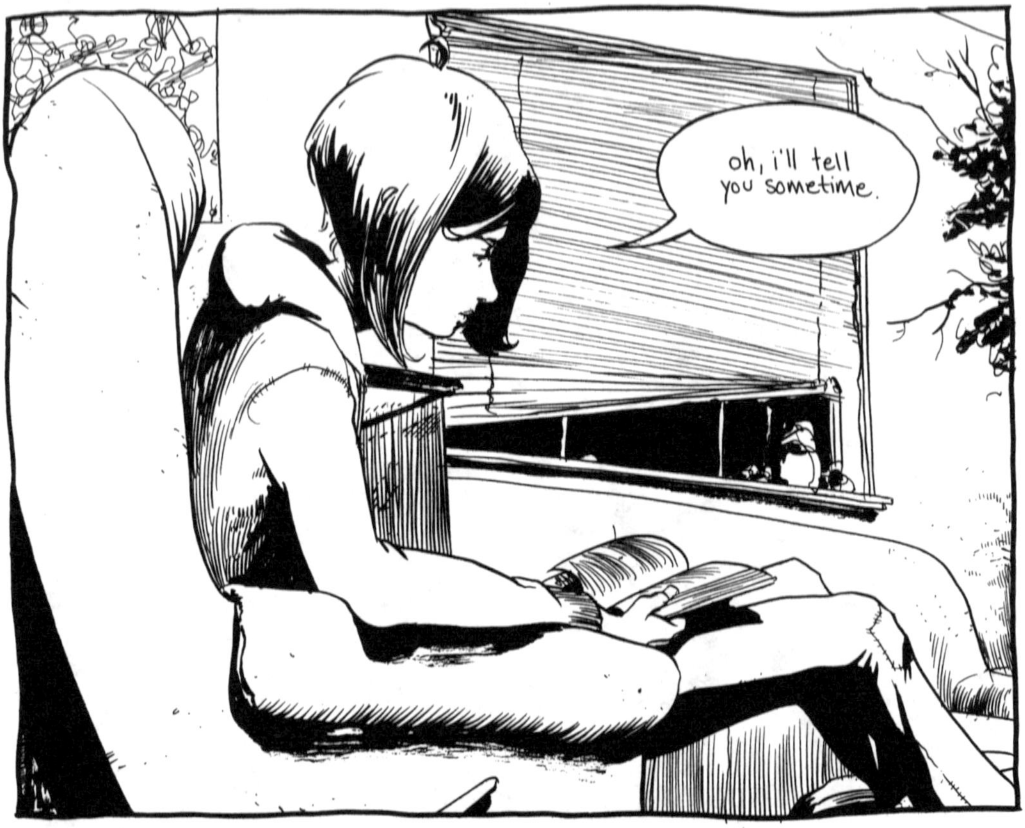
oh, i'll tell you sometime.

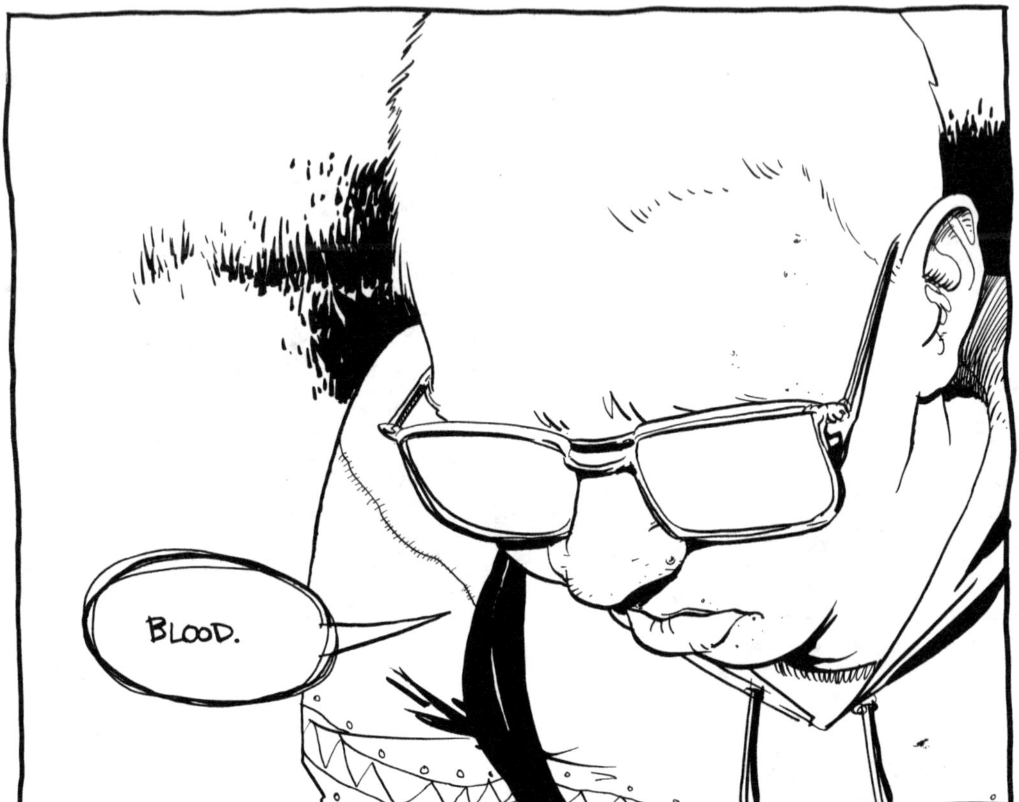
BLOOD.

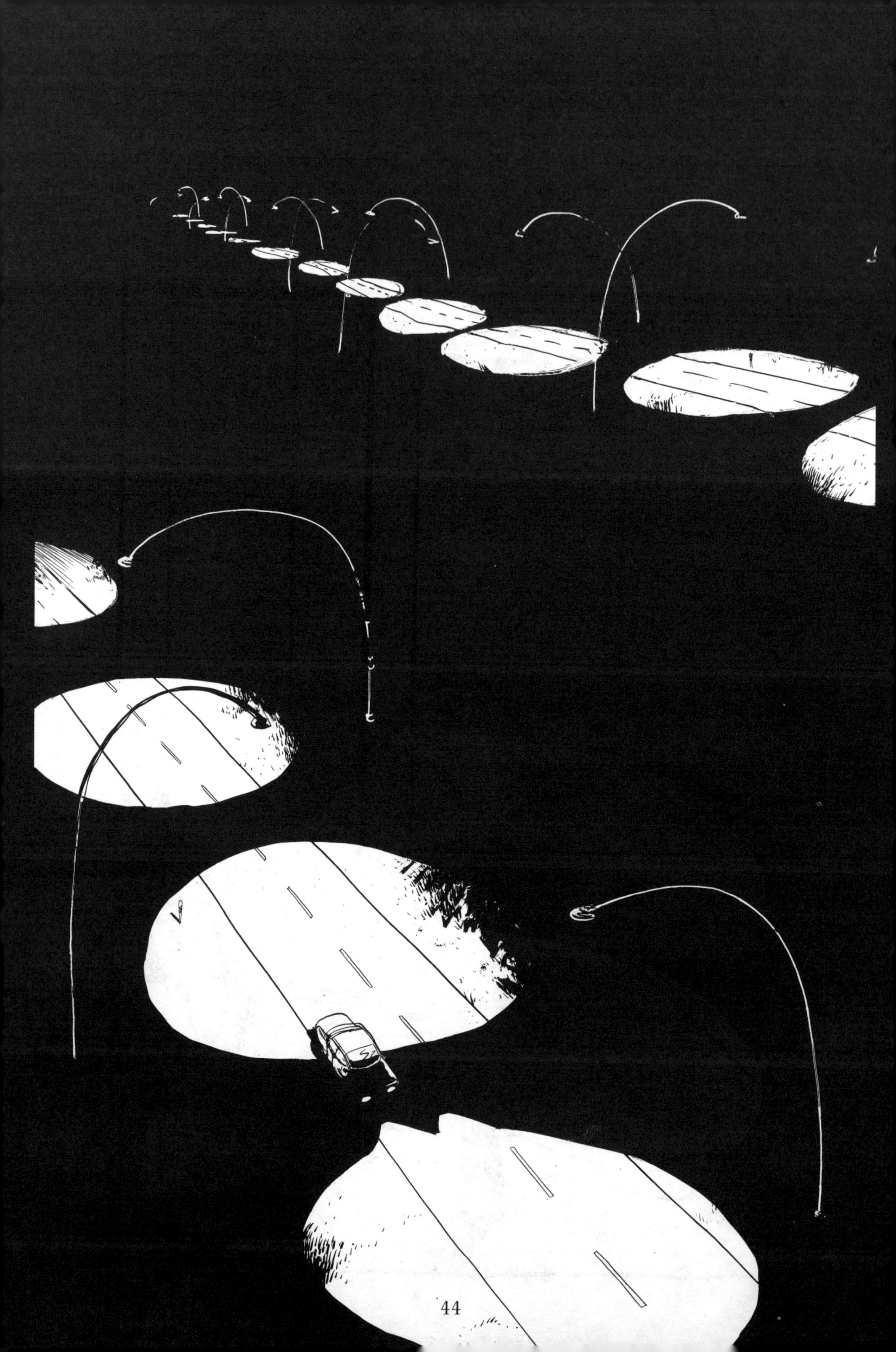

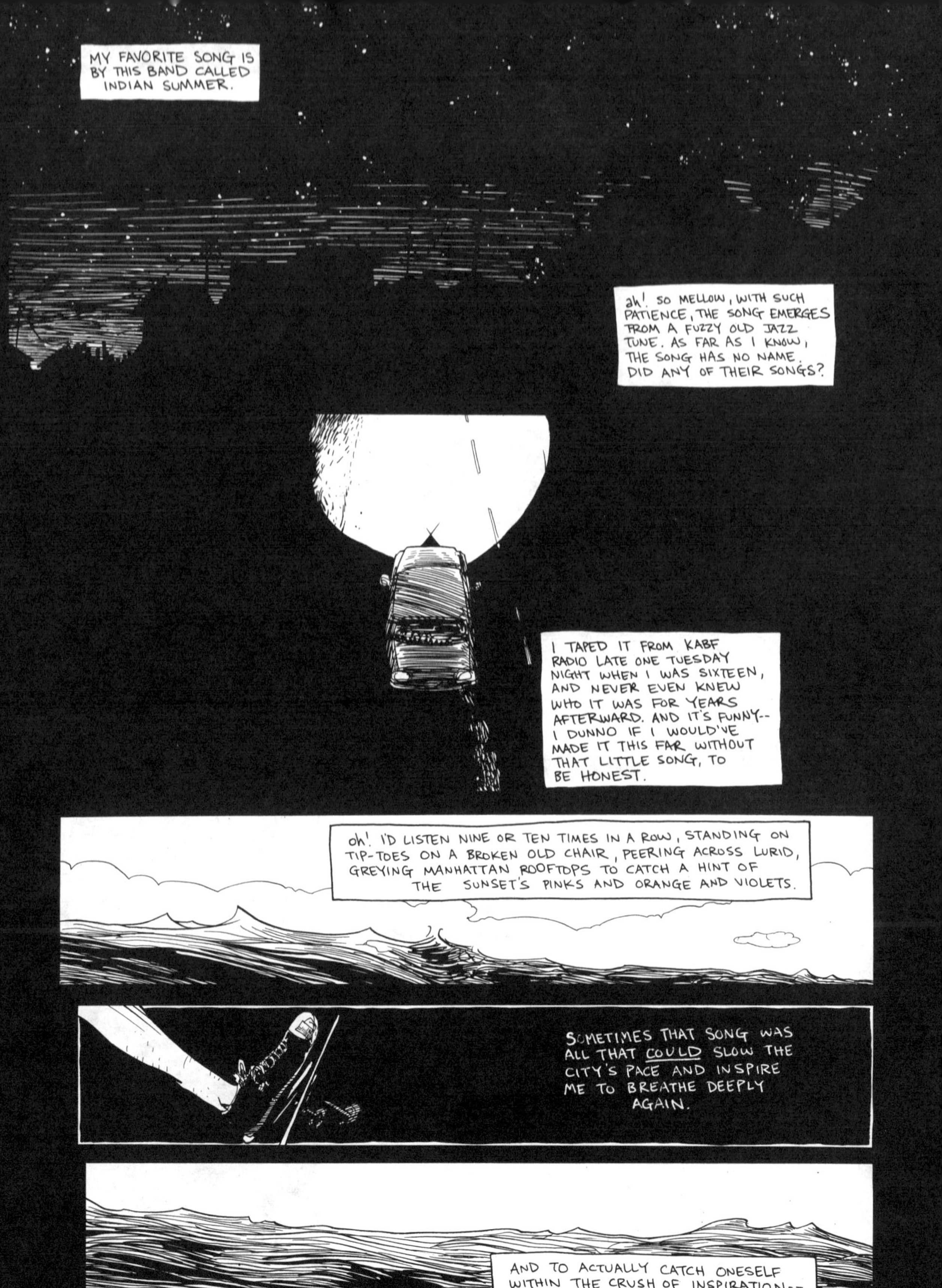
MY FAVORITE SONG IS BY THIS BAND CALLED INDIAN SUMMER.
ah! SO MELLOW, WITH SUCH PATIENCE, THE SONG EMERGES FROM A FUZZY OLD JAZZ TUNE. AS FAR AS I KNOW, THE SONG HAS NO NAME. DID ANY OF THEIR SONGS?
I TAPED IT FROM KABF RADIO LATE ONE TUESDAY NIGHT WHEN I WAS SIXTEEN, AND NEVER EVEN KNEW WHO IT WAS FOR YEARS AFTERWARD. AND IT'S FUNNY-- I DUNNO IF I WOULD'VE MADE IT THIS FAR WITHOUT THAT LITTLE SONG, TO BE HONEST.
oh! I'D LISTEN NINE OR TEN TIMES IN A ROW, STANDING ON TIP-TOES ON A BROKEN OLD CHAIR, PEERING ACROSS LURID, GREYING MANHATTAN ROOFTOPS TO CATCH A HINT OF THE SUNSET'S PINKS AND ORANGE AND VIOLETS.
SOMETIMES THAT SONG WAS ALL THAT COULD SLOW THE CITY'S PACE AND INSPIRE ME TO BREATHE DEEPLY AGAIN.
AND TO ACTUALLY CATCH ONESELF WITHIN THE CRUSH OF INSPIRATION--

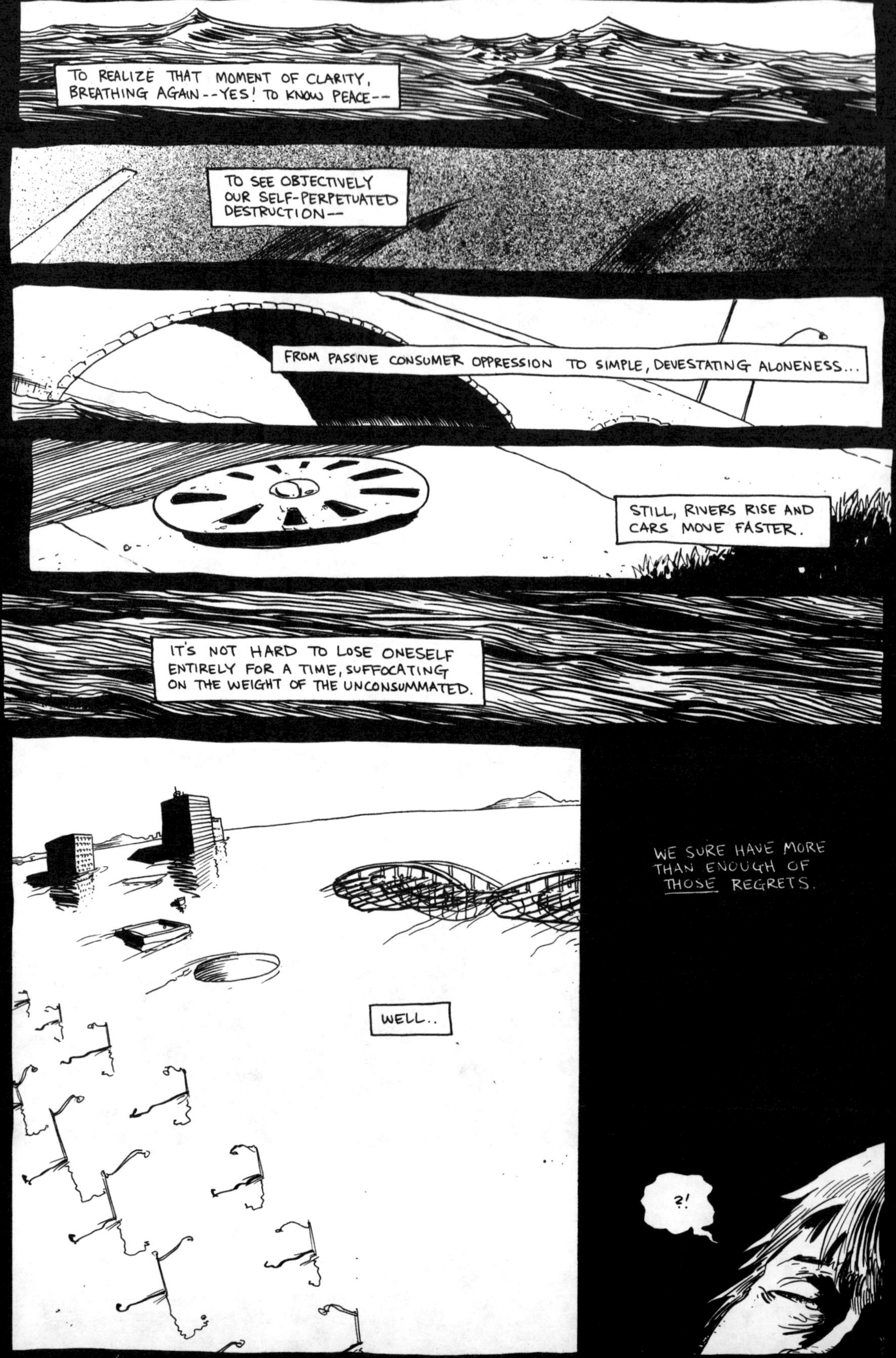
TO REALIZE THAT MOMENT OF CLARITY, BREATHING AGAIN--YES! TO KNOW PEACE--
TO SEE OBJECTIVELY OUR SELF-PERPETUATED DESTRUCTION--
FROM PASSIVE CONSUMER OPPRESSION TO SIMPLE, DEVESTATING ALONENESS...
STILL, RIVERS RISE AND CARS MOVE FASTER.
IT'S NOT HARD TO LOSE ONESELF ENTIRELY FOR A TIME, SUFFOCATING ON THE WEIGHT OF THE UNCONSUMMATED.
WELL..
WE SURE HAVE MORE THAN ENOUGH OF THOSE REGRETS.
?!

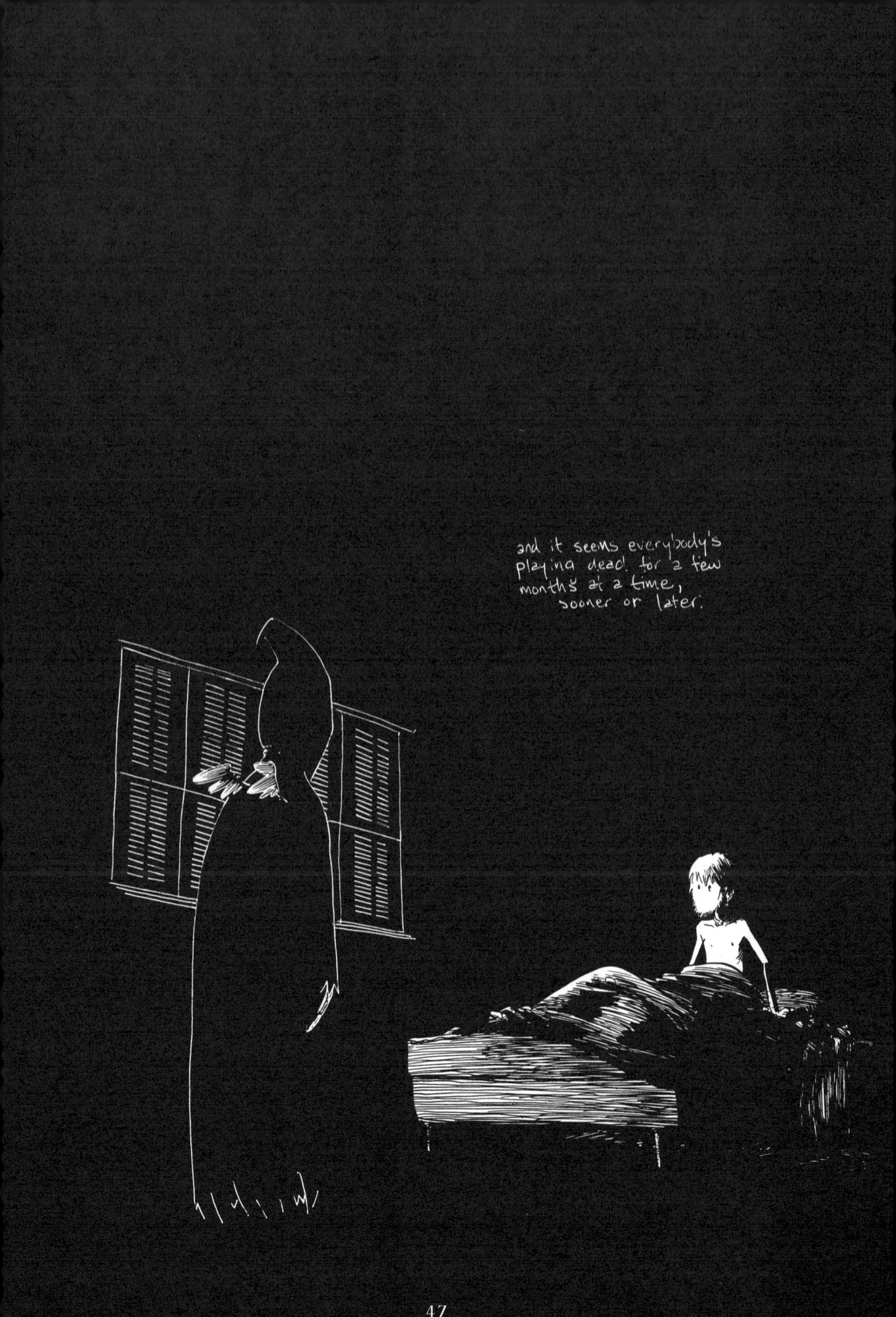
and it seems everybody's playing dead for a few months at a time, sooner or later.

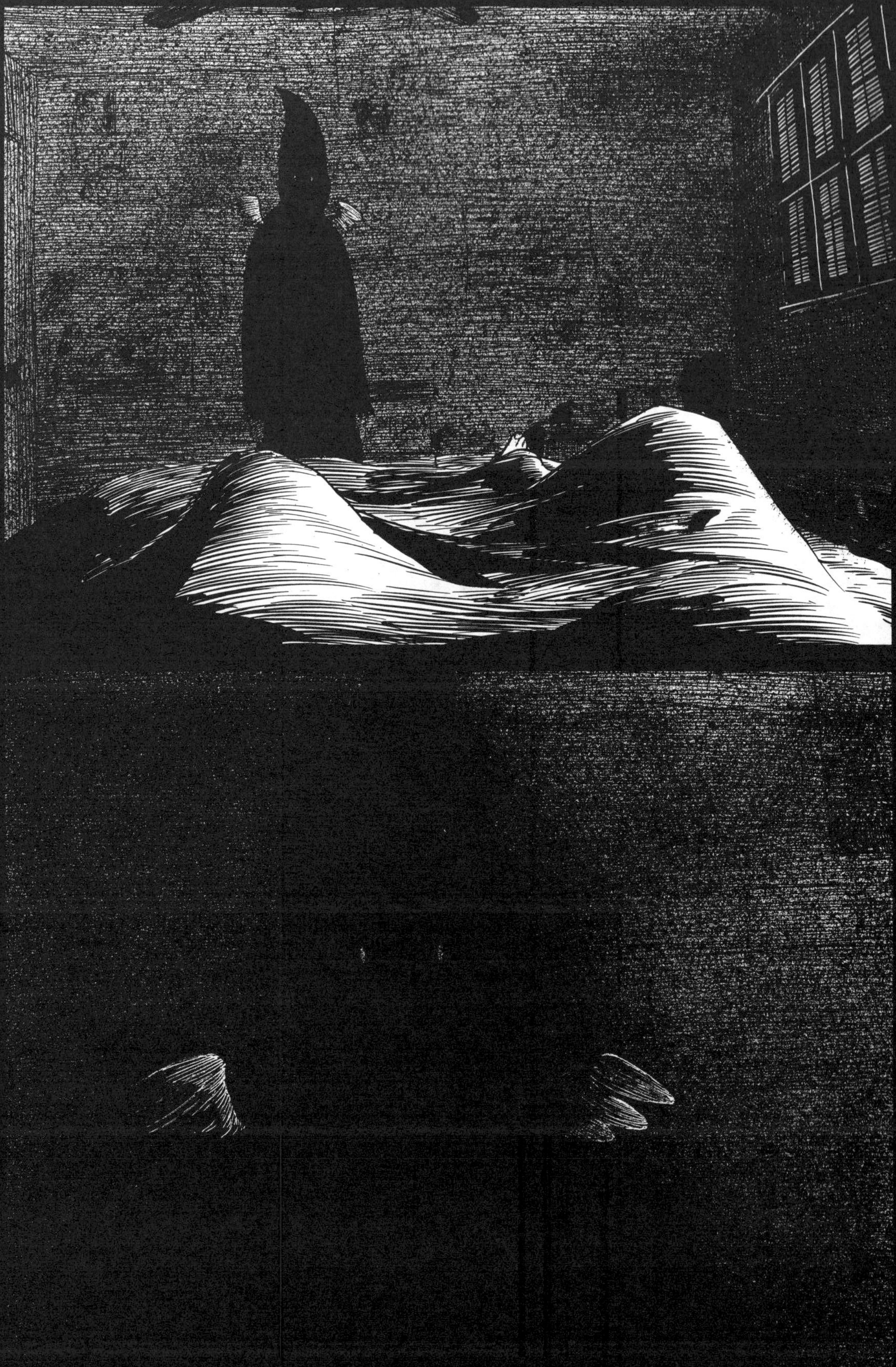

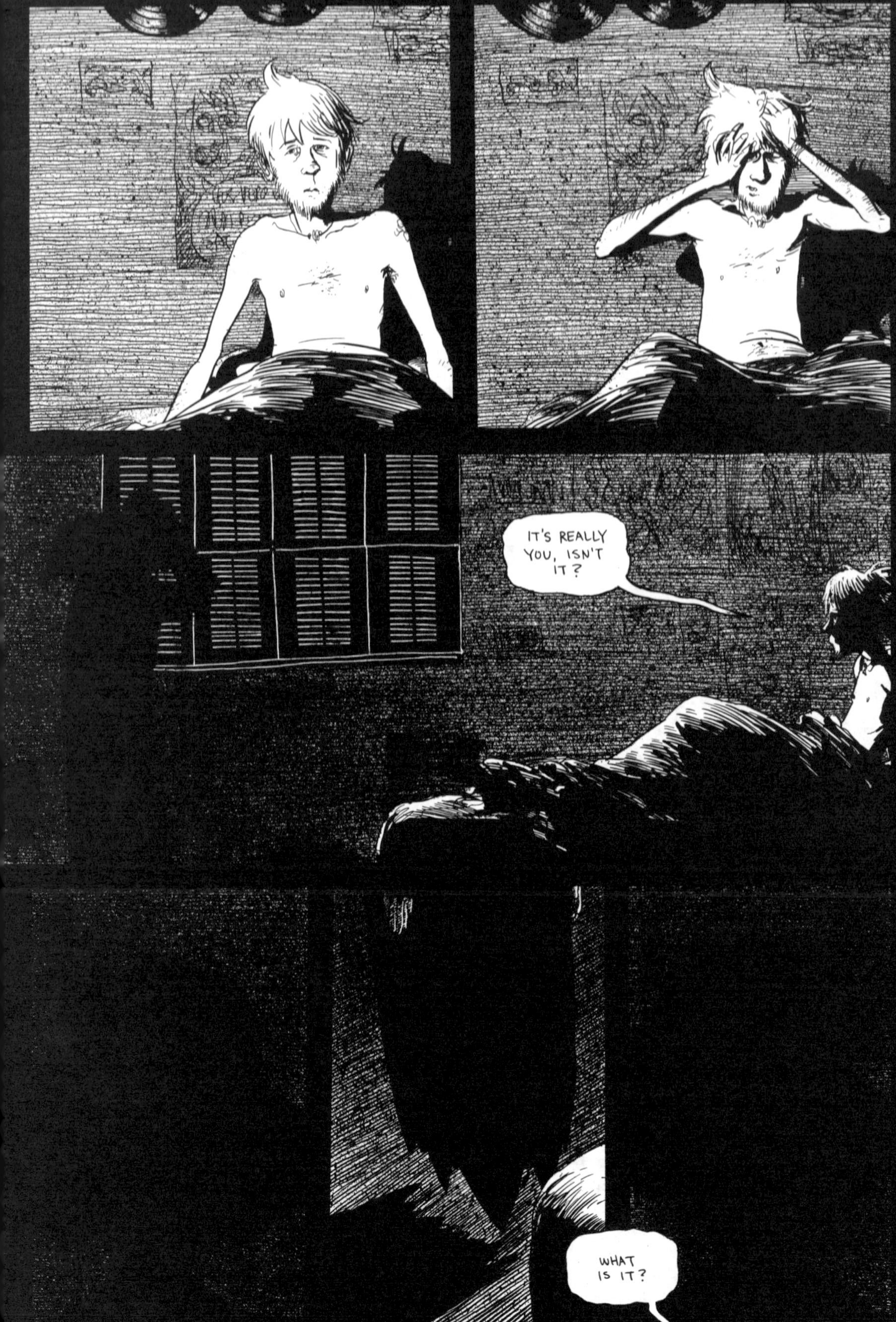
IT'S REALLY YOU, ISN'T IT?
WHAT IS IT?

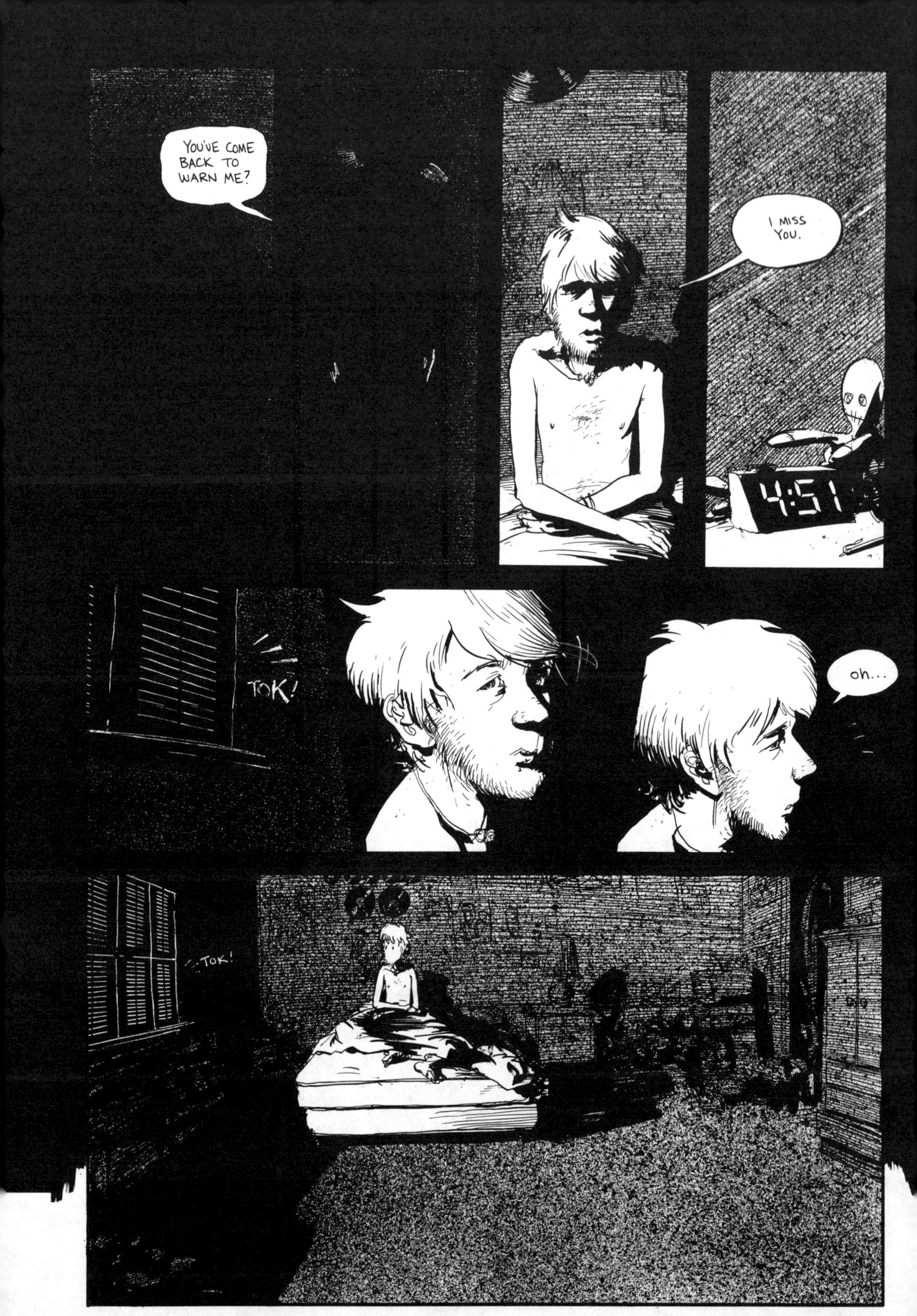
YOU'VE COME BACK TO WARN ME?
I MISS YOU.
4:51
TOK!
oh...
TOK!

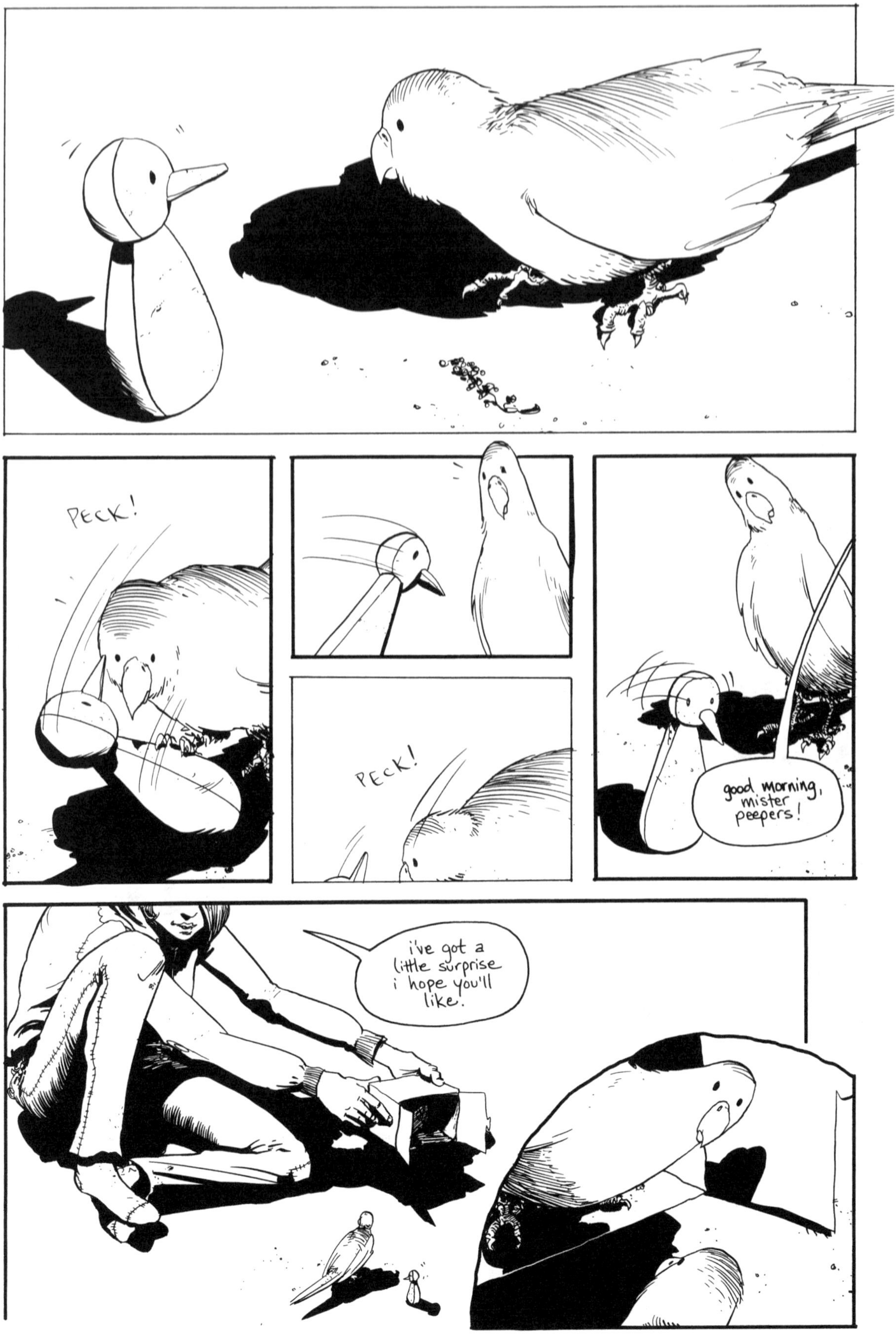
PECK!
PECK!
good morning, mister peepers!
i've got a little surprise i hope you'll like.

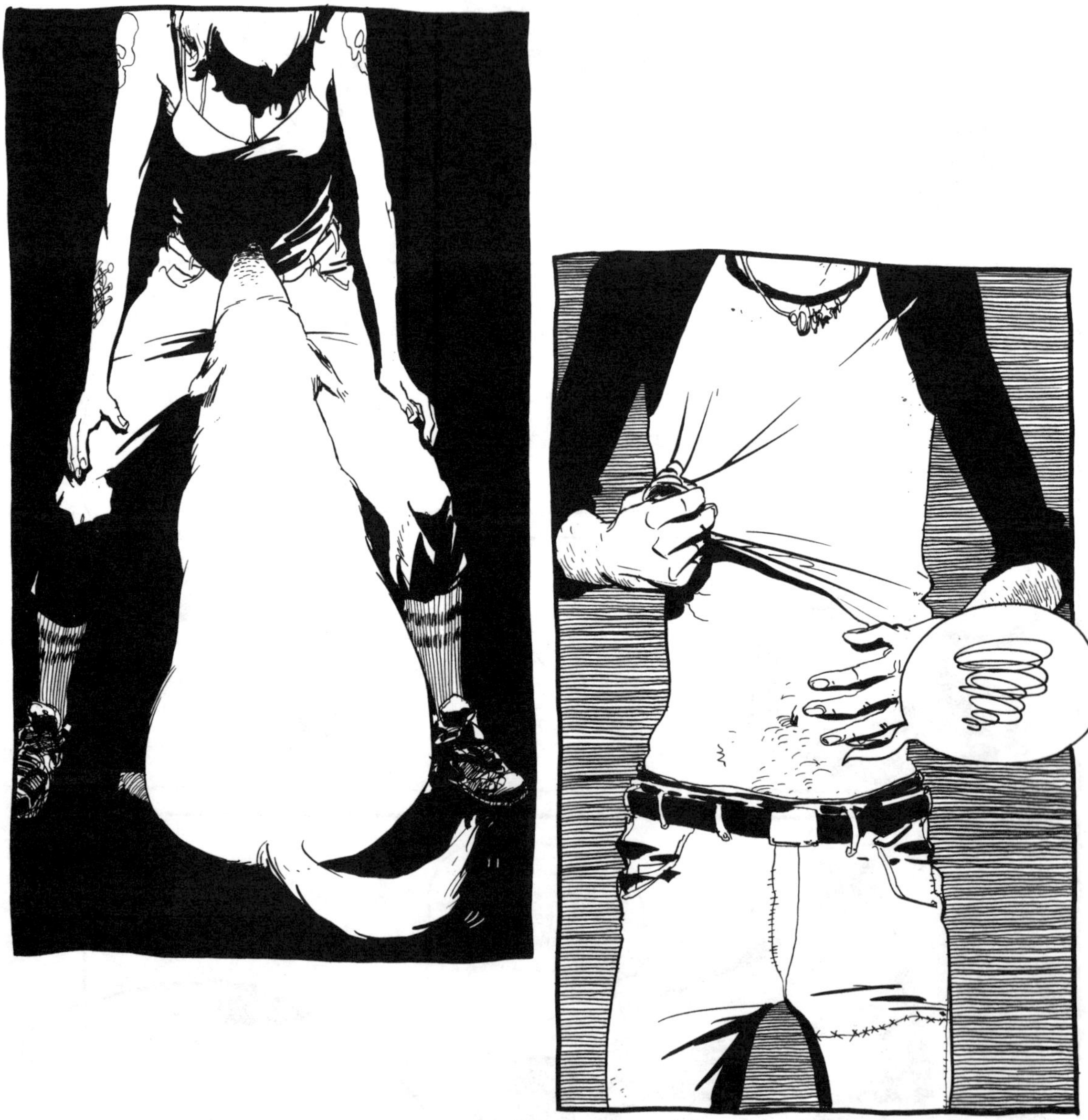

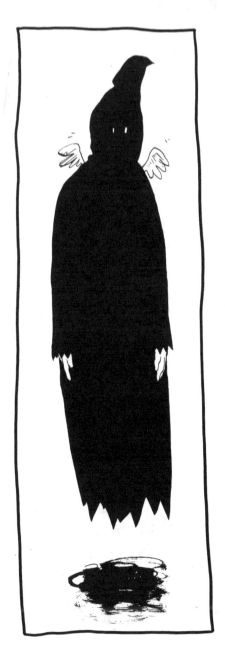

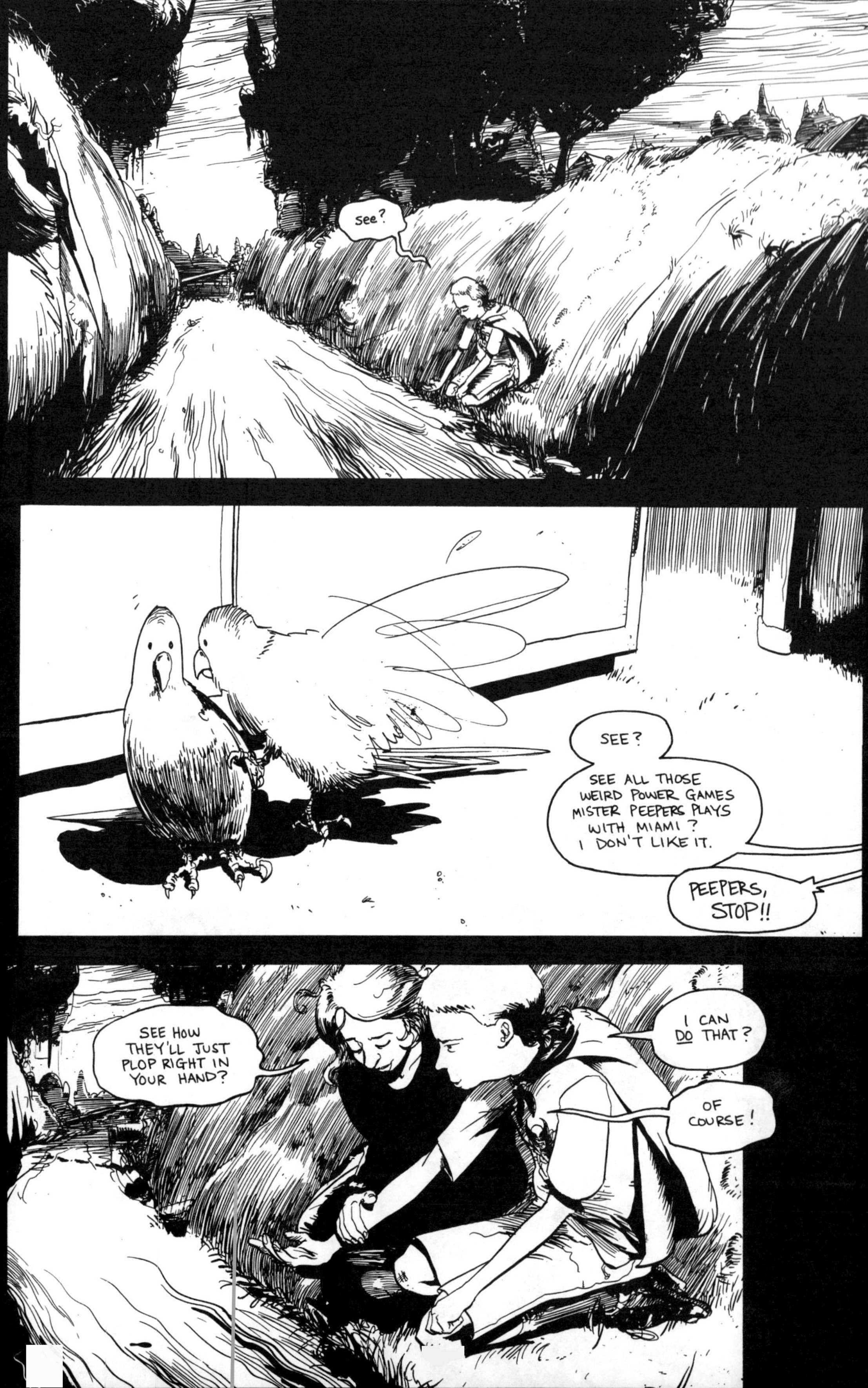

See?
SEE?
SEE ALL THOSE WEIRD POWER GAMES MISTER PEEPERS PLAYS WITH MIAMI? I DON'T LIKE IT.
PEEPERS, STOP!!
SEE HOW THEY'LL JUST PLOP RIGHT IN YOUR HAND?
I CAN DO THAT?
OF COURSE!

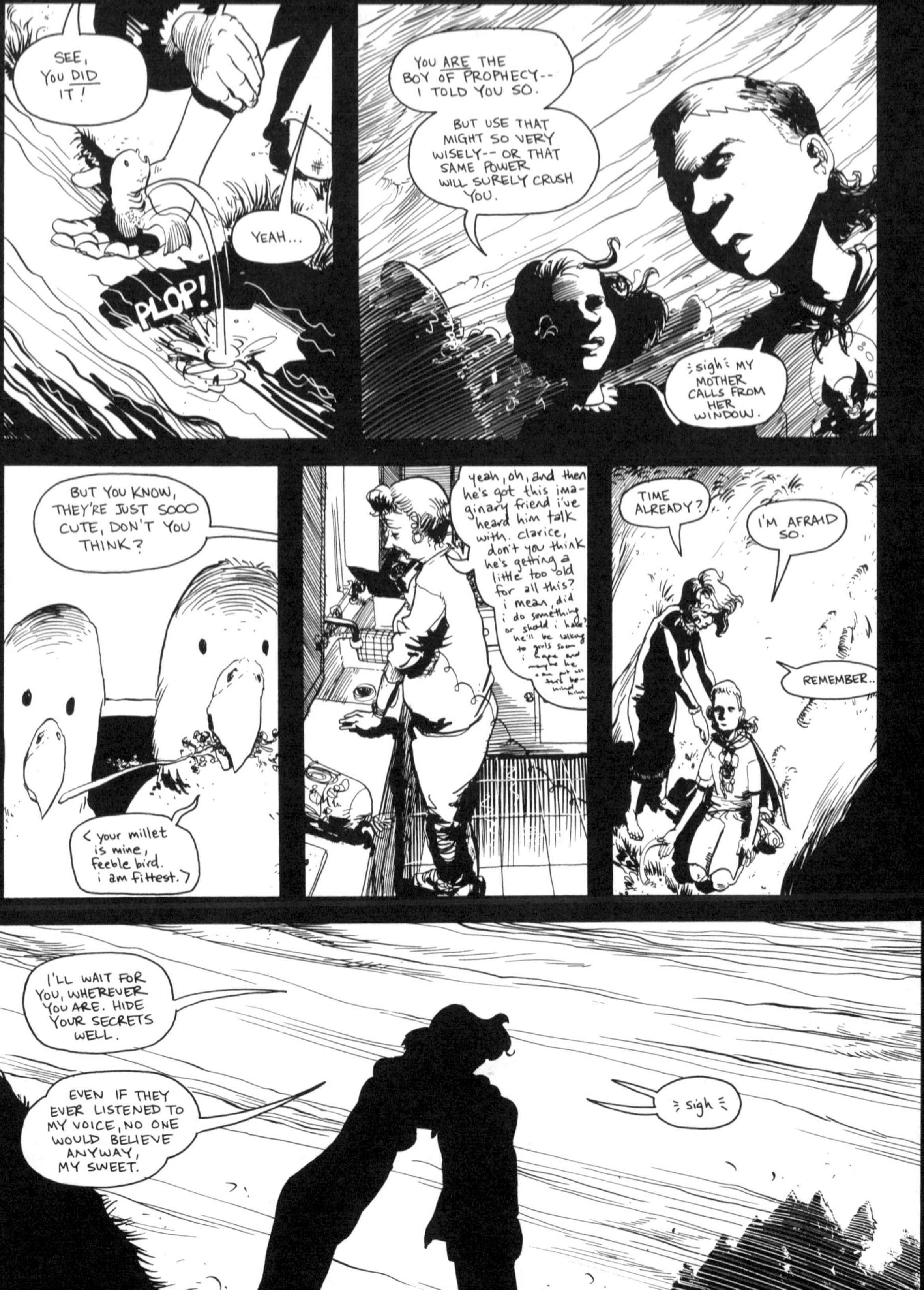
SEE, YOU DID IT!
YEAH...
PLOP!
YOU ARE THE BOY OF PROPHECY-- I TOLD YOU SO.
BUT USE THAT MIGHT SO VERY WISELY-- OR THAT SAME POWER WILL SURELY CRUSH YOU.
⁝sigh⁝ MY MOTHER CALLS FROM HER WINDOW.
BUT YOU KNOW, THEY'RE JUST SOOO CUTE, DON'T YOU THINK?
<your millet is mine, feeble bird. i am fittest.>
yeah, oh, and then he's got this imaginary friend i've heard him talk with. clarice, don't you think he's getting a little too old for all this? i mean, did i do something or should i have? he'll be talking to girls soon i hope and maybe he
TIME ALREADY?
I'M AFRAID SO.
REMEMBER..
I'LL WAIT FOR YOU, WHEREVER YOU ARE. HIDE YOUR SECRETS WELL.
EVEN IF THEY EVER LISTENED TO MY VOICE, NO ONE WOULD BELIEVE ANYWAY, MY SWEET.
⁝sigh⁝

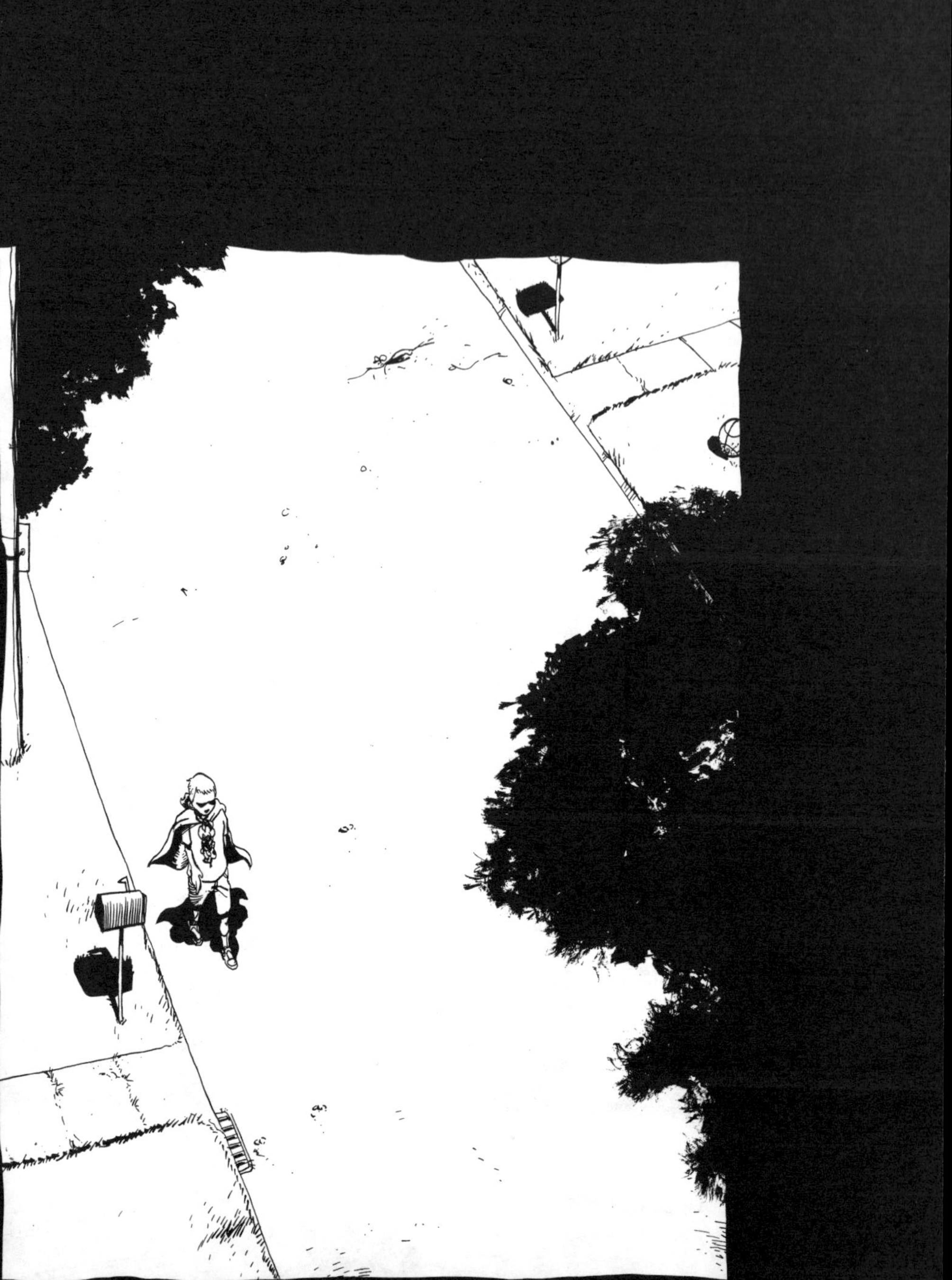

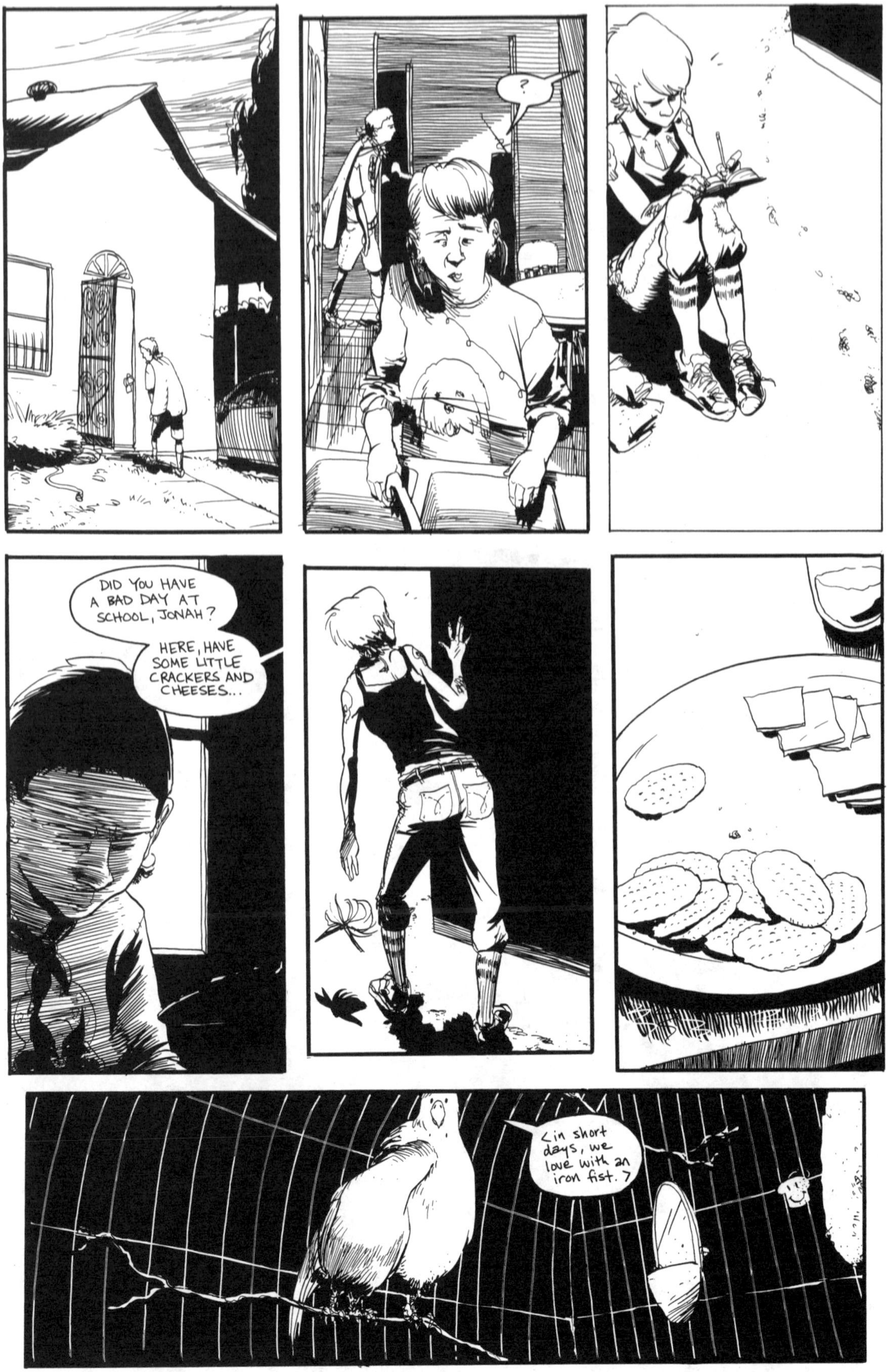
?
DID YOU HAVE A BAD DAY AT SCHOOL, JONAH?
HERE, HAVE SOME LITTLE CRACKERS AND CHEESES...
<in short days, we love with an iron fist.>

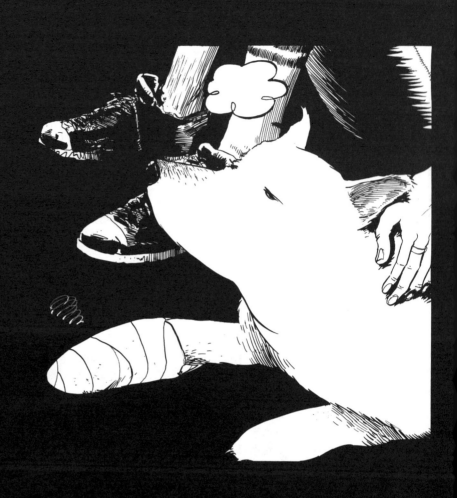

TOK!

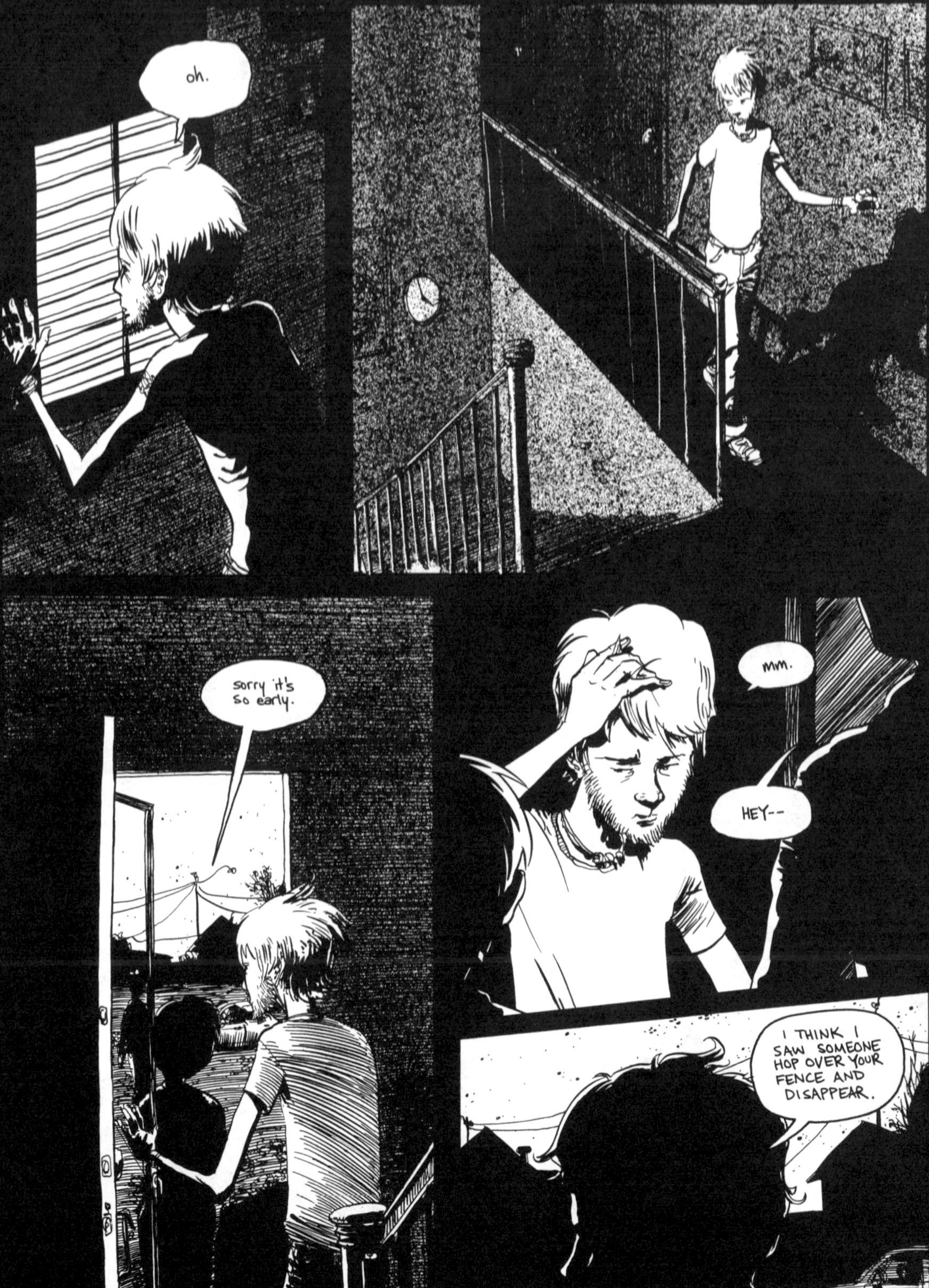
oh.
sorry it's so early.
mm.
HEY--
I THINK I SAW SOMEONE HOP OVER YOUR FENCE AND DISAPPEAR.

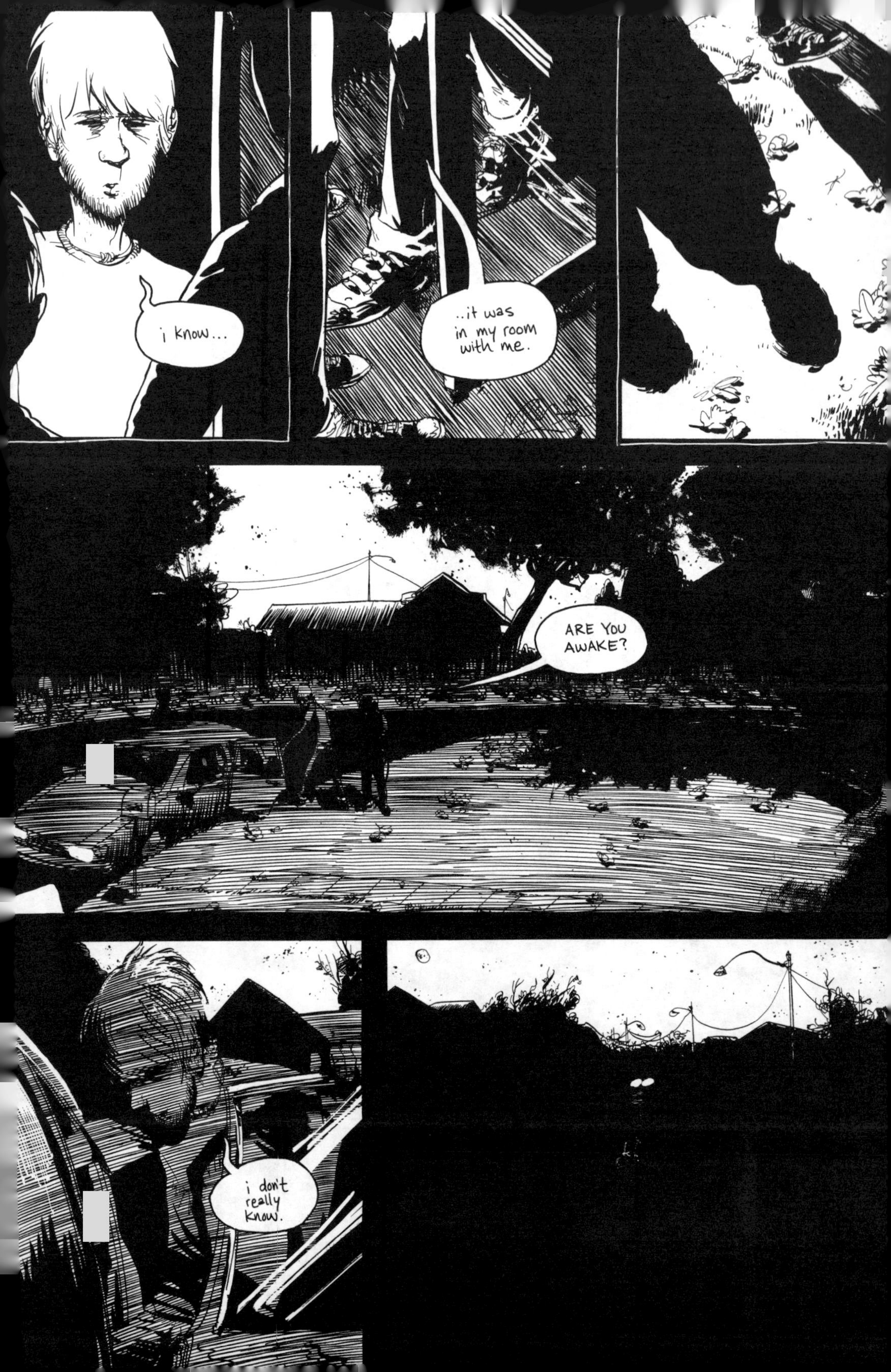
i know...
..it was in my room with me.
ARE YOU AWAKE?
i don't really know.

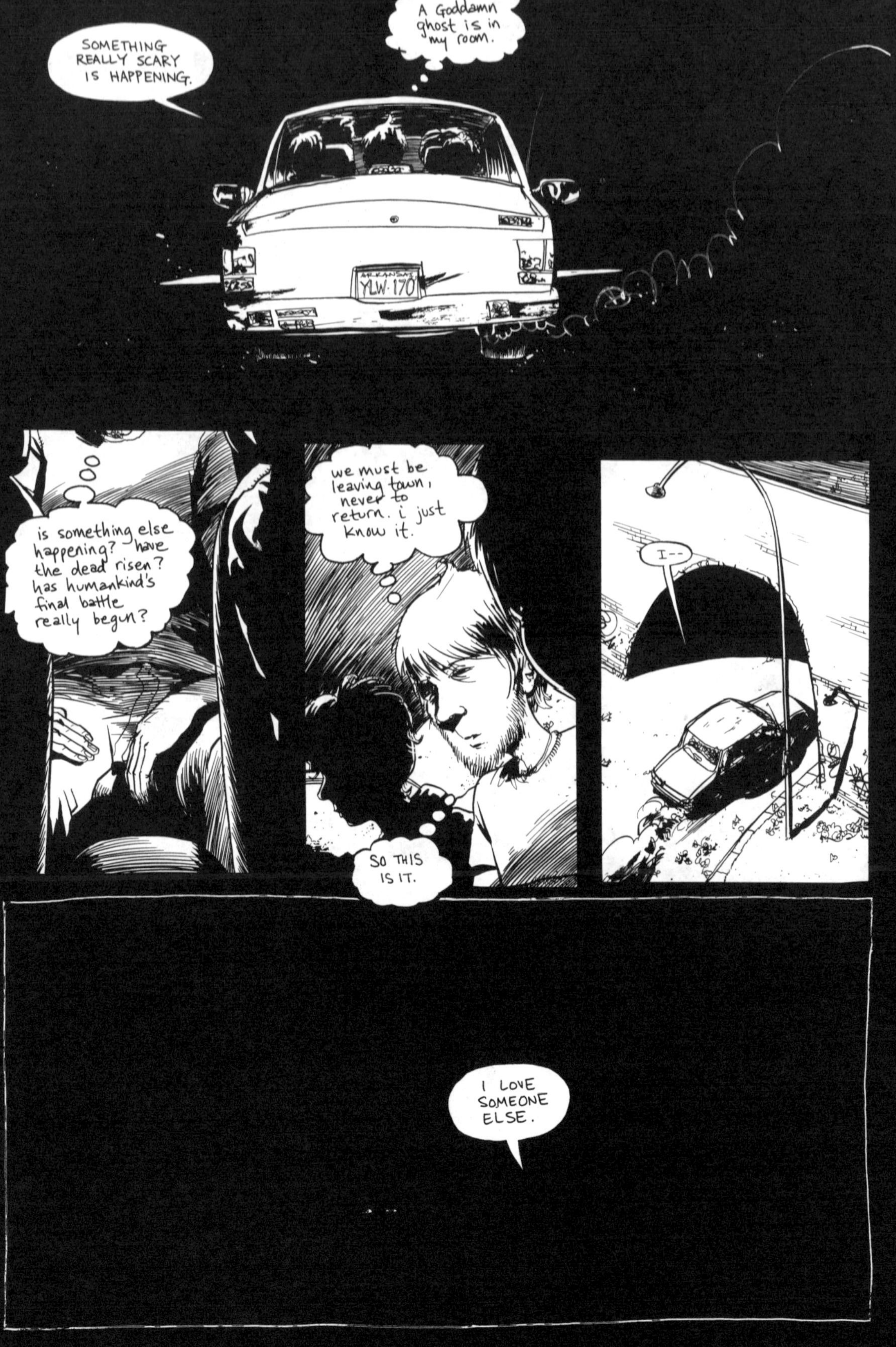

SOMETHING REALLY SCARY IS HAPPENING.
A Goddamn ghost is in my room.
is something else happening? have the dead risen? has humankind's final battle really begun?
we must be leaving town, never to return. i just know it.
SO THIS IS IT.
I--
I LOVE SOMEONE ELSE.

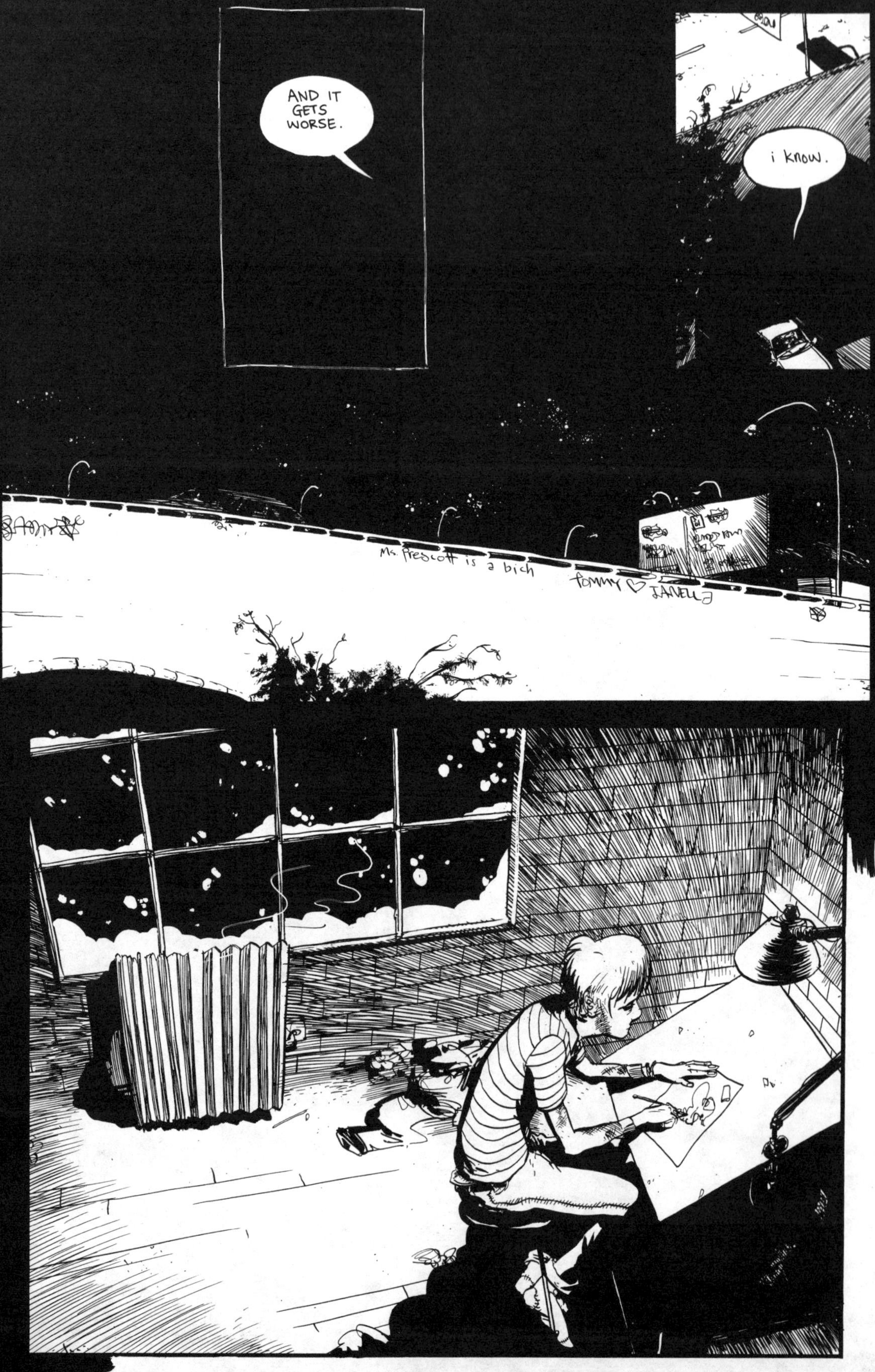
AND IT GETS WORSE.
i know.
Ms. Prescott is a bich
TOMMY ♡ JANELL

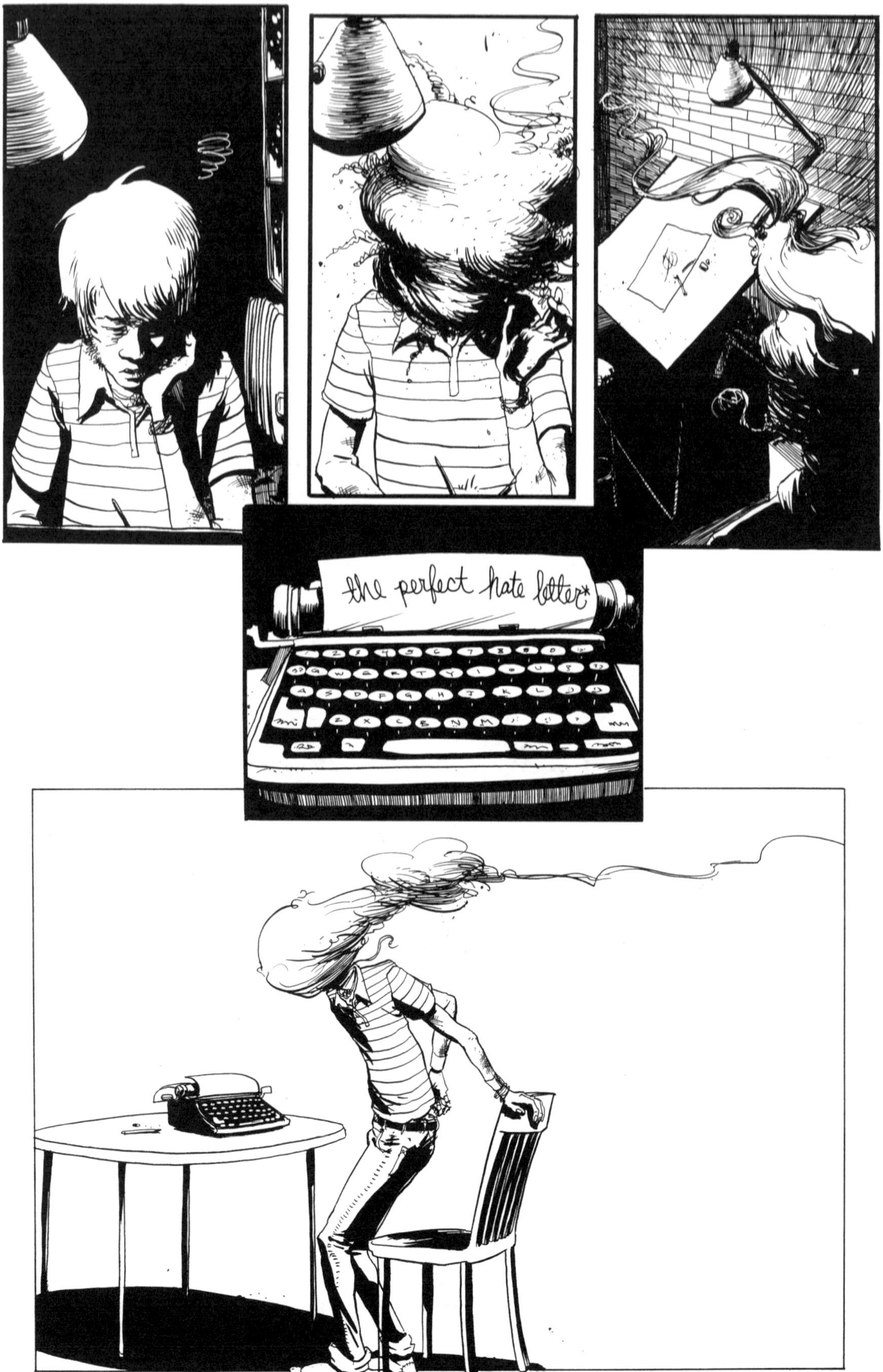
the perfect hate letter*

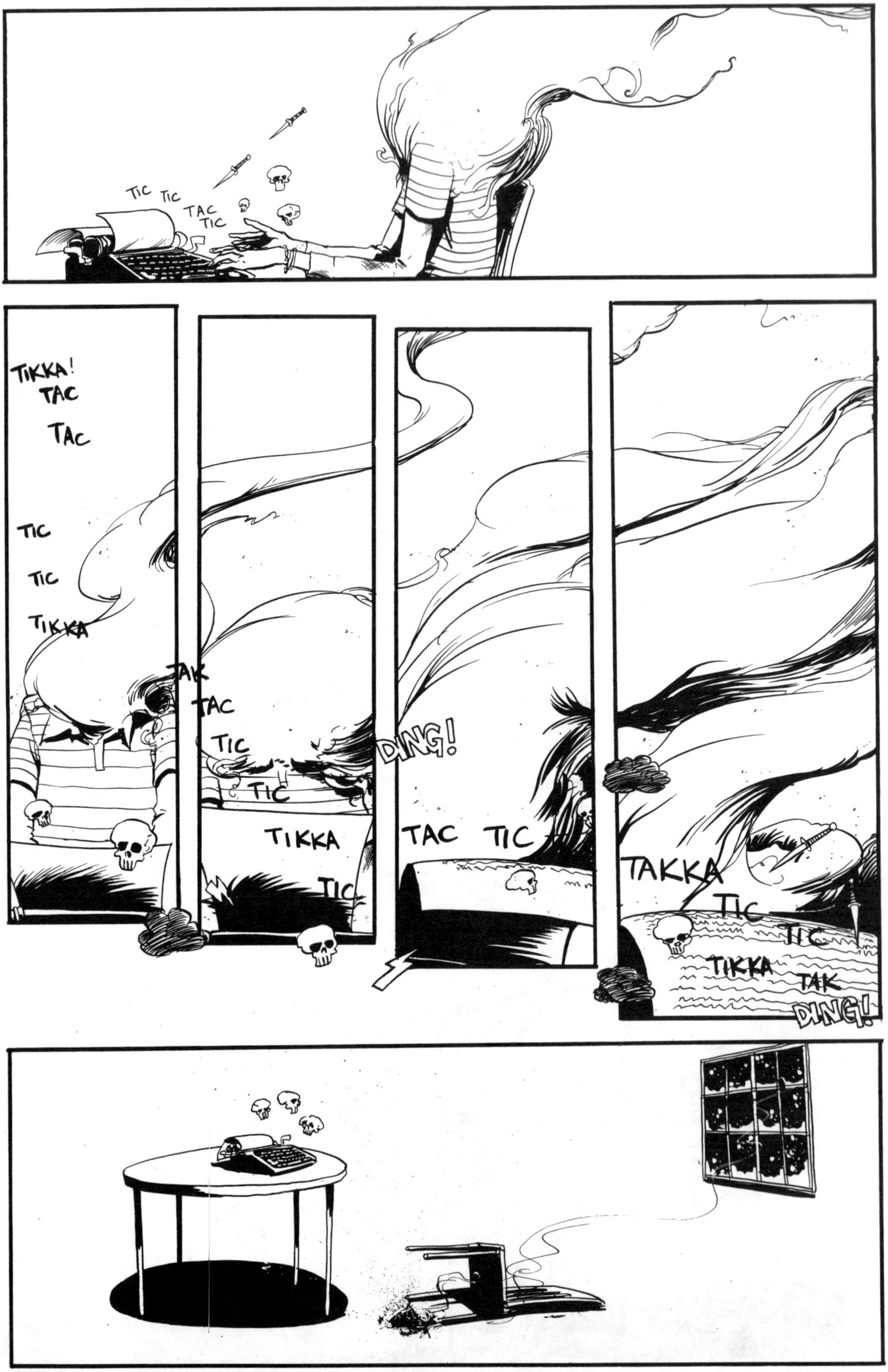
TIC TIC
TAC
TIC
TIKKA!
TAC
TAC
TIC
TIC
TIKKA
TAK
TAC
TIC
TIC
TIKKA
TIC
DING!
TAC TIC
TAKKA
TIC
TIC
TIKKA
TAK
DING!

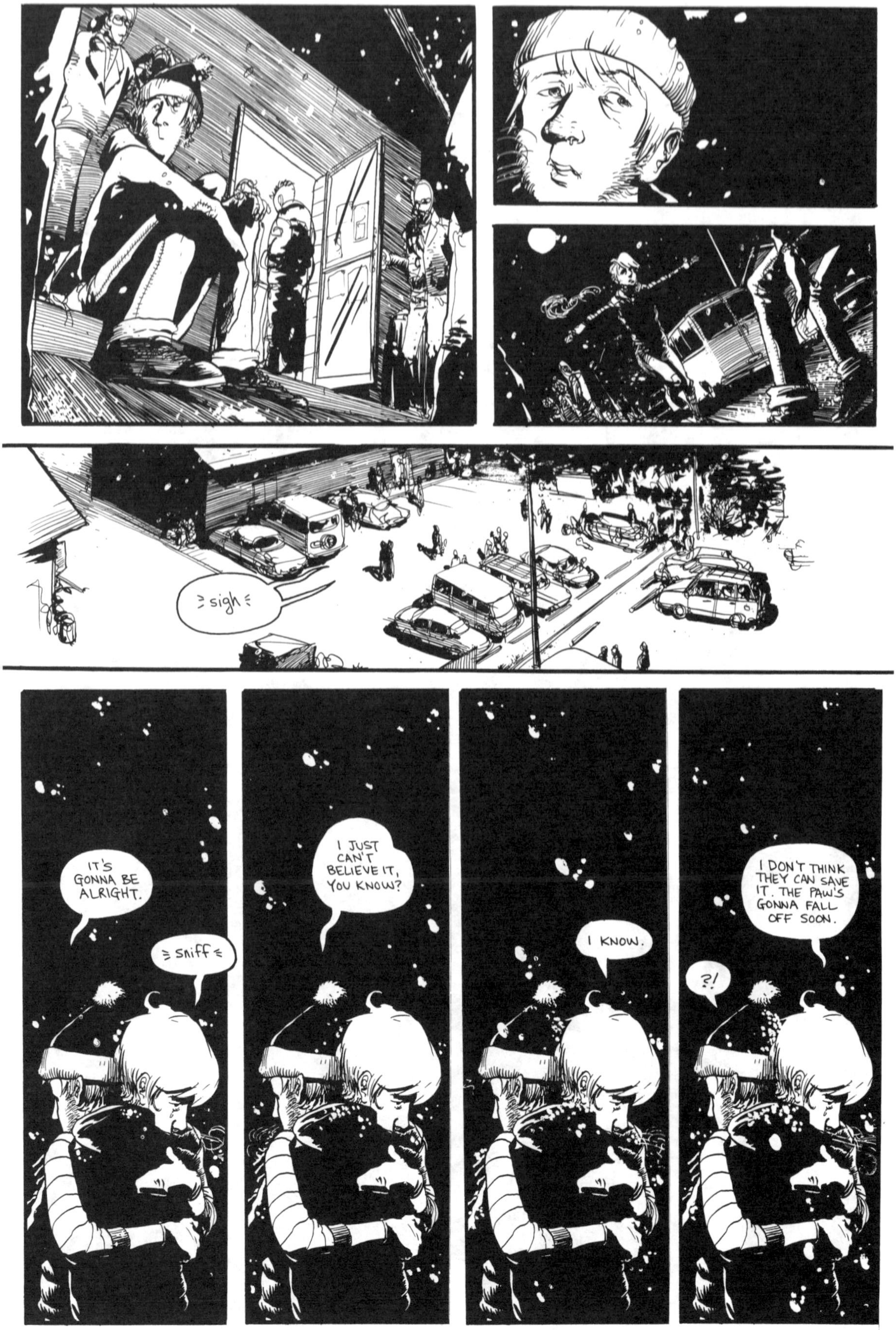
sigh
IT'S GONNA BE ALRIGHT.
sniff
I JUST CAN'T BELIEVE IT, YOU KNOW?
I KNOW.
I DON'T THINK THEY CAN SAVE IT. THE PAW'S GONNA FALL OFF SOON.
?!

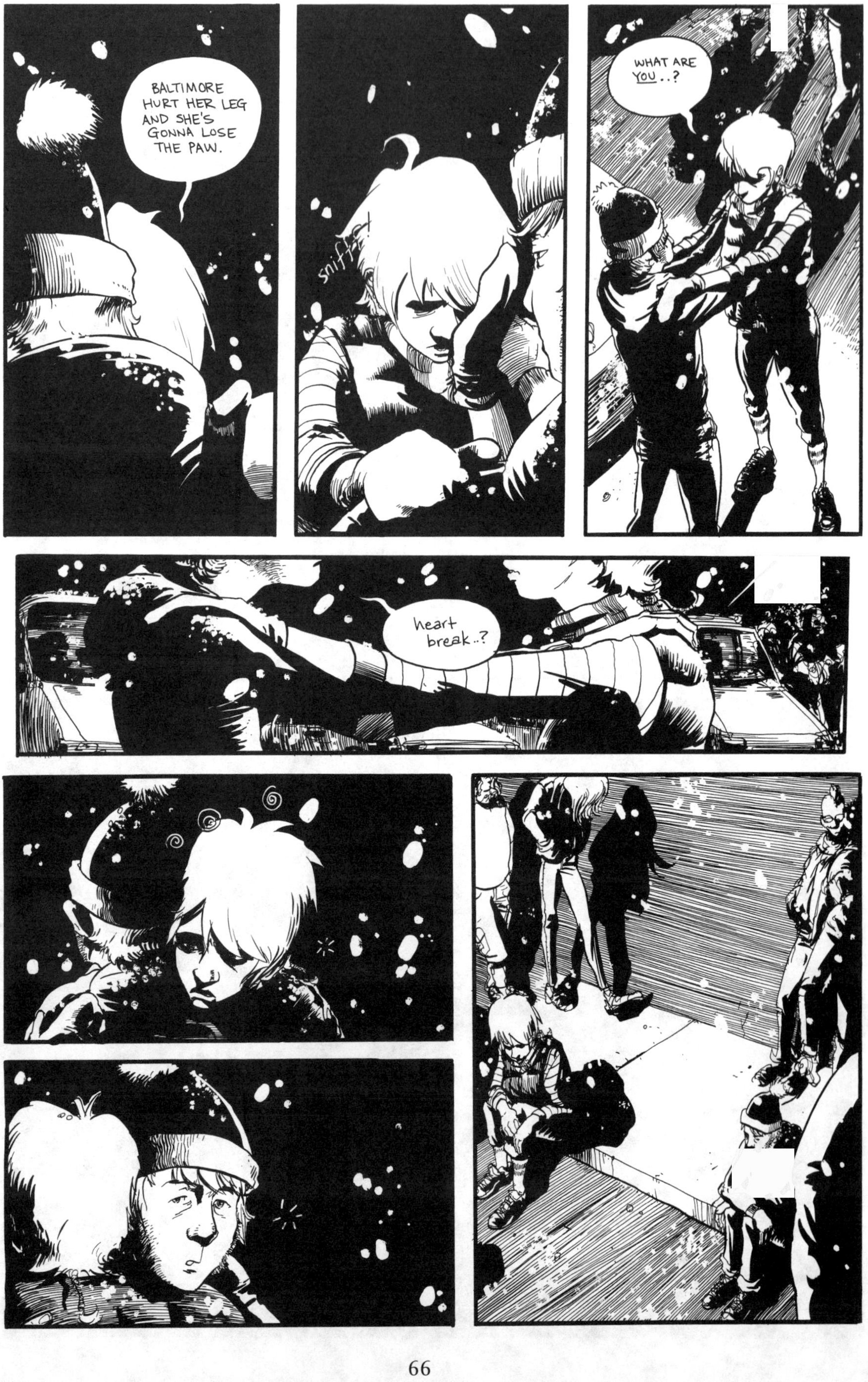
BALTIMORE HURT HER LEG AND SHE'S GONNA LOSE THE PAW.
sniff
WHAT ARE YOU..?
heart break..?

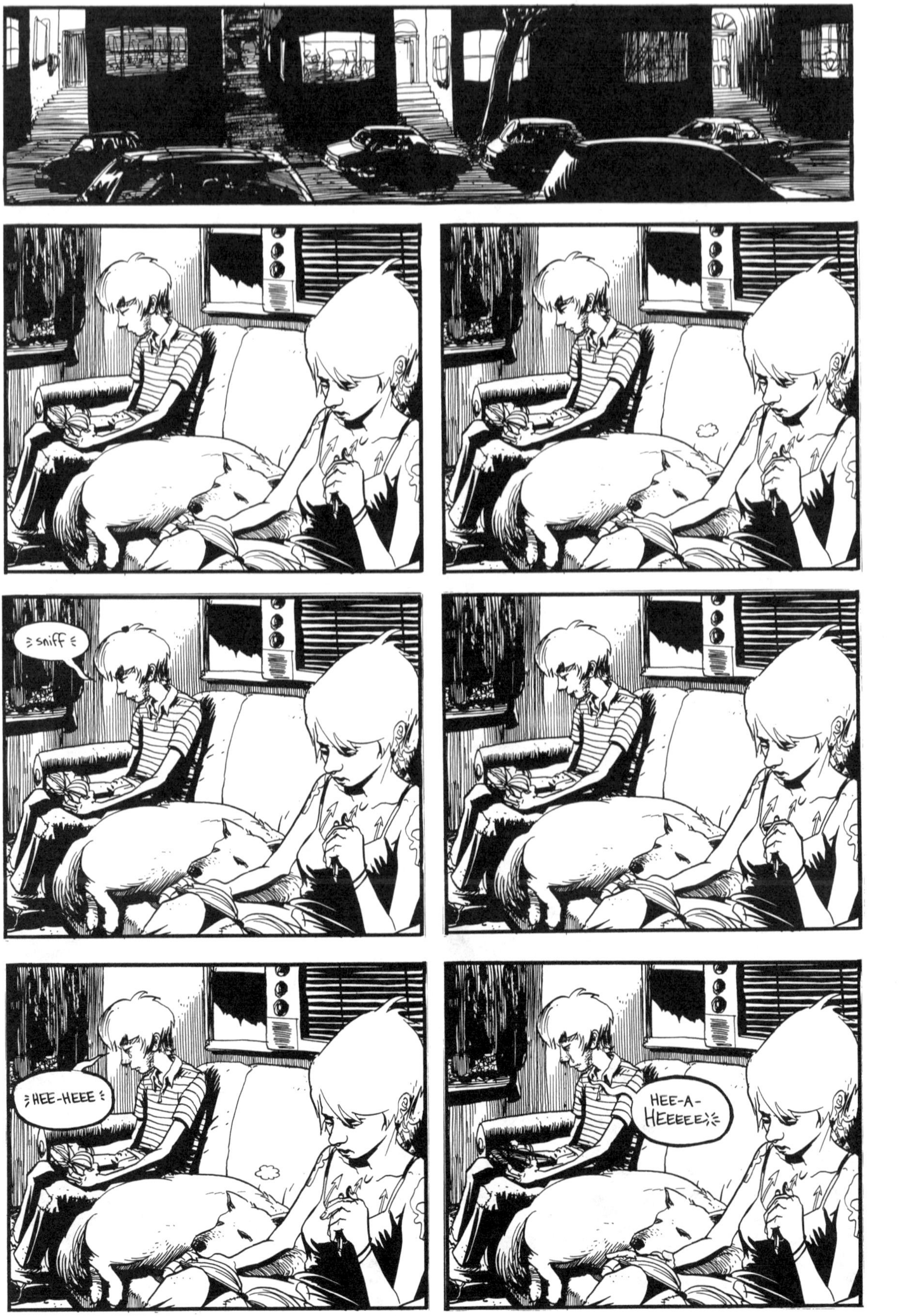
sniff
HEE-HEEE
HEE-A-HEEEEE

BALTIMORE...
snifff
SHE'S A GOOD LITTLE GUY..
Scritch! scritch!
you could say i never felt so alienated--
--but that would only be half of it..

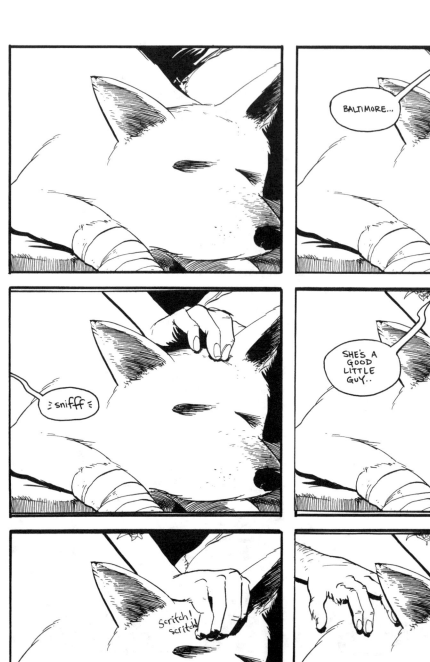

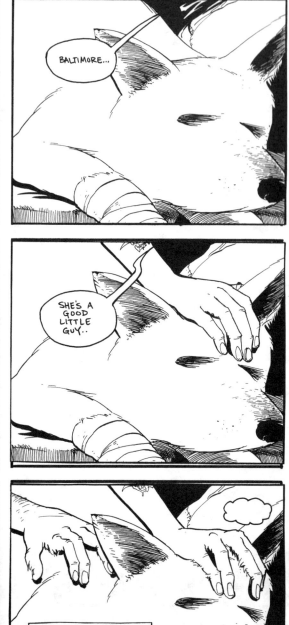

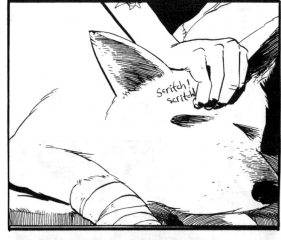

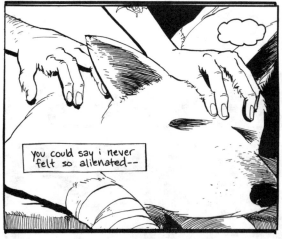

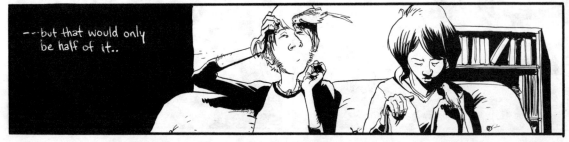

could anything be more wonderful than being in over our heads together?

like heartfelt, half-assed teenage scribble --

kids choke on words, as in some years they'll wake up crying from dreams of feeding worms too deep in dirt.

a young man living in michigan leaves his cartoonist's desk lamp burning one night

as he passes the evenings washing dishes only to dirty them again.

he eventually turns in for the night in the ground-level bedroom of a sweetheart

leaving a night light for his empty mattress in the basement, a bed long abandoned next to a desk virtually untouched since moving in one month prior.

I AM SO VERY HAPPY.

level bedroom of a sweet-heart

leaving a night light for his empty mattress in the basem ed long abandoned next to a desk virtually untouched since moving in one month prior.

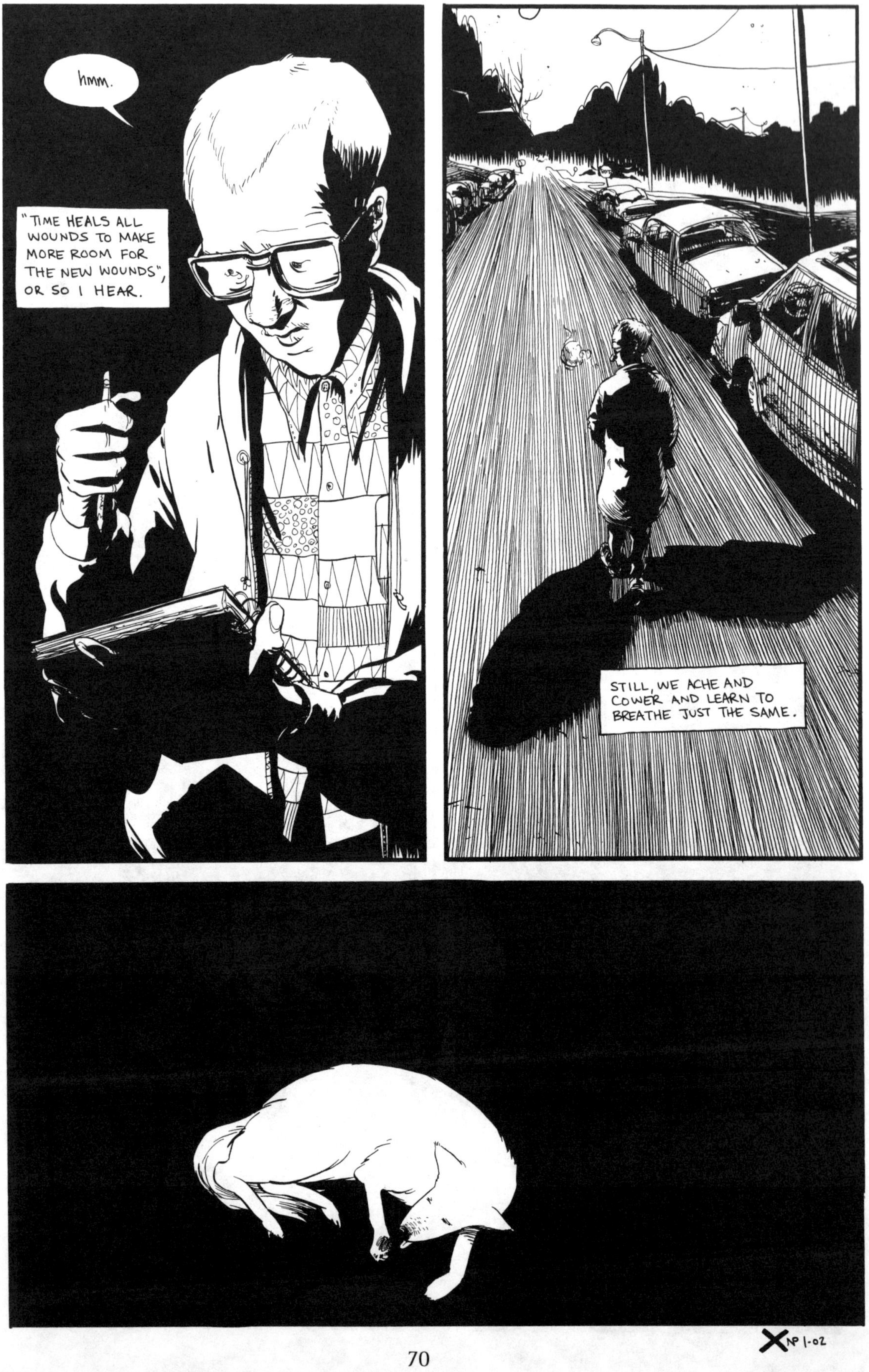
hmm.
"TIME HEALS ALL WOUNDS TO MAKE MORE ROOM FOR THE NEW WOUNDS", OR SO I HEAR.
STILL, WE ACHE AND COWER AND LEARN TO BREATHE JUST THE SAME.

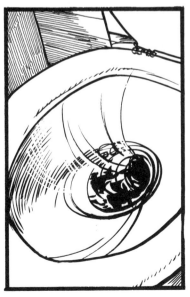

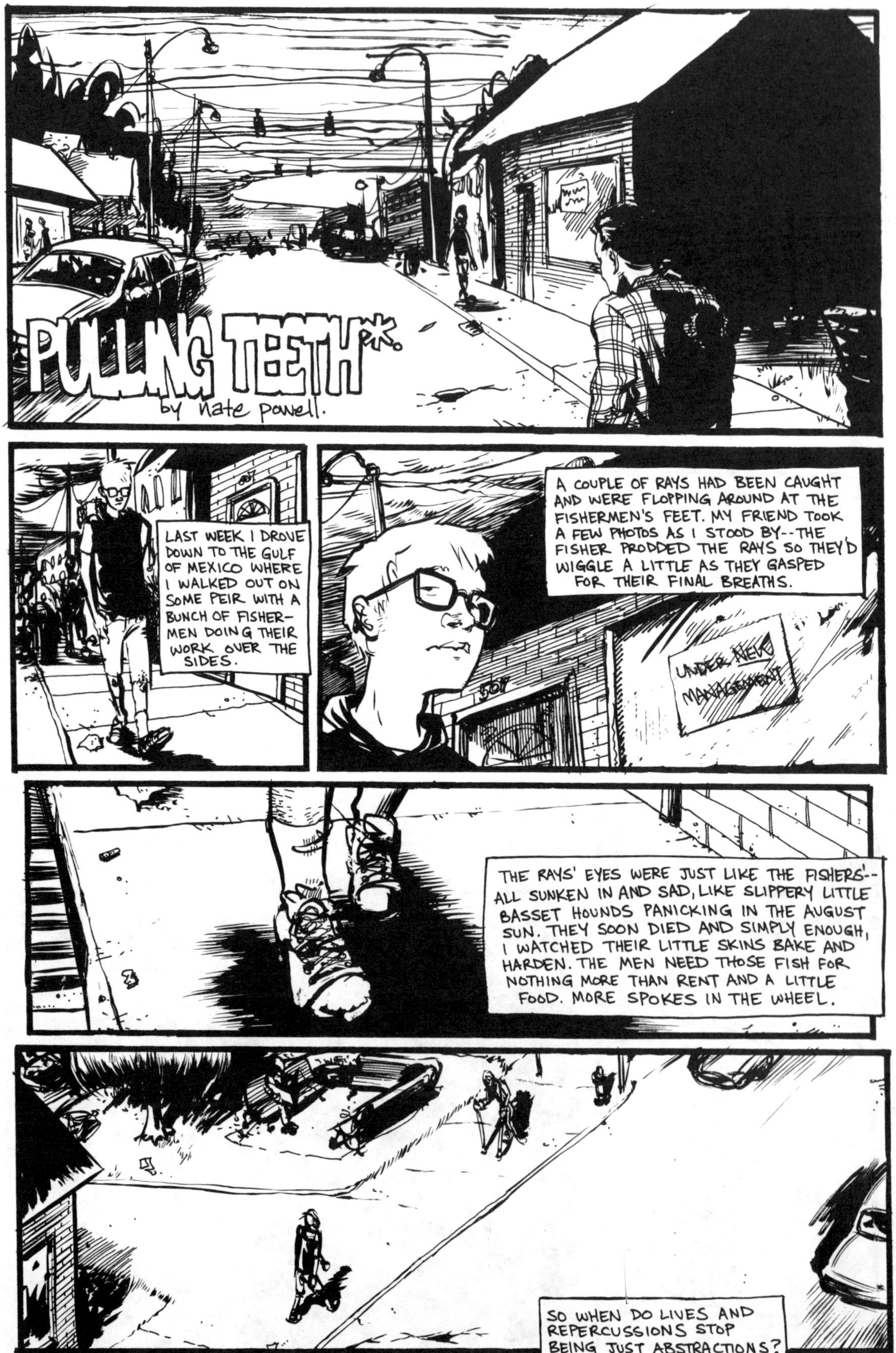
PULLING TEETH*.
by nate powell.
LAST WEEK I DROVE DOWN TO THE GULF OF MEXICO WHERE I WALKED OUT ON SOME PEIR WITH A BUNCH OF FISHER-MEN DOING THEIR WORK OVER THE SIDES.
A COUPLE OF RAYS HAD BEEN CAUGHT AND WERE FLOPPING AROUND AT THE FISHERMEN'S FEET. MY FRIEND TOOK A FEW PHOTOS AS I STOOD BY--THE FISHER PRODDED THE RAYS SO THEY'D WIGGLE A LITTLE AS THEY GASPED FOR THEIR FINAL BREATHS.
UNDER NEW MANAGEMENT
THE RAYS' EYES WERE JUST LIKE THE FISHERS'-- ALL SUNKEN IN AND SAD, LIKE SLIPPERY LITTLE BASSET HOUNDS PANICKING IN THE AUGUST SUN. THEY SOON DIED AND SIMPLY ENOUGH, I WATCHED THEIR LITTLE SKINS BAKE AND HARDEN. THE MEN NEED THOSE FISH FOR NOTHING MORE THAN RENT AND A LITTLE FOOD. MORE SPOKES IN THE WHEEL.
SO WHEN DO LIVES AND REPERCUSSIONS STOP BEING JUST ABSTRACTIONS?

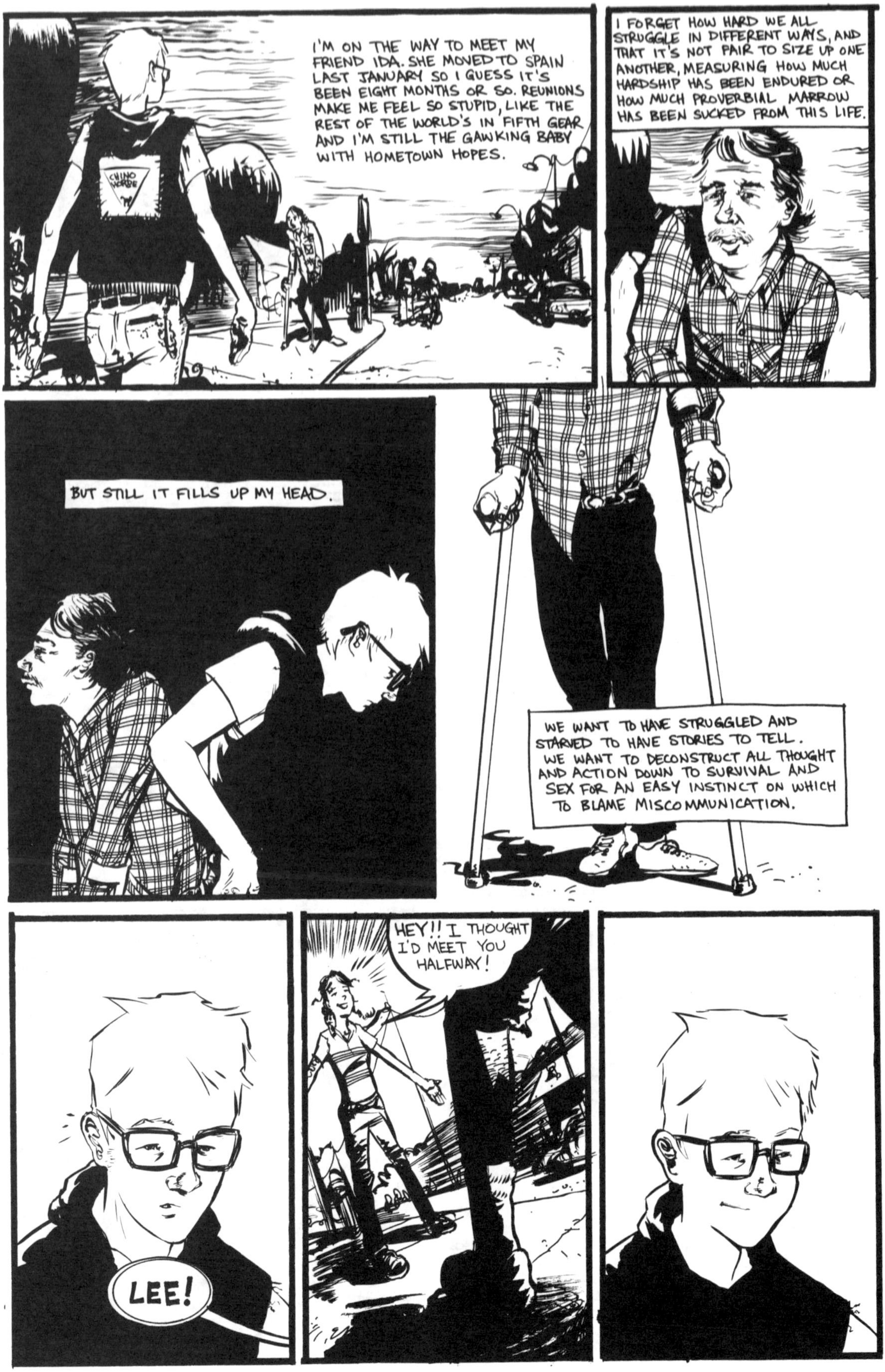
I'M ON THE WAY TO MEET MY FRIEND IDA. SHE MOVED TO SPAIN LAST JANUARY SO I GUESS IT'S BEEN EIGHT MONTHS OR SO. REUNIONS MAKE ME FEEL SO STUPID, LIKE THE REST OF THE WORLD'S IN FIFTH GEAR AND I'M STILL THE GAWKING BABY WITH HOMETOWN HOPES.
CHINO VERDE
I FORGET HOW HARD WE ALL STRUGGLE IN DIFFERENT WAYS, AND THAT IT'S NOT FAIR TO SIZE UP ONE ANOTHER, MEASURING HOW MUCH HARDSHIP HAS BEEN ENDURED OR HOW MUCH PROVERBIAL MARROW HAS BEEN SUCKED FROM THIS LIFE.
BUT STILL IT FILLS UP MY HEAD.
WE WANT TO HAVE STRUGGLED AND STARVED TO HAVE STORIES TO TELL. WE WANT TO DECONSTRUCT ALL THOUGHT AND ACTION DOWN TO SURVIVAL AND SEX FOR AN EASY INSTINCT ON WHICH TO BLAME MISCOMMUNICATION.
LEE!
HEY!! I THOUGHT I'D MEET YOU HALFWAY!

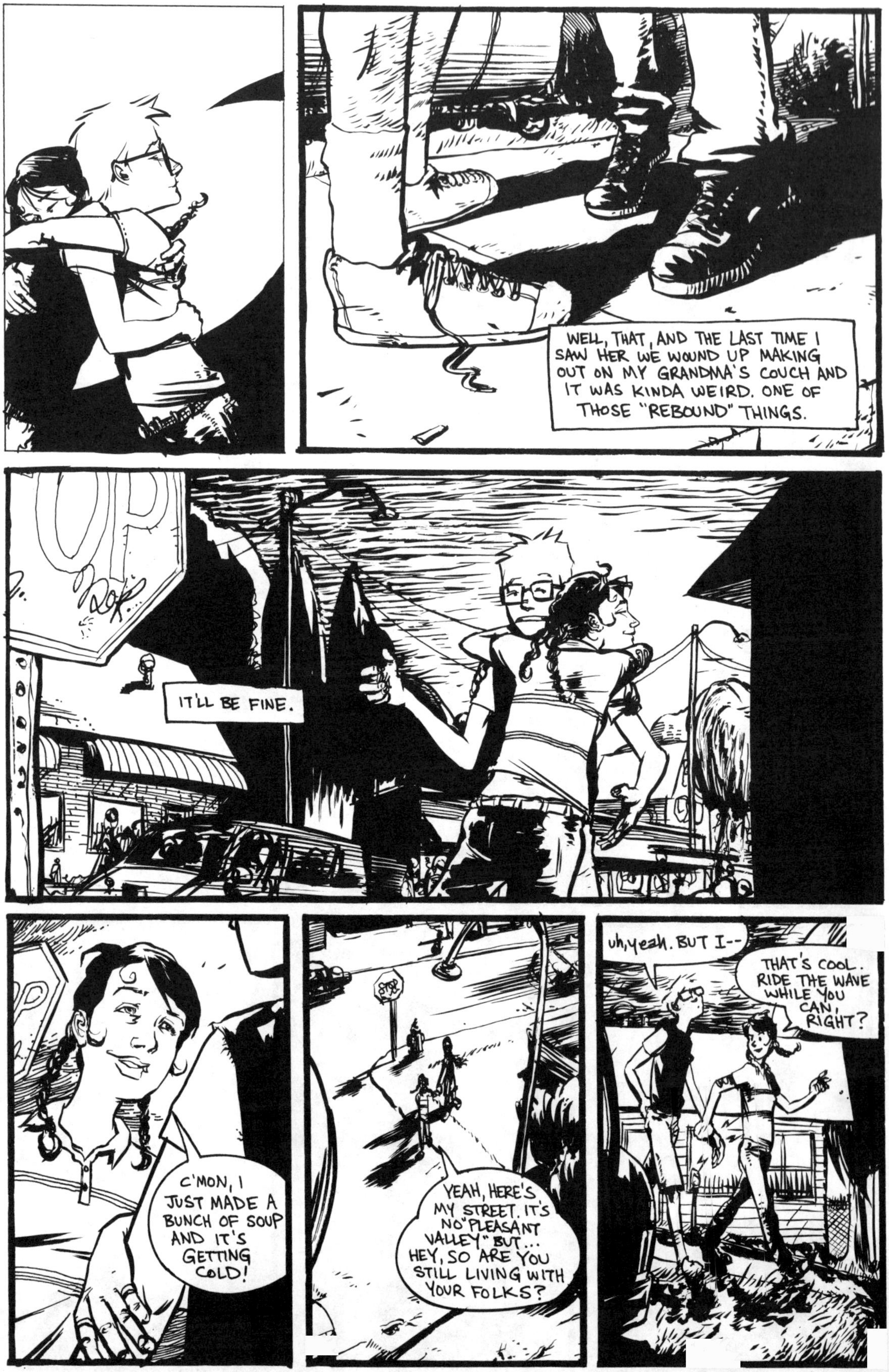
WELL, THAT, AND THE LAST TIME I SAW HER WE WOUND UP MAKING OUT ON MY GRANDMA'S COUCH AND IT WAS KINDA WEIRD. ONE OF THOSE "REBOUND" THINGS.
IT'LL BE FINE.
C'MON, I JUST MADE A BUNCH OF SOUP AND IT'S GETTING COLD!
YEAH, HERE'S MY STREET. IT'S NO "PLEASANT VALLEY" BUT... HEY, SO ARE YOU STILL LIVING WITH YOUR FOLKS?
uh, yeah. BUT I--
THAT'S COOL. RIDE THE WAVE WHILE YOU CAN, RIGHT?

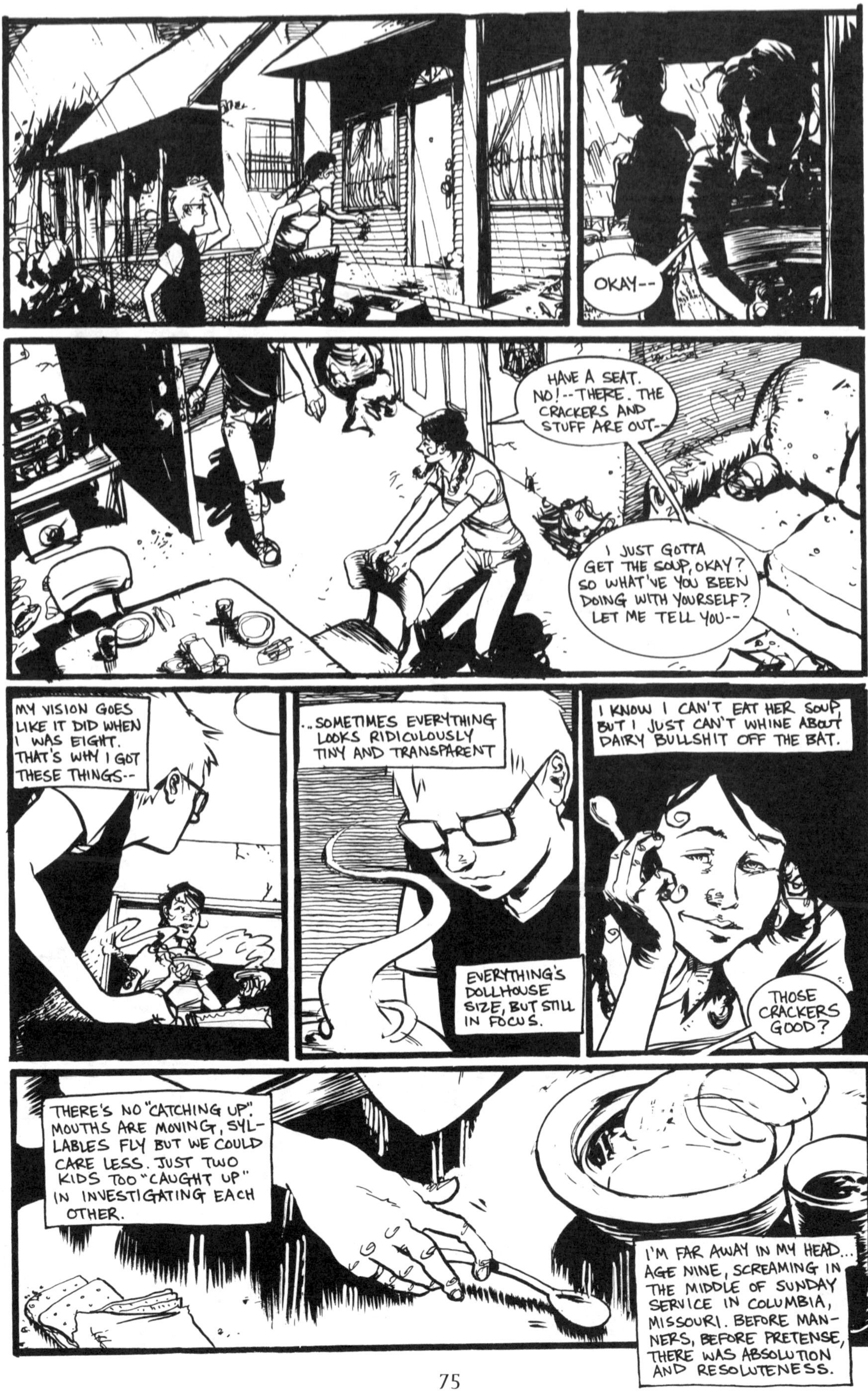
OKAY--
HAVE A SEAT. NO!--THERE. THE CRACKERS AND STUFF ARE OUT--
I JUST GOTTA GET THE SOUP, OKAY? SO WHAT'VE YOU BEEN DOING WITH YOURSELF? LET ME TELL YOU--
MY VISION GOES LIKE IT DID WHEN I WAS EIGHT. THAT'S WHY I GOT THESE THINGS--
..SOMETIMES EVERYTHING LOOKS RIDICULOUSLY TINY AND TRANSPARENT
EVERYTHING'S DOLLHOUSE SIZE, BUT STILL IN FOCUS.
I KNOW I CAN'T EAT HER SOUP, BUT I JUST CAN'T WHINE ABOUT DAIRY BULLSHIT OFF THE BAT.
THOSE CRACKERS GOOD?
THERE'S NO "CATCHING UP". MOUTHS ARE MOVING, SYLLABLES FLY BUT WE COULD CARE LESS. JUST TWO KIDS TOO "CAUGHT UP" IN INVESTIGATING EACH OTHER.
I'M FAR AWAY IN MY HEAD... AGE NINE, SCREAMING IN THE MIDDLE OF SUNDAY SERVICE IN COLUMBIA, MISSOURI. BEFORE MANNERS, BEFORE PRETENSE, THERE WAS ABSOLUTION AND RESOLUTENESS.

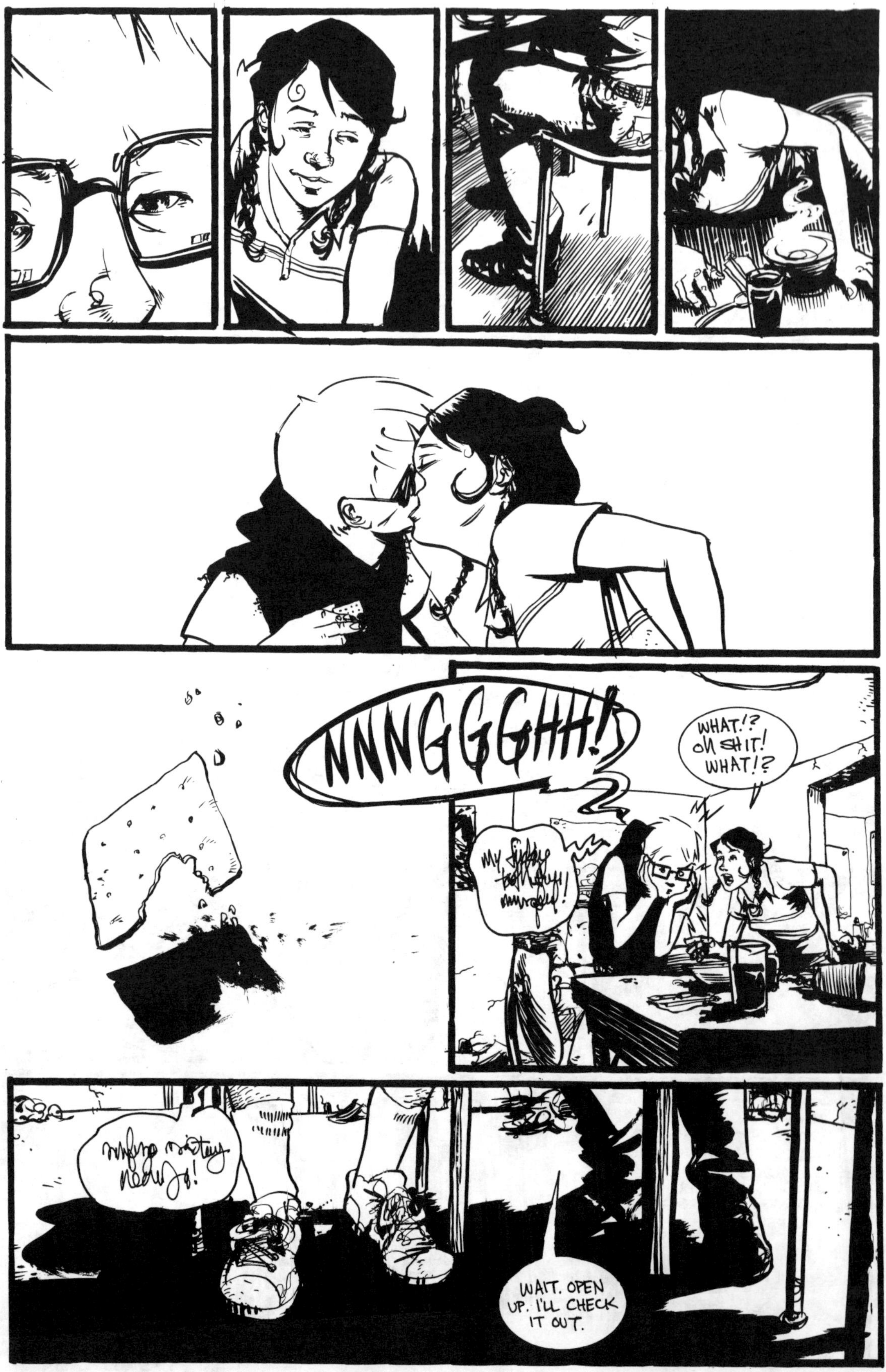
NNNGGGHH!
WHAT!? OH SHIT! WHAT!?
WAIT. OPEN UP. I'LL CHECK IT OUT.

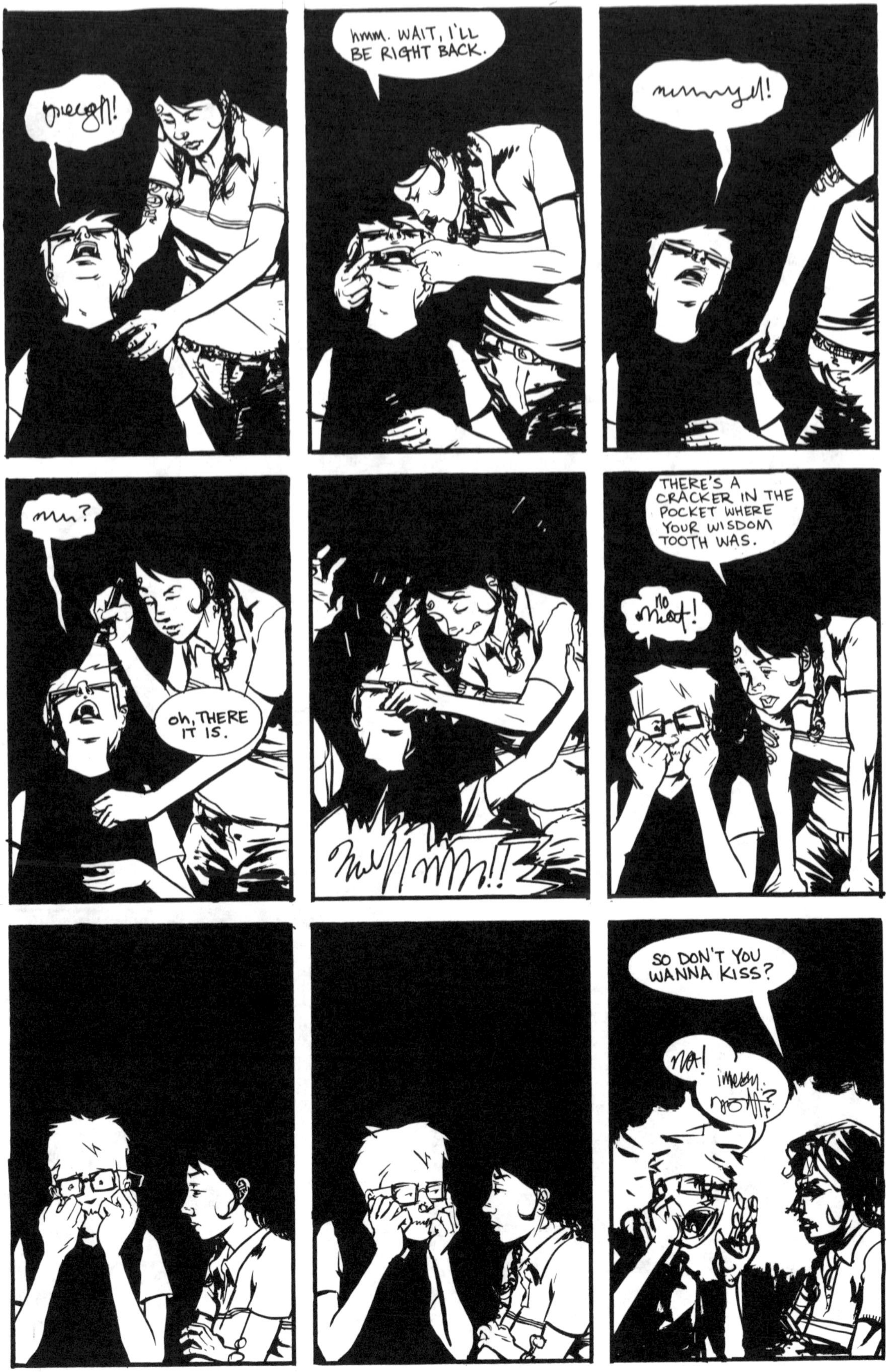
hmm. WAIT, I'LL BE RIGHT BACK.
oh, THERE IT IS.
THERE'S A CRACKER IN THE POCKET WHERE YOUR WISDOM TOOTH WAS.
SO DON'T YOU WANNA KISS?

WHAT? WHAT IS IT? LOOK, I...

I'M GOING TO THE HEALTH CLINIC...

IT WAS JUST A DUMB KISS, ALL RIGHT...?

NO--UM, I MEAN, it's not--SHIT... I'M SORRY.

OW!

IT'S THE OBJECTIVITY OF ID.

CHINO

BECAUSE NO MATTER WHAT, AT THE CORE OF RELATIONSHIPS, OF WORK AND NEIGHBORHOODS AND BROKEN BONES, HUNGER PANGS, ROAD TRIPS, MILKSHAKES, AND THE BACK NINE OF ANY MAJOR GOLF COURSE IS SURVIVAL AND REPRODUCTION.

WE STUMBLE AROUND, CORRUPTING OUR FOOT-STEPS WITH THE NOTION THAT OUR OWN EMOTIONS ARE INHERENTLY DUALIST.

SO WHAT FILLS A KID WITH SO MUCH CON-FUSION WHEN AN ASEXUAL RELATIONSHIP REDEFINES ITSELF?

oh shit...

AND WHAT GAVE ME THE NOTION THAT ANY-THING IS ASEXUAL?

BY THE TIME WE'VE FULLY SURRENDERED TO IMPOSED MORALITY, RELATIONSHIPS AND HEARTBEATS ARE JUST NAILS IN EMPTY COFFINS.

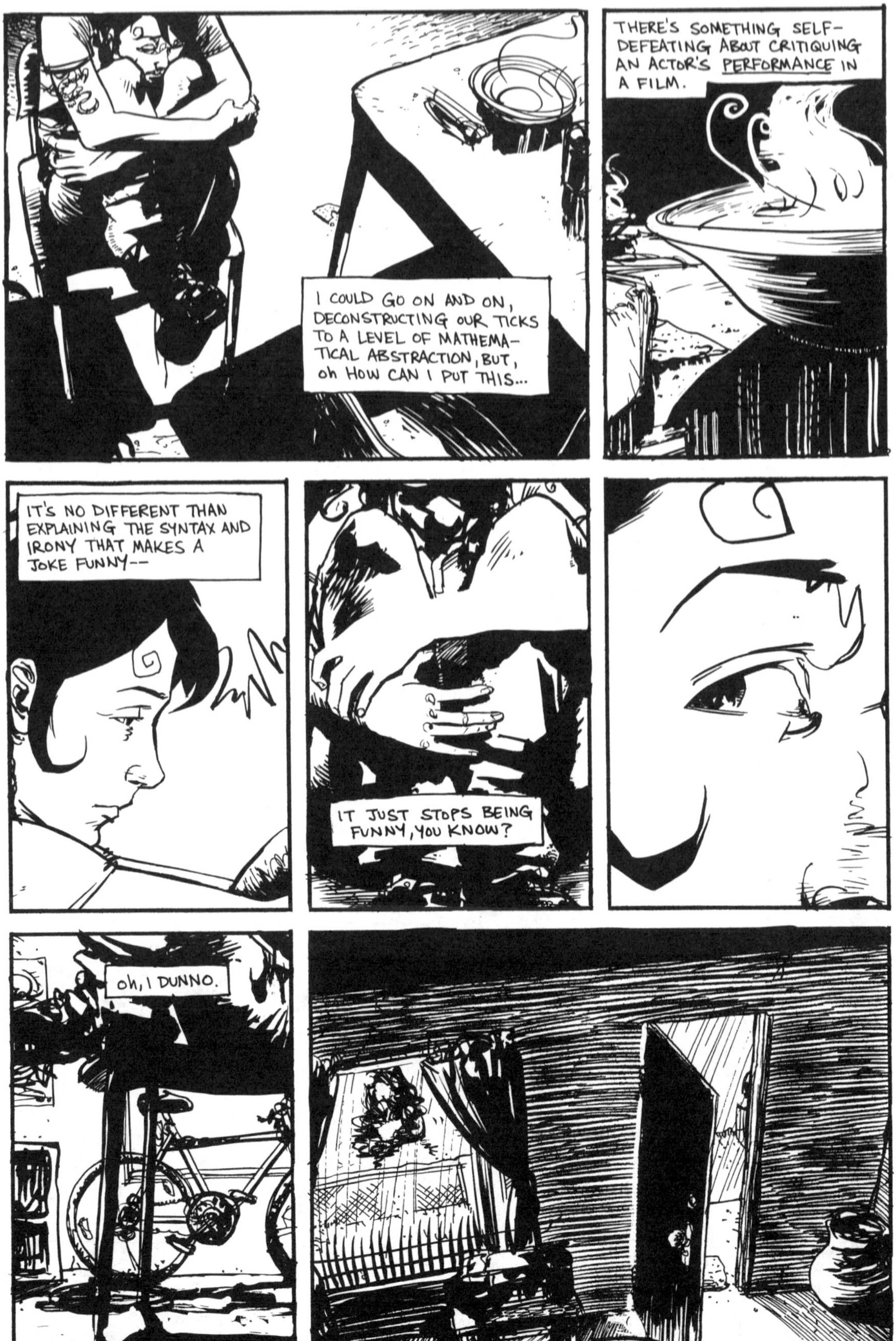
I COULD GO ON AND ON, DECONSTRUCTING OUR TICKS TO A LEVEL OF MATHEMATICAL ABSTRACTION, BUT, oh HOW CAN I PUT THIS...
THERE'S SOMETHING SELF-DEFEATING ABOUT CRITIQUING AN ACTOR'S PERFORMANCE IN A FILM.
IT'S NO DIFFERENT THAN EXPLAINING THE SYNTAX AND IRONY THAT MAKES A JOKE FUNNY--
IT JUST STOPS BEING FUNNY, YOU KNOW?
oh, I DUNNO.

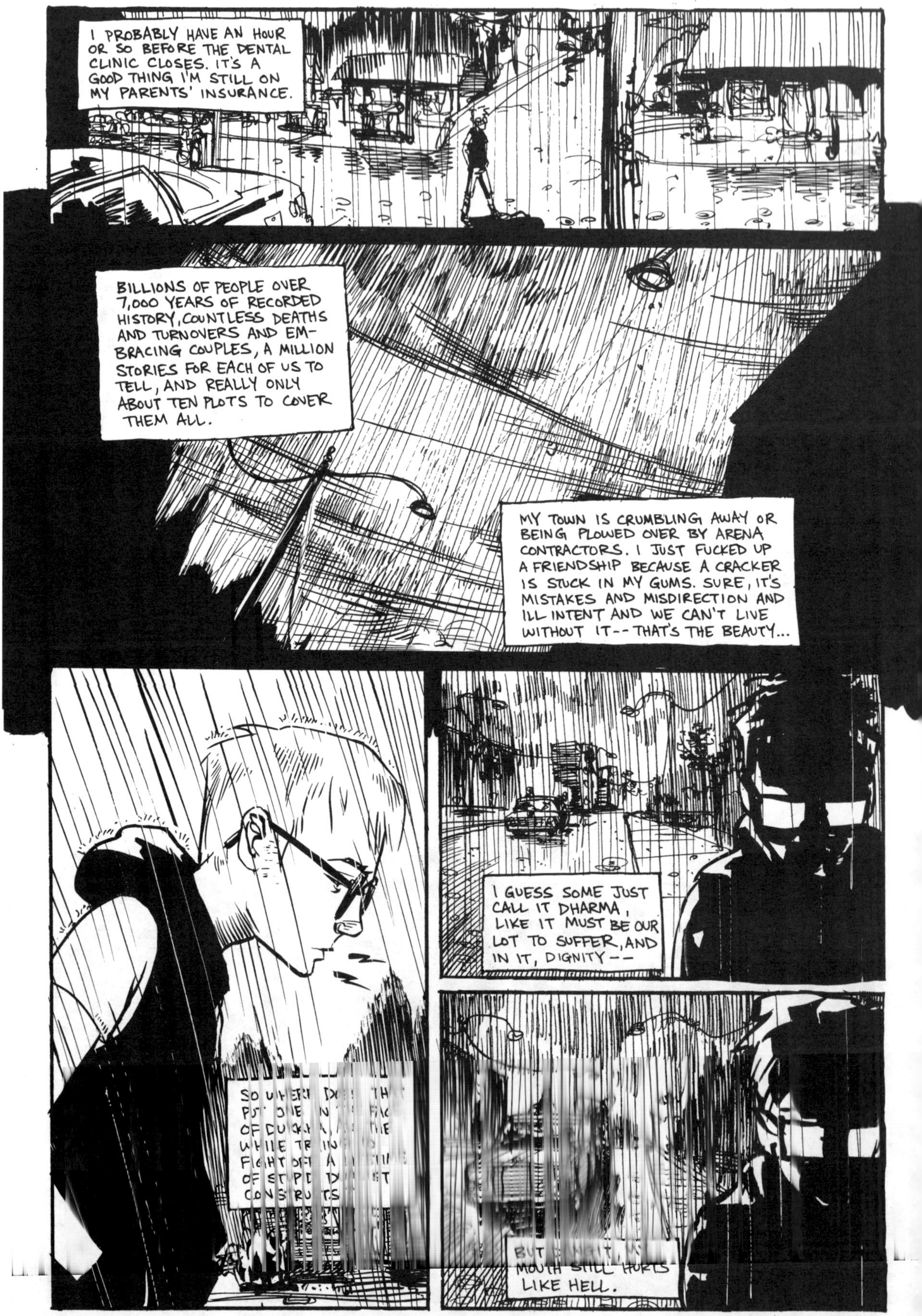
I PROBABLY HAVE AN HOUR OR SO BEFORE THE DENTAL CLINIC CLOSES. IT'S A GOOD THING I'M STILL ON MY PARENTS' INSURANCE.
BILLIONS OF PEOPLE OVER 7,000 YEARS OF RECORDED HISTORY, COUNTLESS DEATHS AND TURNOVERS AND EMBRACING COUPLES, A MILLION STORIES FOR EACH OF US TO TELL, AND REALLY ONLY ABOUT TEN PLOTS TO COVER THEM ALL.
MY TOWN IS CRUMBLING AWAY OR BEING PLOWED OVER BY ARENA CONTRACTORS. I JUST FUCKED UP A FRIENDSHIP BECAUSE A CRACKER IS STUCK IN MY GUMS. SURE, IT'S MISTAKES AND MISDIRECTION AND ILL INTENT AND WE CAN'T LIVE WITHOUT IT-- THAT'S THE BEAUTY...
I GUESS SOME JUST CALL IT DHARMA, LIKE IT MUST BE OUR LOT TO SUFFER, AND IN IT, DIGNITY--
MOUTH STILL HURTS
LIKE HELL.

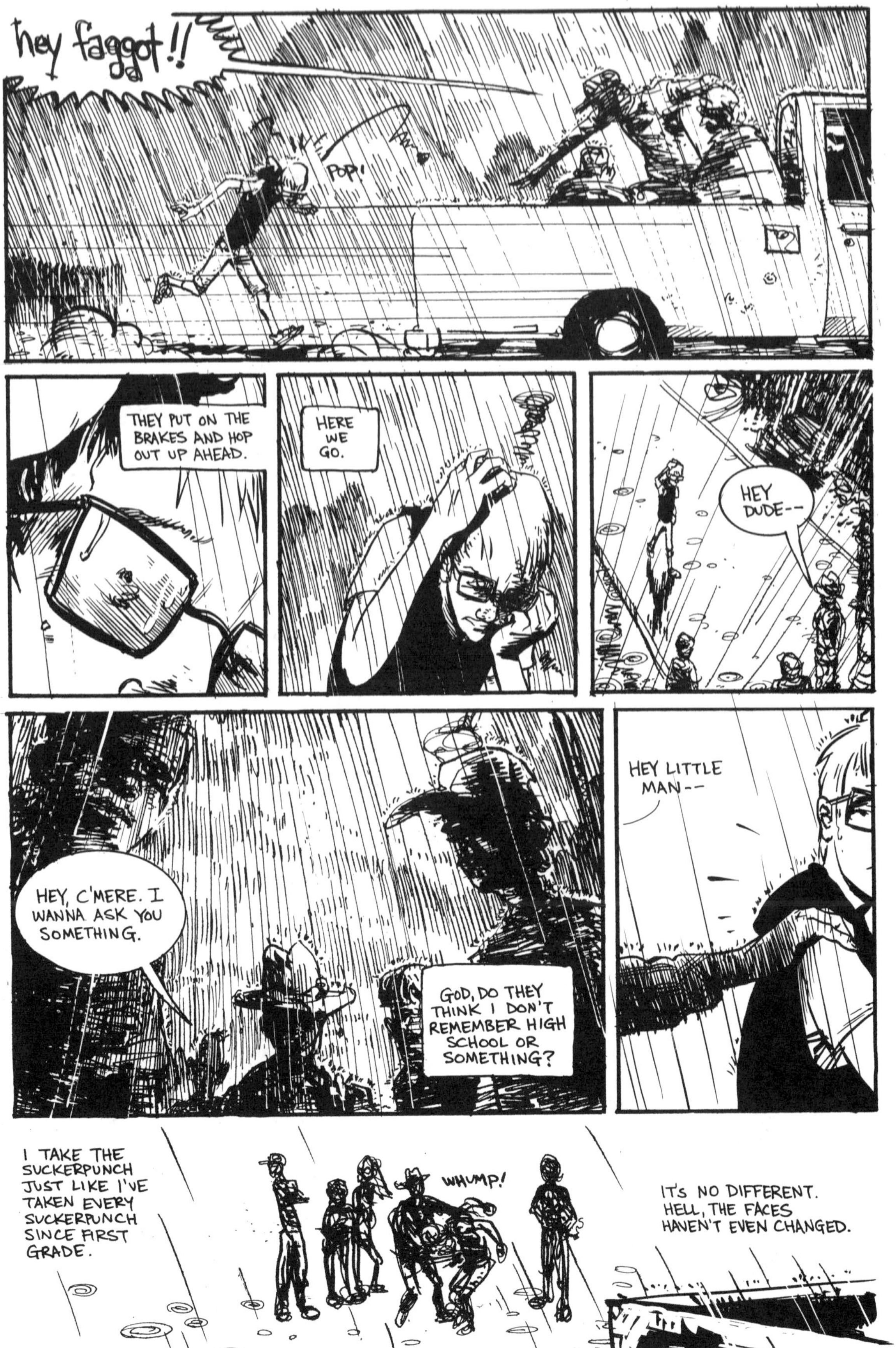
hey faggot!!
POP!
THEY PUT ON THE BRAKES AND HOP OUT UP AHEAD.
HERE WE GO.
HEY DUDE--
HEY, C'MERE. I WANNA ASK YOU SOMETHING.
GOD, DO THEY THINK I DON'T REMEMBER HIGH SCHOOL OR SOMETHING?
HEY LITTLE MAN--
I TAKE THE SUCKERPUNCH JUST LIKE I'VE TAKEN EVERY SUCKERPUNCH SINCE FIRST GRADE.
WHUMP!
IT'S NO DIFFERENT. HELL, THE FACES HAVEN'T EVEN CHANGED.

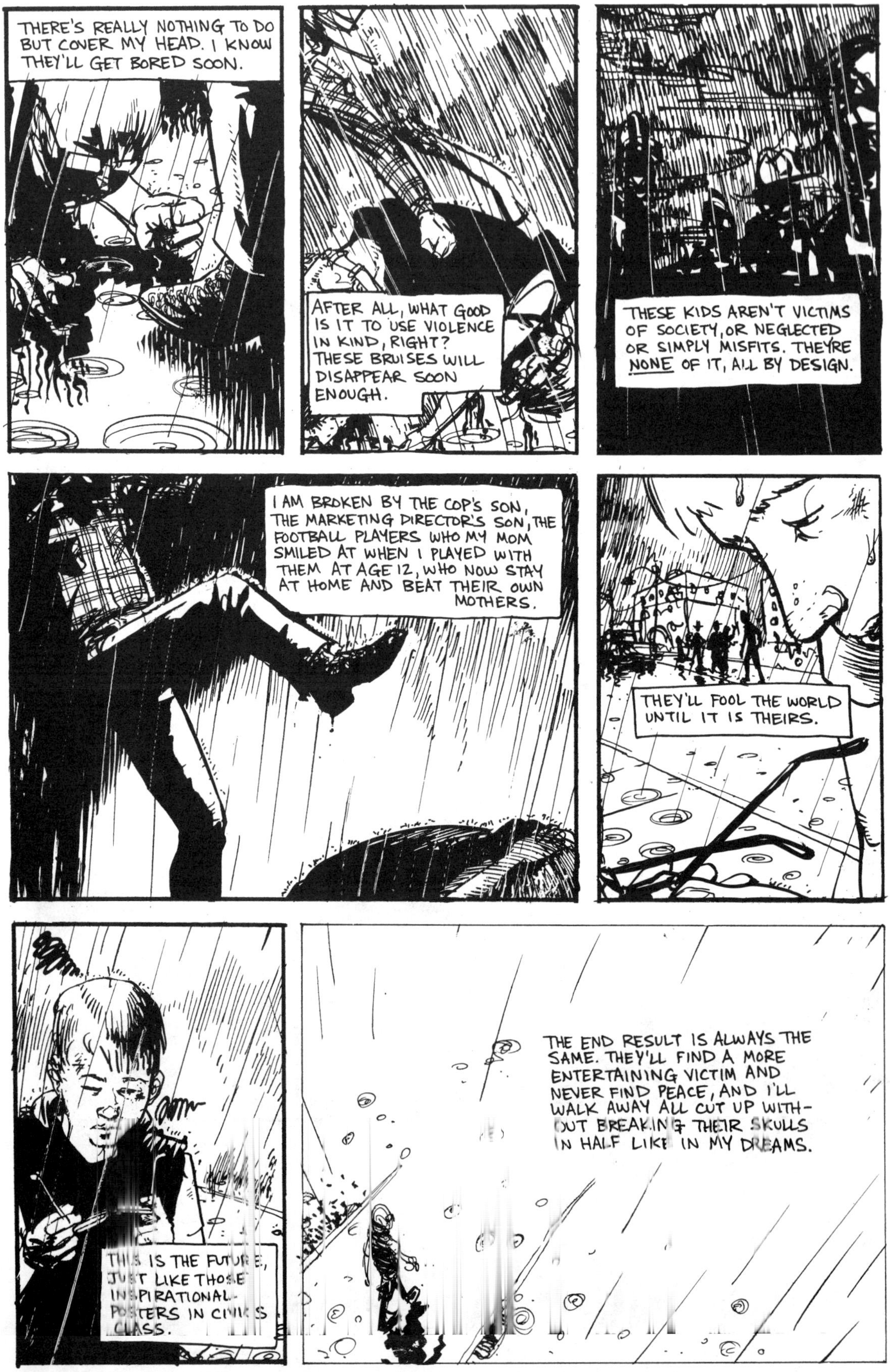
THERE'S REALLY NOTHING TO DO BUT COVER MY HEAD. I KNOW THEY'LL GET BORED SOON.
AFTER ALL, WHAT GOOD IS IT TO USE VIOLENCE IN KIND, RIGHT? THESE BRUISES WILL DISAPPEAR SOON ENOUGH.
THESE KIDS AREN'T VICTIMS OF SOCIETY, OR NEGLECTED OR SIMPLY MISFITS. THEY'RE NONE OF IT, ALL BY DESIGN.
I AM BROKEN BY THE COP'S SON, THE MARKETING DIRECTOR'S SON, THE FOOTBALL PLAYERS WHO MY MOM SMILED AT WHEN I PLAYED WITH THEM AT AGE 12, WHO NOW STAY AT HOME AND BEAT THEIR OWN MOTHERS.
THEY'LL FOOL THE WORLD UNTIL IT IS THEIRS.
THIS IS THE FUTURE, JUST LIKE THOSE INSPIRATIONAL POSTERS IN CIVICS CLASS.
THE END RESULT IS ALWAYS THE SAME. THEY'LL FIND A MORE ENTERTAINING VICTIM AND NEVER FIND PEACE, AND I'LL WALK AWAY ALL CUT UP WITHOUT BREAKING THEIR SKULLS IN HALF LIKE IN MY DREAMS.

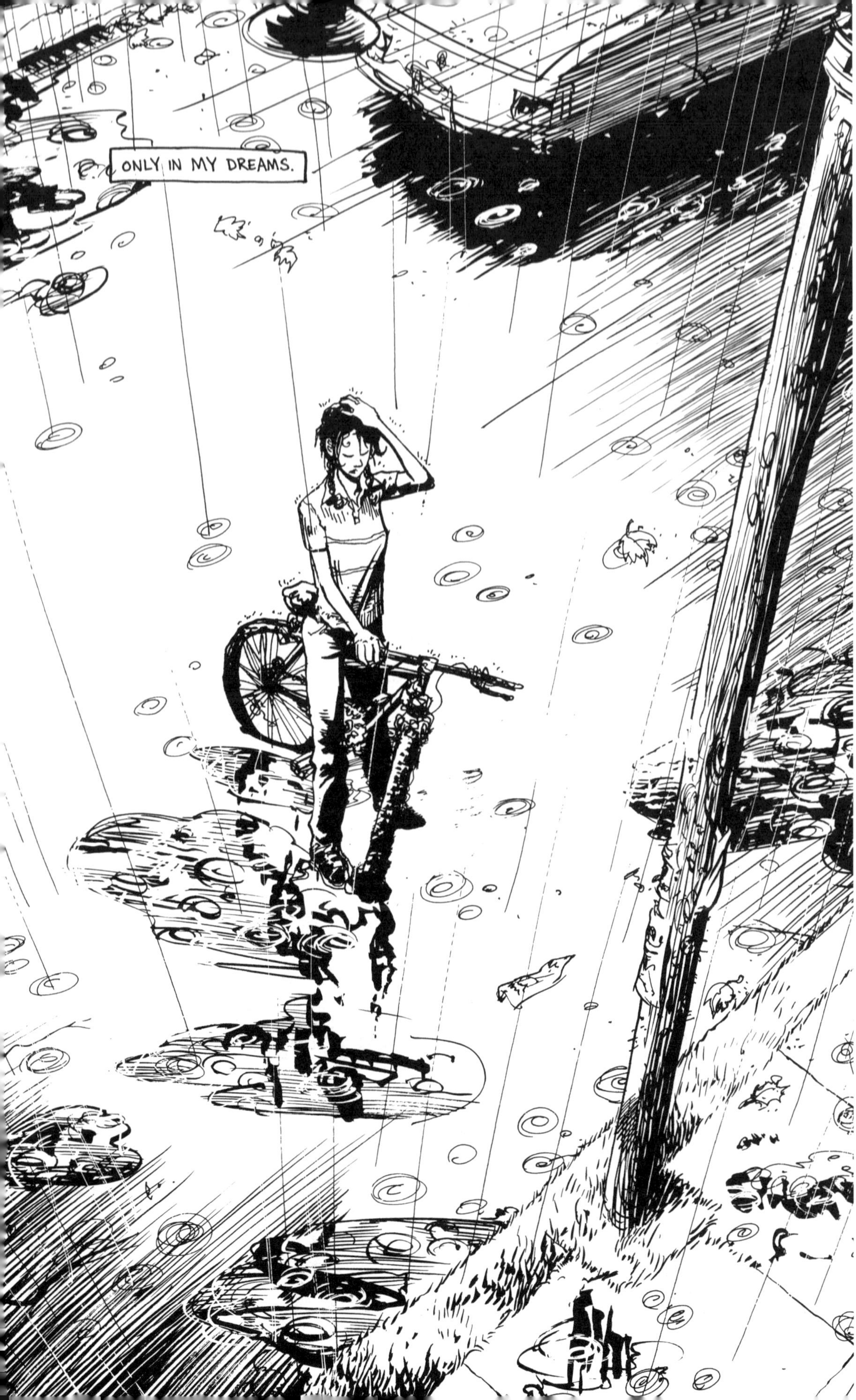
ONLY IN MY DREAMS.

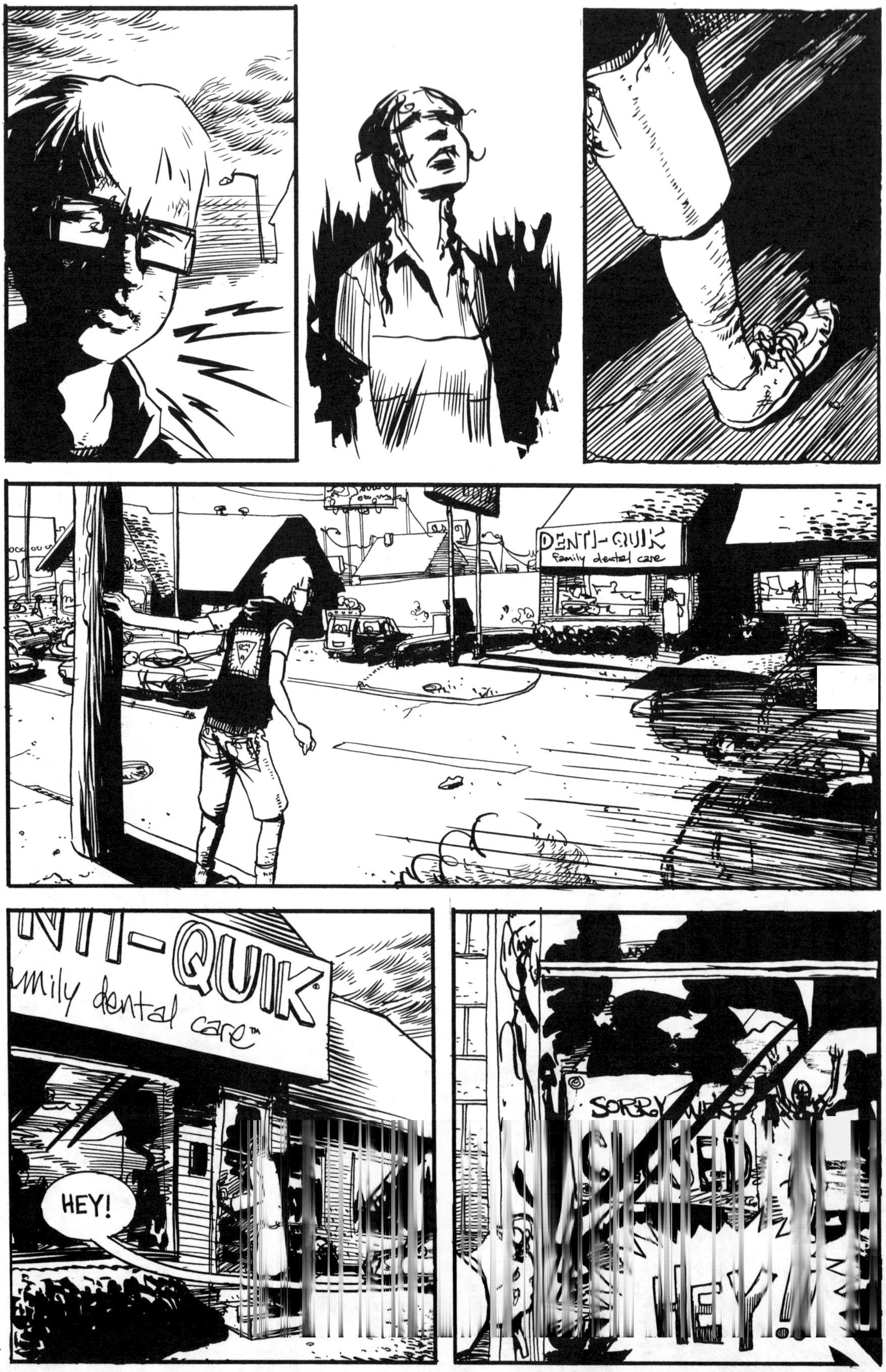
DENTI-QUIK
family dental care
NTI-QUIK
mily dental care™
HEY!

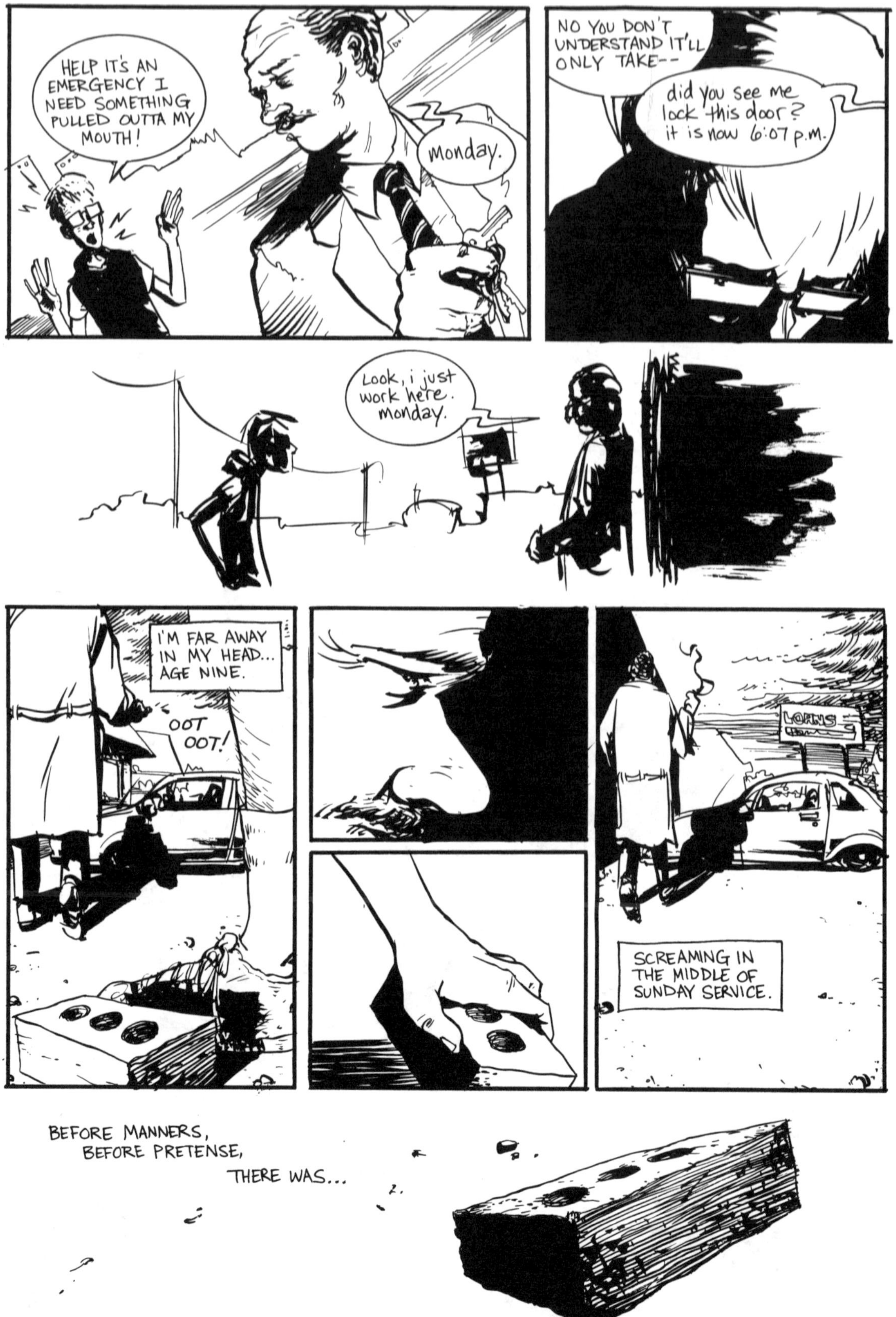
HELP IT'S AN EMERGENCY I NEED SOMETHING PULLED OUTTA MY MOUTH!
monday.
NO YOU DON'T UNDERSTAND IT'LL ONLY TAKE--
did you see me lock this door? it is now 6:07 p.m.
Look, i just work here. monday.
I'M FAR AWAY IN MY HEAD... AGE NINE.
OOT OOT!
SCREAMING IN THE MIDDLE OF SUNDAY SERVICE.
BEFORE MANNERS,
BEFORE PRETENSE,
THERE WAS...

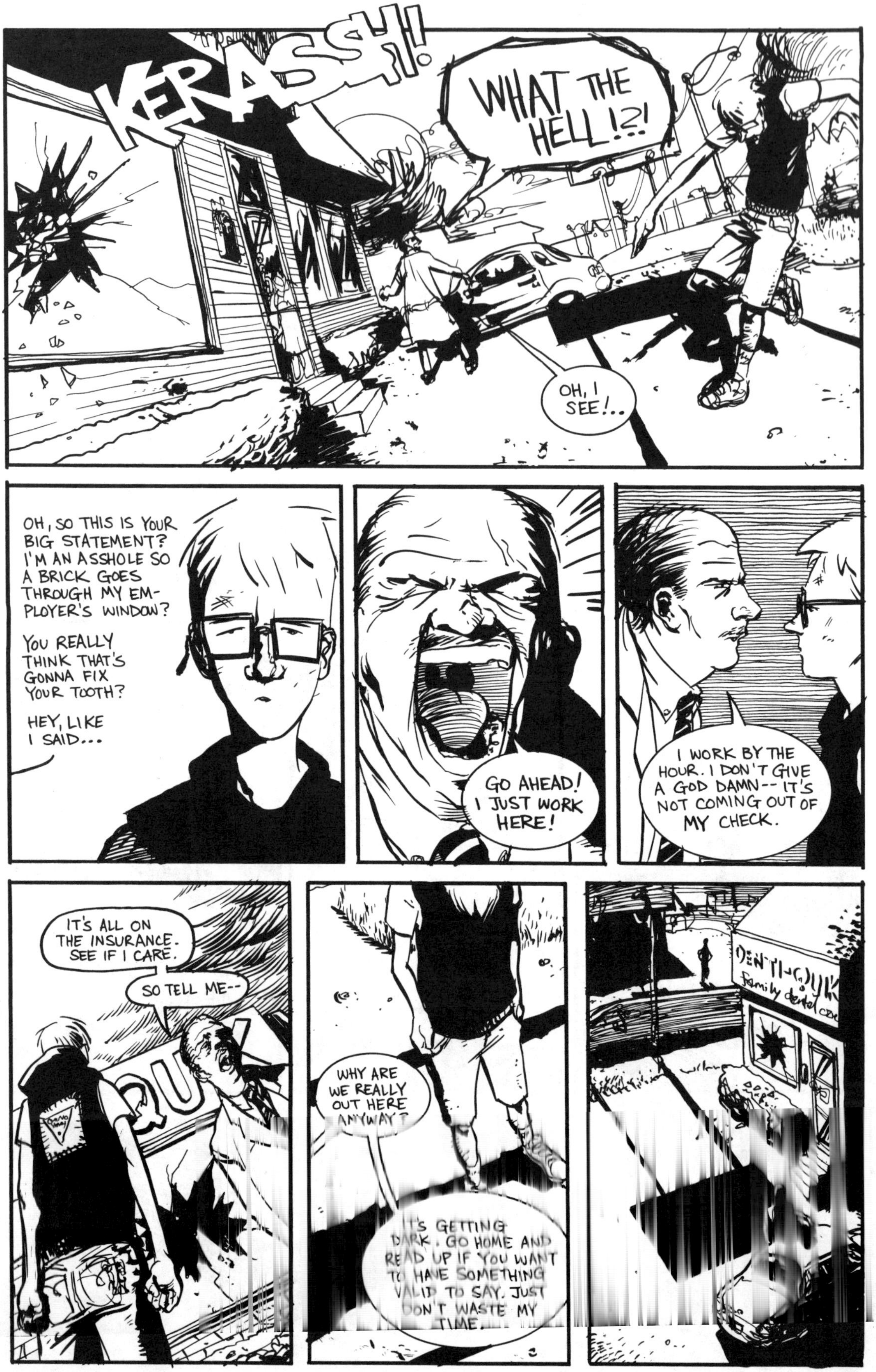
KERASSH!
WHAT THE HELL!?!
OH, I SEE!..
OH, SO THIS IS YOUR BIG STATEMENT? I'M AN ASSHOLE SO A BRICK GOES THROUGH MY EMPLOYER'S WINDOW?
YOU REALLY THINK THAT'S GONNA FIX YOUR TOOTH?
HEY, LIKE I SAID...
GO AHEAD! I JUST WORK HERE!
I WORK BY THE HOUR. I DON'T GIVE A GOD DAMN-- IT'S NOT COMING OUT OF MY CHECK.
IT'S ALL ON THE INSURANCE. SEE IF I CARE.
SO TELL ME--
WHY ARE WE REALLY OUT HERE ANYWAY?
IT'S GETTING DARK. GO HOME AND READ UP IF YOU WANT TO HAVE SOMETHING VALID TO SAY. JUST DON'T WASTE MY TIME.
family dental care

yeah. walk briskly home.

bunny ears, "home".

mace in left pocket. hurry. undo snap in case i need it.

dickhead slows down. stupid truck matching my pace.

he whistles—smiles—looking back.

he's proud of himself. he can drive and whistle at the same time.

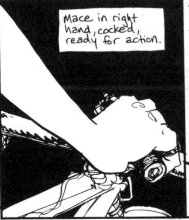

Mace in right hand, cocked, ready for action.

i'm amazed at the automatic reflex of middle finger.

left hand too.

the word "chicken" comes to mind. middle finger=chicken. who knows why.

a dirty word and a prayer at the same time.

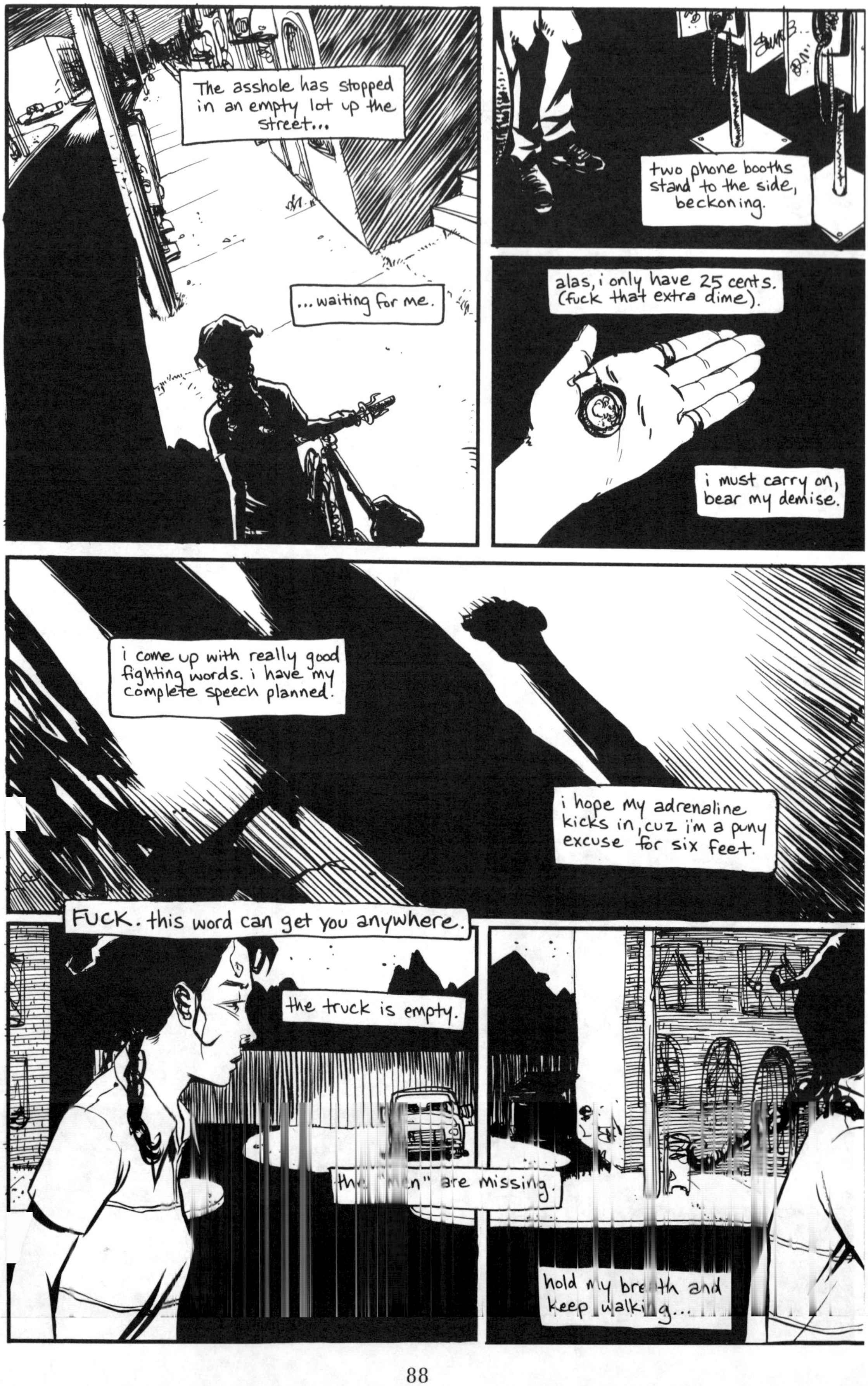
The asshole has stopped in an empty lot up the street...
...waiting for me.
two phone booths stand to the side, beckoning.
alas, i only have 25 cents. (fuck that extra dime).
i must carry on, bear my demise.
i come up with really good fighting words. i have my complete speech planned.
i hope my adrenaline kicks in, cuz i'm a puny excuse for six feet.
FUCK. this word can get you anywhere.
the truck is empty.
the "men" are missing.
hold my breath and keep walking...

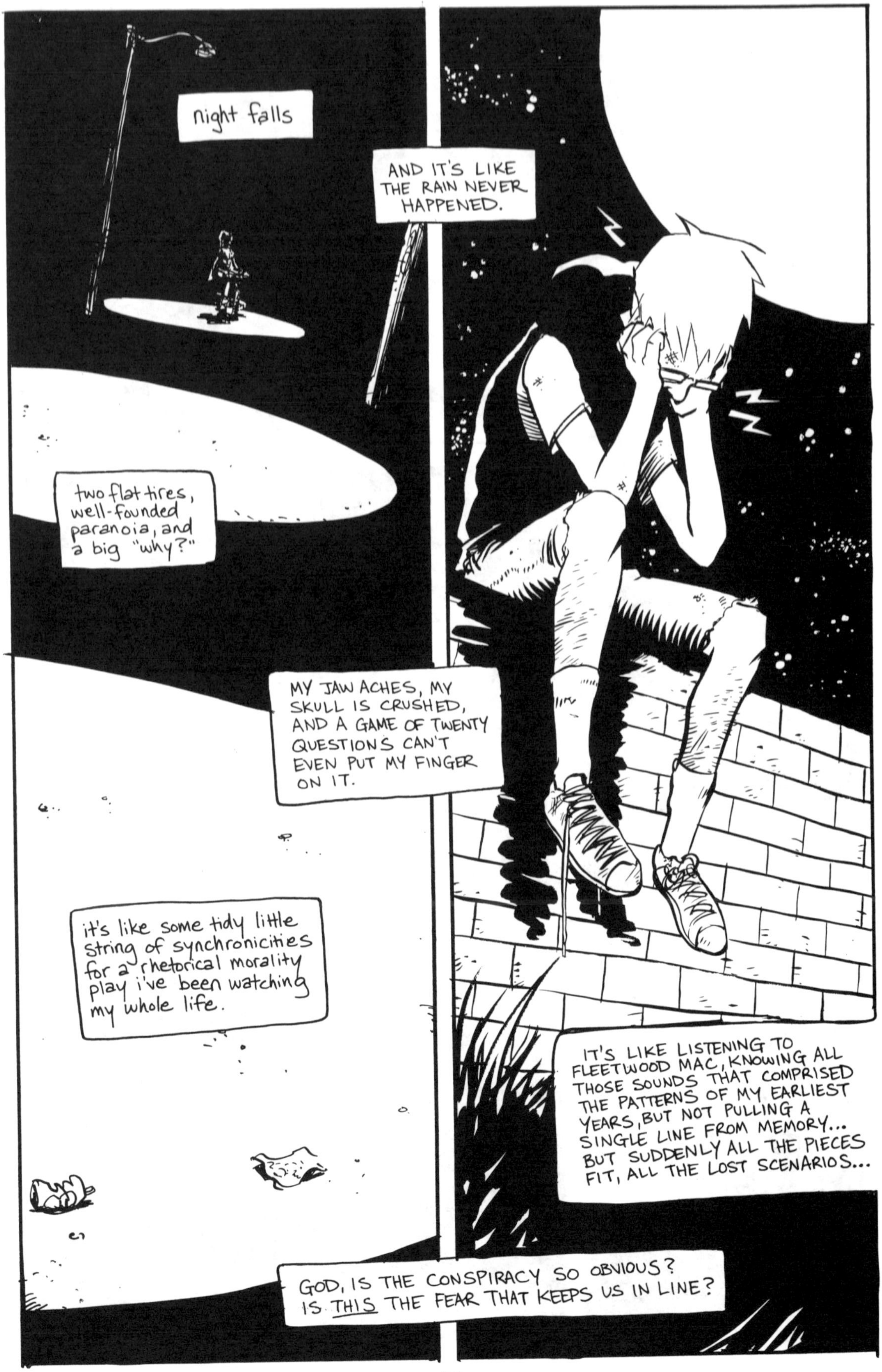
night falls
two flat tires, well-founded paranoia, and a big "why?"
AND IT'S LIKE THE RAIN NEVER HAPPENED.
MY JAW ACHES, MY SKULL IS CRUSHED, AND A GAME OF TWENTY QUESTIONS CAN'T EVEN PUT MY FINGER ON IT.
it's like some tidy little string of synchronicities for a rhetorical morality play i've been watching my whole life.
IT'S LIKE LISTENING TO FLEETWOOD MAC, KNOWING ALL THOSE SOUNDS THAT COMPRISED THE PATTERNS OF MY EARLIEST YEARS, BUT NOT PULLING A SINGLE LINE FROM MEMORY... BUT SUDDENLY ALL THE PIECES FIT, ALL THE LOST SCENARIOS...
GOD, IS THE CONSPIRACY SO OBVIOUS? IS THIS THE FEAR THAT KEEPS US IN LINE?

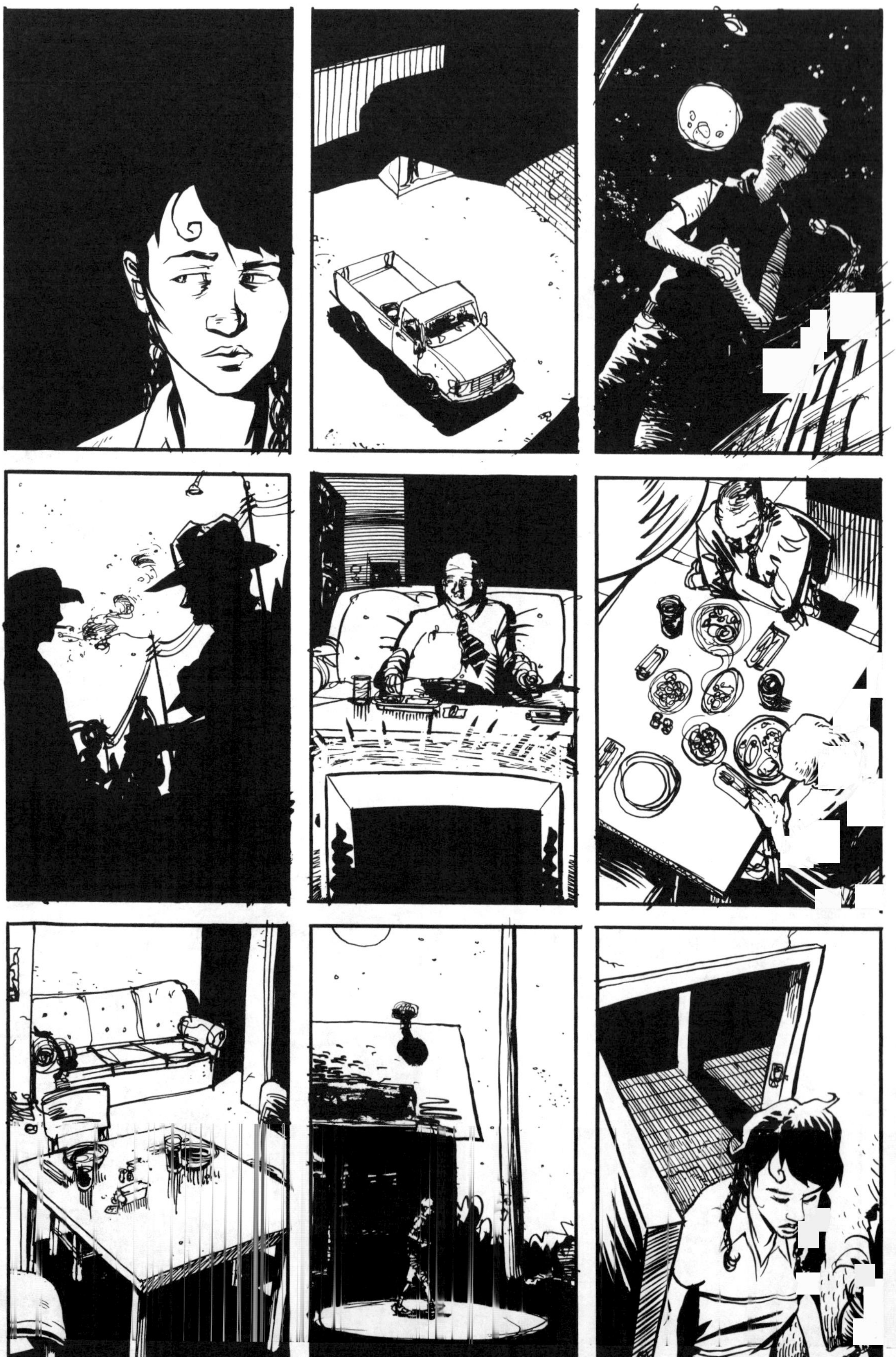

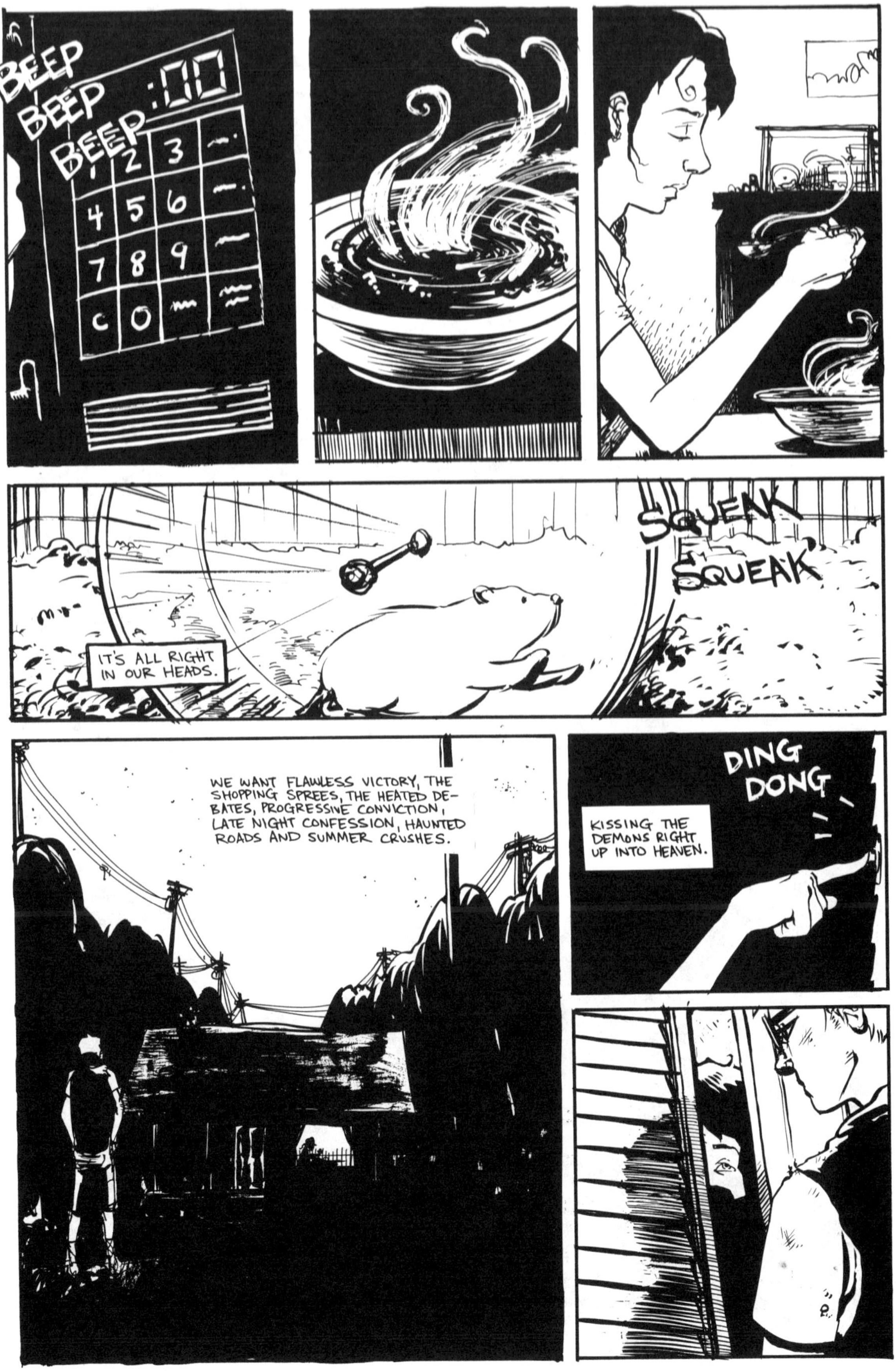
BEEP
BEEP
BEEP
:00
1 2 3
4 5 6
7 8 9
C 0
SQUEAK
SQUEAK
IT'S ALL RIGHT IN OUR HEADS.
WE WANT FLAWLESS VICTORY, THE SHOPPING SPREES, THE HEATED DE-BATES, PROGRESSIVE CONVICTION, LATE NIGHT CONFESSION, HAUNTED ROADS AND SUMMER CRUSHES.
DING DONG
KISSING THE DEMONS RIGHT UP INTO HEAVEN.

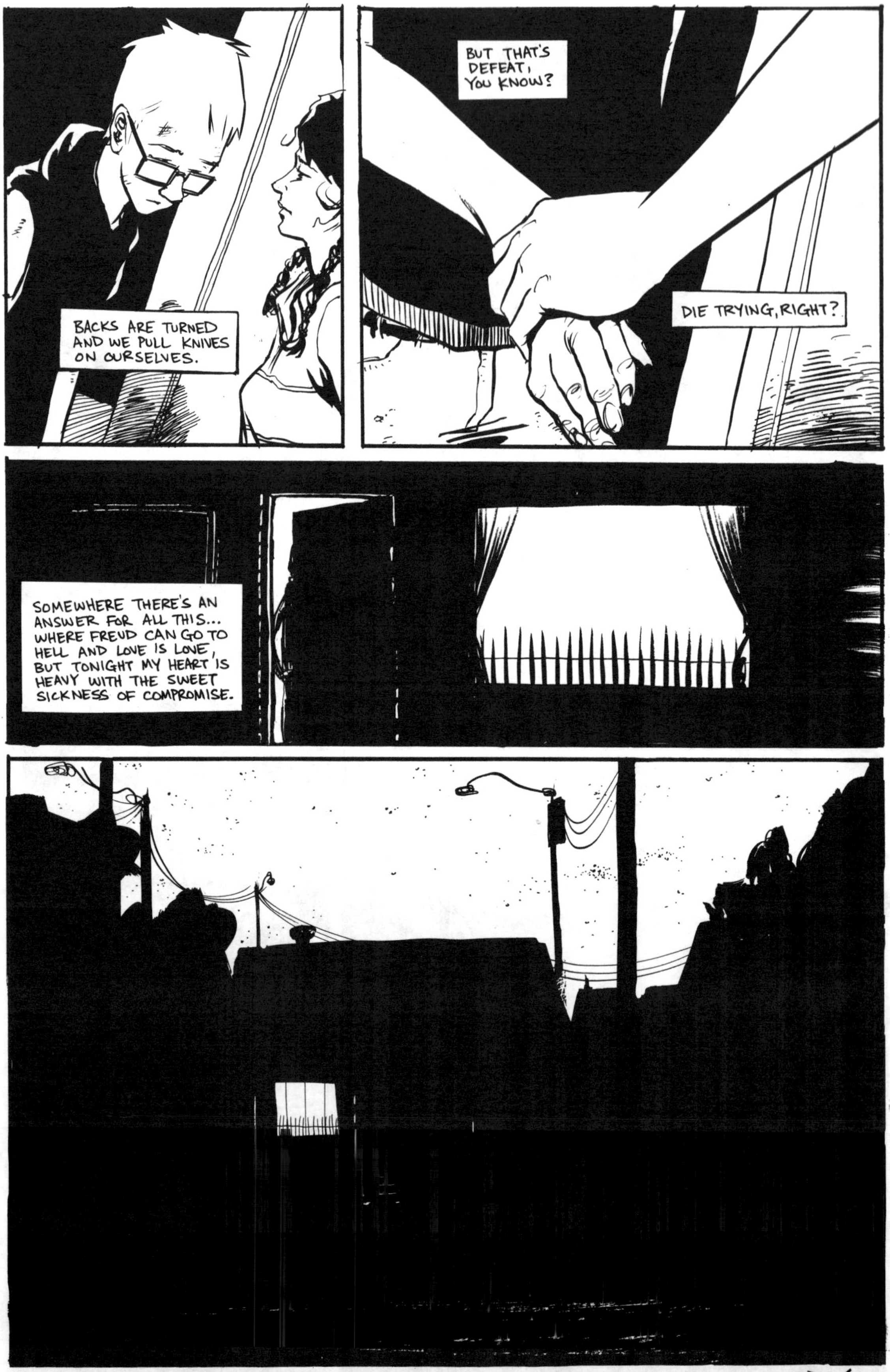
BACKS ARE TURNED AND WE PULL KNIVES ON OURSELVES.
BUT THAT'S DEFEAT, YOU KNOW?
DIE TRYING, RIGHT?
SOMEWHERE THERE'S AN ANSWER FOR ALL THIS... WHERE FREUD CAN GO TO HELL AND LOVE IS LOVE, BUT TONIGHT MY HEART IS HEAVY WITH THE SWEET SICKNESS OF COMPROMISE.
N.P. 4-00 X

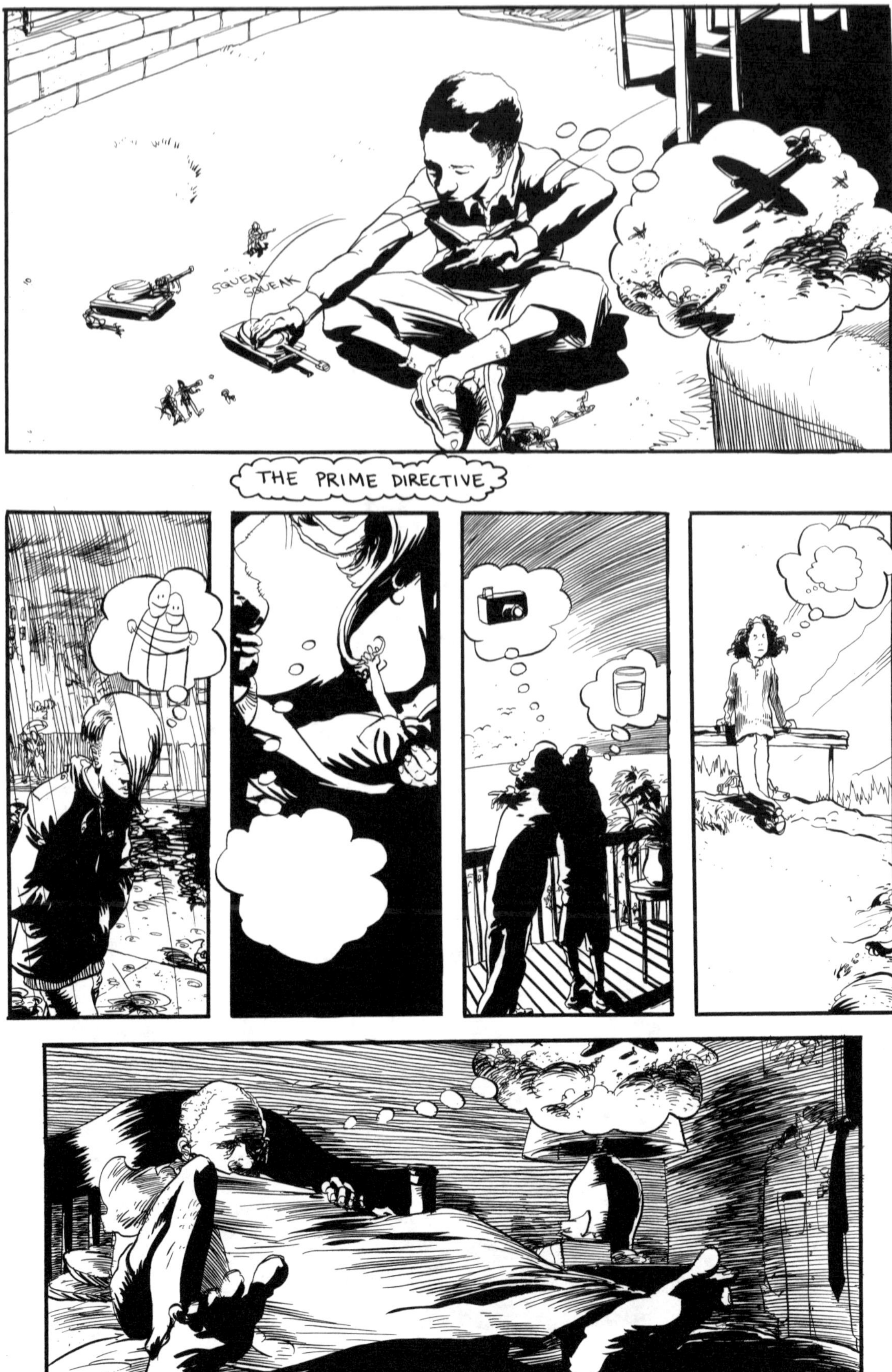
SQUEAK SQUEAK
THE PRIME DIRECTIVE

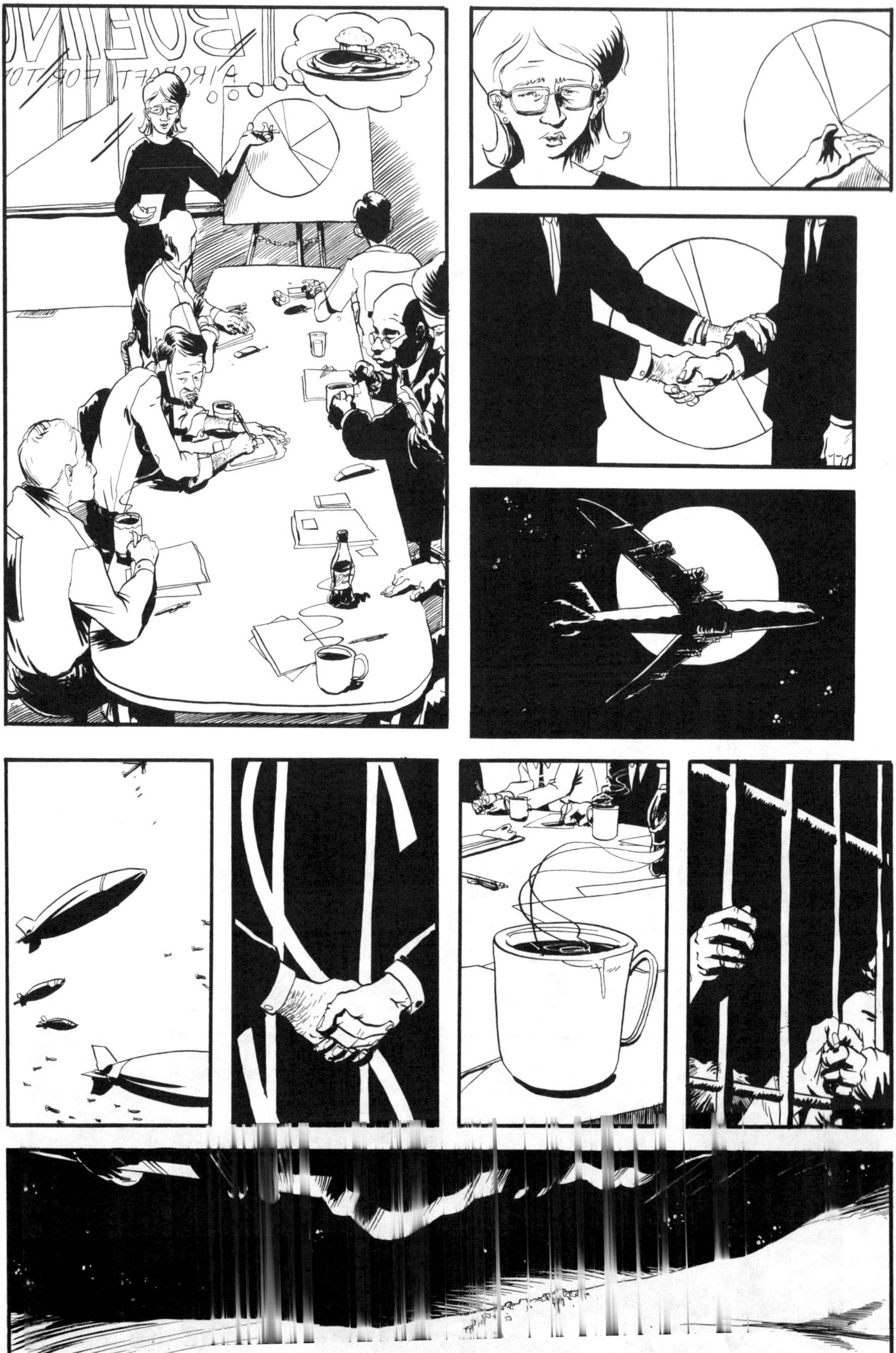

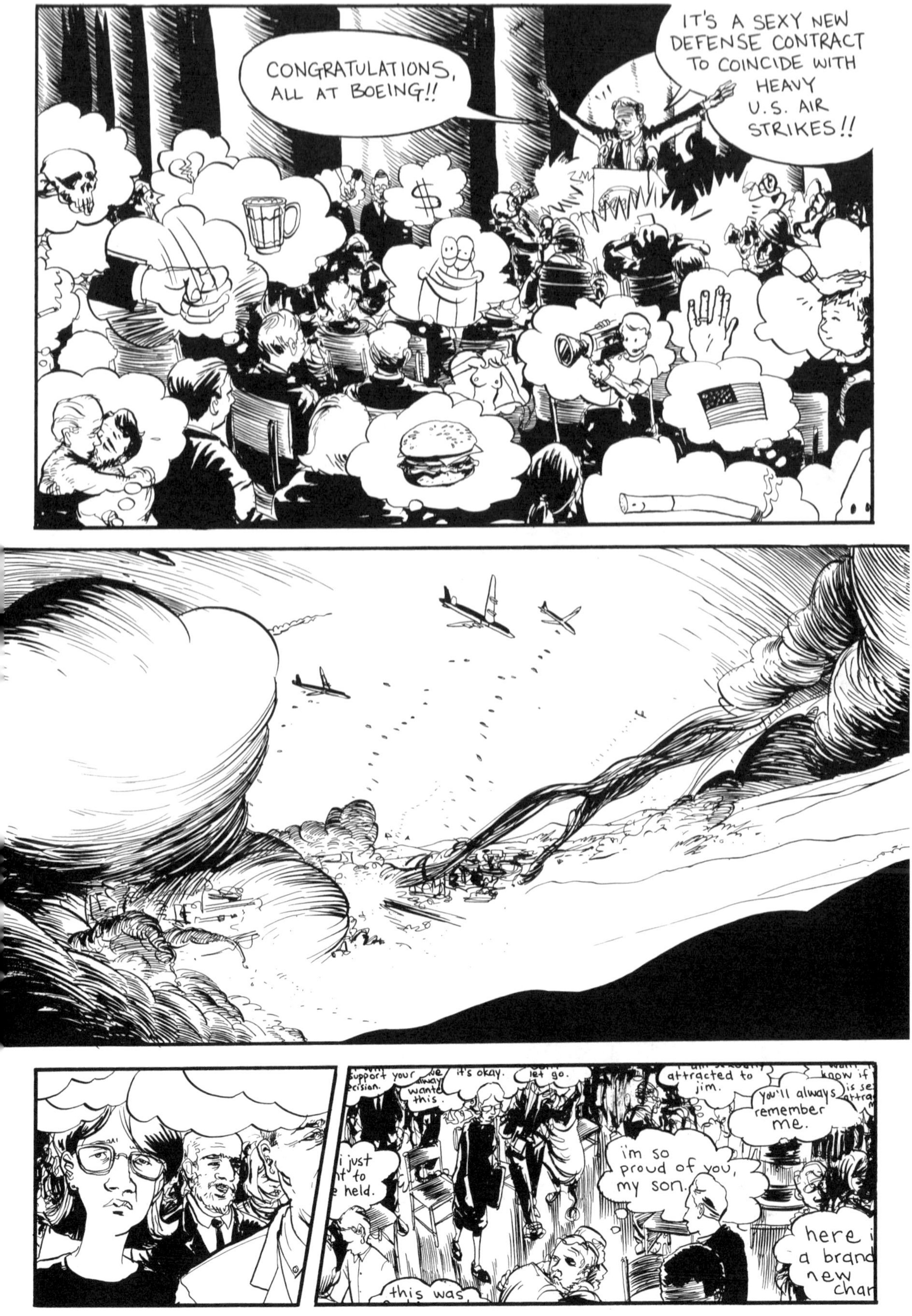
CONGRATULATIONS, ALL AT BOEING!!
IT'S A SEXY NEW DEFENSE CONTRACT TO COINCIDE WITH HEAVY U.S. AIR STRIKES!!
support your
ecision.
wante
this.
it's okay.
let go.
attracted to
jim.
know if
you'll always remember me.
i just
t to
held.
i'm so proud of you, my son.
here
a brand
new
char
this was

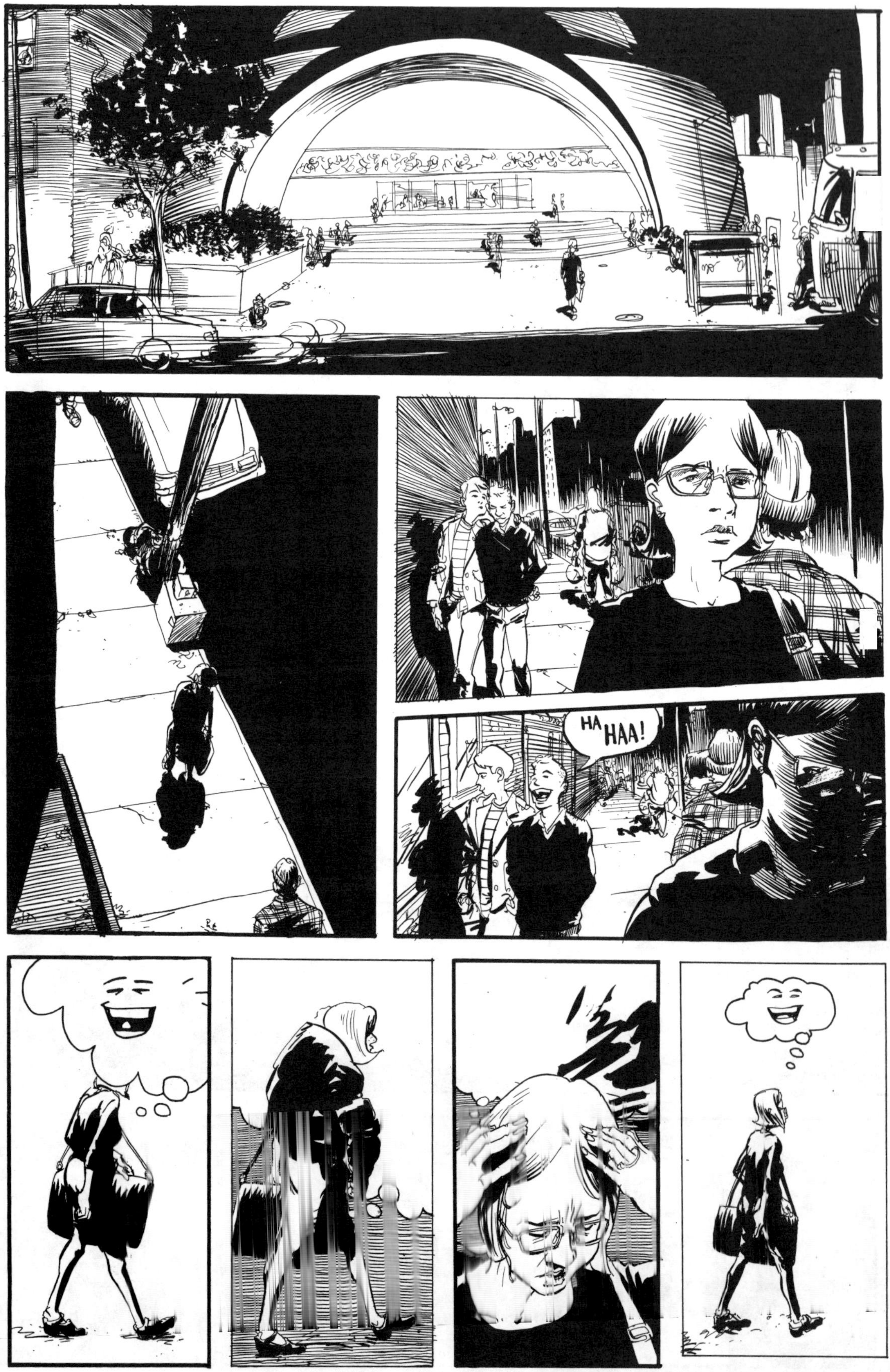
HA HAA!

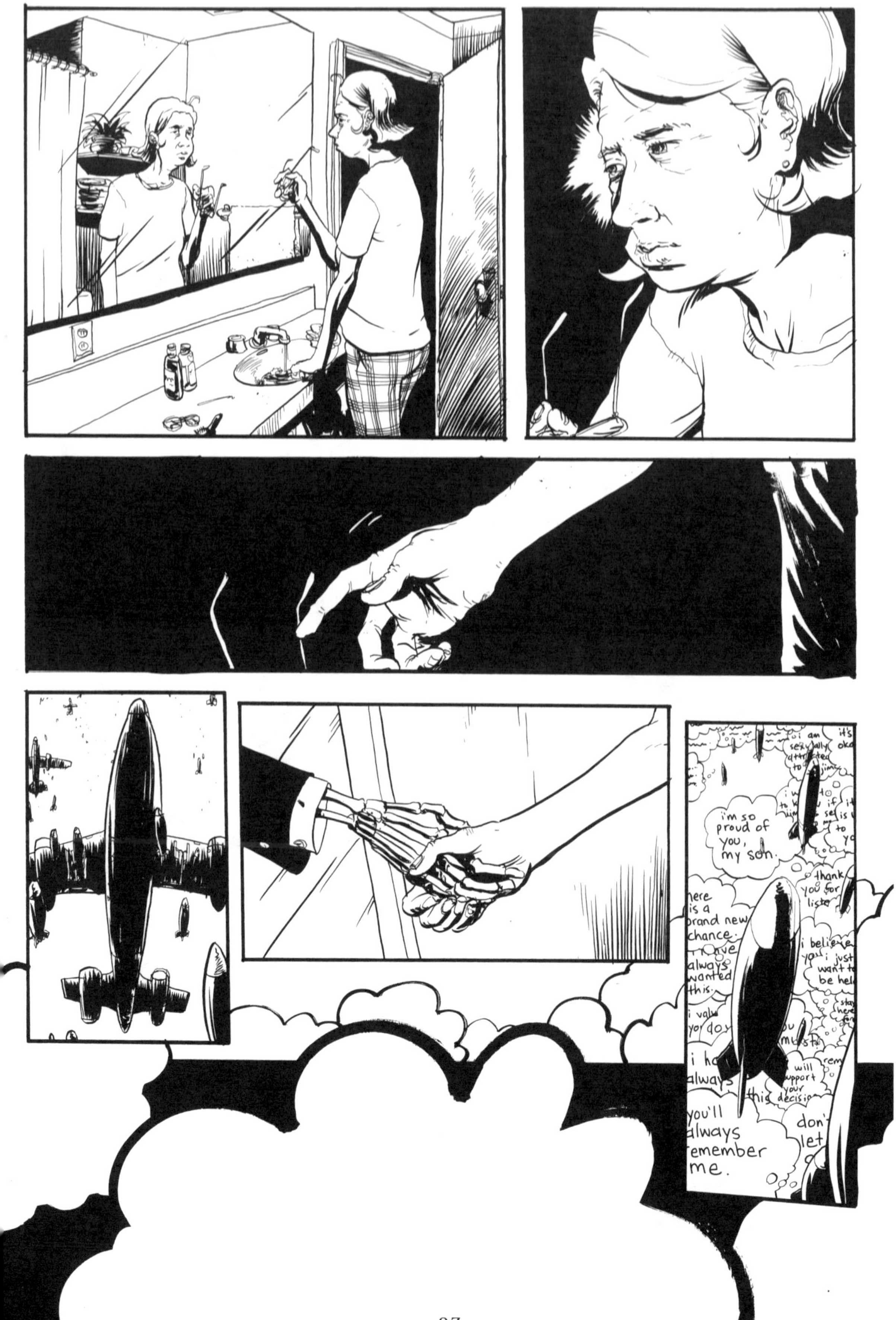
i am sexually attracted to jim
it's oka
i'm so proud of you, my son.
thank you for liste
ere is a rand new chance.
always wanted this.
i believe you
i just want t be hel
will upport your decisio
you'll always emember me.
don' let

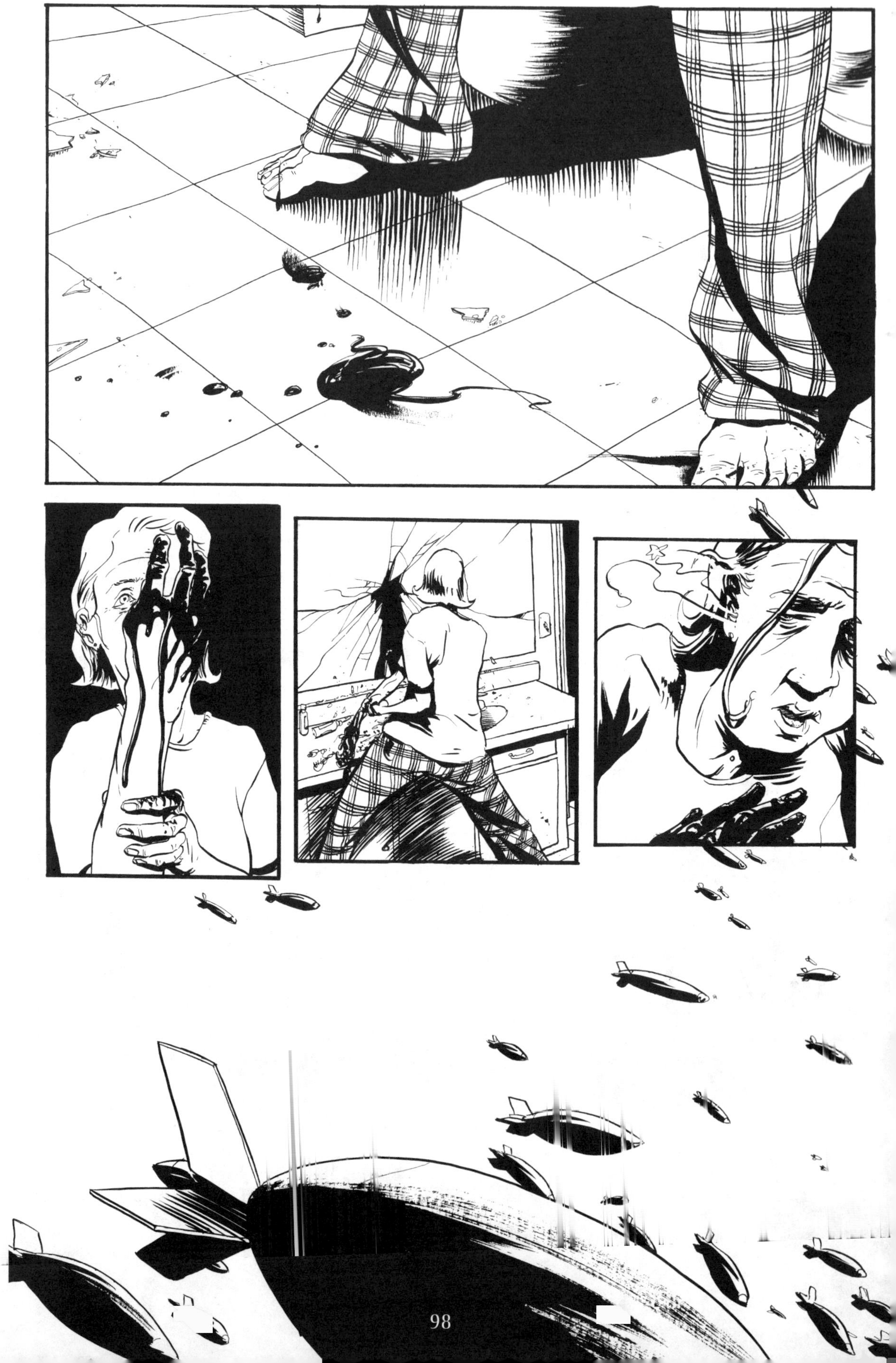

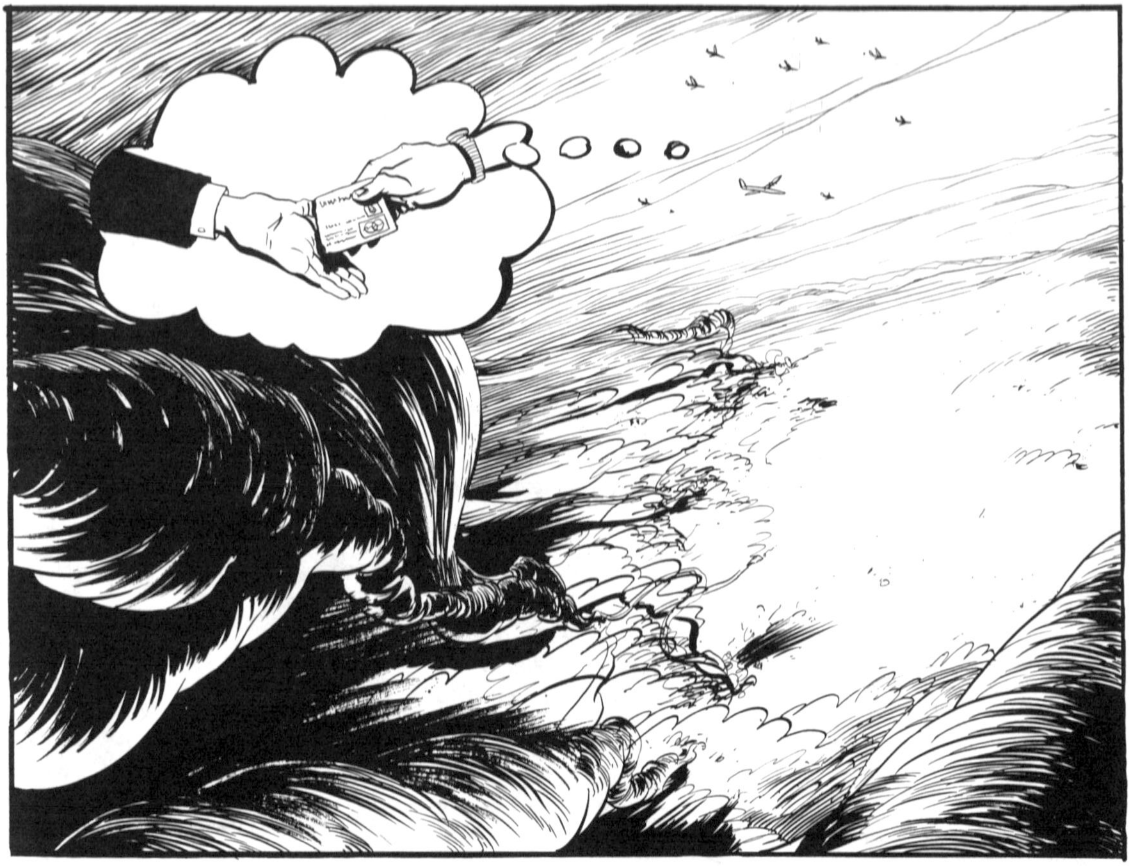

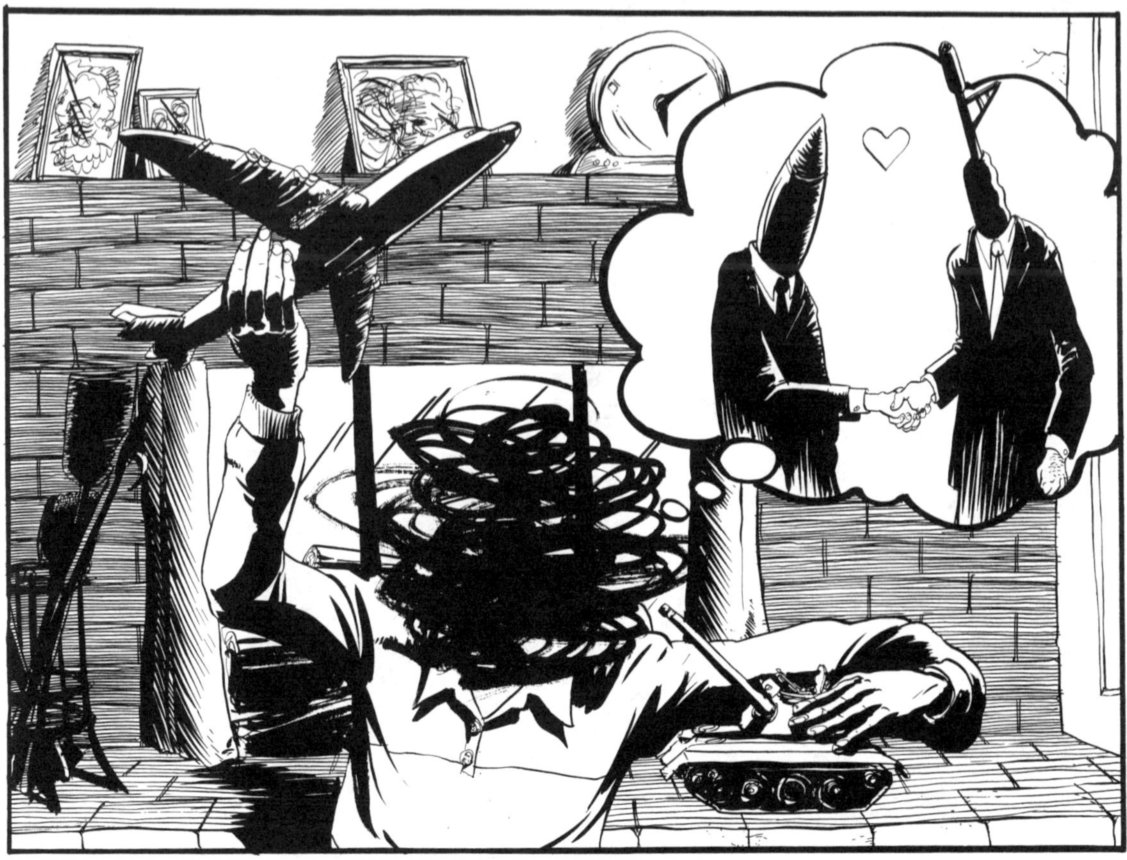

the astronomer's club*

hey tracy... my daddy said the gas still don't work.

ASSHOLE DON'T ¿oof? GIVE A SHIT BOUT US.

AND TODAY MY COUSIN JERRY,

YOU REMEMBER COUSIN JERRY--

--HE GAVE ME A BLACK EYE ON ACCOUNT A THE PLACE NOT BEIN STRAIGHT AND ALL.

FUCK YOU MOTHERFUCKER.

YOU AIN'T EVEN MY DADDY.

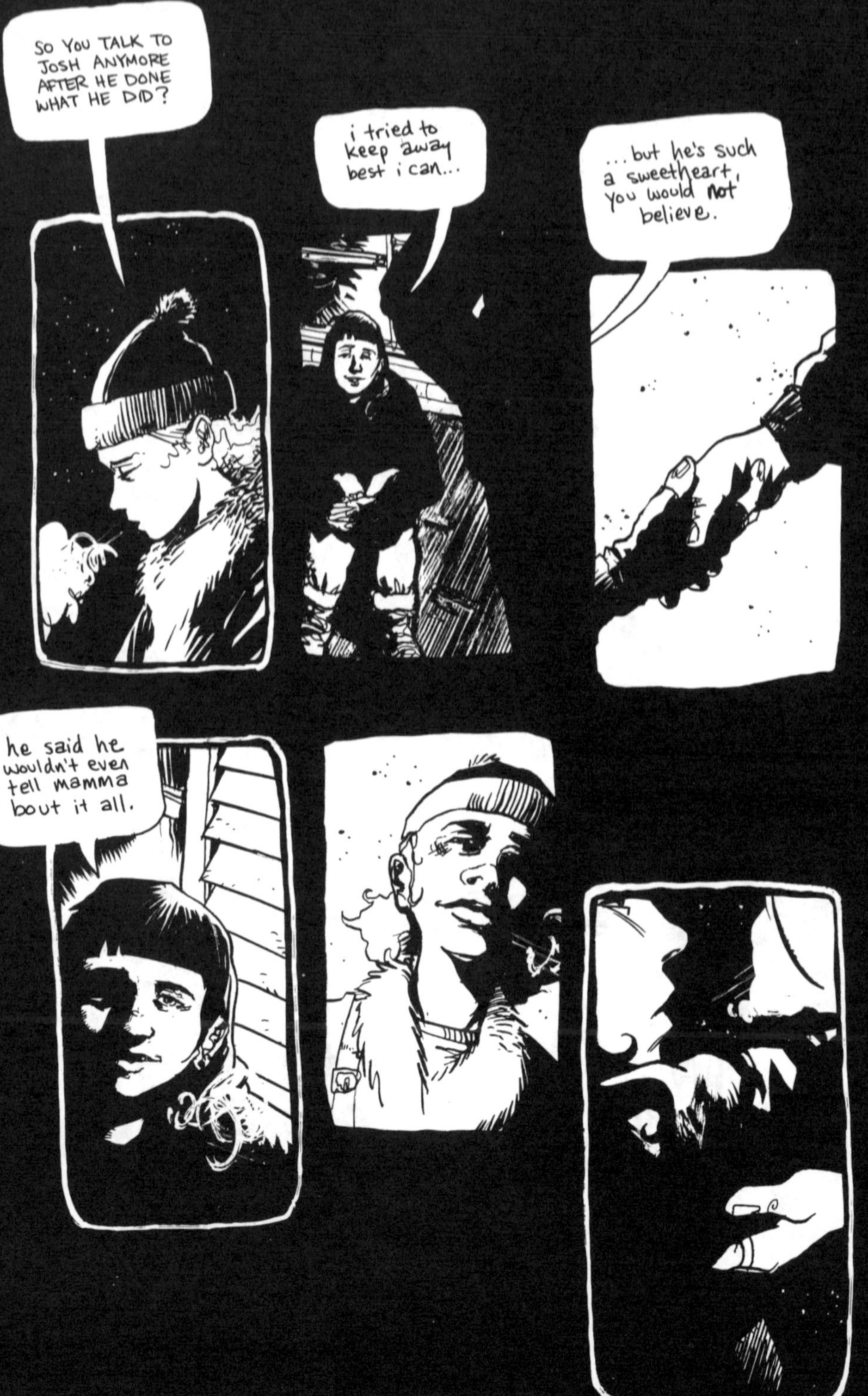
SO YOU TALK TO JOSH ANYMORE AFTER HE DONE WHAT HE DID?
i tried to keep away best i can...
...but he's such a sweetheart, you would not believe.
he said he wouldn't even tell mamma bout it all.

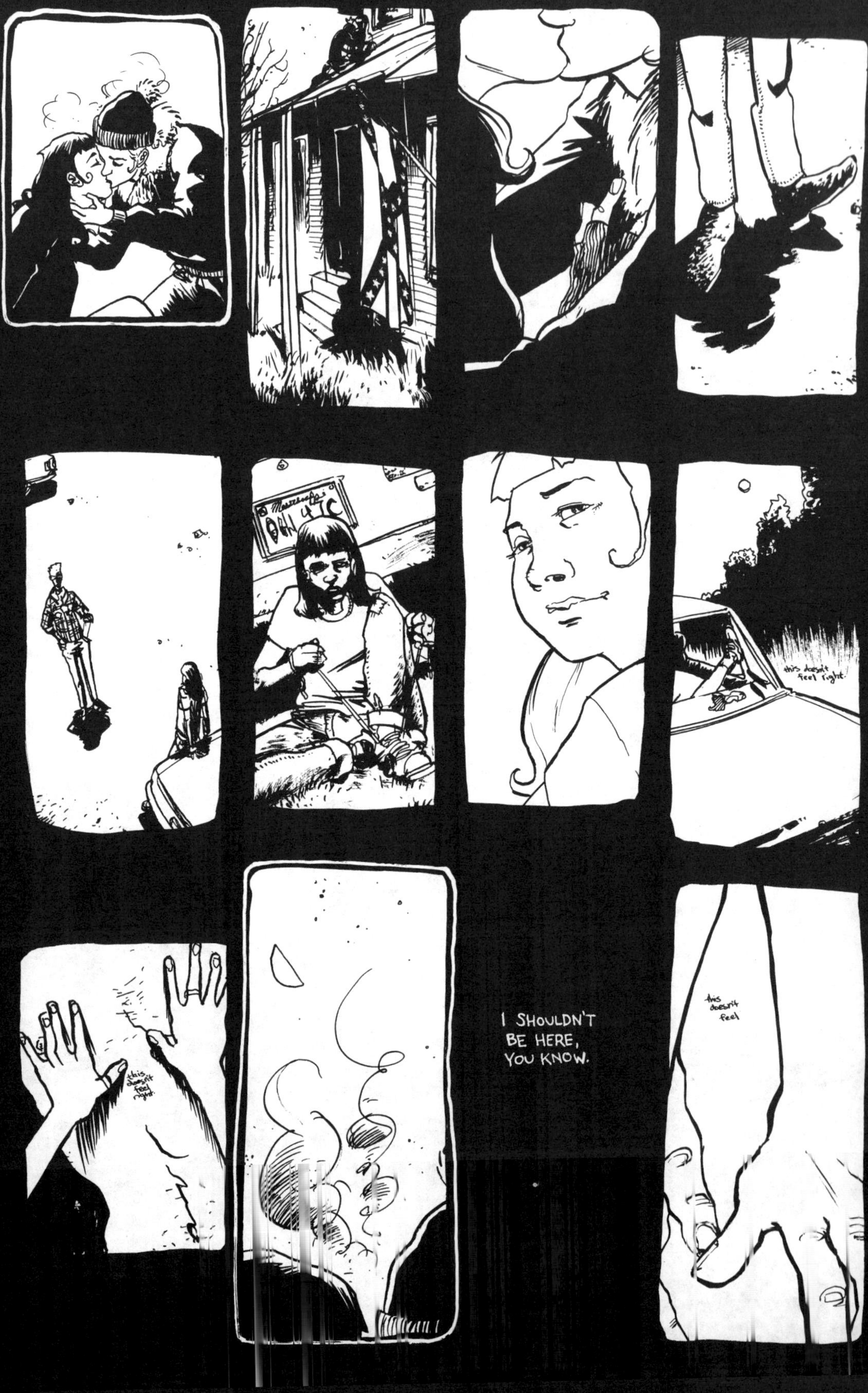
this doesn't feel right.
this doesn't feel right.
I SHOULDN'T BE HERE, YOU KNOW.
this doesn't feel

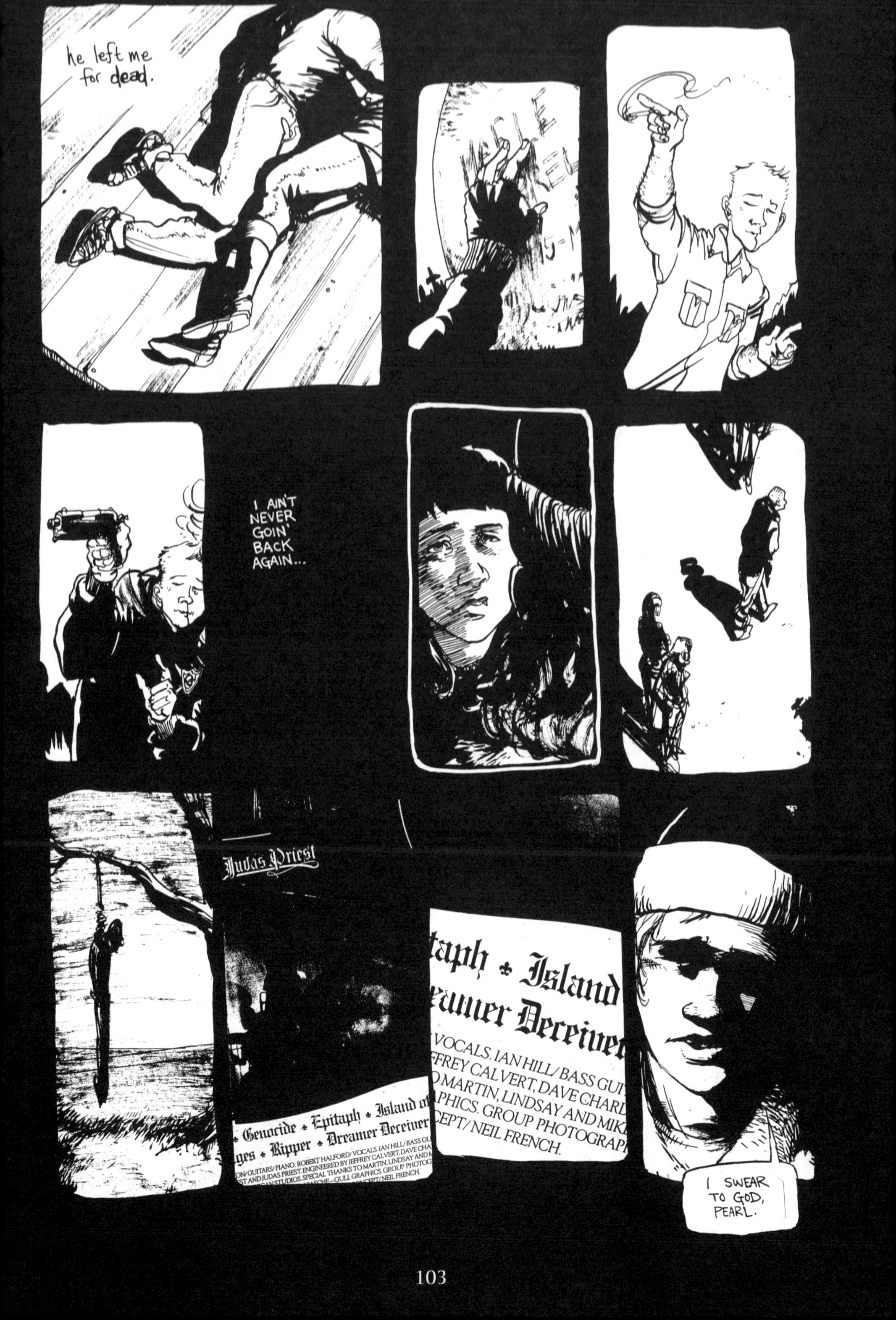
he left me for dead.
I AIN'T NEVER GOIN' BACK AGAIN...
Judas Priest
Genocide • Epitaph • Island of
ges • Ripper • Dreamer Deceiver
taph • Island
eamer Deceiver
VOCALS. IAN HILL/ BASS GUI
FFREY CALVERT, DAVE CHARL
D MARTIN, LINDSAY AND MIK
PHICS. GROUP PHOTOGRAP
CEPT/ NEIL FRENCH.
I SWEAR TO GOD, PEARL.

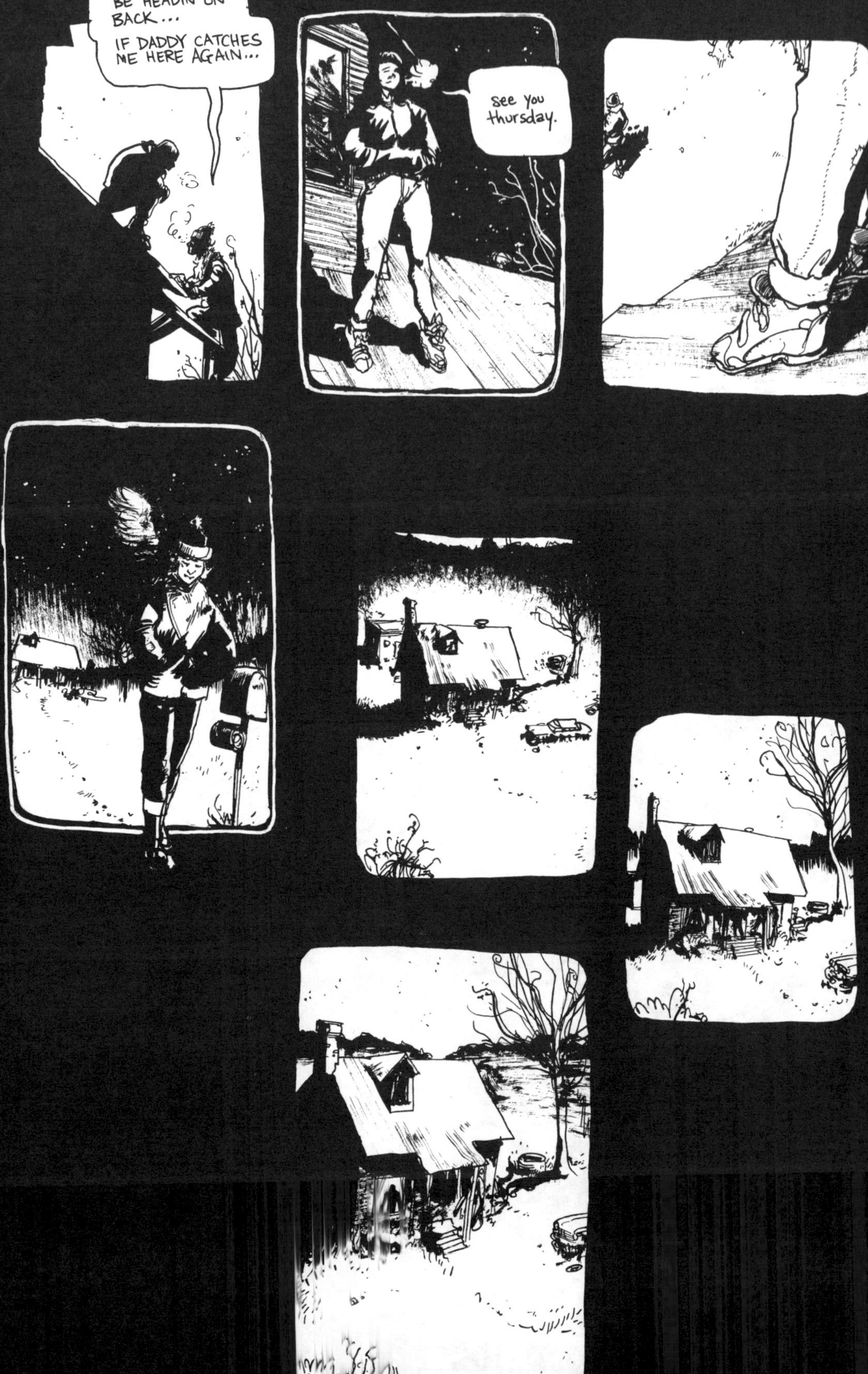
WELL, I BEST BE HEADIN' ON BACK...
IF DADDY CATCHES ME HERE AGAIN...
see you thursday.

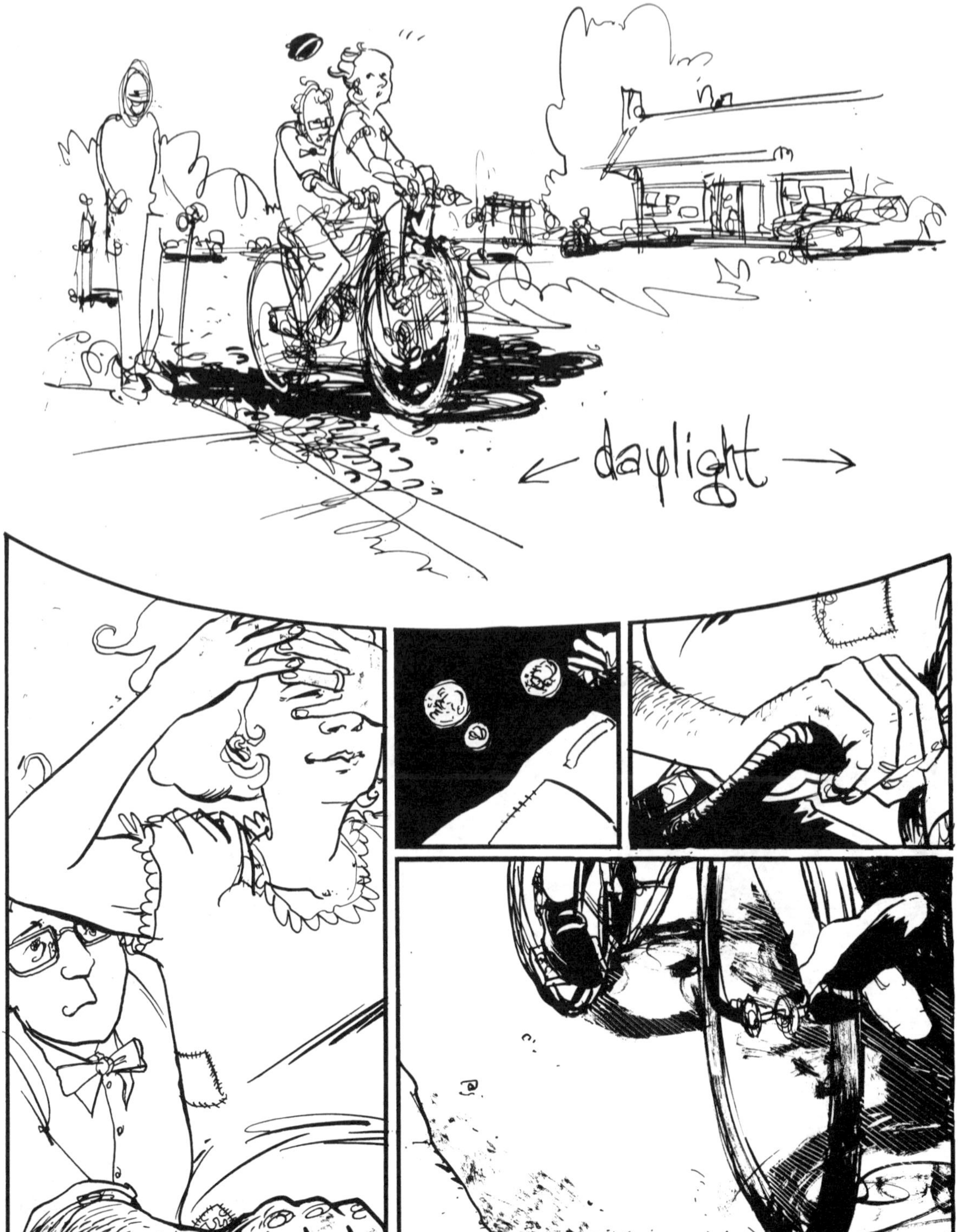
daylight

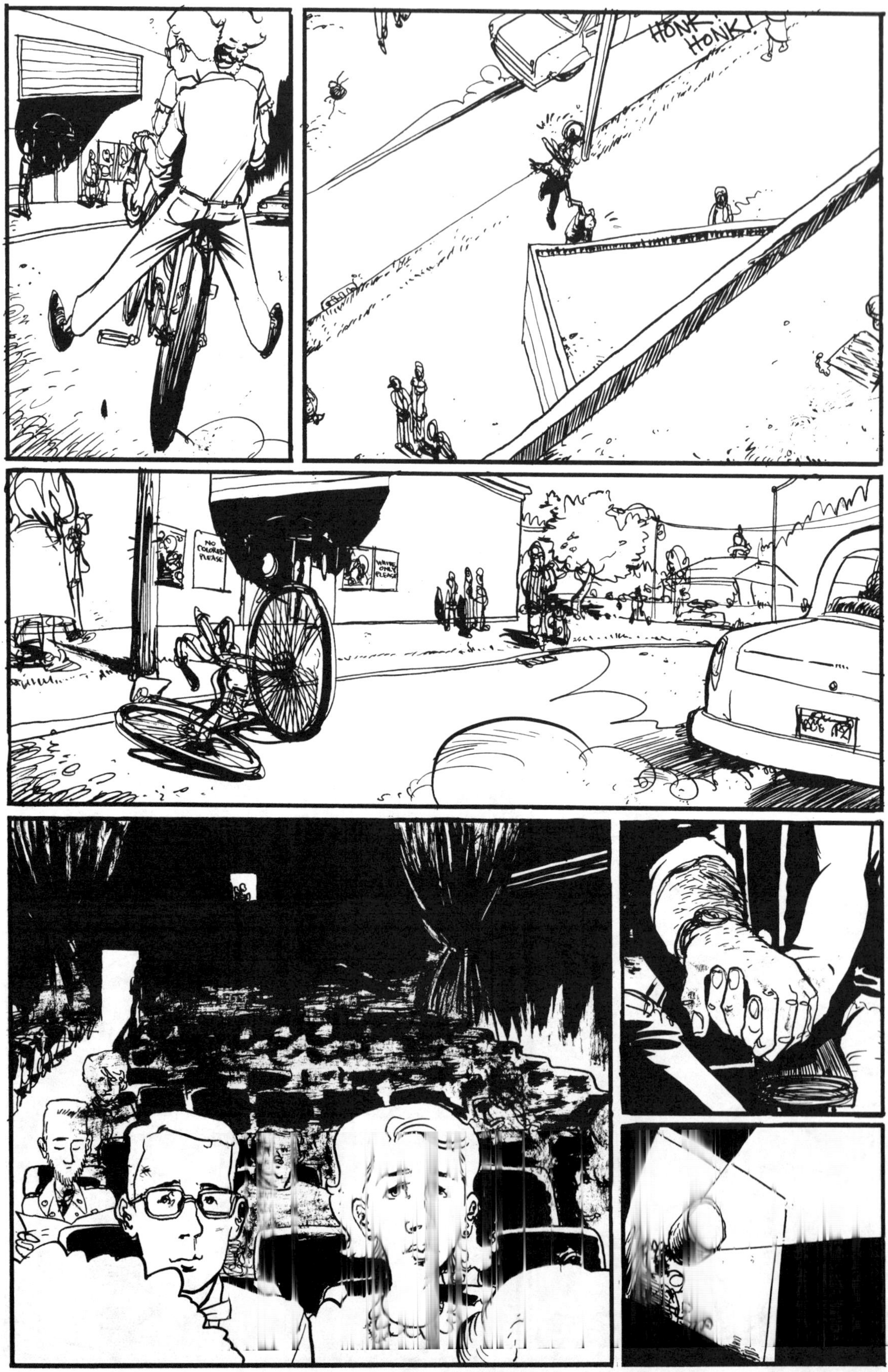
HONK HONK!
NO COLORED PLEASE
WHITE ONLY PLEASE

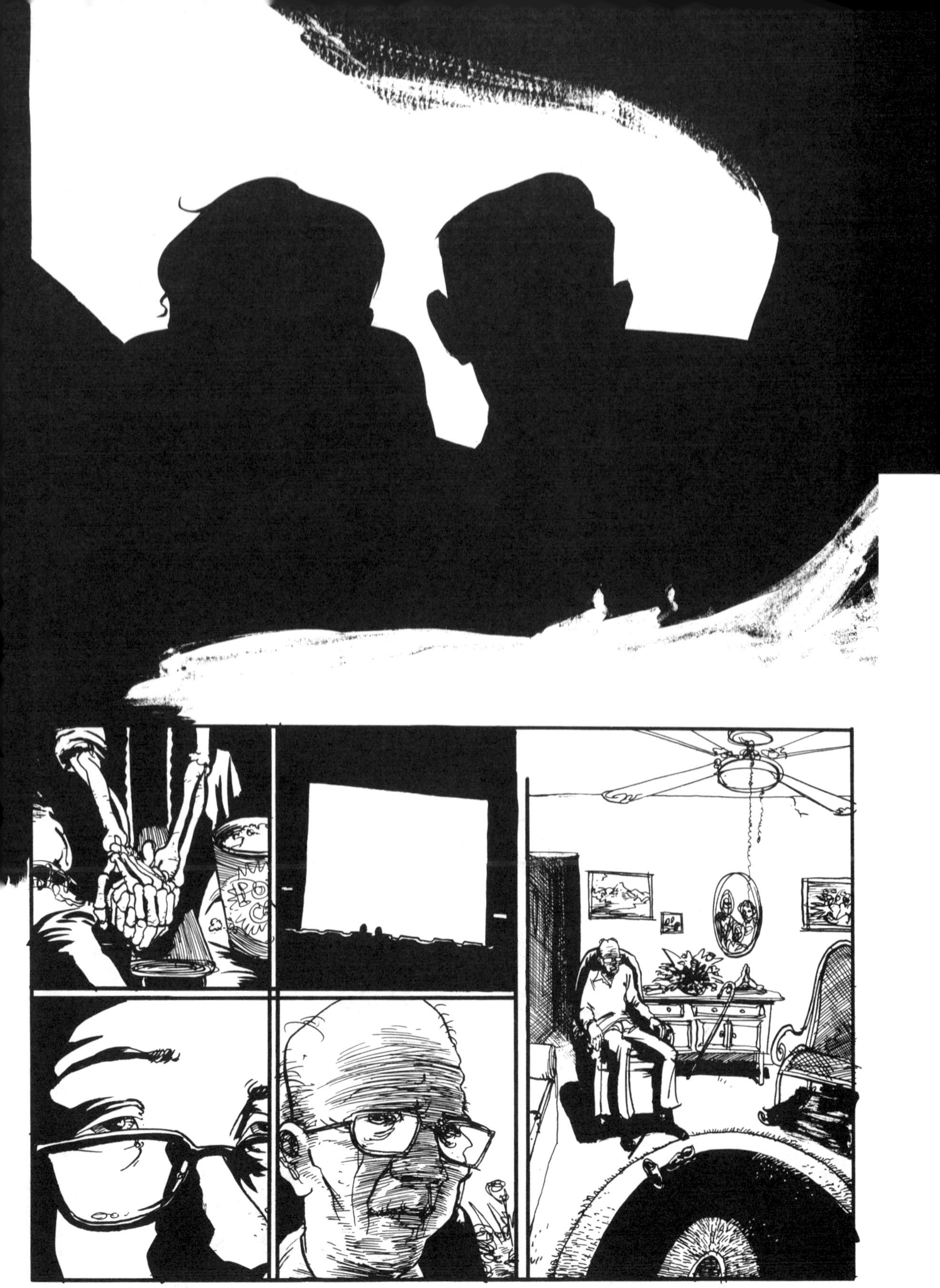

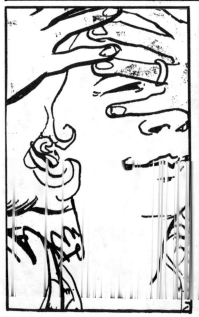

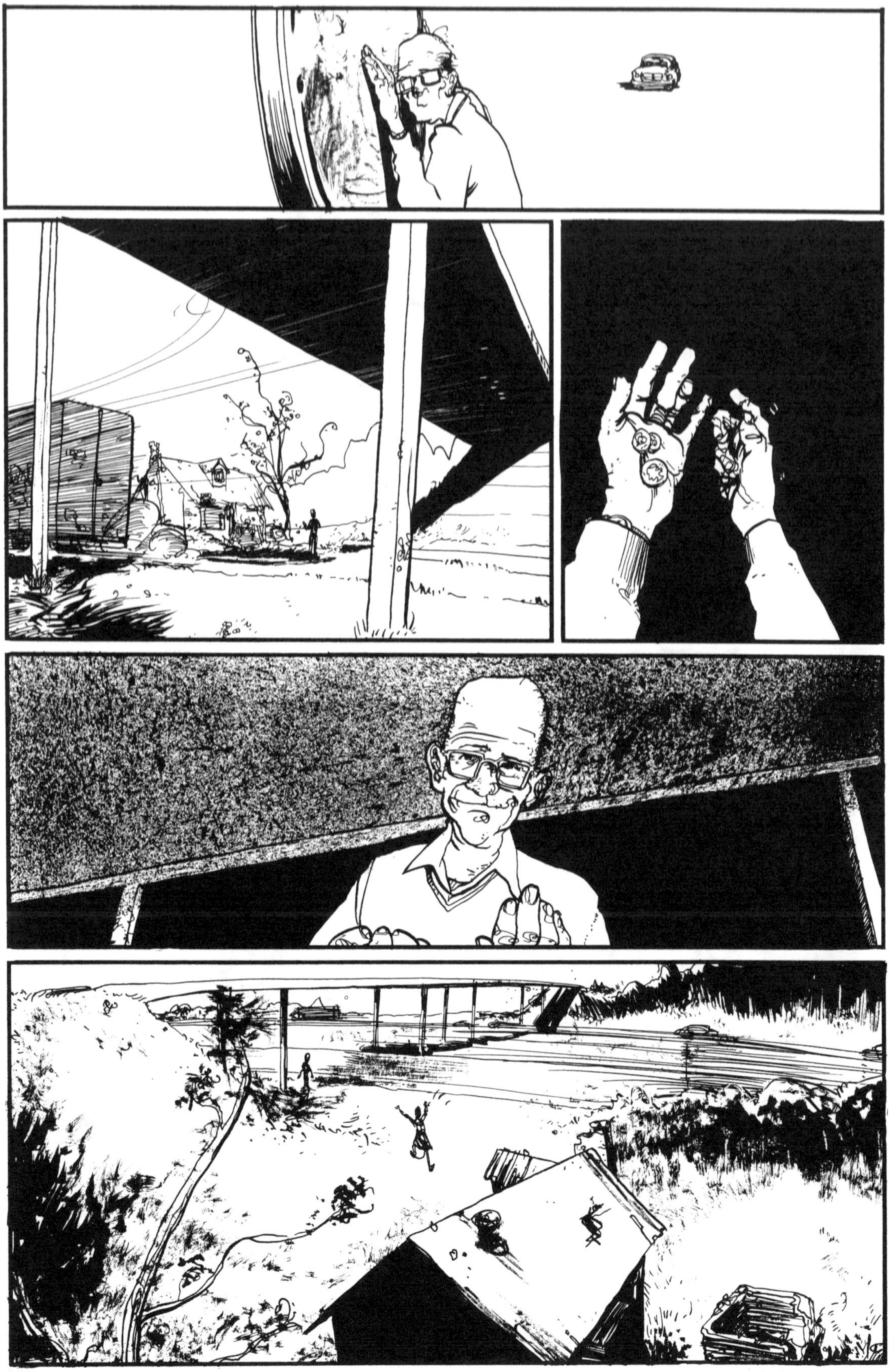

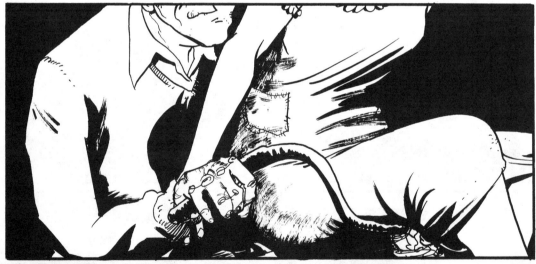

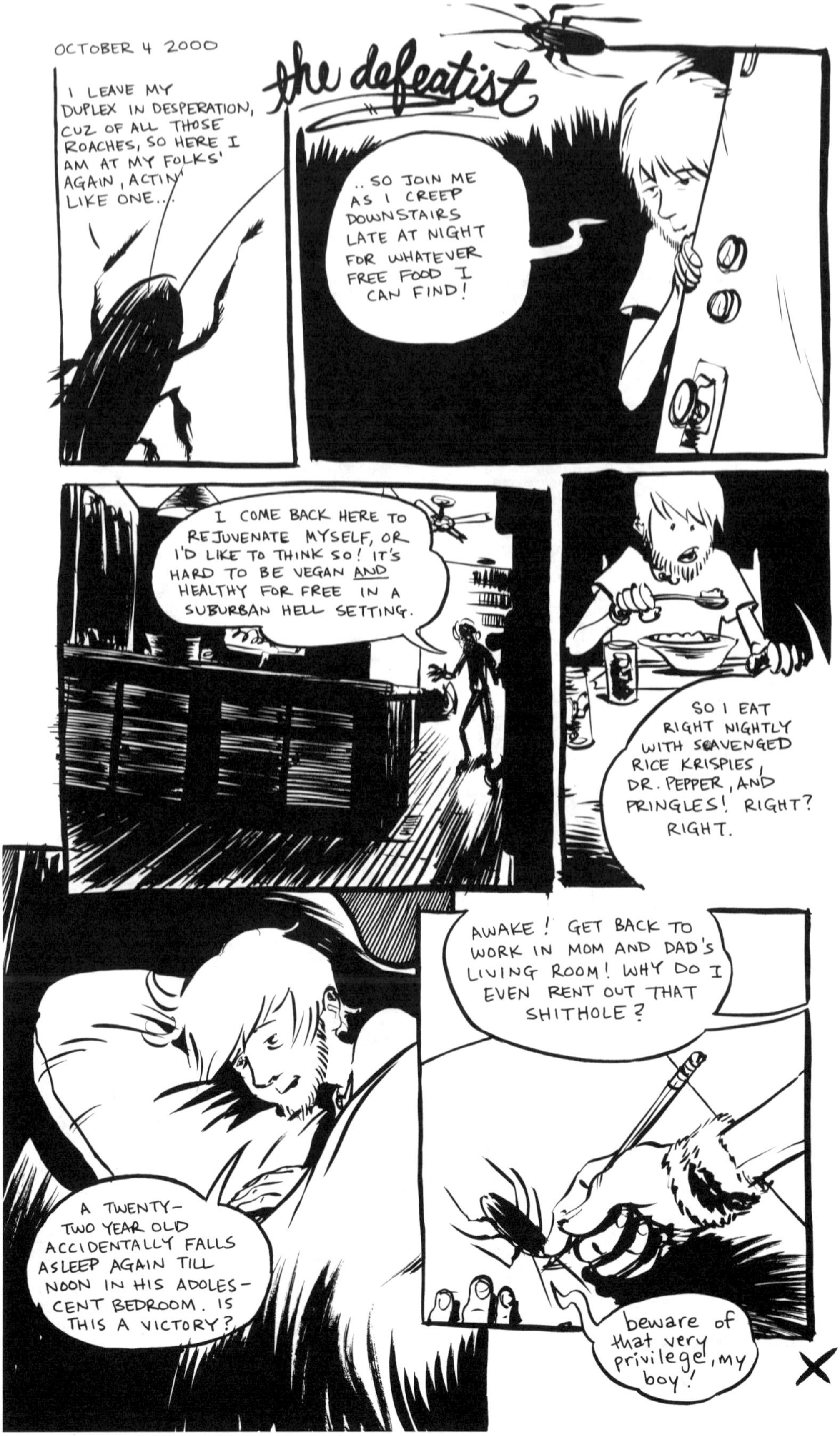
the defeatist
OCTOBER 4 2000
I LEAVE MY DUPLEX IN DESPERATION, CUZ OF ALL THOSE ROACHES, SO HERE I AM AT MY FOLKS' AGAIN, ACTIN' LIKE ONE...
..SO JOIN ME AS I CREEP DOWNSTAIRS LATE AT NIGHT FOR WHATEVER FREE FOOD I CAN FIND!
I COME BACK HERE TO REJUVENATE MYSELF, OR I'D LIKE TO THINK SO! IT'S HARD TO BE VEGAN AND HEALTHY FOR FREE IN A SUBURBAN HELL SETTING.
SO I EAT RIGHT NIGHTLY WITH SCAVENGED RICE KRISPIES, DR. PEPPER, AND PRINGLES! RIGHT? RIGHT.
A TWENTY-TWO YEAR OLD ACCIDENTALLY FALLS ASLEEP AGAIN TILL NOON IN HIS ADOLESCENT BEDROOM. IS THIS A VICTORY?
AWAKE! GET BACK TO WORK IN MOM AND DAD'S LIVING ROOM! WHY DO I EVEN RENT OUT THAT SHITHOLE?
beware of that very privilege, my boy!

1. mercury

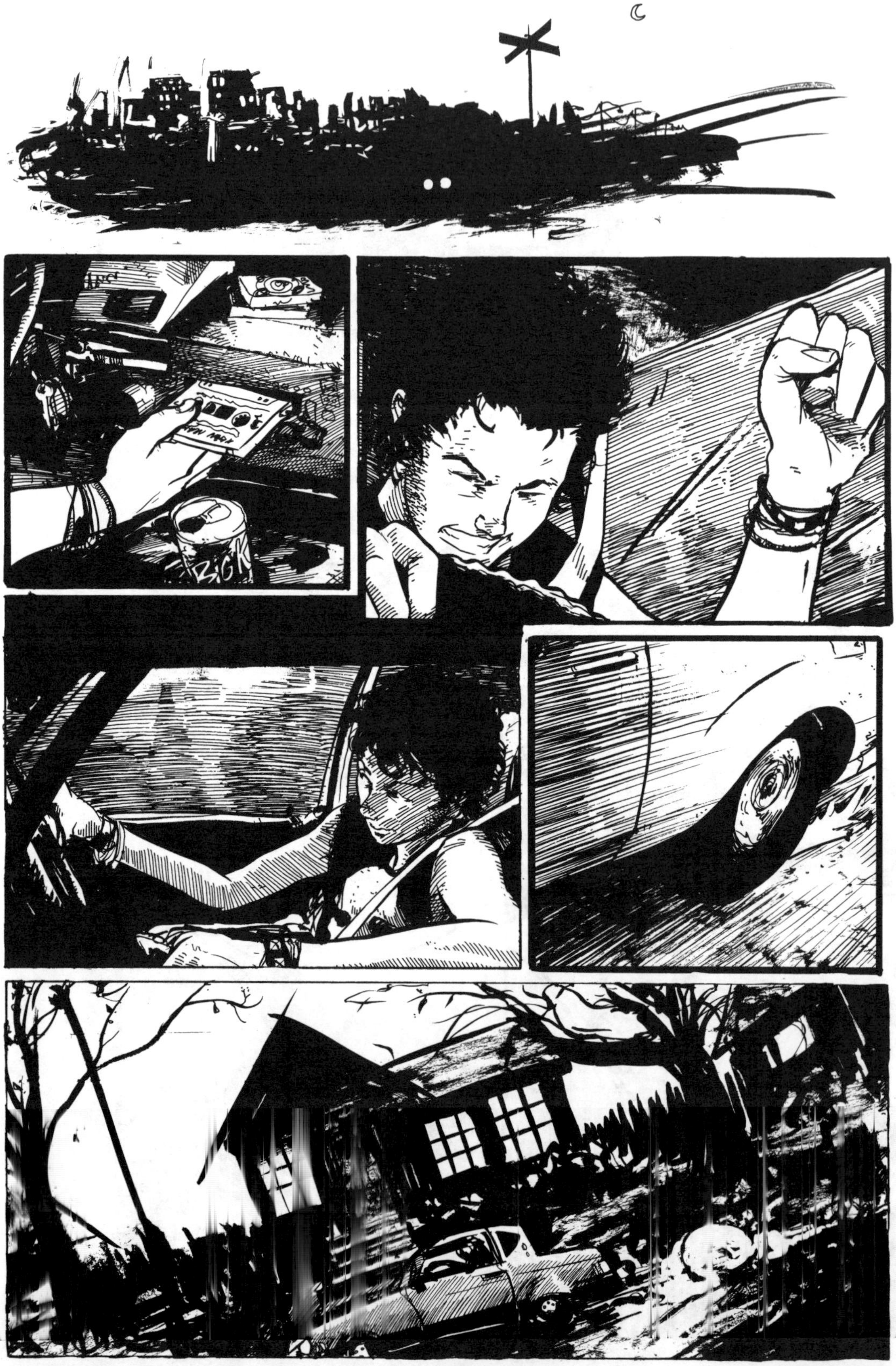

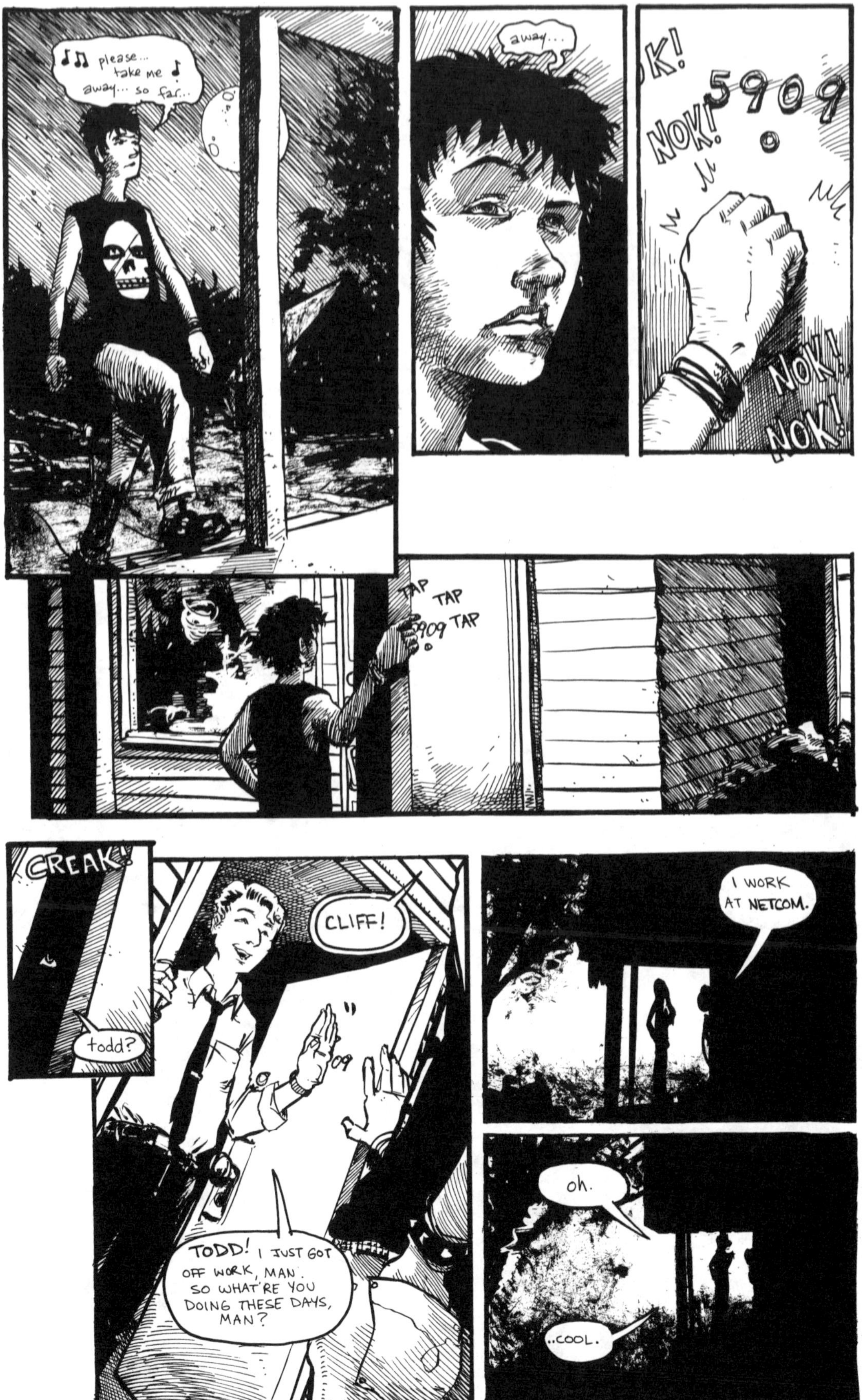
♪♫ please... take me ♪ away... so far...
away...
OK!
5909
NOK!
NOK!
NOK!
TAP TAP TAP
CREAK!
todd?
CLIFF!
TODD! I JUST GOT OFF WORK, MAN. SO WHAT'RE YOU DOING THESE DAYS, MAN?
I WORK AT NETCOM.
oh.
..COOL.

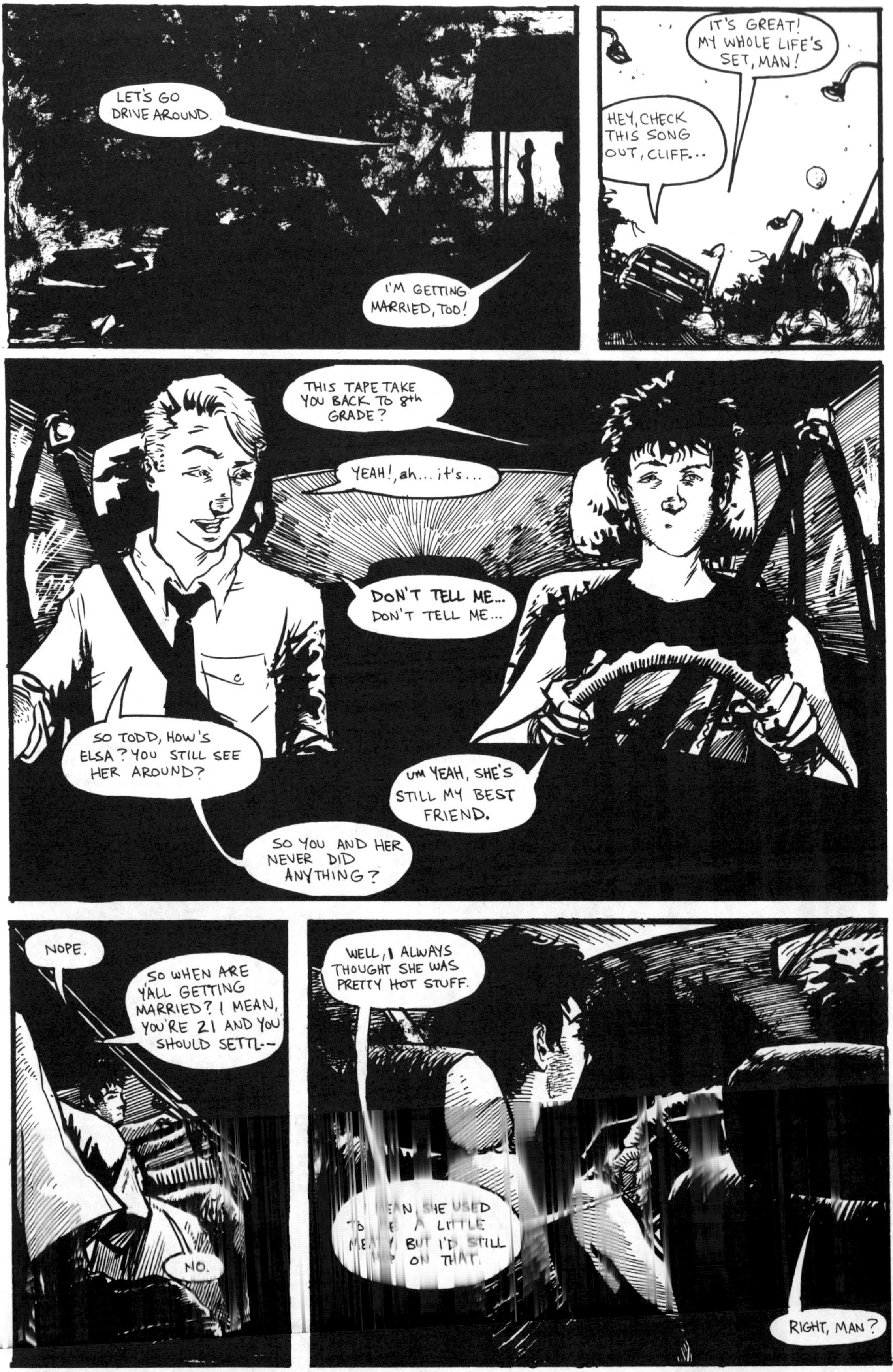
LET'S GO DRIVE AROUND.
I'M GETTING MARRIED, TOO!
IT'S GREAT! MY WHOLE LIFE'S SET, MAN!
HEY, CHECK THIS SONG OUT, CLIFF...
THIS TAPE TAKE YOU BACK TO 8th GRADE?
YEAH!, ah... it's...
DON'T TELL ME... DON'T TELL ME...
SO TODD, HOW'S ELSA? YOU STILL SEE HER AROUND?
UM YEAH, SHE'S STILL MY BEST FRIEND.
SO YOU AND HER NEVER DID ANYTHING?
NOPE.
SO WHEN ARE Y'ALL GETTING MARRIED? I MEAN, YOU'RE 21 AND YOU SHOULD SETTL--
NO.
WELL, I ALWAYS THOUGHT SHE WAS PRETTY HOT STUFF.
SHE USED A LITTLE BUT I'D STILL ON THAT.
RIGHT, MAN?

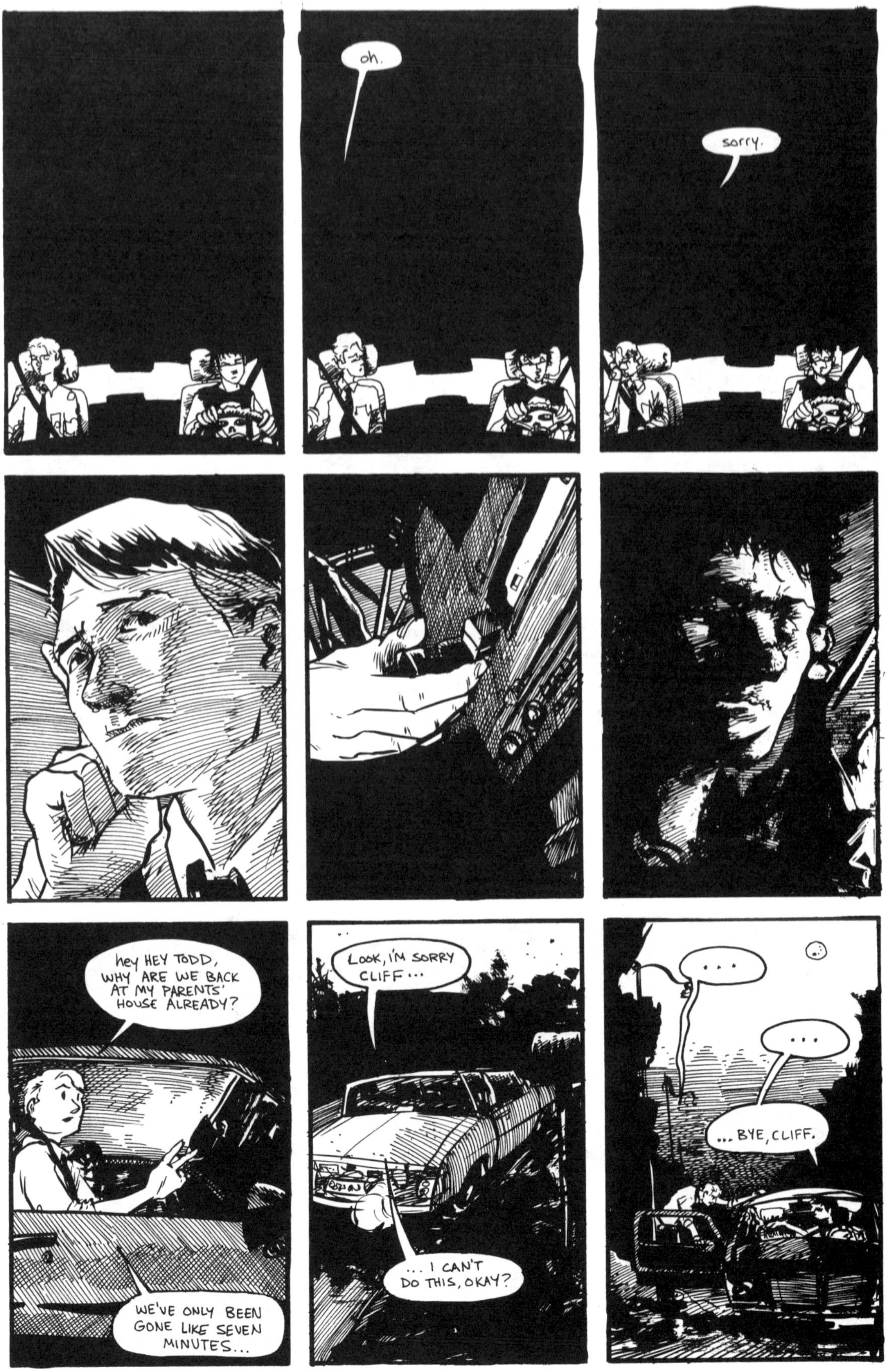

oh.
sorry.
hey HEY TODD, WHY ARE WE BACK AT MY PARENTS' HOUSE ALREADY?
WE'VE ONLY BEEN GONE LIKE SEVEN MINUTES...
LOOK, I'M SORRY CLIFF...
... I CAN'T DO THIS, OKAY?
. . .
. . .
... BYE, CLIFF.

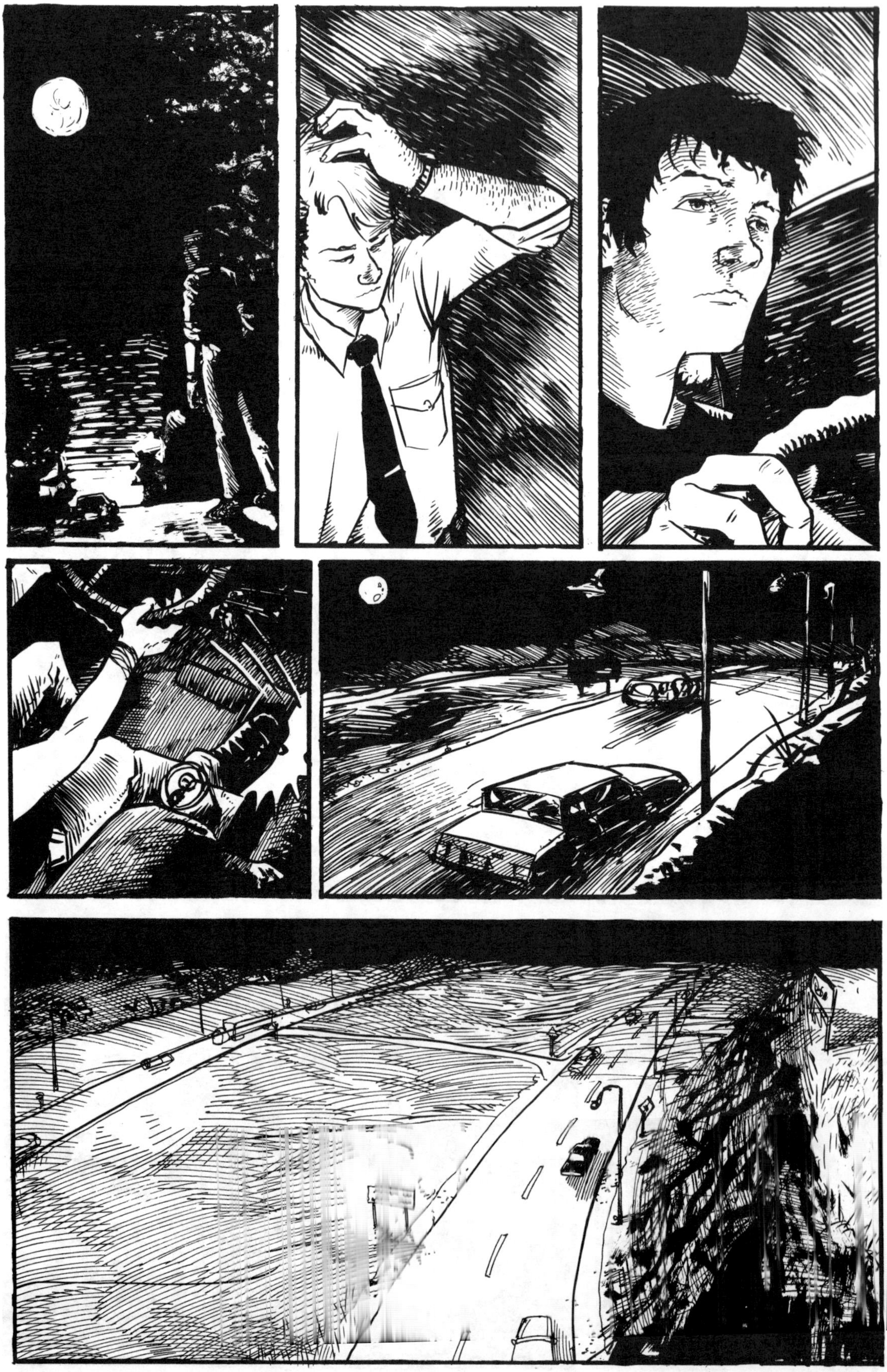

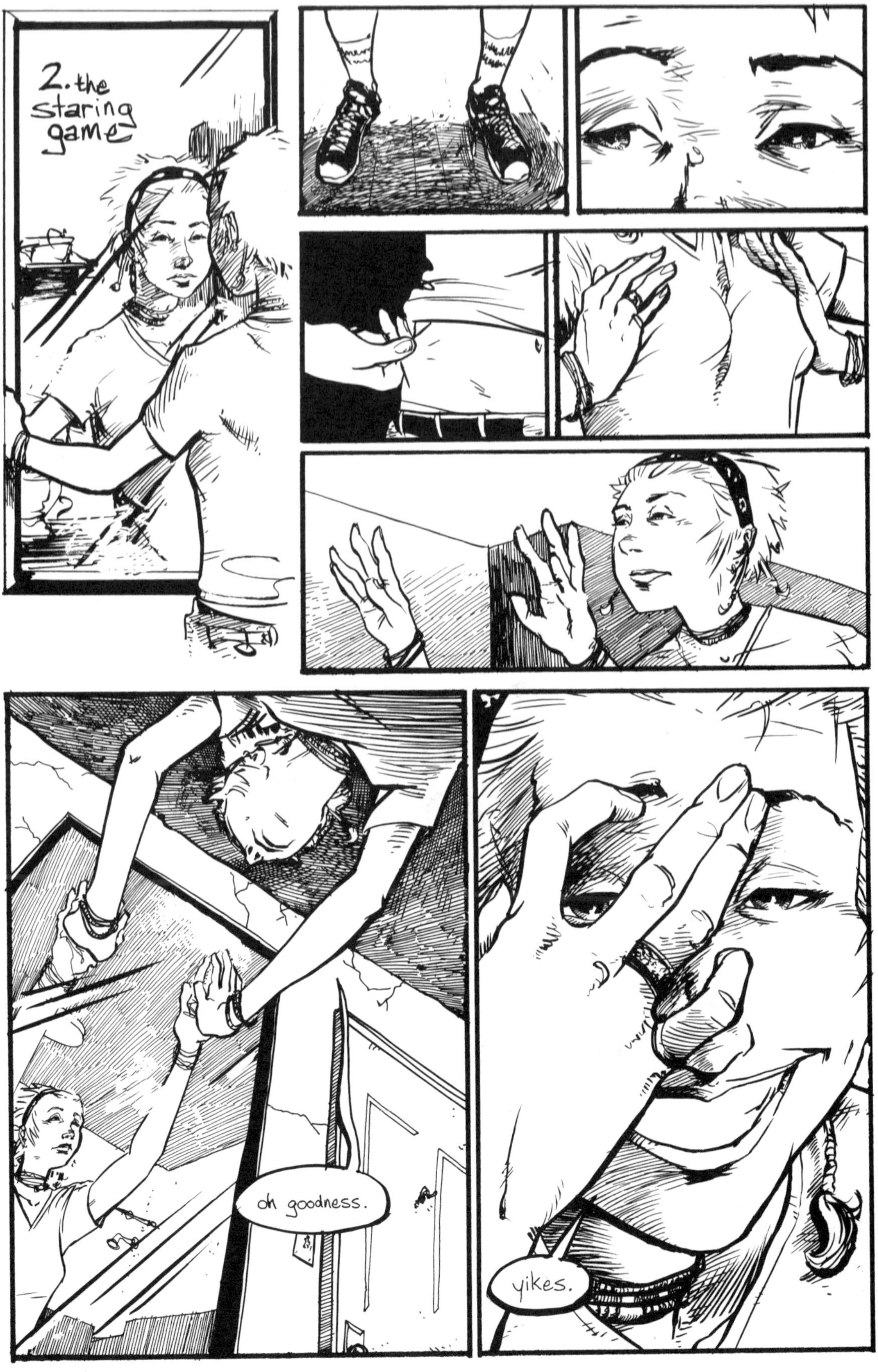
2. the staring game
oh goodness.
yikes.

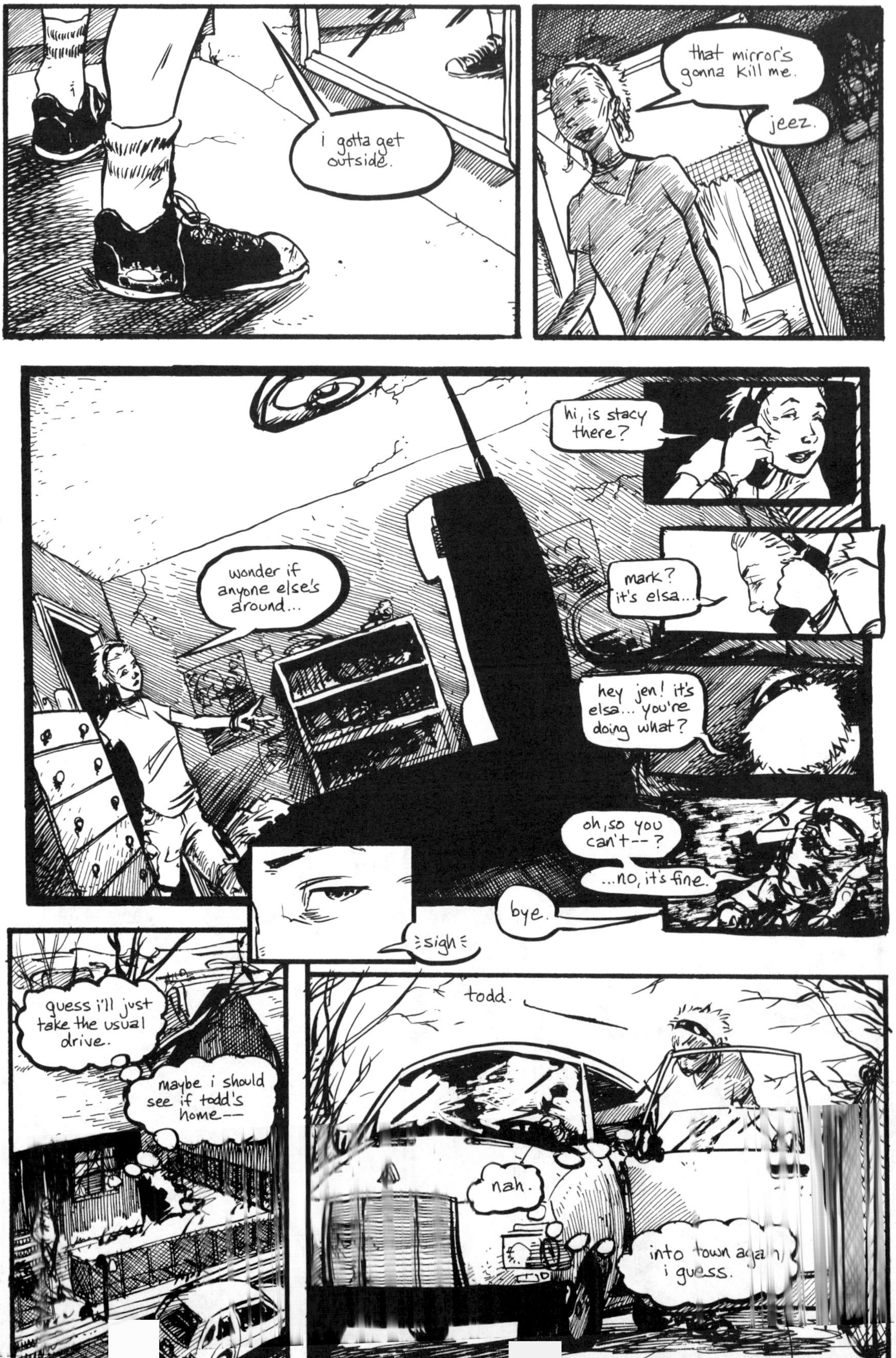
i gotta get outside.
that mirror's gonna kill me.
jeez.
wonder if anyone else's around...
hi, is stacy there?
mark? it's elsa...
hey jen! it's elsa... you're doing what?
oh, so you can't--?
...no, it's fine.
bye.
sigh
guess i'll just take the usual drive.
maybe i should see if todd's home--
todd.
nah.
into town again i guess.

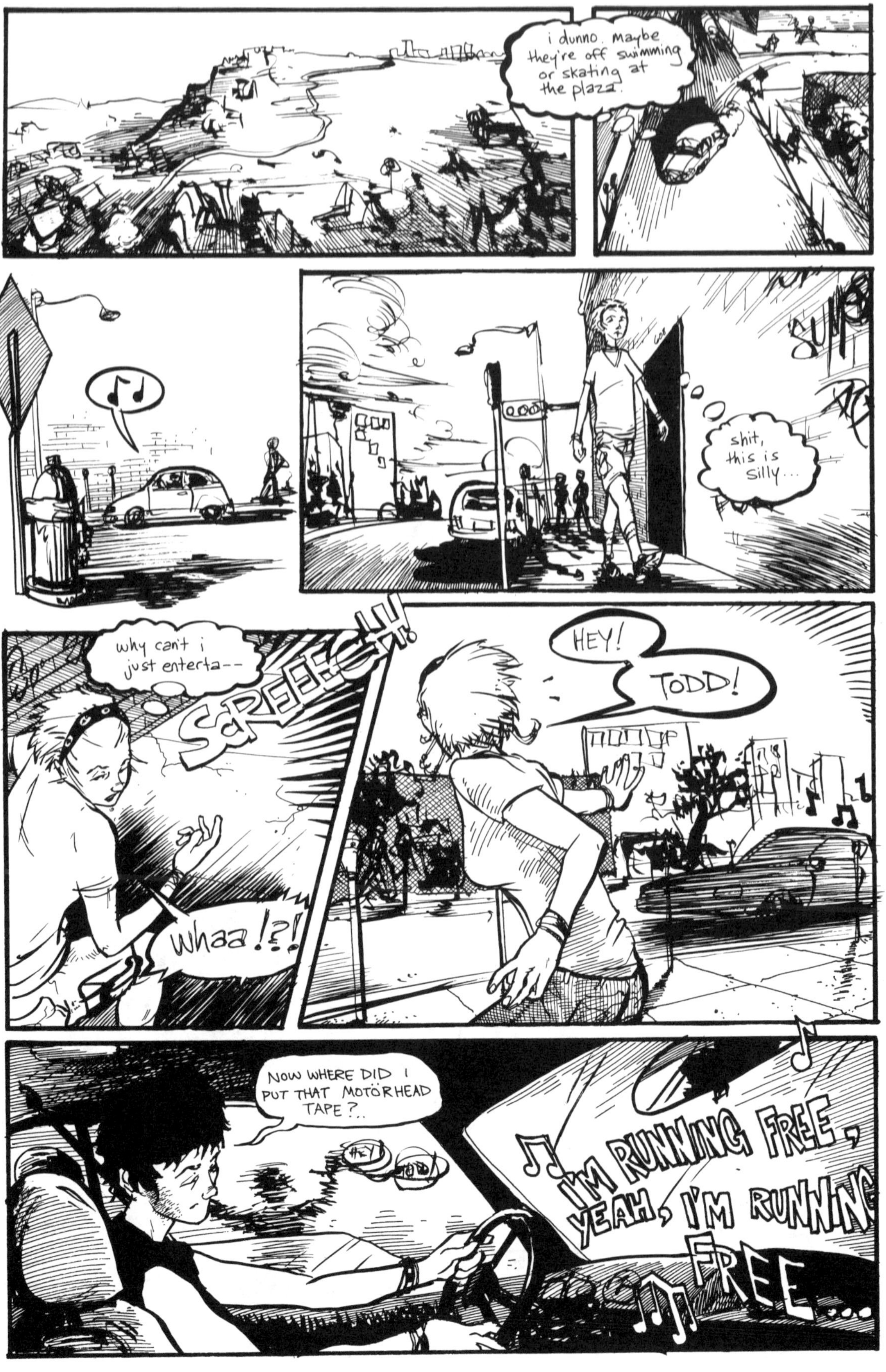
i dunno. maybe they're off swimming or skating at the plaza.
shit, this is silly...
why can't i just enterta--
SCREEECH!
whaa!?!
HEY!
TODD!
NOW WHERE DID I PUT THAT MOTÖRHEAD TAPE?..
I'M RUNNING FREE, YEAH, I'M RUNNING FREE...

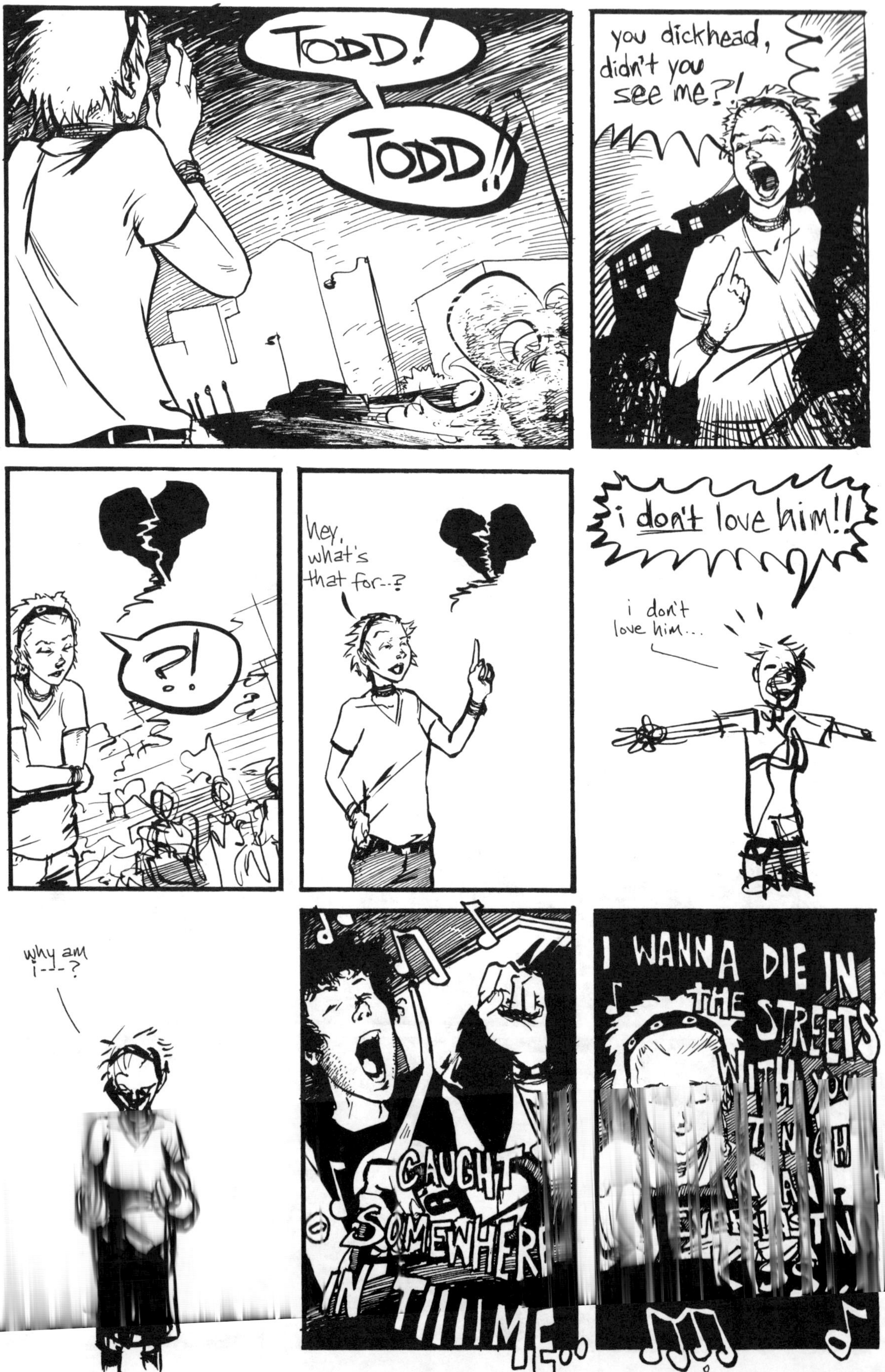
TODD!
TODD!!
you dickhead, didn't you see me?!
?!
hey, what's that for--?
i don't love him!!
i don't love him...
why am i---?
CAUGHT SOMEWHERE IN TIIIIME...
I WANNA DIE IN THE STREETS WITH

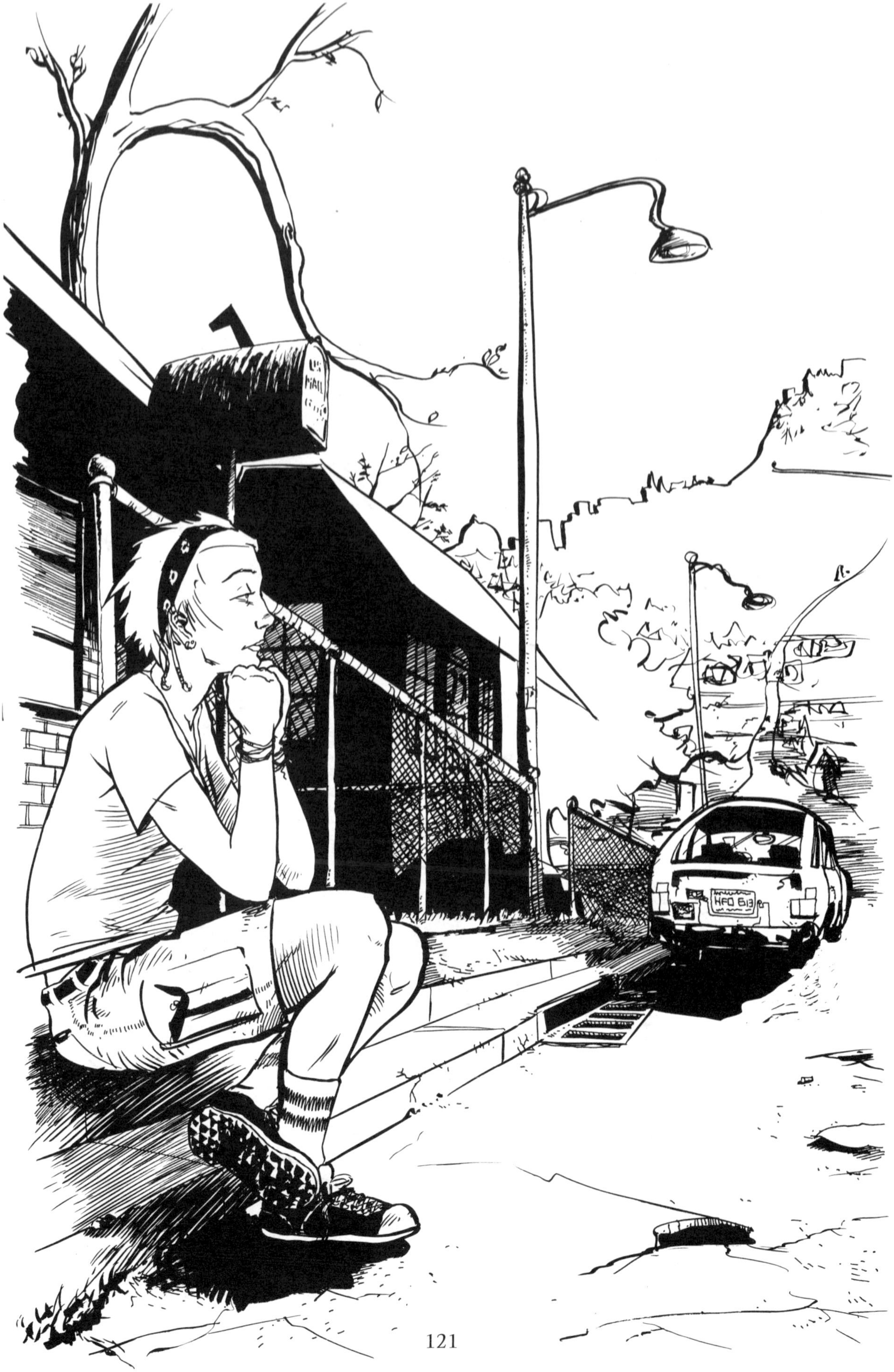
HFO 613

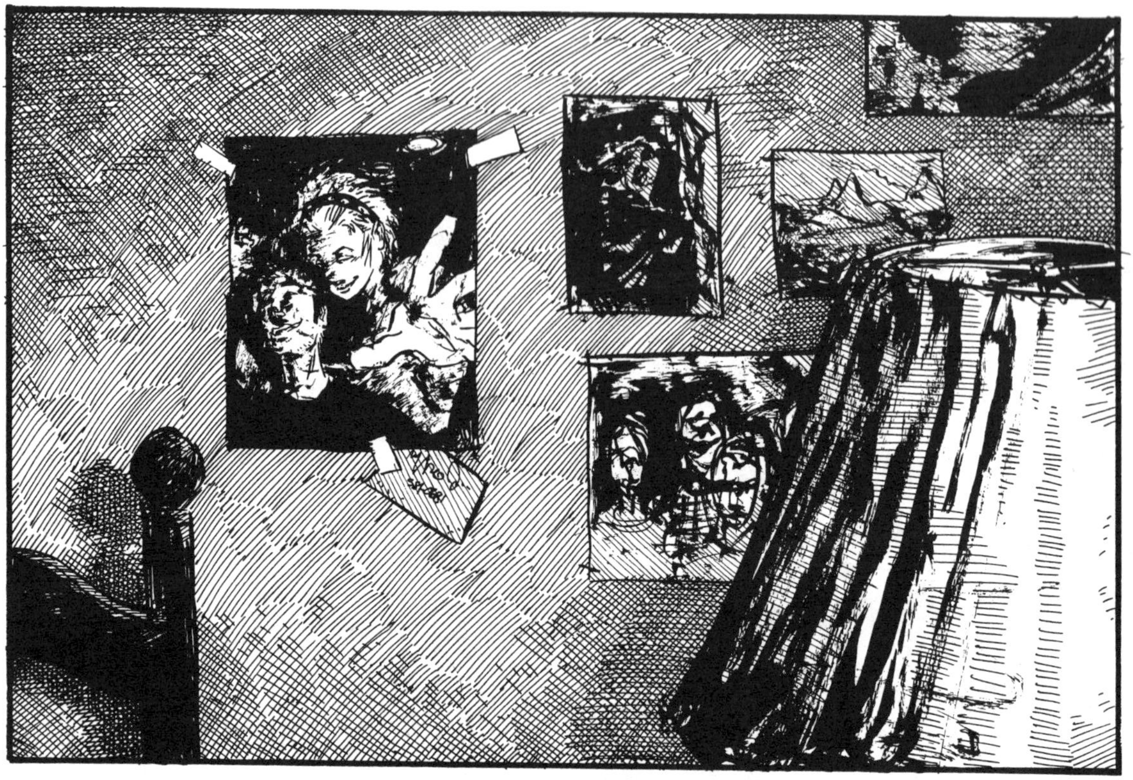

3. the mission

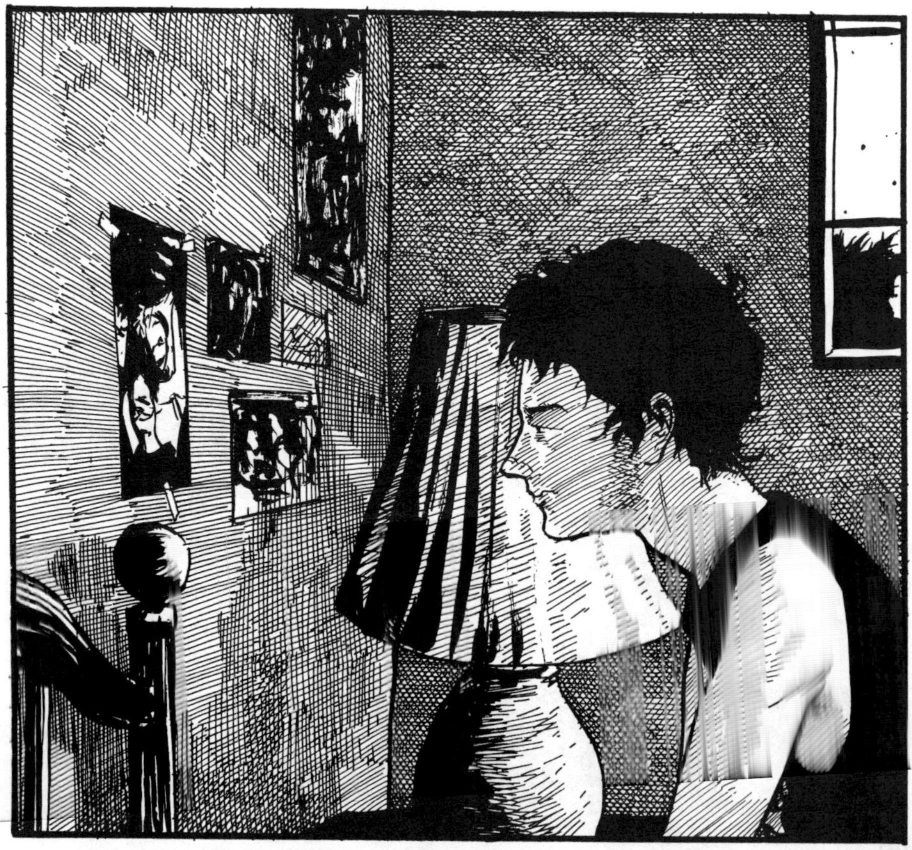

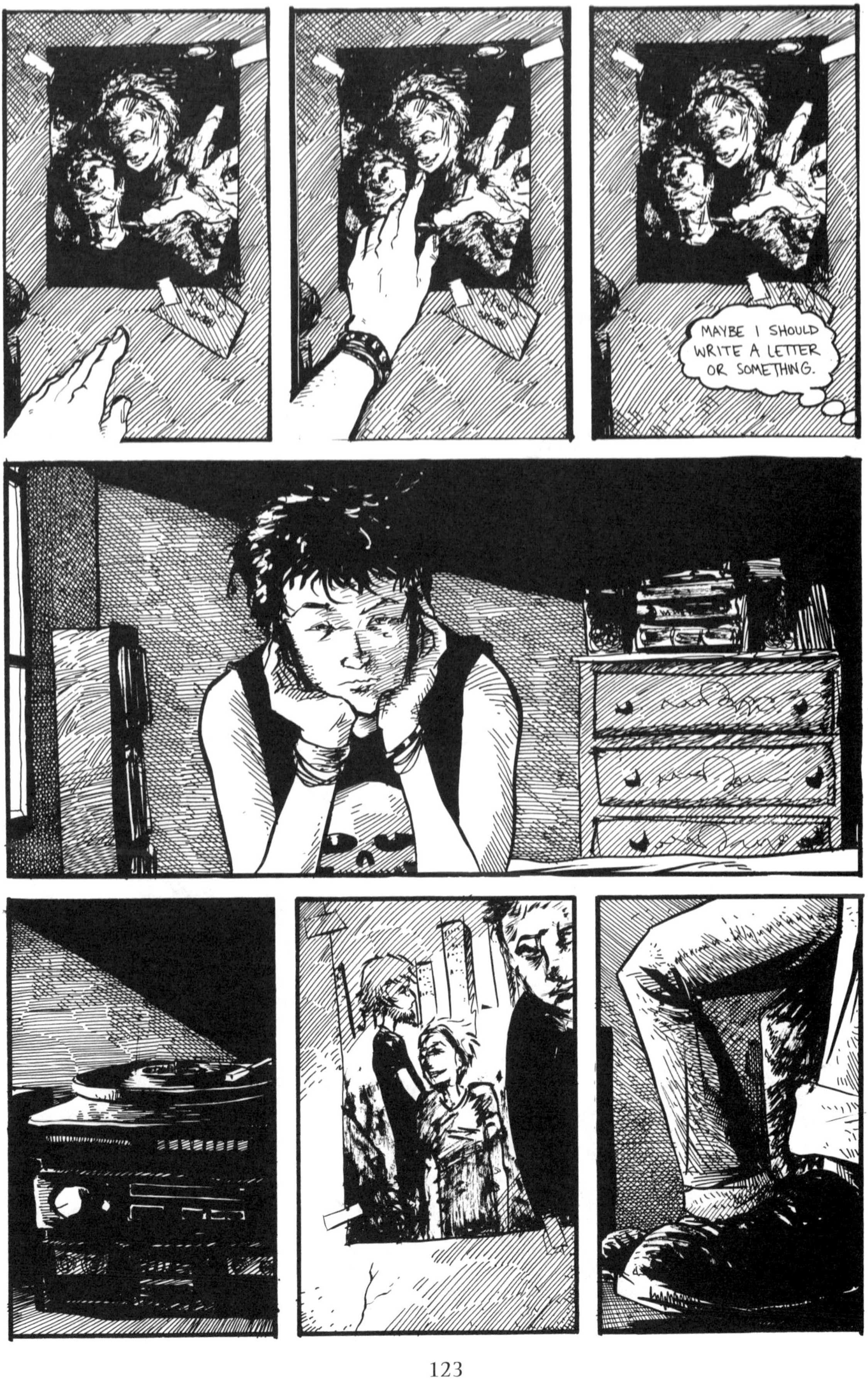
MAYBE I SHOULD WRITE A LETTER OR SOMETHING.

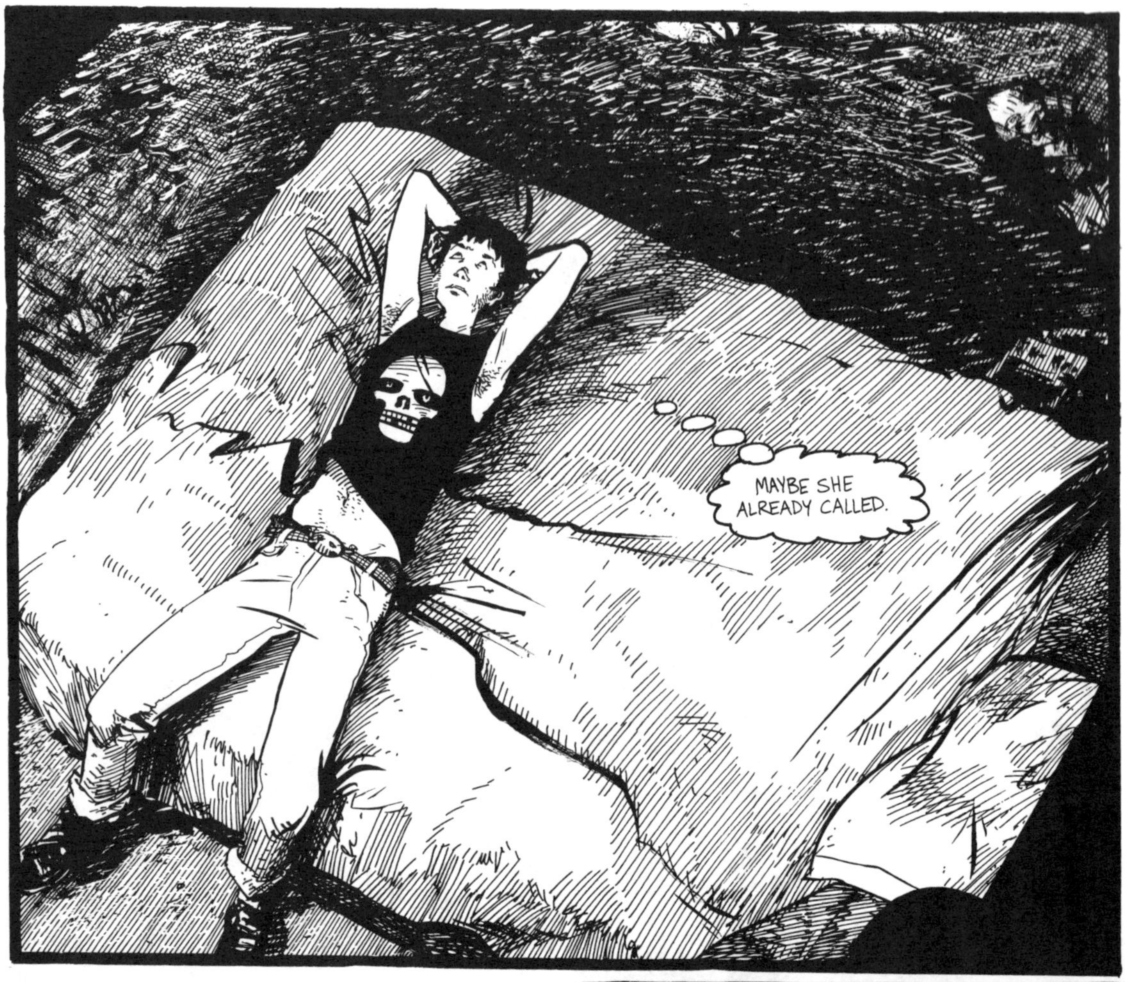
MAYBE SHE ALREADY CALLED.

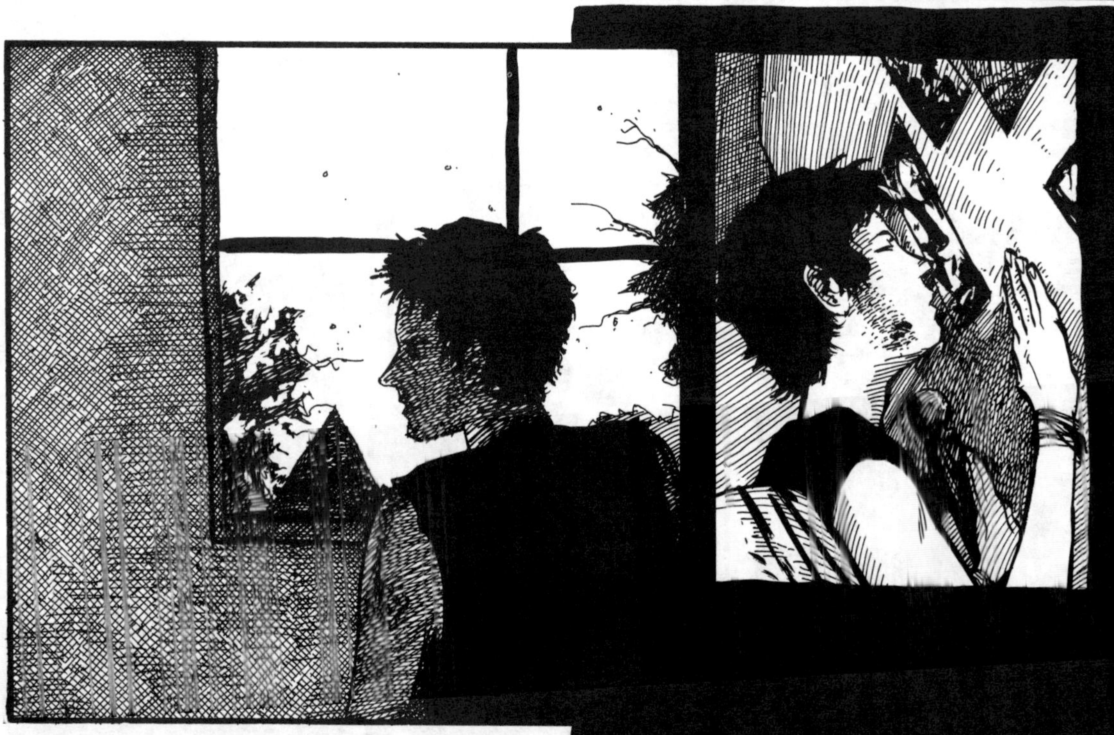

4. CLOCKS

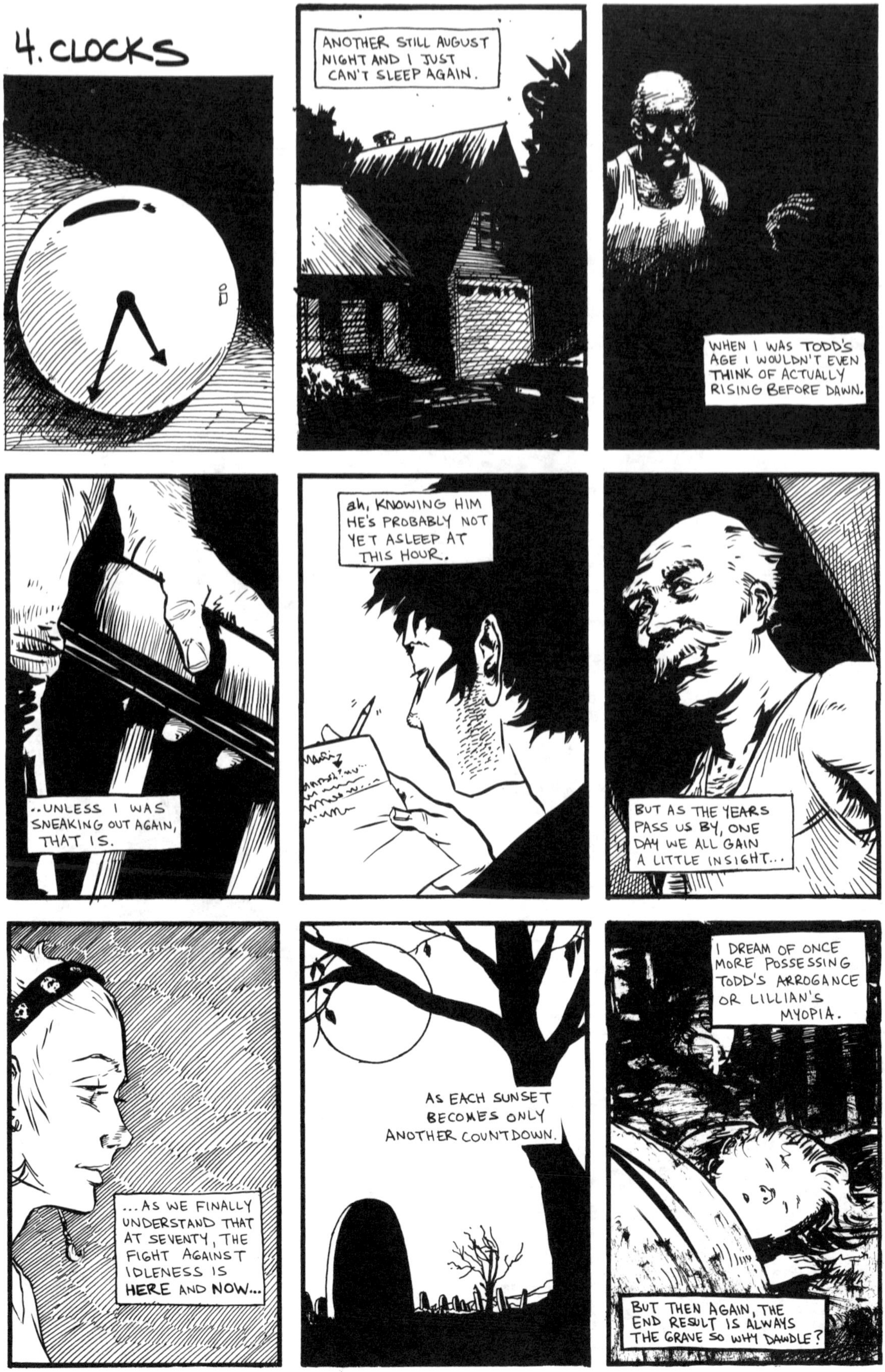
ANOTHER STILL AUGUST NIGHT AND I JUST CAN'T SLEEP AGAIN.
WHEN I WAS TODD'S AGE I WOULDN'T EVEN THINK OF ACTUALLY RISING BEFORE DAWN.
..UNLESS I WAS SNEAKING OUT AGAIN, THAT IS.
ah, KNOWING HIM HE'S PROBABLY NOT YET ASLEEP AT THIS HOUR.
BUT AS THE YEARS PASS US BY, ONE DAY WE ALL GAIN A LITTLE INSIGHT...
...AS WE FINALLY UNDERSTAND THAT AT SEVENTY, THE FIGHT AGAINST IDLENESS IS HERE AND NOW...
AS EACH SUNSET BECOMES ONLY ANOTHER COUNTDOWN.
I DREAM OF ONCE MORE POSSESSING TODD'S ARROGANCE OR LILLIAN'S MYOPIA.
BUT THEN AGAIN, THE END RESULT IS ALWAYS THE GRAVE SO WHY DAWDLE?

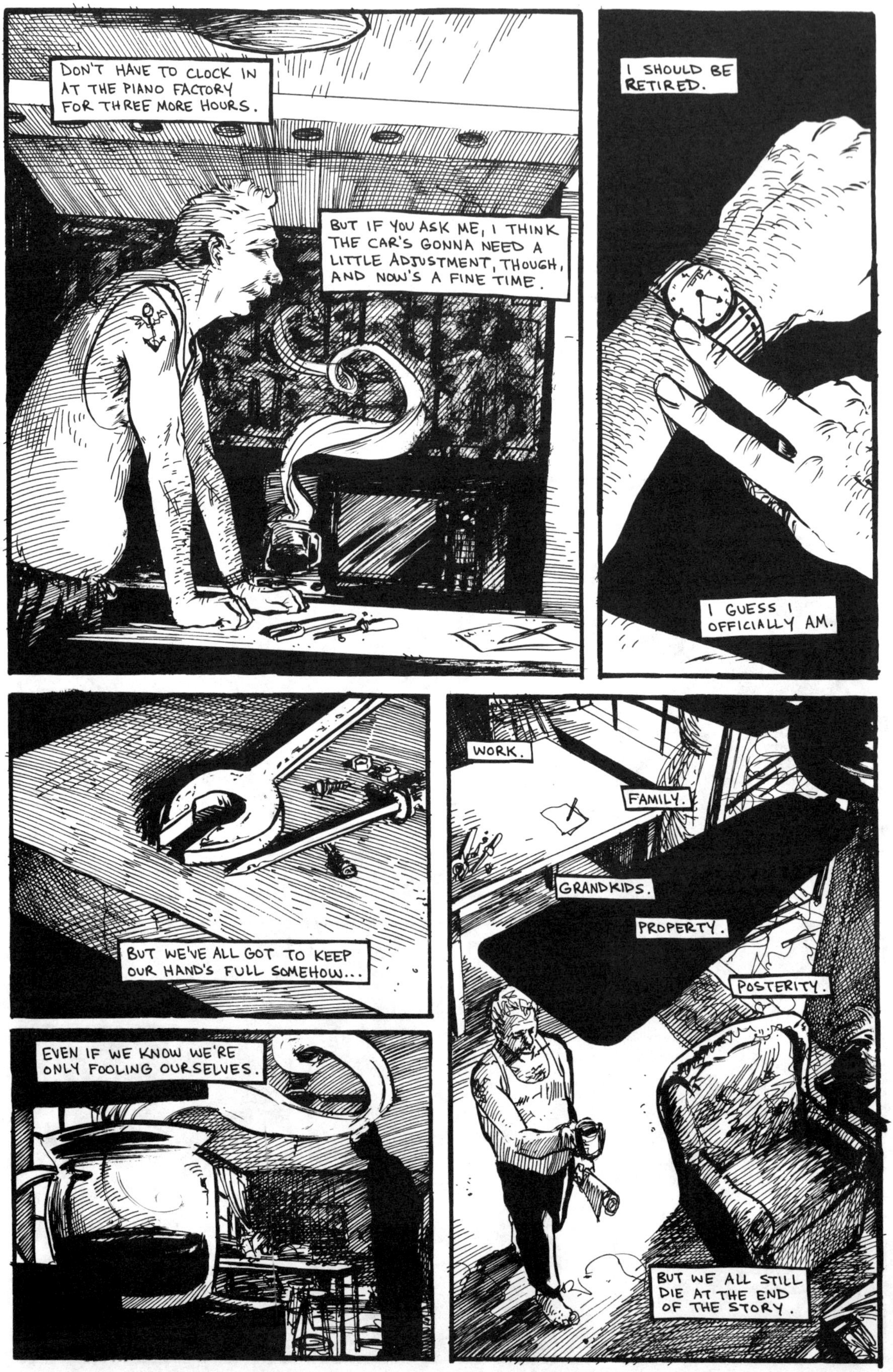
DON'T HAVE TO CLOCK IN AT THE PIANO FACTORY FOR THREE MORE HOURS.
BUT IF YOU ASK ME, I THINK THE CAR'S GONNA NEED A LITTLE ADJUSTMENT, THOUGH, AND NOW'S A FINE TIME.
I SHOULD BE RETIRED.
I GUESS I OFFICIALLY AM.
BUT WE'VE ALL GOT TO KEEP OUR HAND'S FULL SOMEHOW...
EVEN IF WE KNOW WE'RE ONLY FOOLING OURSELVES.
WORK.
FAMILY.
GRANDKIDS.
PROPERTY.
POSTERITY.
BUT WE ALL STILL DIE AT THE END OF THE STORY.

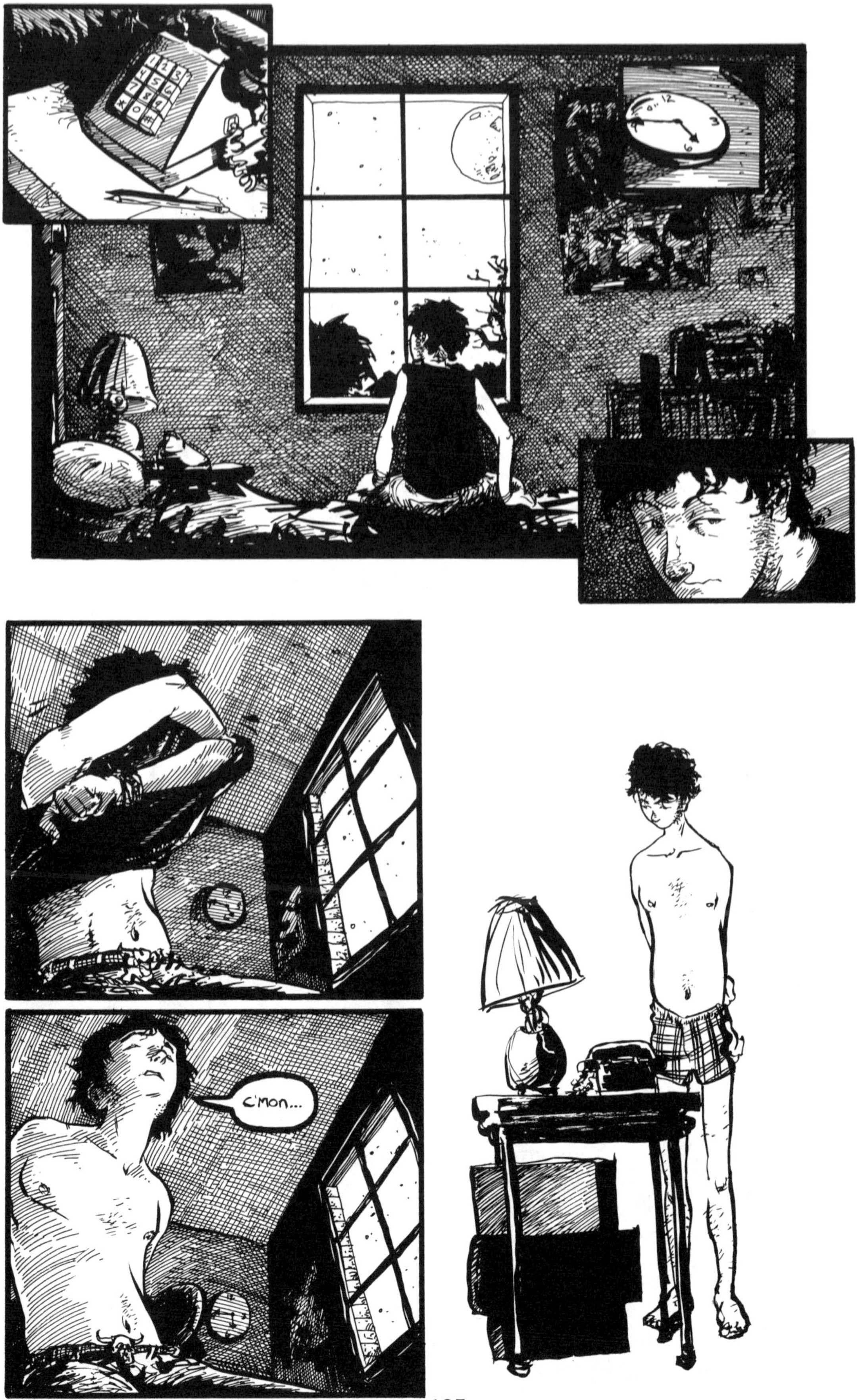
C'MON...

THAT'S WHY SLEEP WILL ALWAYS BE THE ENEMY.

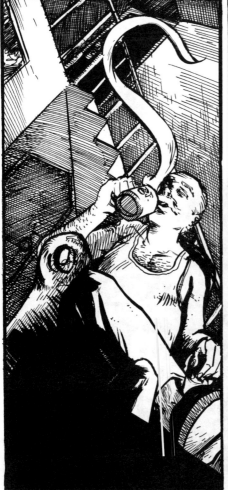

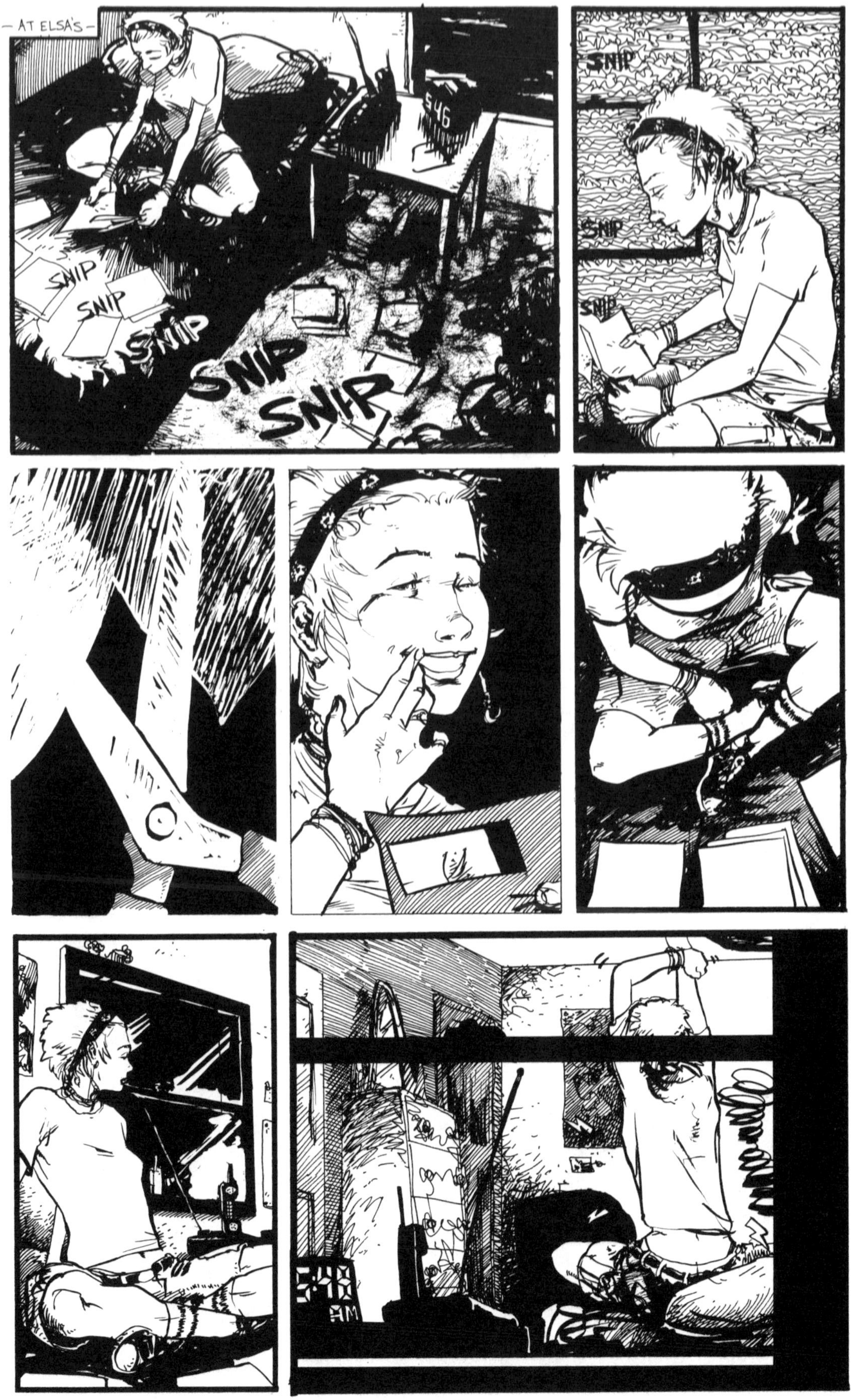

— AT ELSA'S —
546
SNIP
SNIP
SNIP
SNIP
SNIP
SNIP
SNIP
SNIP
AM

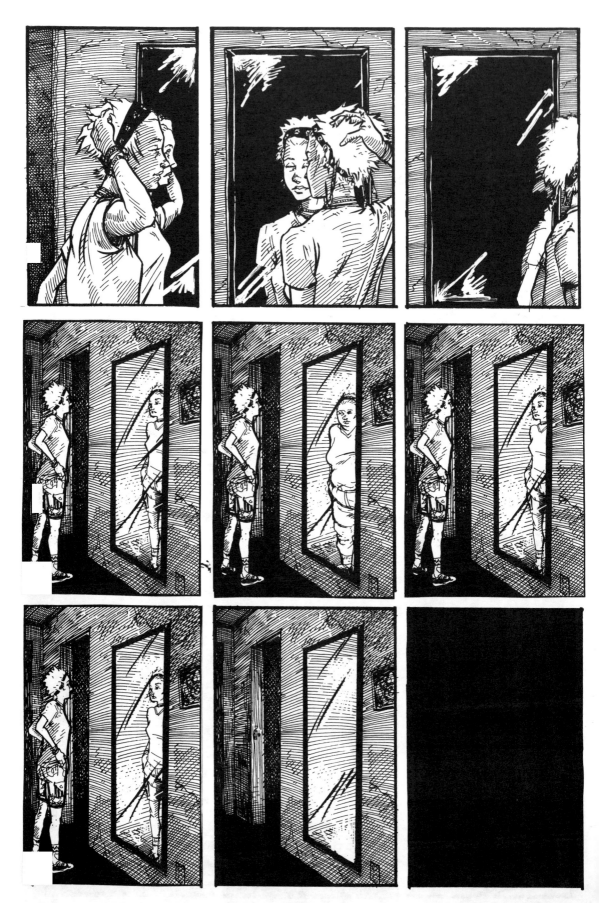

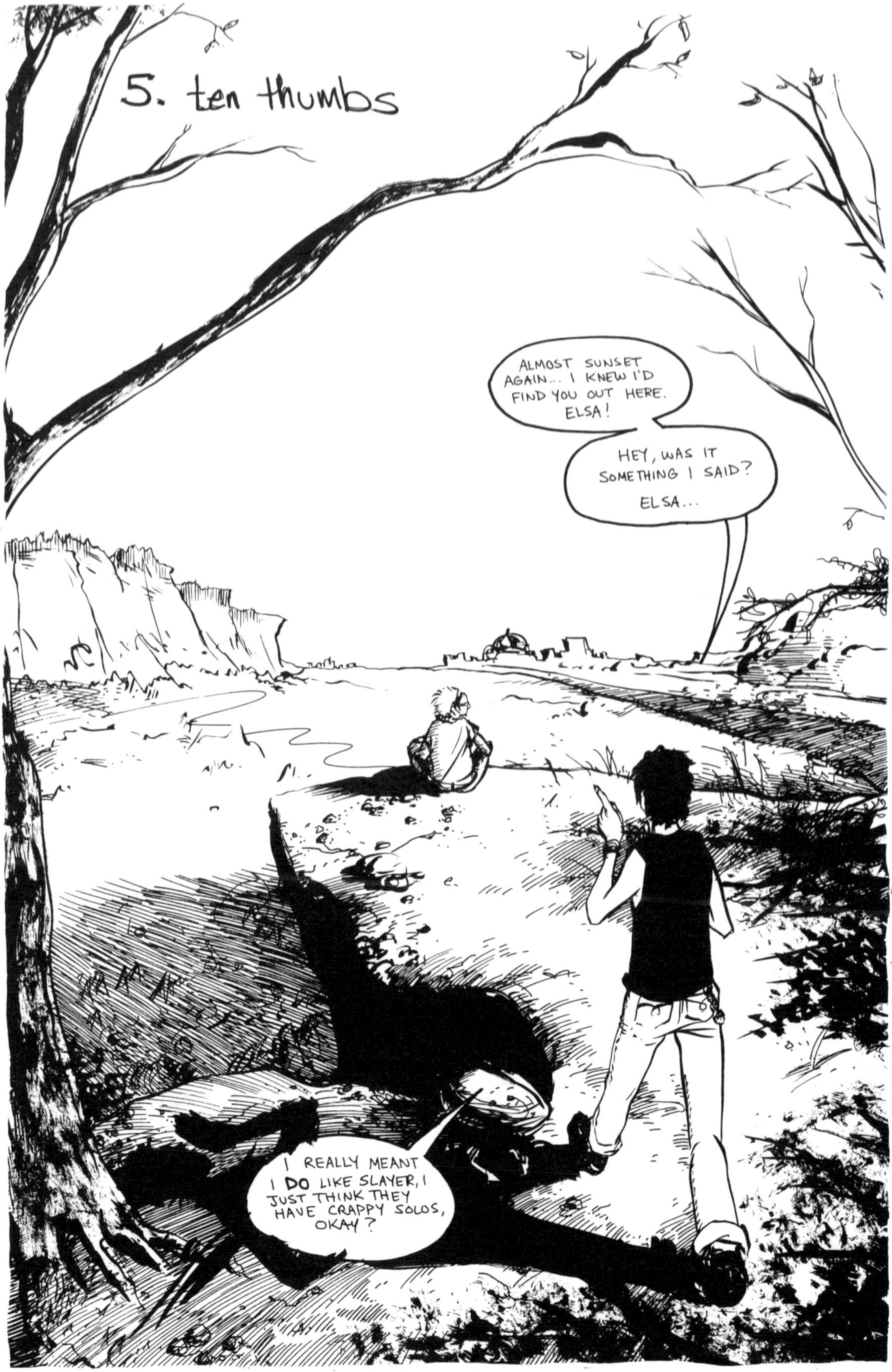
5. ten thumbs
ALMOST SUNSET AGAIN... I KNEW I'D FIND YOU OUT HERE. ELSA!
HEY, WAS IT SOMETHING I SAID? ELSA...
I REALLY MEANT I DO LIKE SLAYER, I JUST THINK THEY HAVE CRAPPY SOLOS, OKAY?

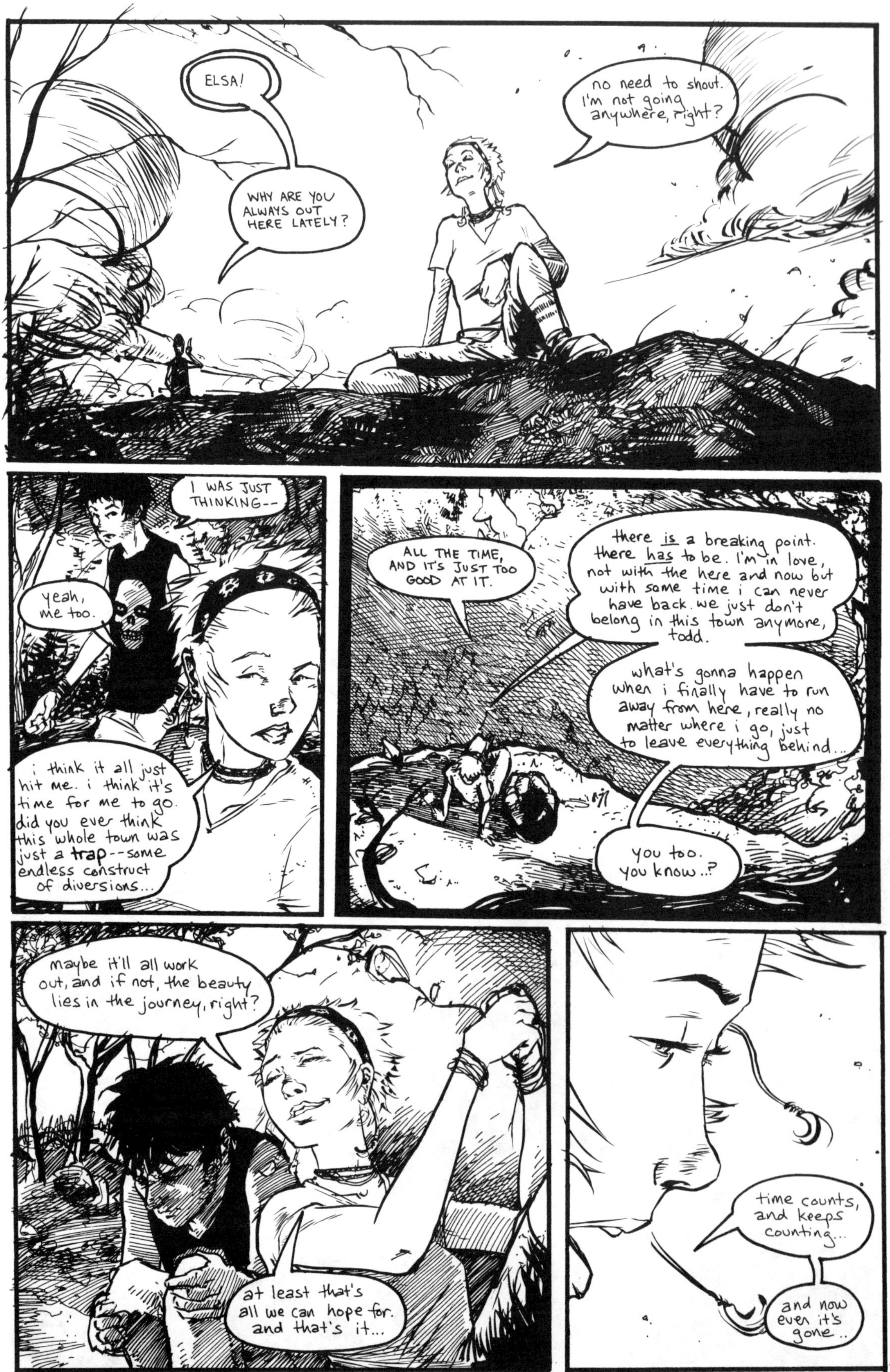
ELSA!
WHY ARE YOU ALWAYS OUT HERE LATELY?
no need to shout. I'm not going anywhere, right?
I WAS JUST THINKING--
yeah, me too.
i think it all just hit me. i think it's time for me to go. did you ever think this whole town was just a trap--some endless construct of diversions...
ALL THE TIME, AND IT'S JUST TOO GOOD AT IT.
there is a breaking point. there has to be. I'm in love, not with the here and now but with some time i can never have back. we just don't belong in this town anymore, todd.
what's gonna happen when i finally have to run away from here, really no matter where i go, just to leave everything behind...
you too. you know..?
maybe it'll all work out, and if not, the beauty lies in the journey, right?
at least that's all we can hope for. and that's it...
time counts, and keeps counting...
and now even it's gone..

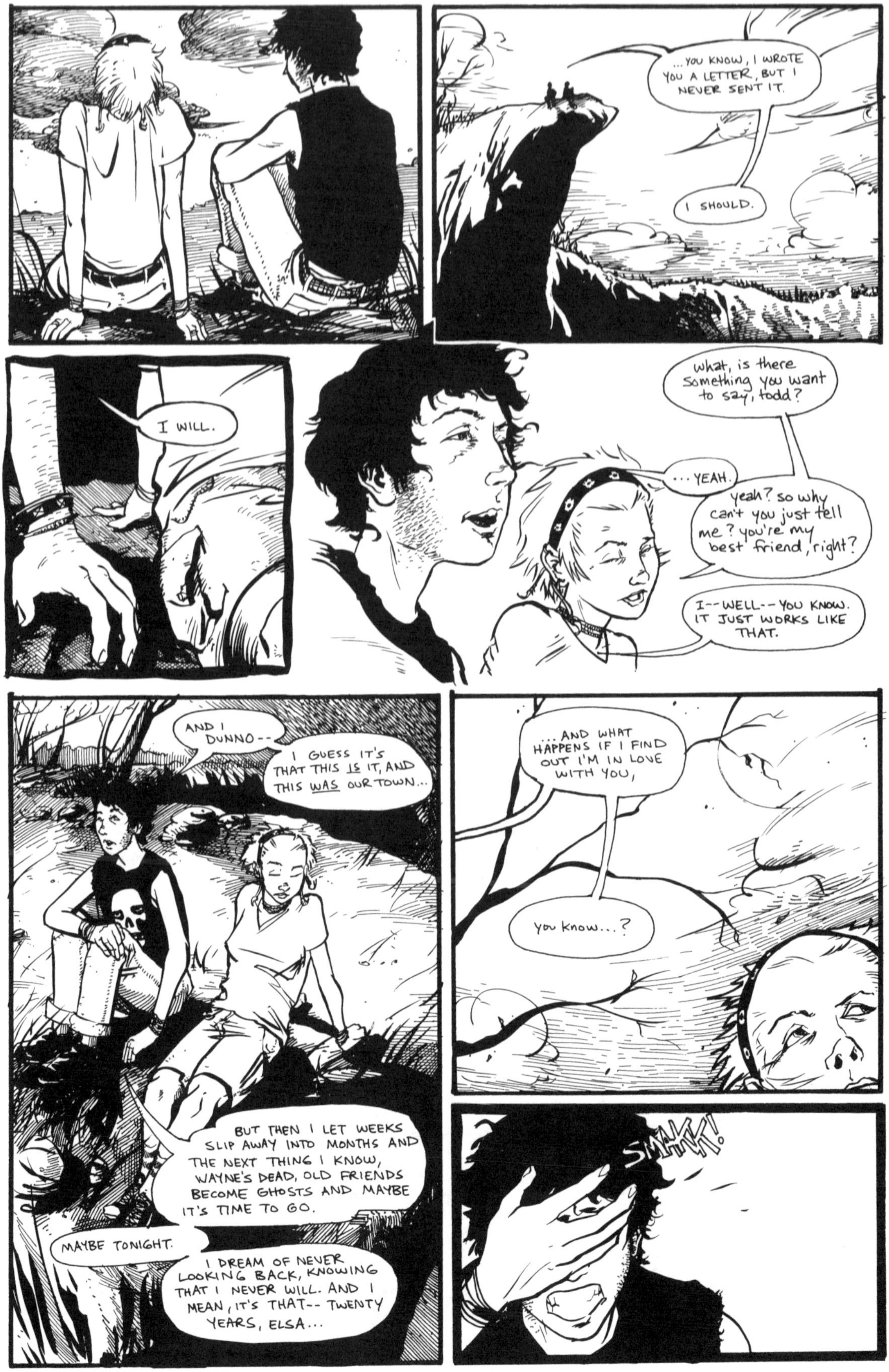
...YOU KNOW, I WROTE YOU A LETTER, BUT I NEVER SENT IT.
I SHOULD.
I WILL.
what, is there something you want to say, todd?
...YEAH.
yeah? so why can't you just tell me? you're my best friend, right?
I--WELL--YOU KNOW. IT JUST WORKS LIKE THAT.
AND I DUNNO--
I GUESS IT'S THAT THIS IS IT, AND THIS WAS OUR TOWN...
BUT THEN I LET WEEKS SLIP AWAY INTO MONTHS AND THE NEXT THING I KNOW, WAYNE'S DEAD, OLD FRIENDS BECOME GHOSTS AND MAYBE IT'S TIME TO GO.
MAYBE TONIGHT.
I DREAM OF NEVER LOOKING BACK, KNOWING THAT I NEVER WILL. AND I MEAN, IT'S THAT-- TWENTY YEARS, ELSA...
...AND WHAT HAPPENS IF I FIND OUT I'M IN LOVE WITH YOU,
you know...?
SMAKK!

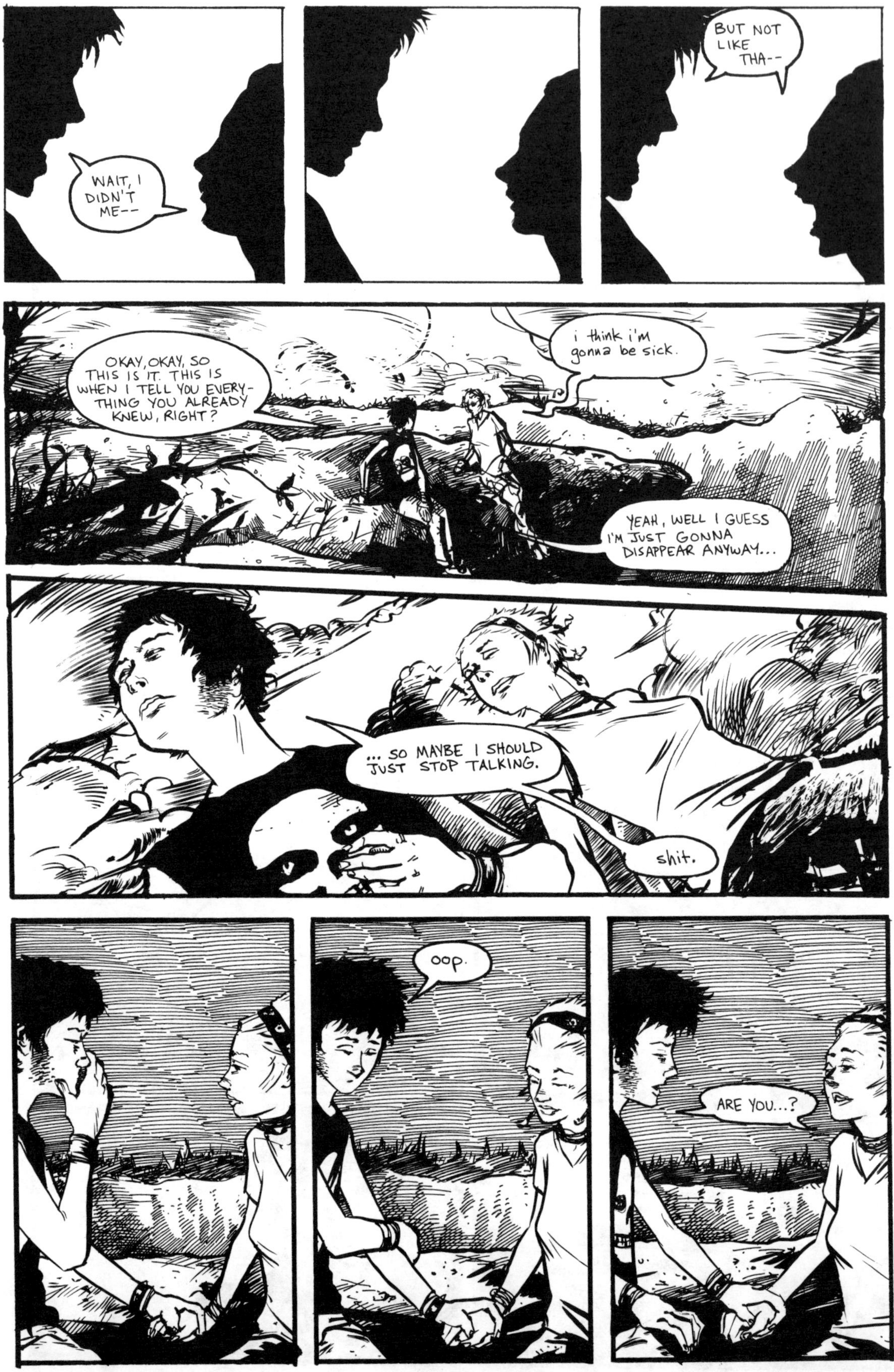
WAIT, I DIDN'T ME--
BUT NOT LIKE THA--
OKAY, OKAY, SO THIS IS IT. THIS IS WHEN I TELL YOU EVERYTHING YOU ALREADY KNEW, RIGHT?
i think i'm gonna be sick.
YEAH, WELL I GUESS I'M JUST GONNA DISAPPEAR ANYWAY...
... SO MAYBE I SHOULD JUST STOP TALKING.
shit.
oop.
ARE YOU...?

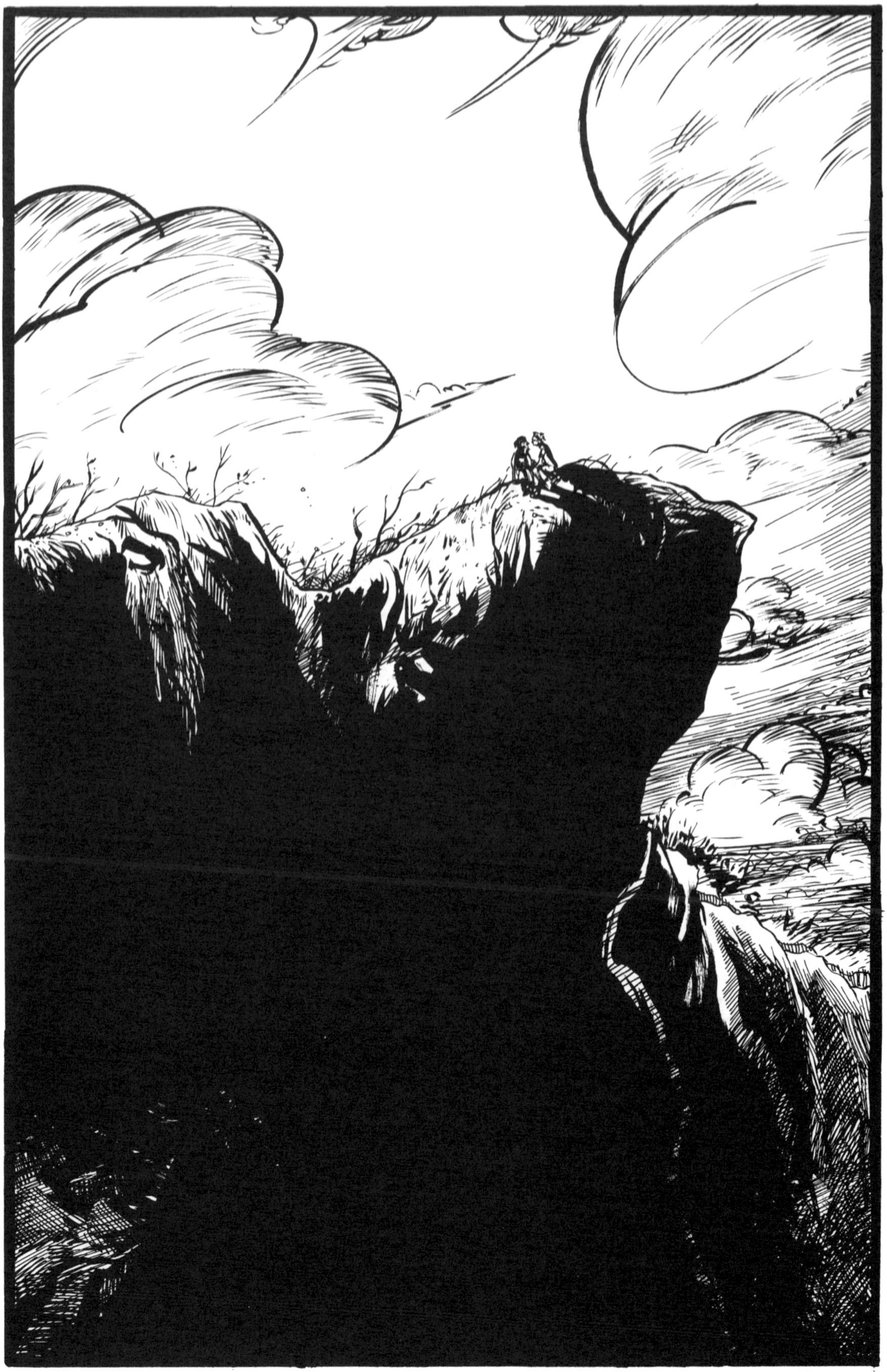

6. NEVER ENDER

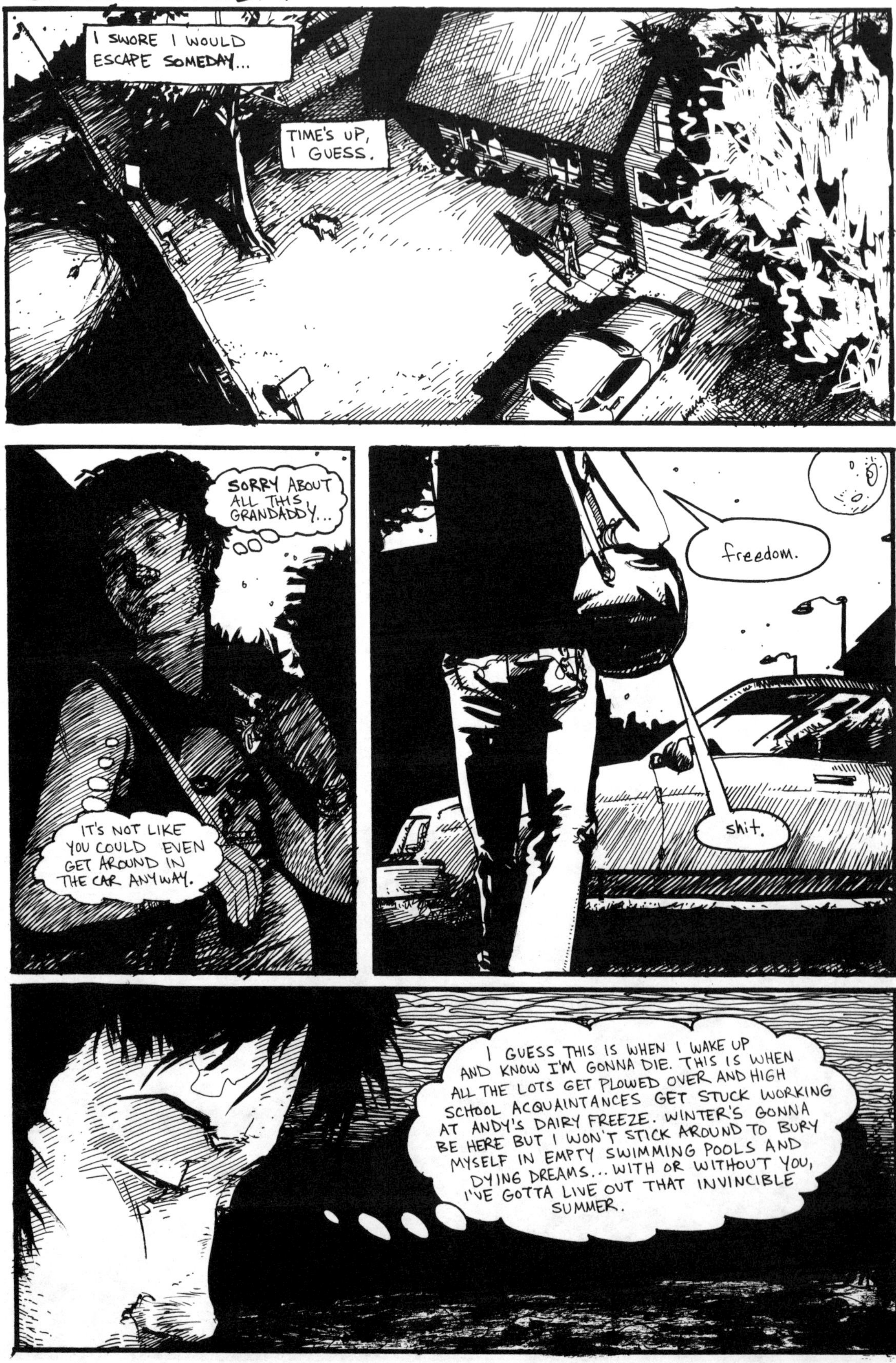

I SWORE I WOULD ESCAPE SOMEDAY...
TIME'S UP, I GUESS.
SORRY ABOUT ALL THIS, GRANDADDY...
IT'S NOT LIKE YOU COULD EVEN GET AROUND IN THE CAR ANYWAY.
freedom.
shit.
I GUESS THIS IS WHEN I WAKE UP AND KNOW I'M GONNA DIE. THIS IS WHEN ALL THE LOTS GET PLOWED OVER AND HIGH SCHOOL ACQUAINTANCES GET STUCK WORKING AT ANDY'S DAIRY FREEZE. WINTER'S GONNA BE HERE BUT I WON'T STICK AROUND TO BURY MYSELF IN EMPTY SWIMMING POOLS AND DYING DREAMS... WITH OR WITHOUT YOU, I'VE GOTTA LIVE OUT THAT INVINCIBLE SUMMER.

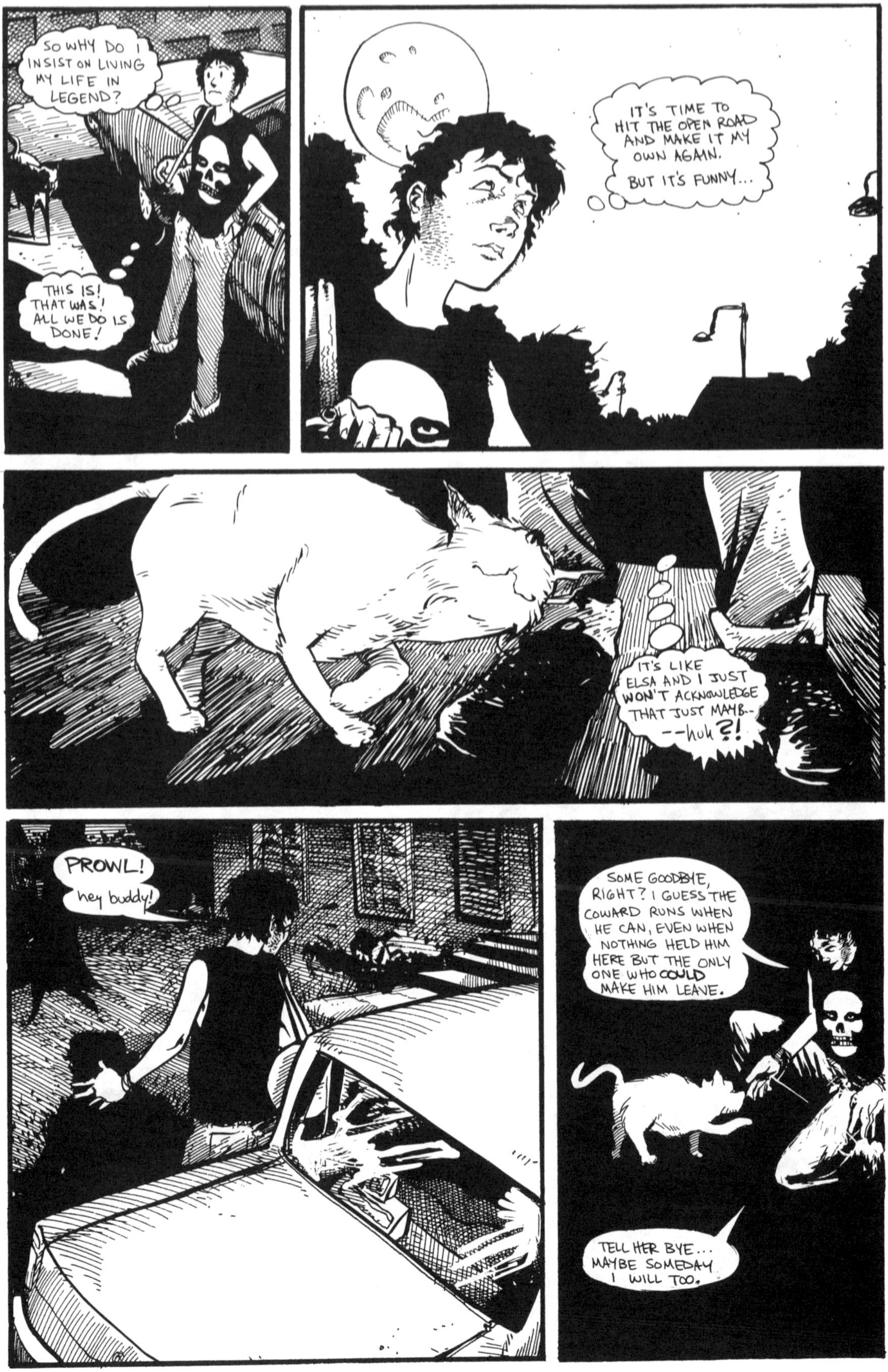
SO WHY DO I INSIST ON LIVING MY LIFE IN LEGEND?
THIS IS! THAT WAS! ALL WE DO IS DONE!
IT'S TIME TO HIT THE OPEN ROAD AND MAKE IT MY OWN AGAIN.
BUT IT'S FUNNY...
IT'S LIKE ELSA AND I JUST WON'T ACKNOWLEDGE THAT JUST MAYB--
--huh?!
PROWL!
hey buddy!
SOME GOODBYE, RIGHT? I GUESS THE COWARD RUNS WHEN HE CAN, EVEN WHEN NOTHING HELD HIM HERE BUT THE ONLY ONE WHO COULD MAKE HIM LEAVE.
TELL HER BYE... MAYBE SOMEDAY I WILL TOO.

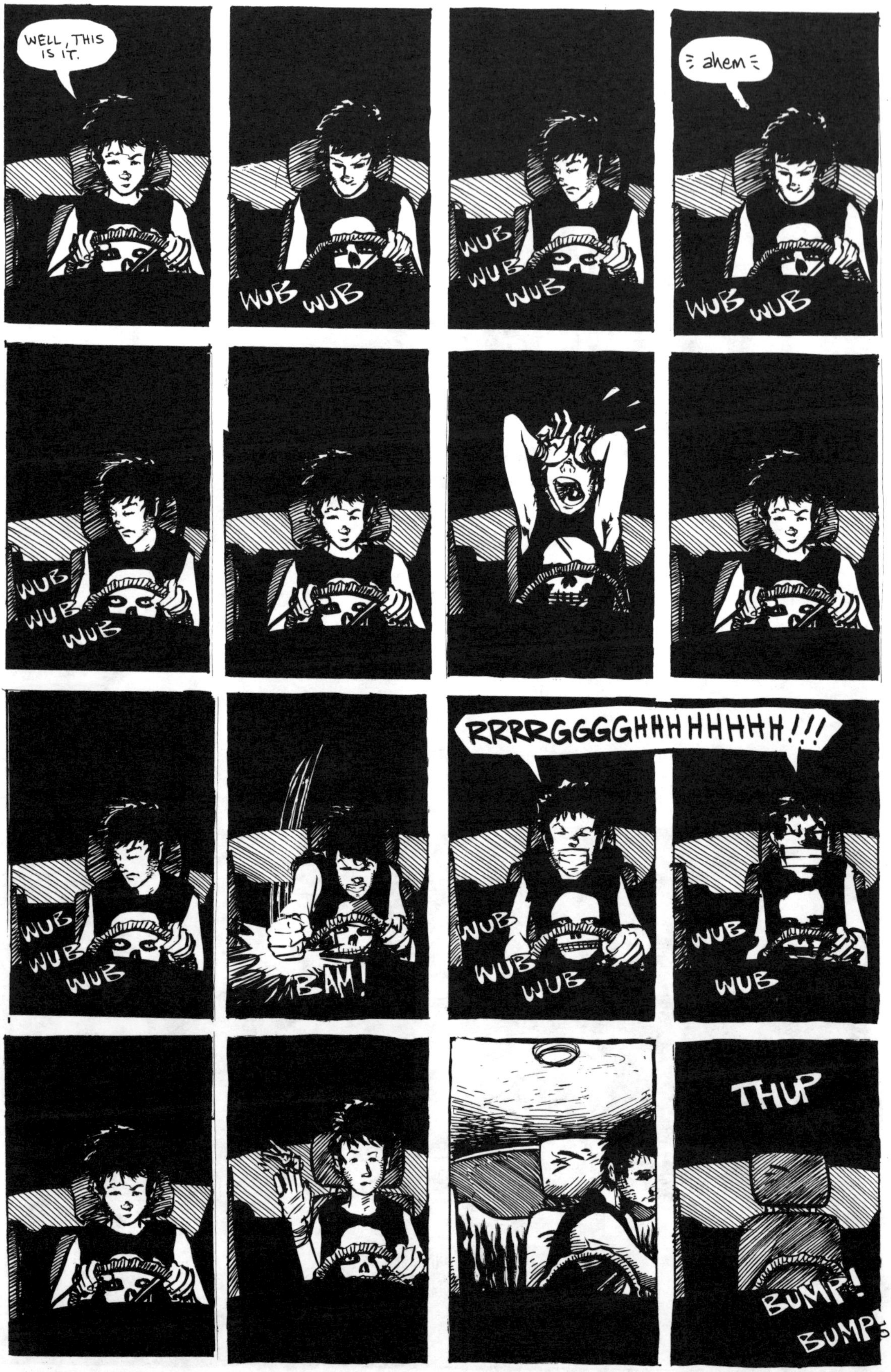
WELL, THIS IS IT.
WUB WUB
WUB WUB WUB
ahem
WUB WUB
WUB WUB WUB
WUB WUB WUB
BAM!
RRRRGGGGHHHHHHH!!!
WUB WUB WUB
WUB WUB
THUP
BUMP! BUMP!

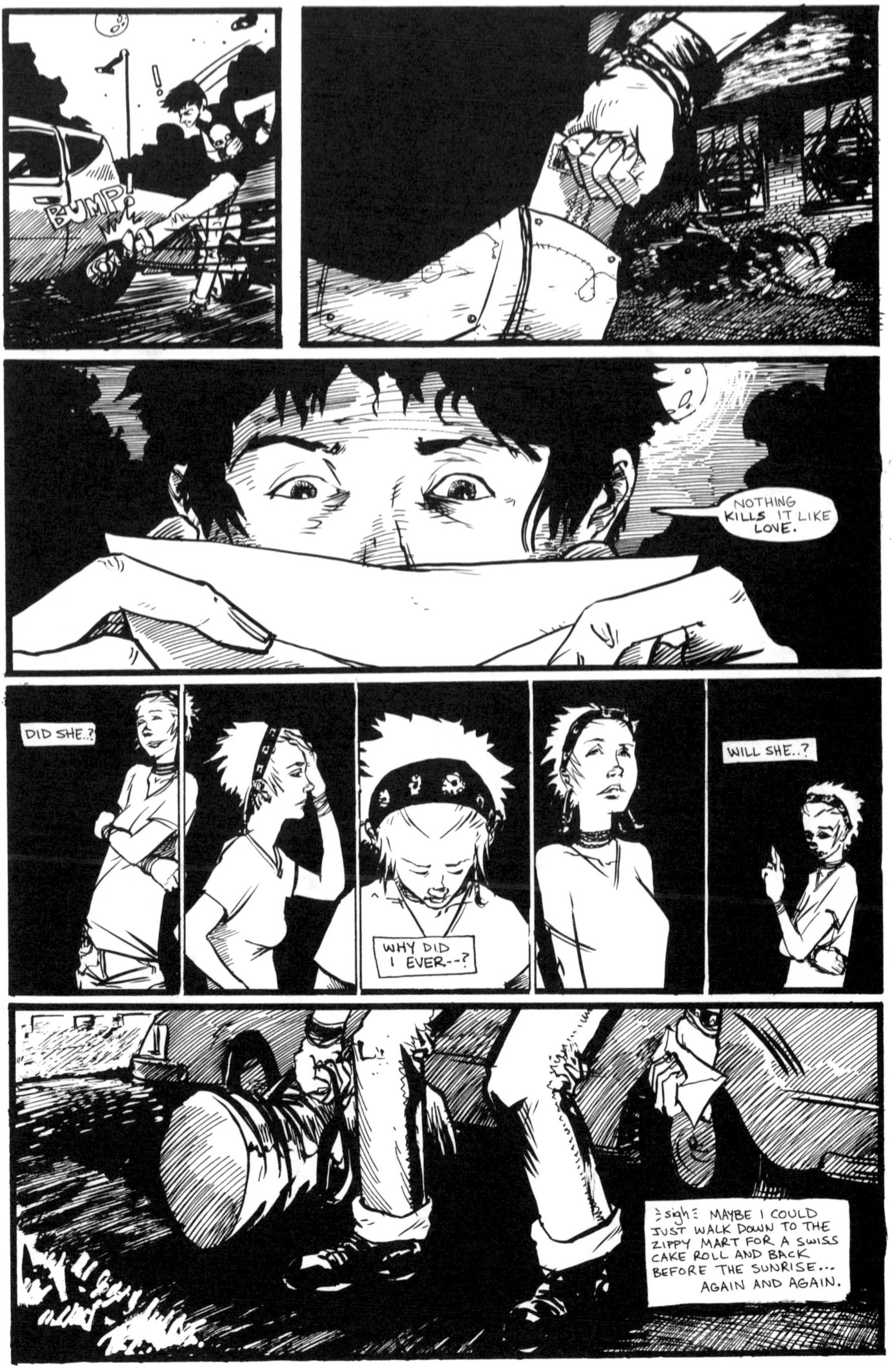
!
BUMP!
NOTHING KILLS IT LIKE LOVE.
DID SHE..?
WHY DID I EVER--?
WILL SHE..?
≷sigh≶ MAYBE I COULD JUST WALK DOWN TO THE ZIPPY MART FOR A SWISS CAKE ROLL AND BACK BEFORE THE SUNRISE... AGAIN AND AGAIN.

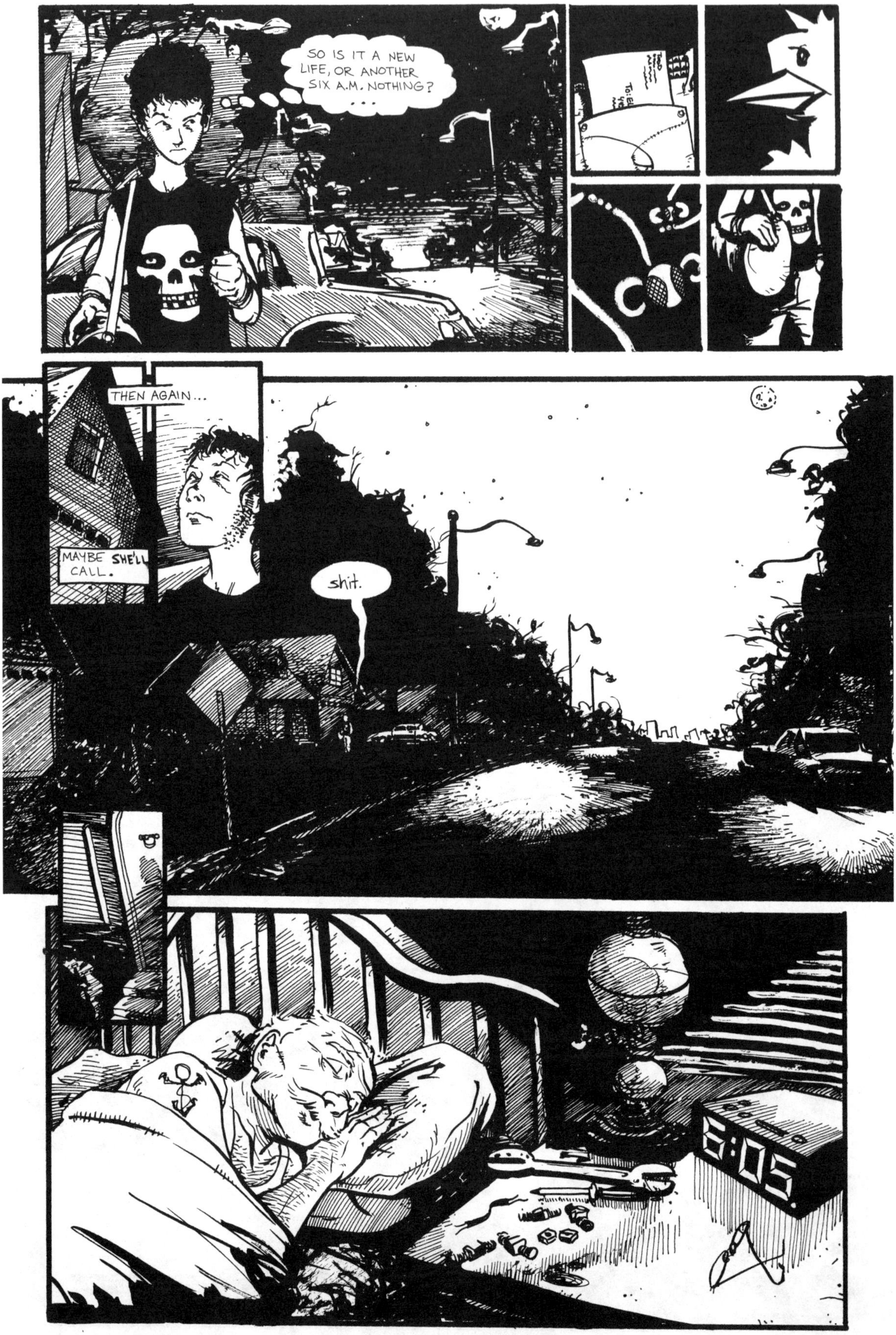
SO IS IT A NEW LIFE, OR ANOTHER SIX A.M. NOTHING? . . .
THEN AGAIN...
MAYBE SHE'LL CALL.
shit.
6:05

7. EPILOGUE

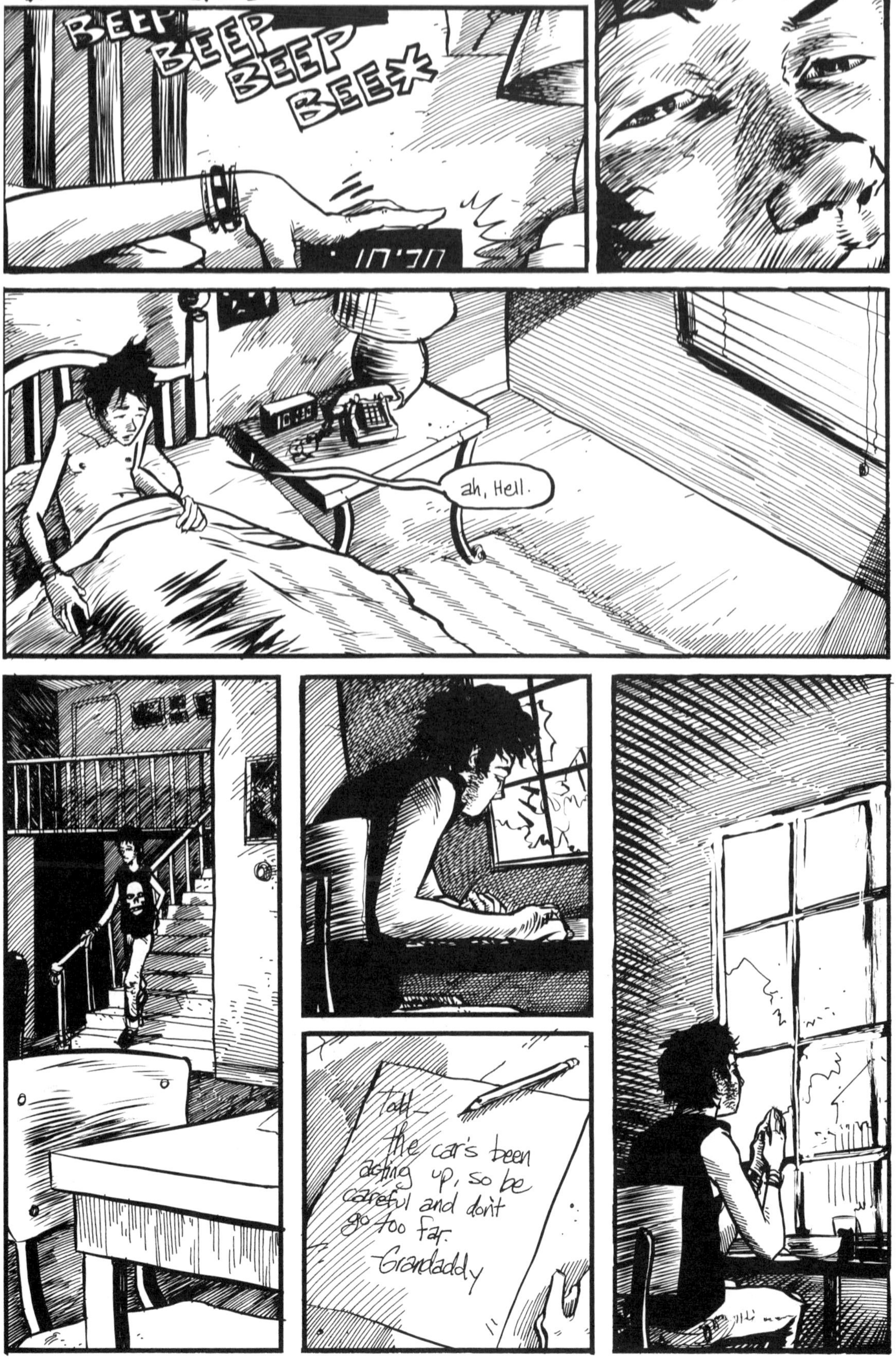
BEEP BEEP BEEP BEE*
ah, Hell.
Todd—
the car's been acting up, so be careful and don't go too far.
-Grandaddy

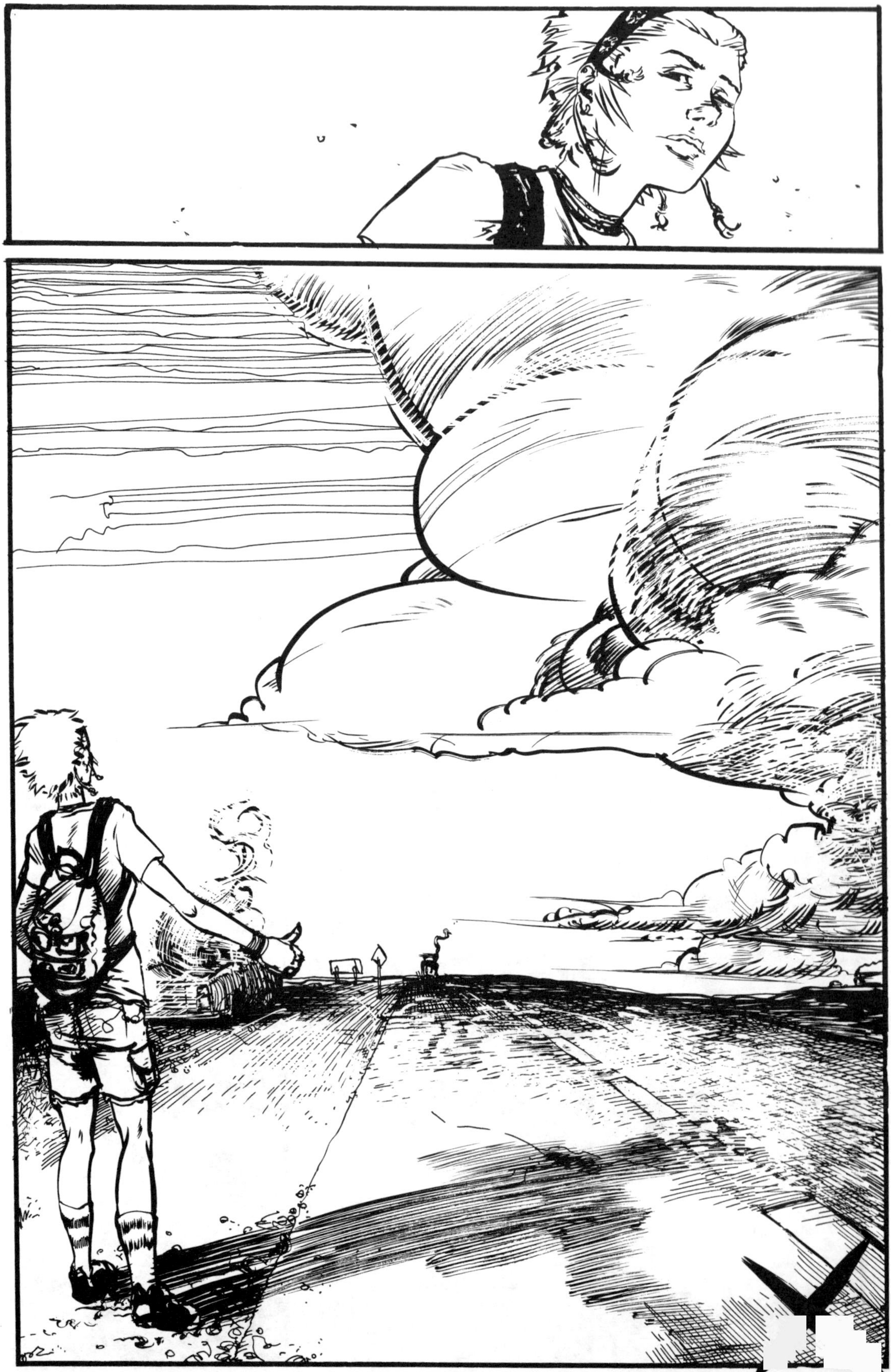

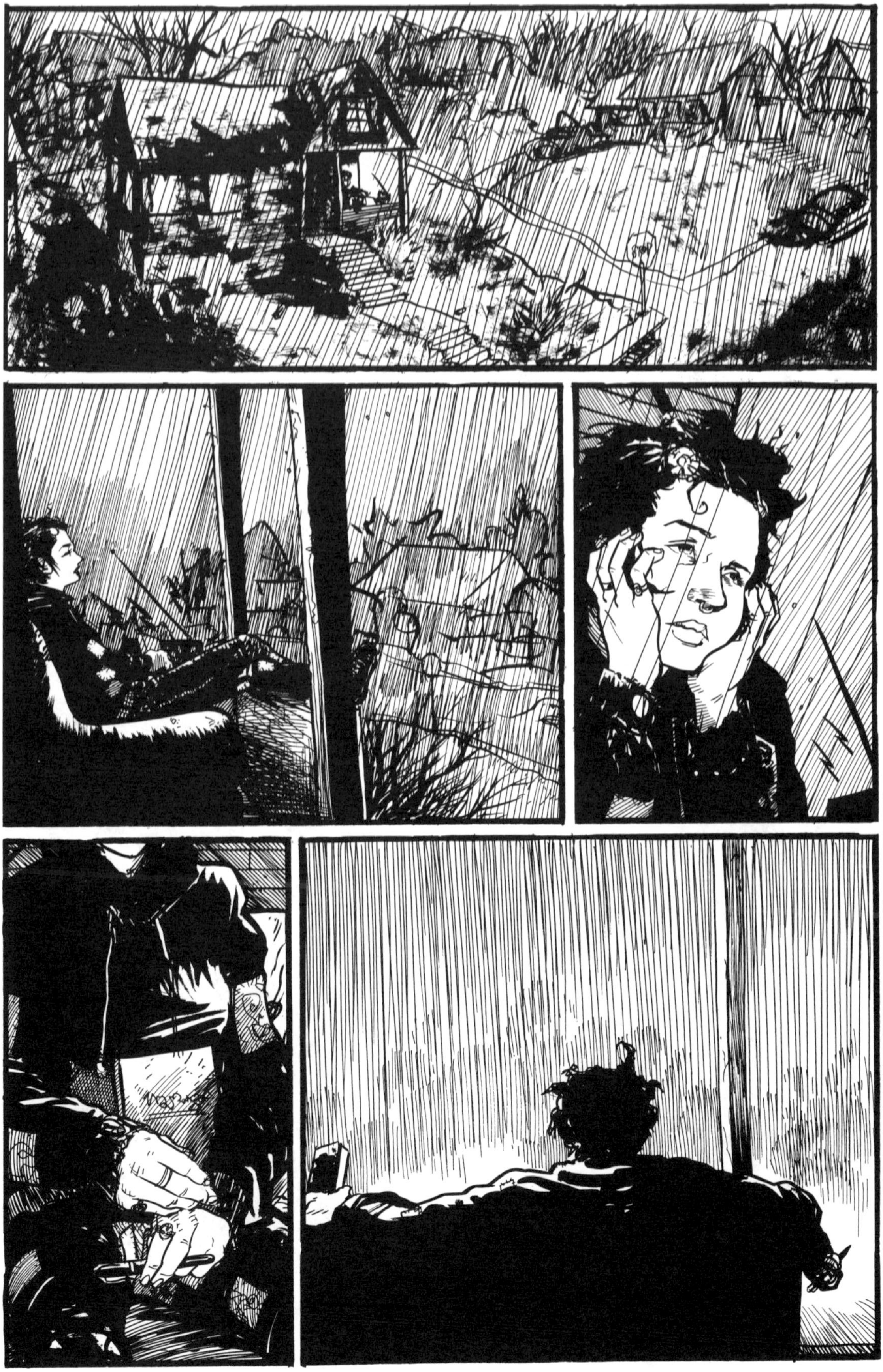

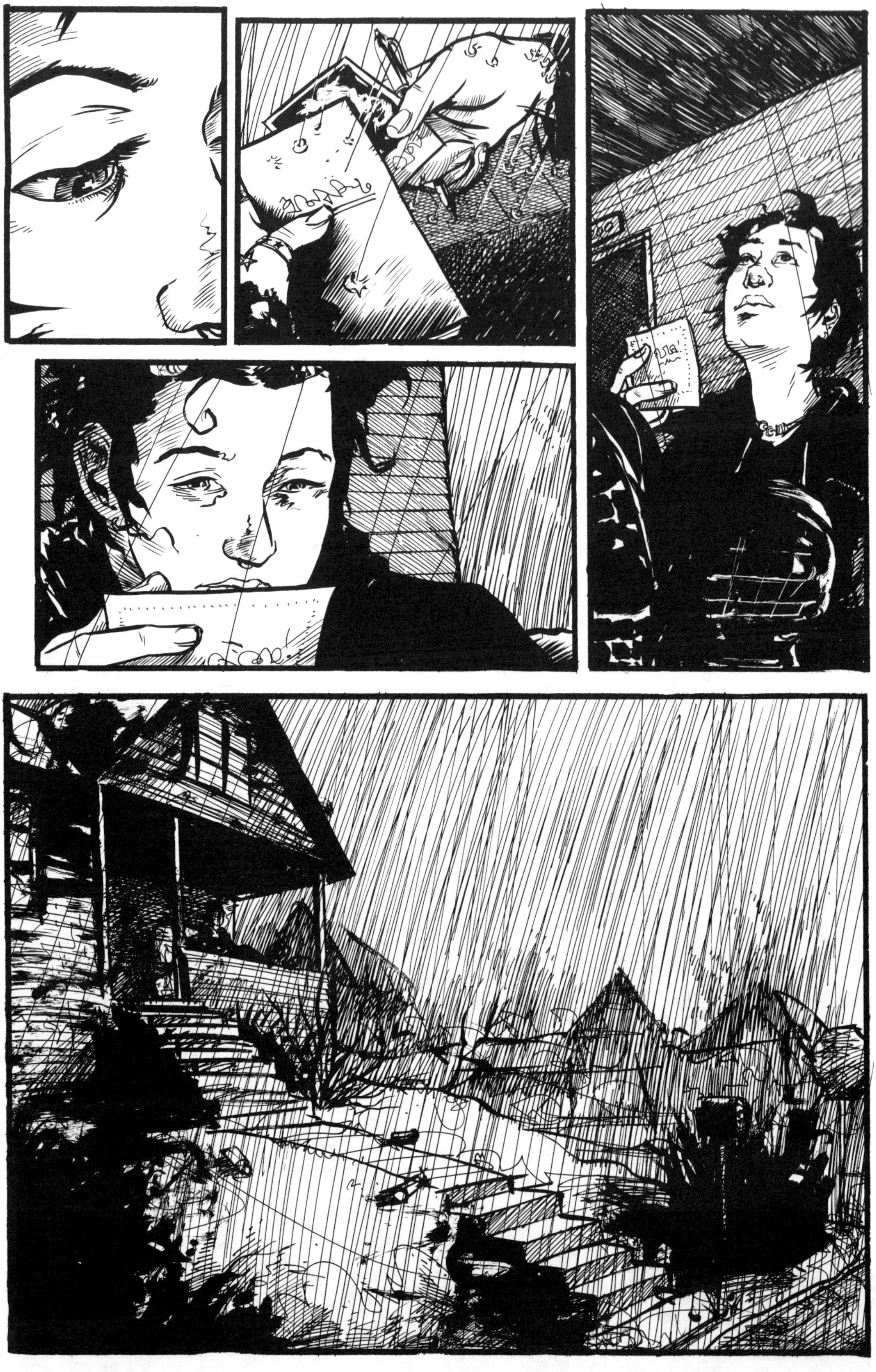

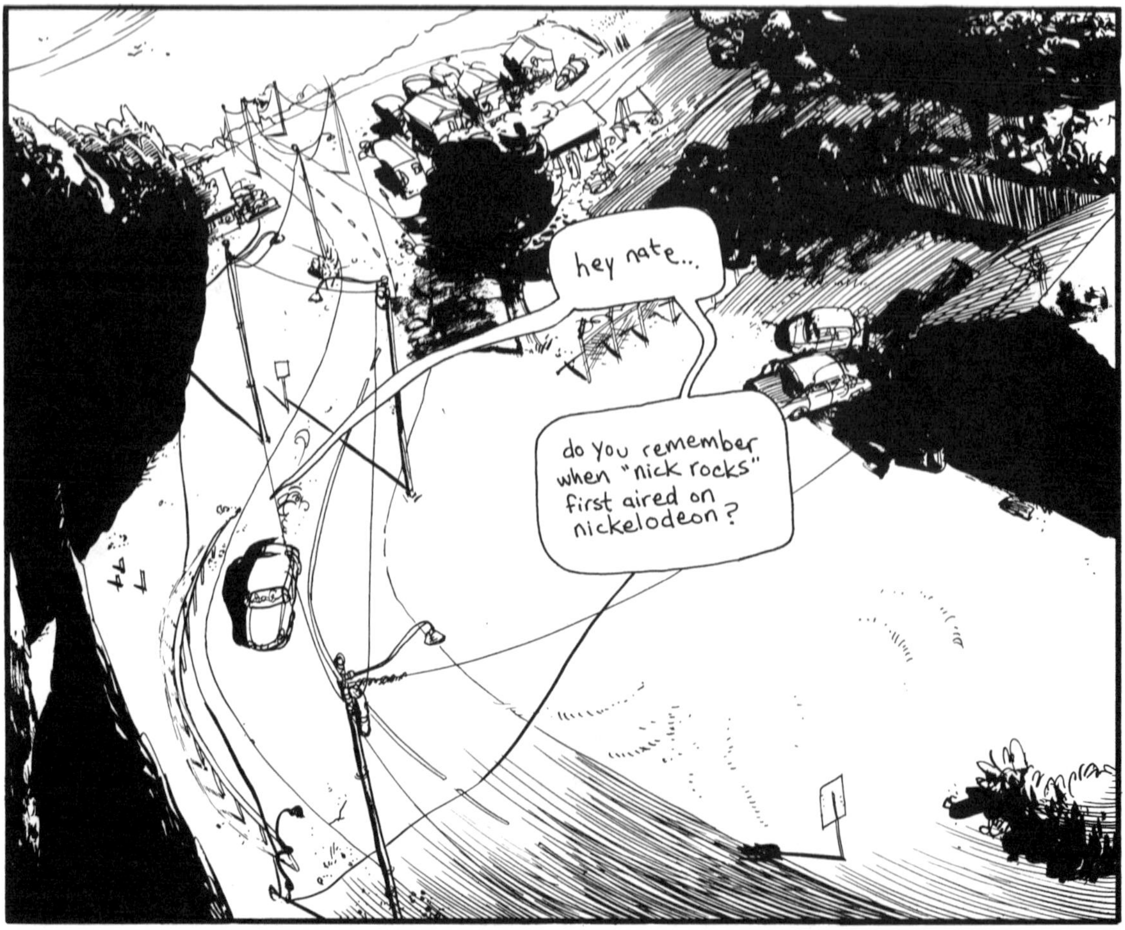
hey nate...
do you remember when "nick rocks" first aired on nickelodeon?

C O M P A N Y *

← by nate powell →

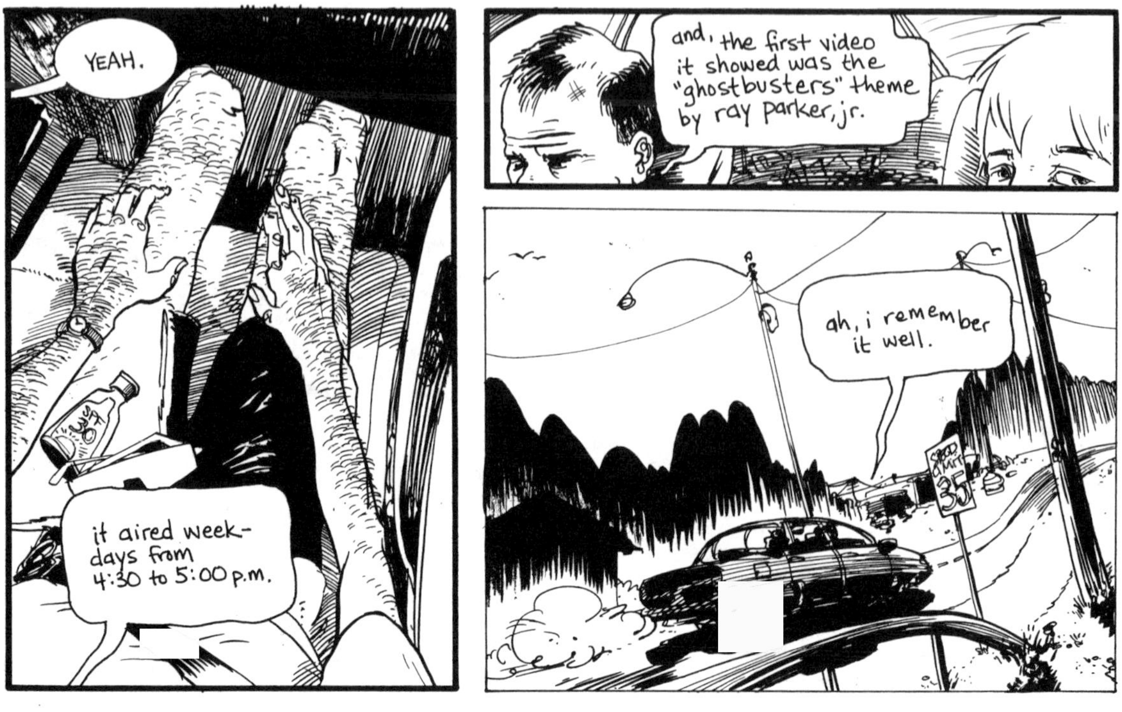
YEAH.
it aired week-days from 4:30 to 5:00 p.m.
and, the first video it showed was the "ghostbusters" theme by ray parker, jr.
ah, i remember it well.

NO BECAUSE
hey, DUUUUDE!
FM
94.5
hmph?
2 NEXT
hey, did you ever like IRON MAIDEN?
YEAH...
YEAH, I STILL DO.
i like that song where he says...
"I AM NOT A NUMBAH!! I AM A FREE MAN!!
YEAH, "THE PRISONER"!
ME TOO..
hey nate...
MM-HMM?
what about JUDAST PR-R-RIEST?
d-did you like him?

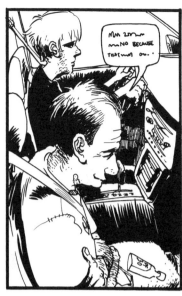

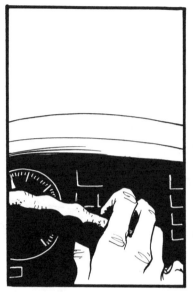

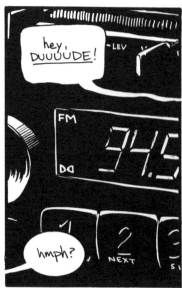

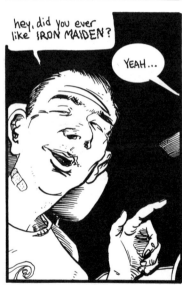

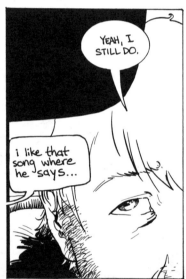

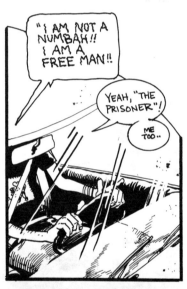

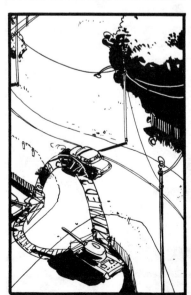

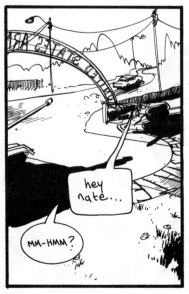

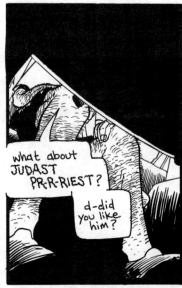

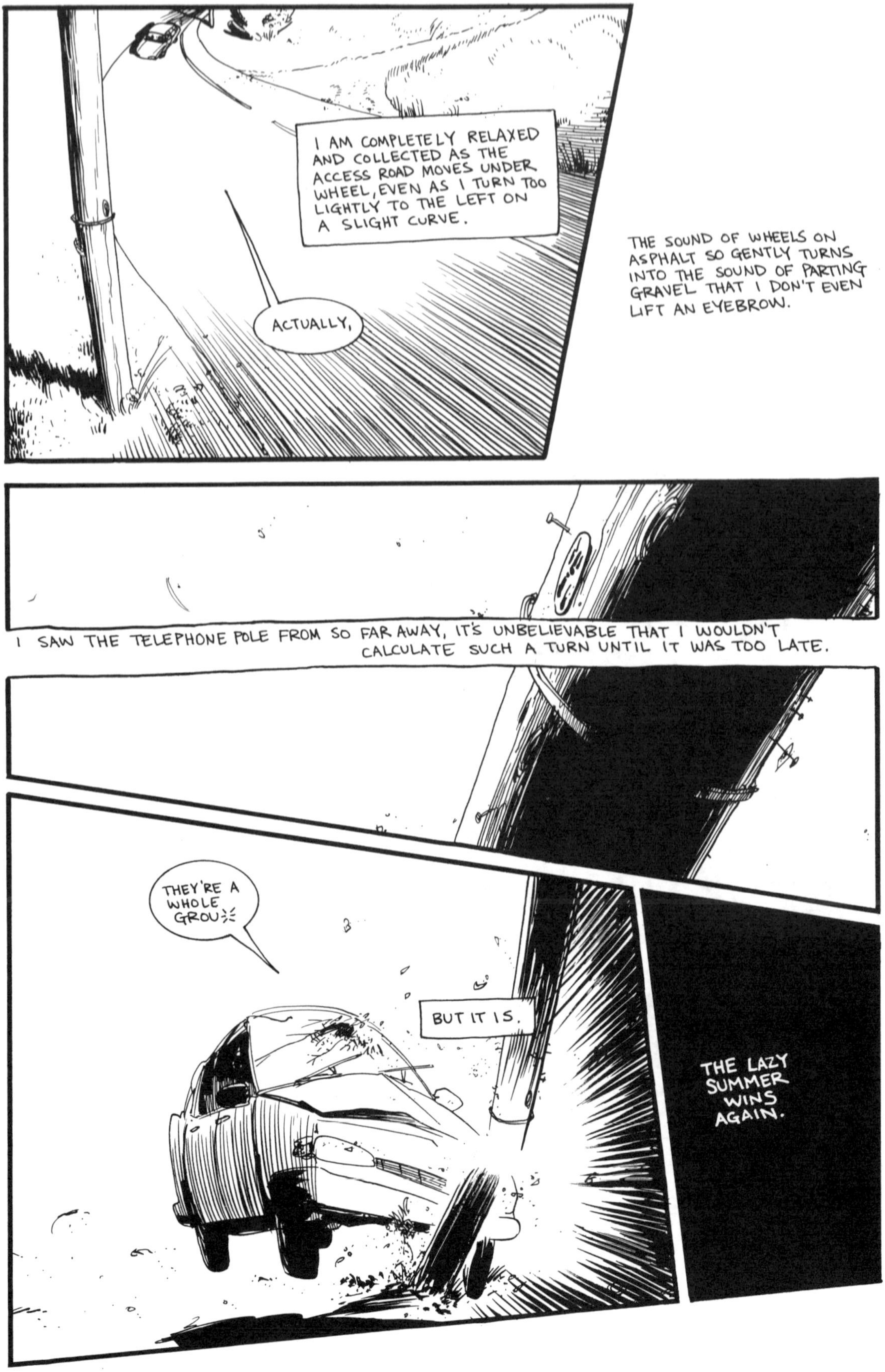
I AM COMPLETELY RELAXED AND COLLECTED AS THE ACCESS ROAD MOVES UNDER WHEEL, EVEN AS I TURN TOO LIGHTLY TO THE LEFT ON A SLIGHT CURVE.
ACTUALLY,
THE SOUND OF WHEELS ON ASPHALT SO GENTLY TURNS INTO THE SOUND OF PARTING GRAVEL THAT I DON'T EVEN LIFT AN EYEBROW.
I SAW THE TELEPHONE POLE FROM SO FAR AWAY, IT'S UNBELIEVABLE THAT I WOULDN'T CALCULATE SUCH A TURN UNTIL IT WAS TOO LATE.
THEY'RE A WHOLE GROU
BUT IT IS.
THE LAZY SUMMER WINS AGAIN.

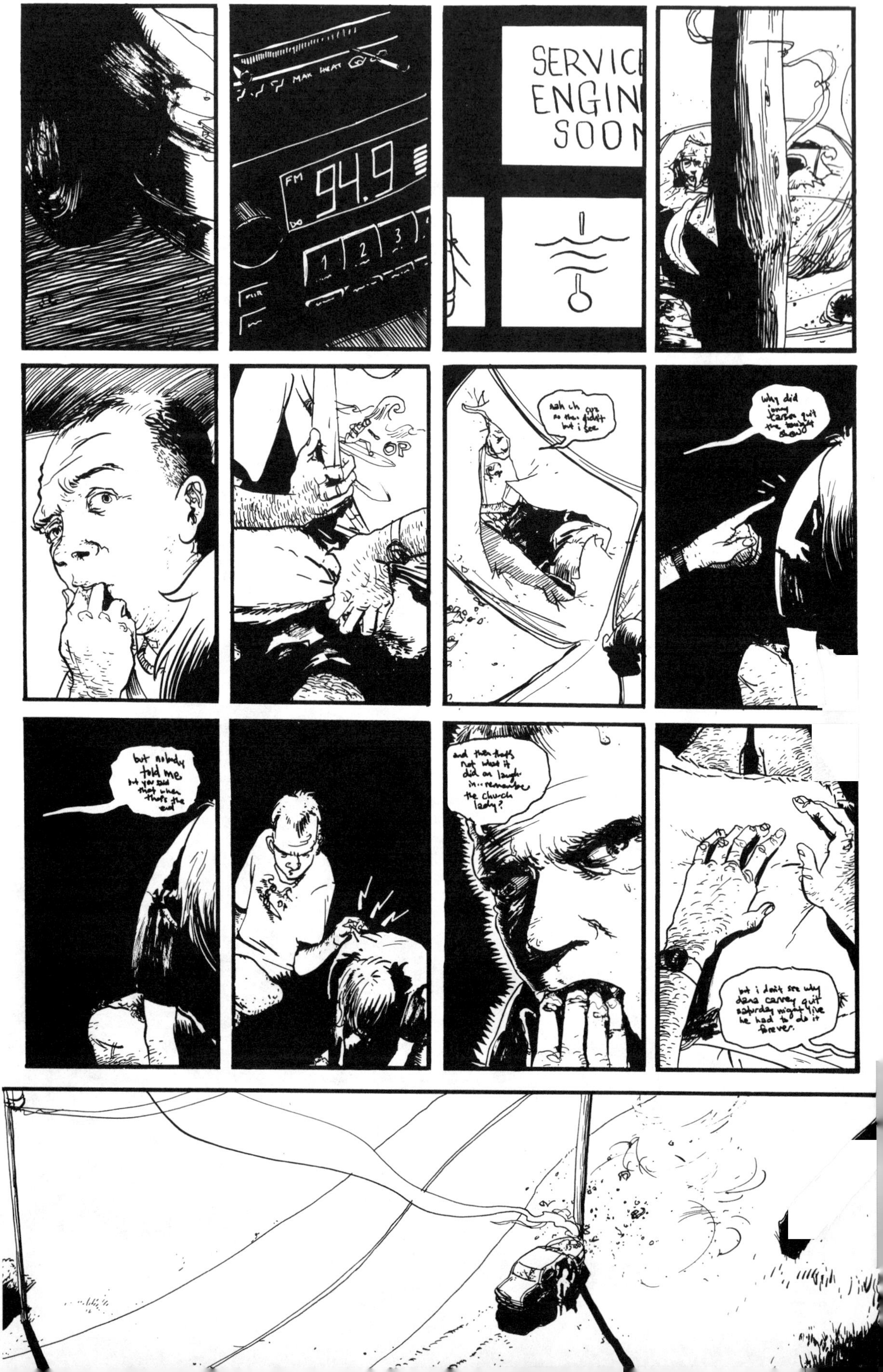
MAX HEAT
FM 94.9
1 2 3
SERVICE ENGINE SOON
aah uh cuz so the didn't but i see
why did jonny carson quit the tonight show
but nobody told me but you said that when that's the end
and then that's not what it did on laugh in.. remember the church lady?
but i don't see why dana carvey quit saturday night live he had to do it forever.

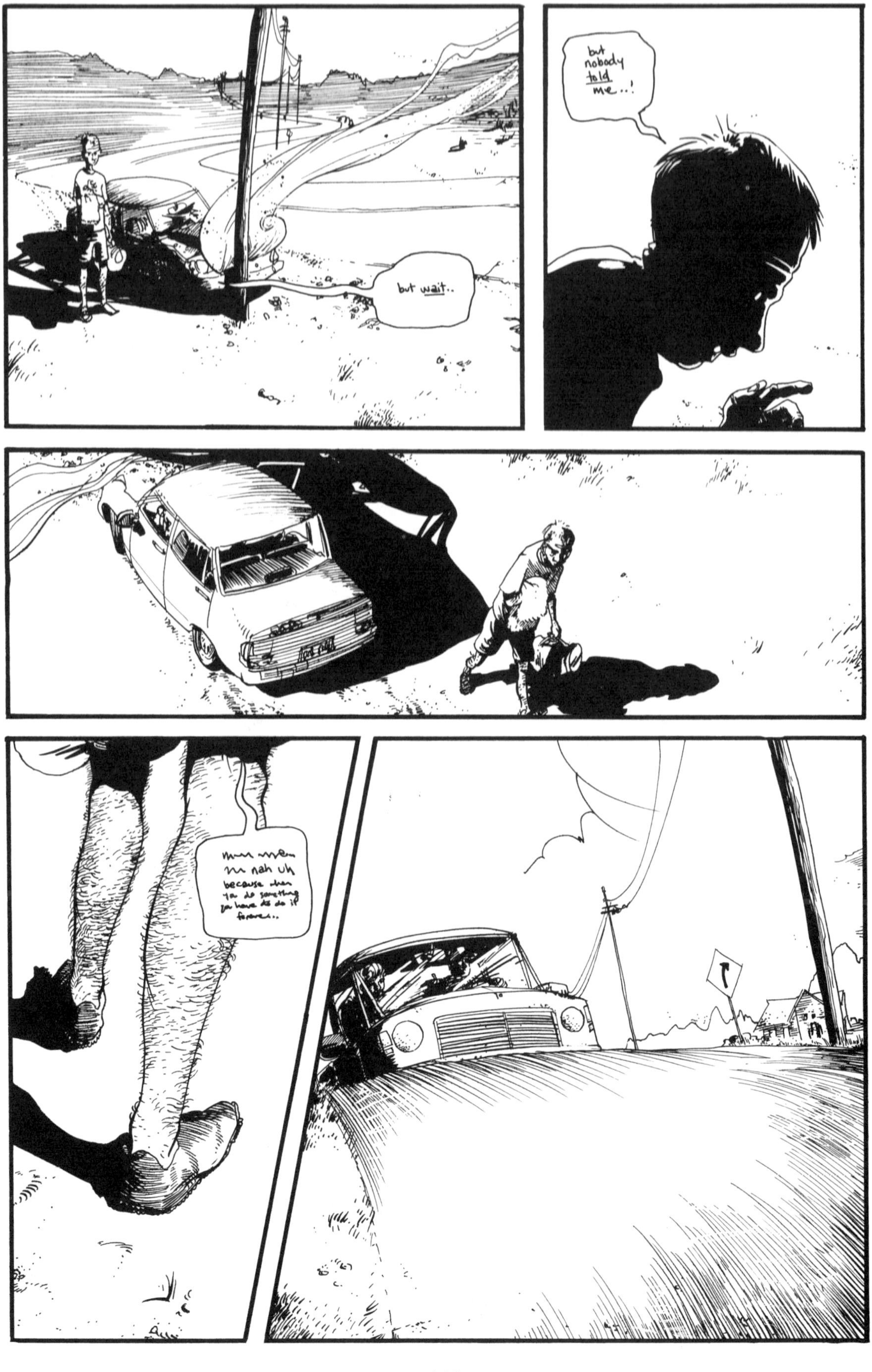
but wait..
but nobody told me..!
nah uh
because when
ya do something
ya have to do it
forever..

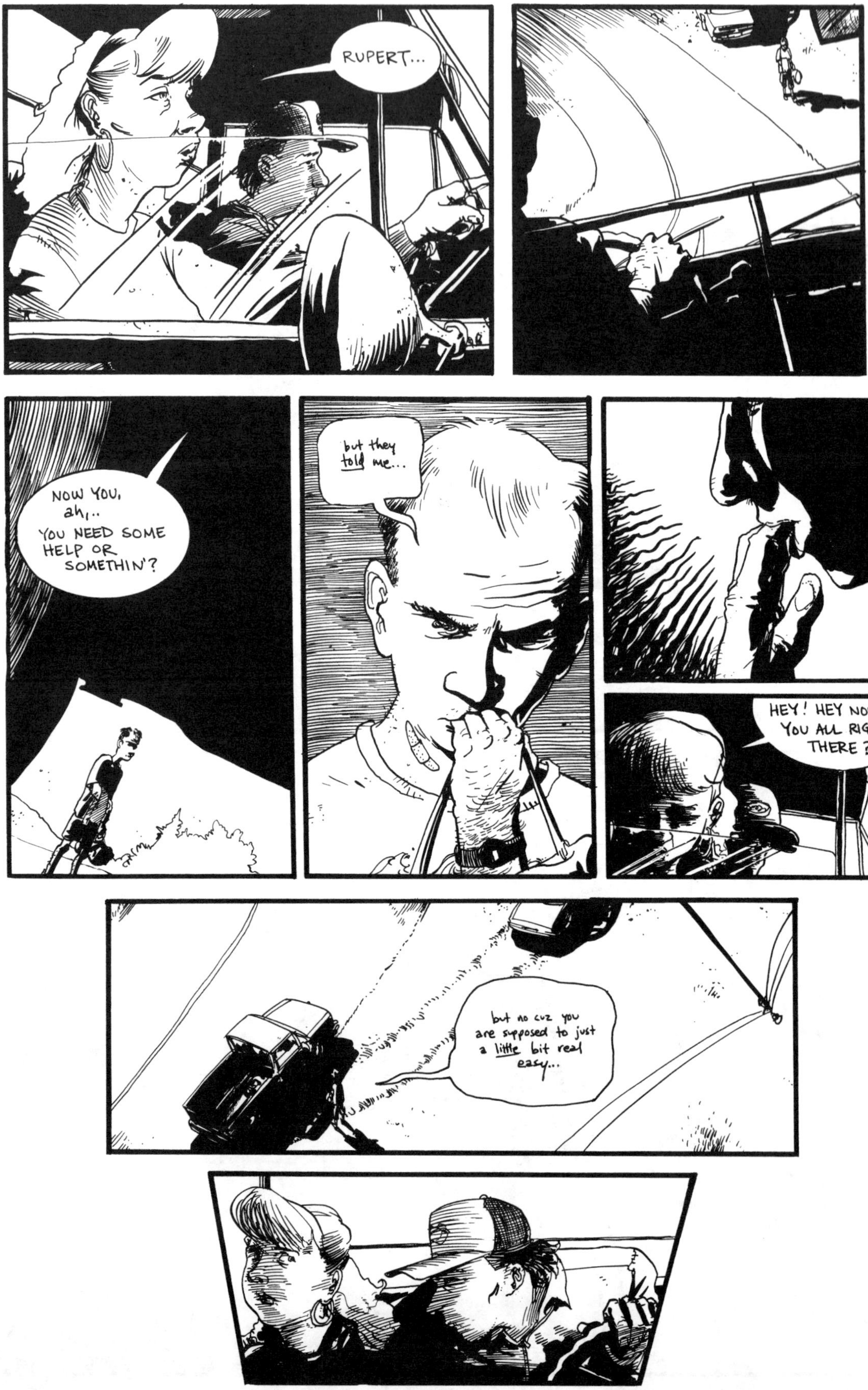
RUPERT...
NOW YOU, ah,.. YOU NEED SOME HELP OR SOMETHIN'?
but they told me...
HEY! HEY NOW, YOU ALL RIGHT THERE?
but no cuz you are supposed to just a little bit real easy...

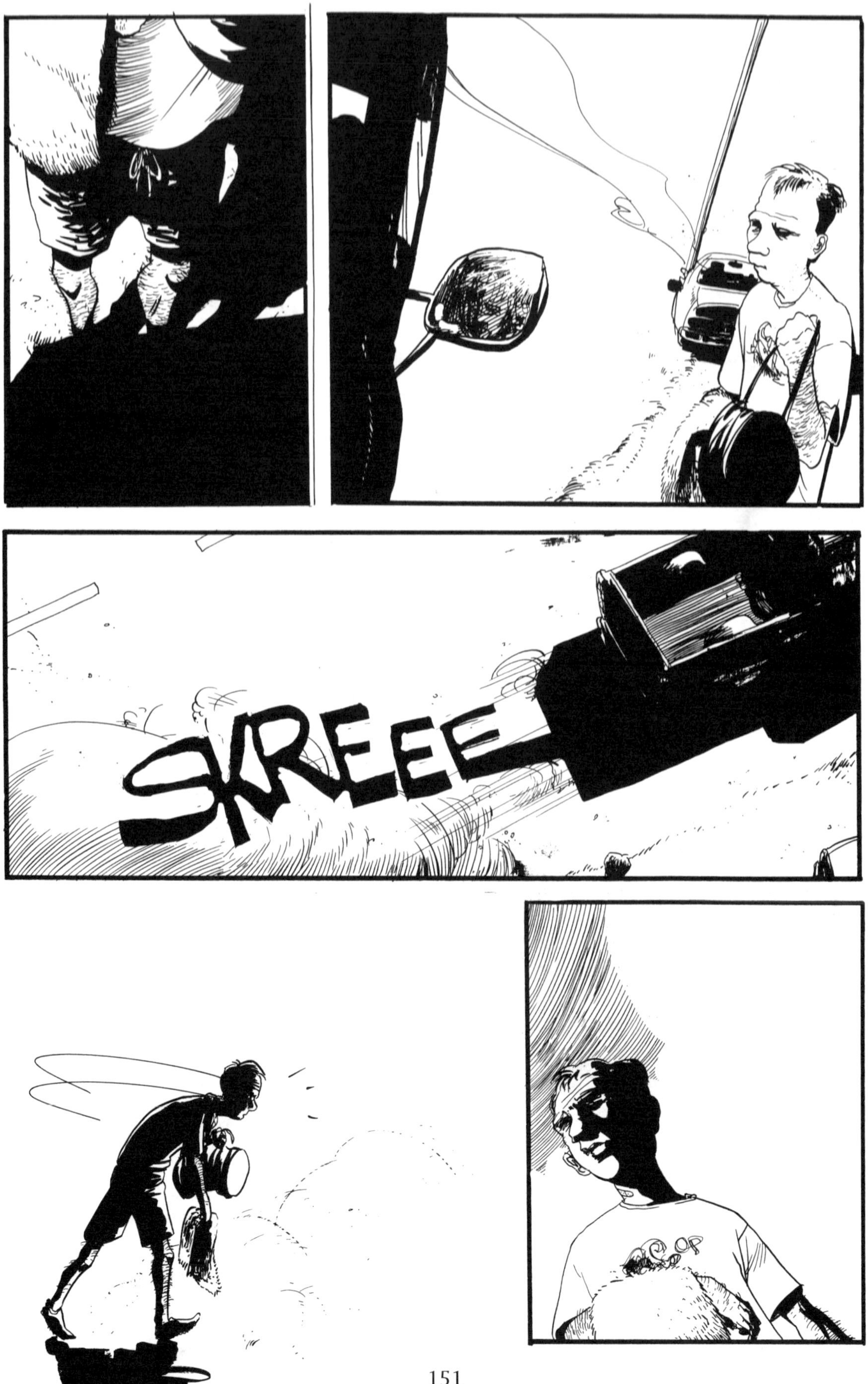
SKREEE

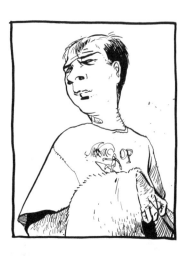

So i said who's the first baseman. who. the guy playing first base. who. who's on first. what.

no what's on second. who. who's on first. i don't know you tell me. no he's our third baseman. who. he's on first.

well what's the name of your catcher. tomorrow. why can't you tell me now? what's his name. second base. who. who's on first. i don't know what you're talking about. third base.

(a work of fiction dedicated to my brother, in hopes that he and others with developmental disabilities might be able to live their lives more fully and with dignity.)
x

152

N° 10/01.

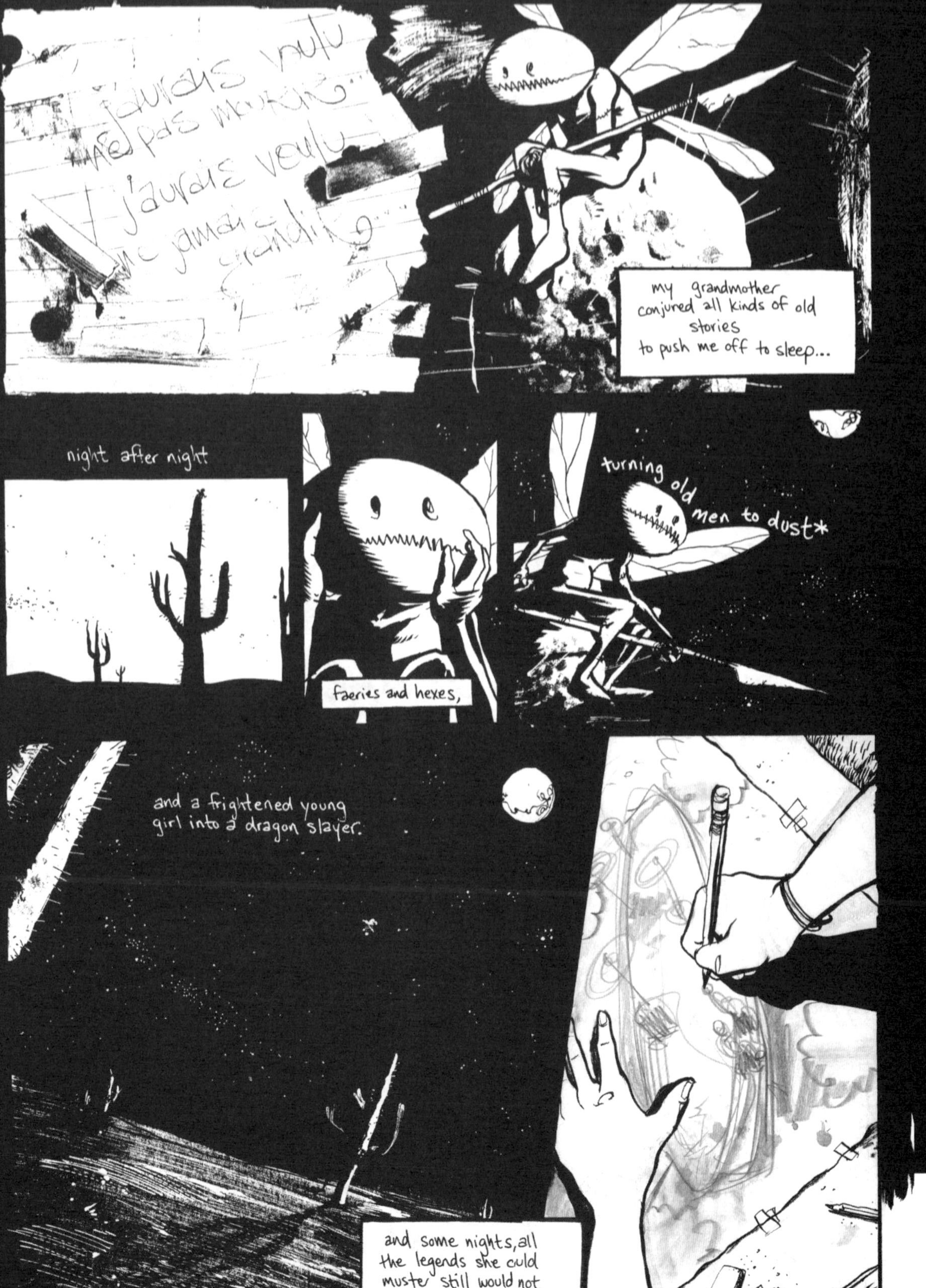
J'aurais voulu
ne pas mourir...
J'aurais voulu
ne jamais
grandir...
my grandmother conjured all kinds of old stories to push me off to sleep...
night after night
faeries and hexes,
turning old men to dust*
and a frightened young girl into a dragon slayer.
and some nights, all the legends she culd muste still would not take me to slumber...

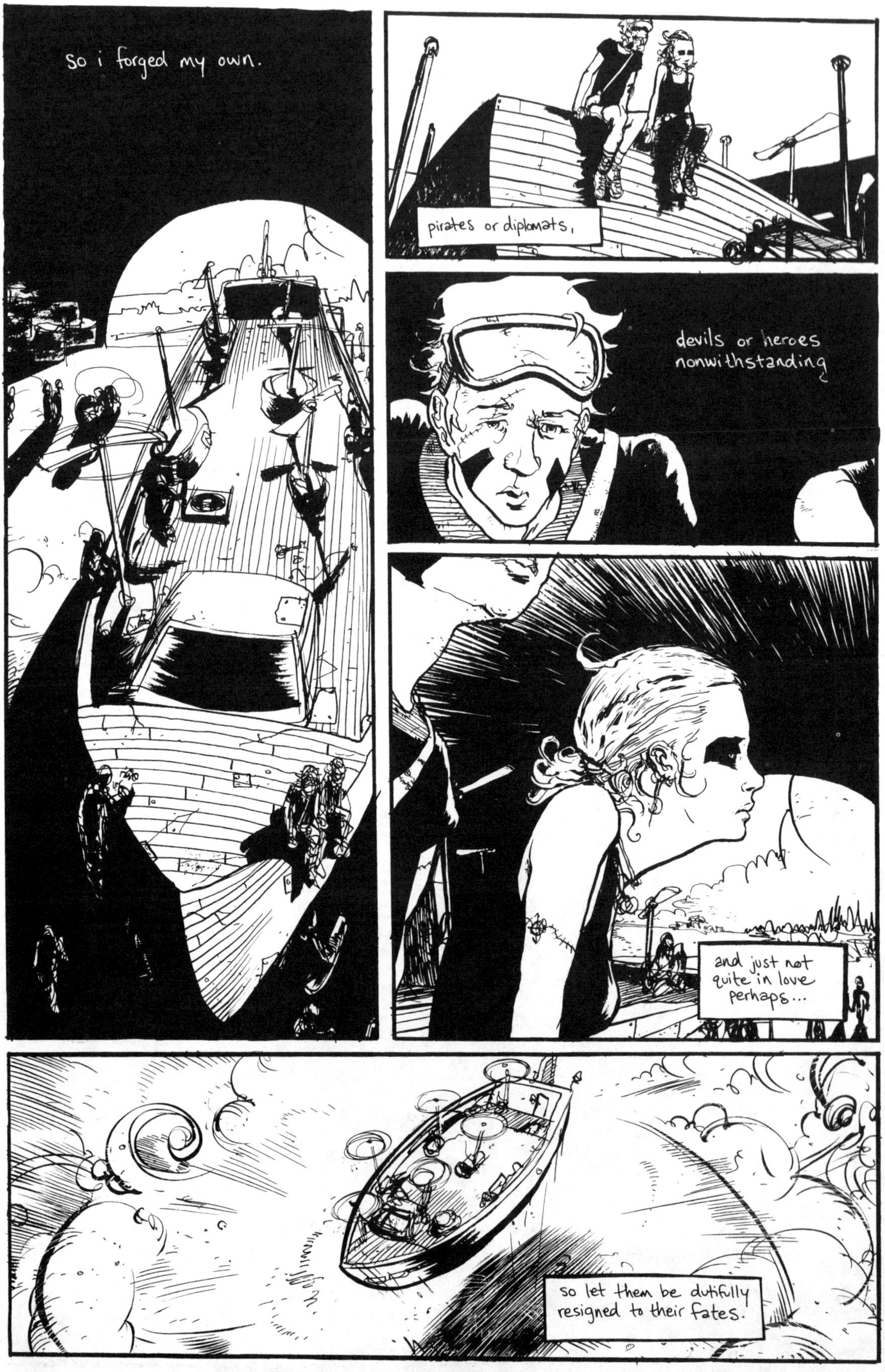
so i forged my own.
pirates or diplomats,
devils or heroes nonwithstanding
and just not quite in love perhaps...
so let them be dutifully resigned to their fates.

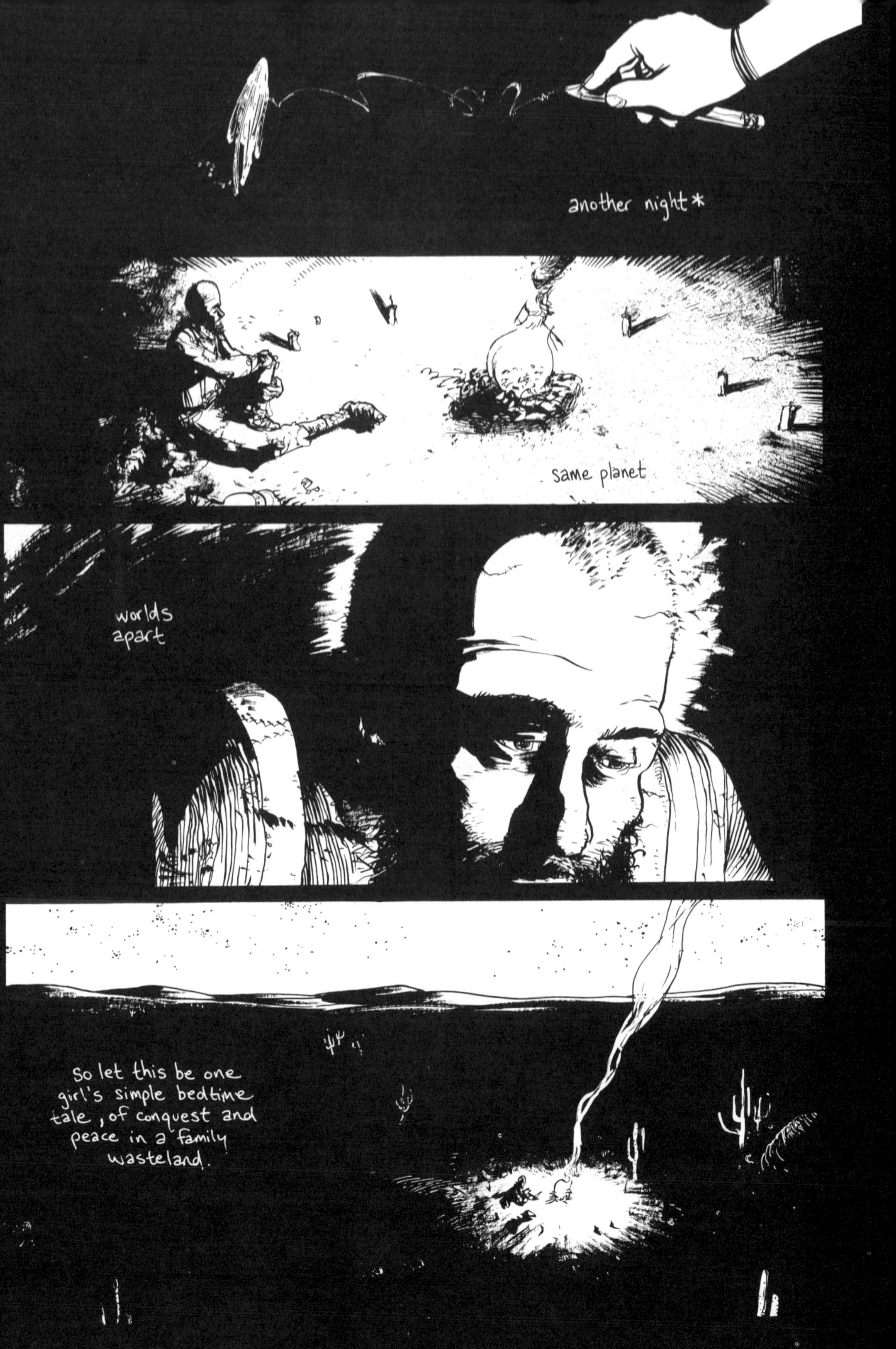

another night*
same planet
worlds apart
so let this be one girl's simple bedtime tale, of conquest and peace in a family wasteland.

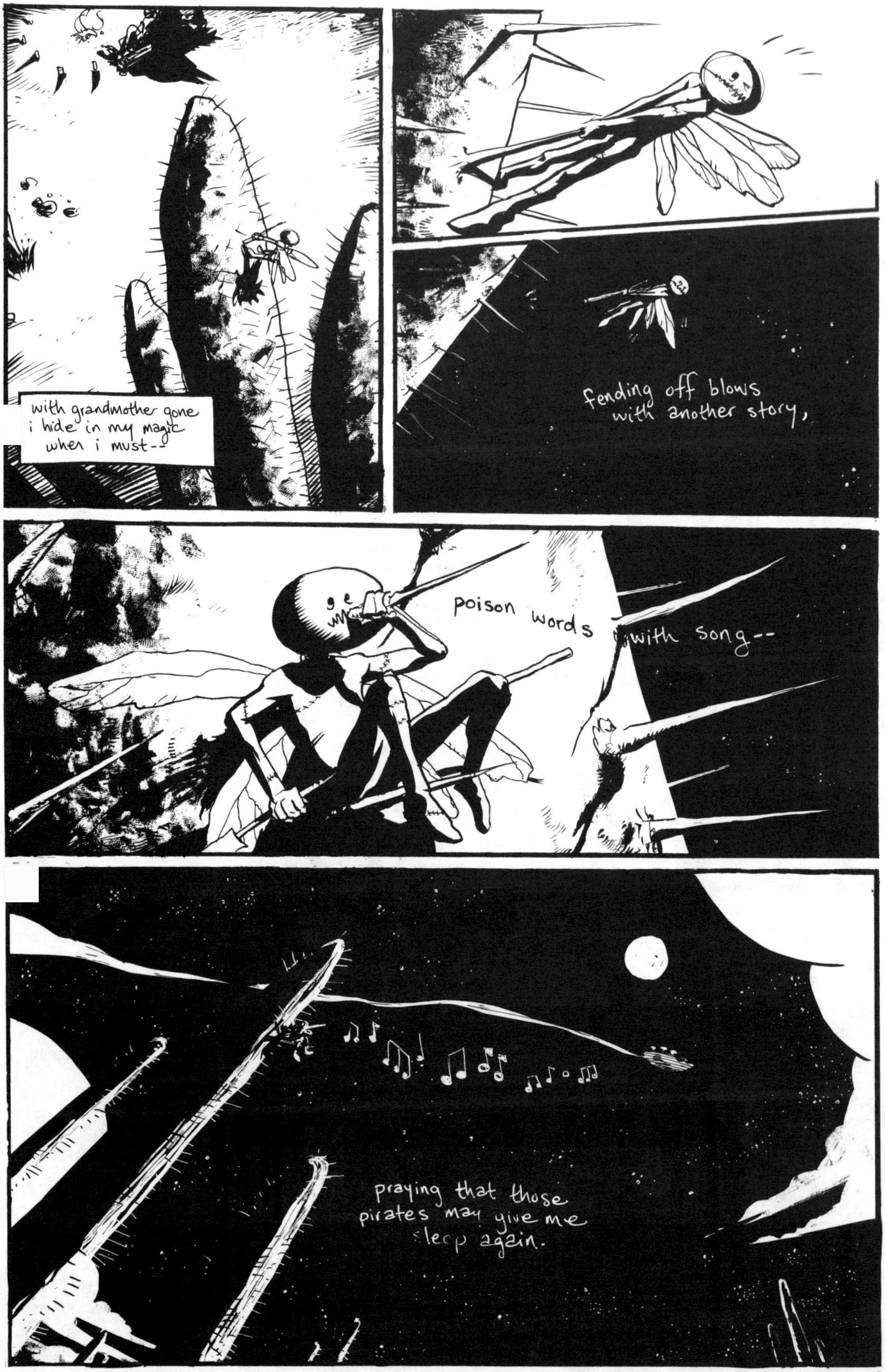
with grandmother gone
i hide in my magic
when i must--
fending off blows
with another story,
poison words with song--
praying that those
pirates may give me
sleep again.

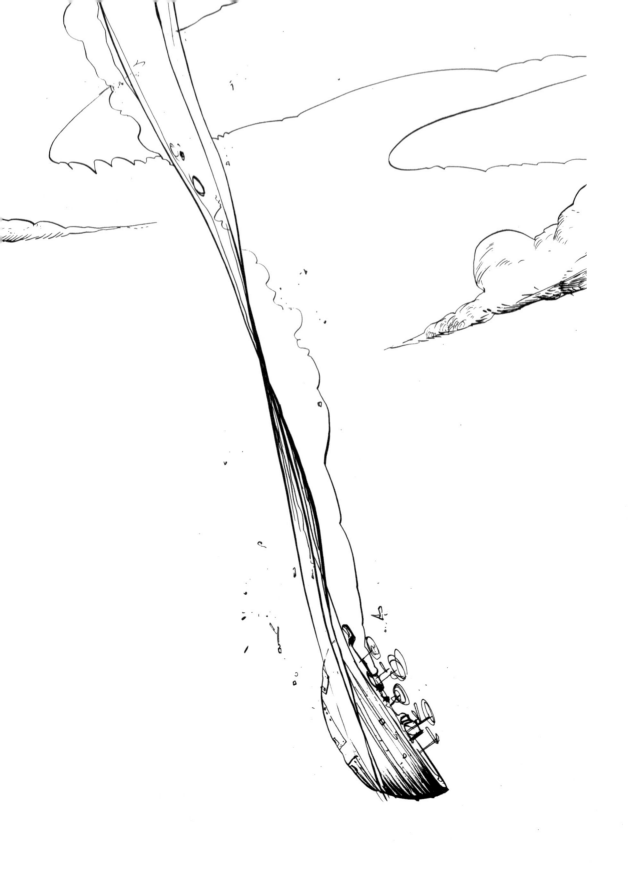

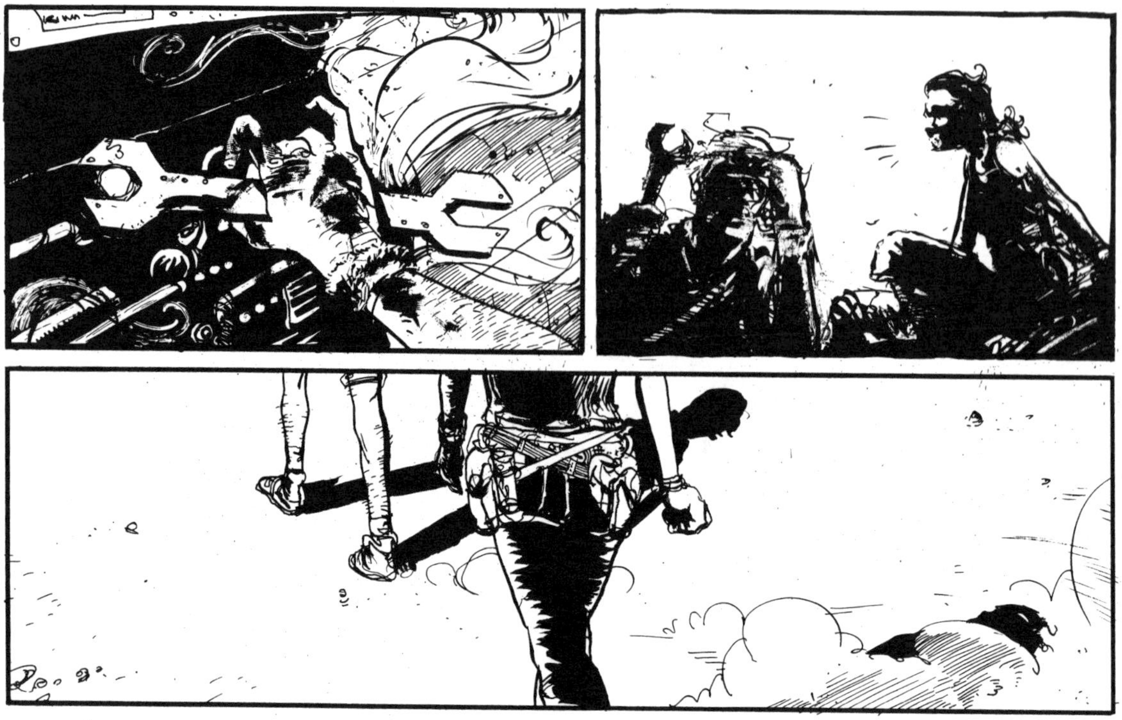

AUTOPILOT*

by nate powell

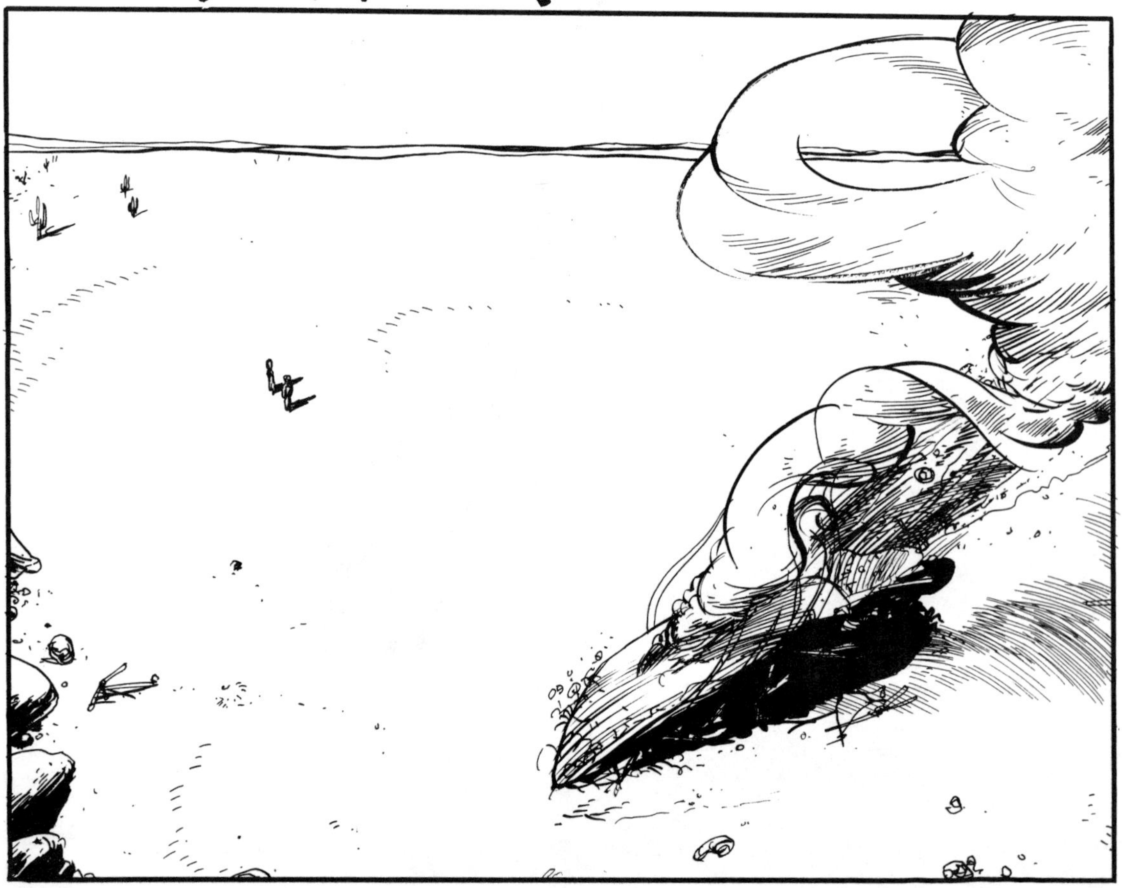

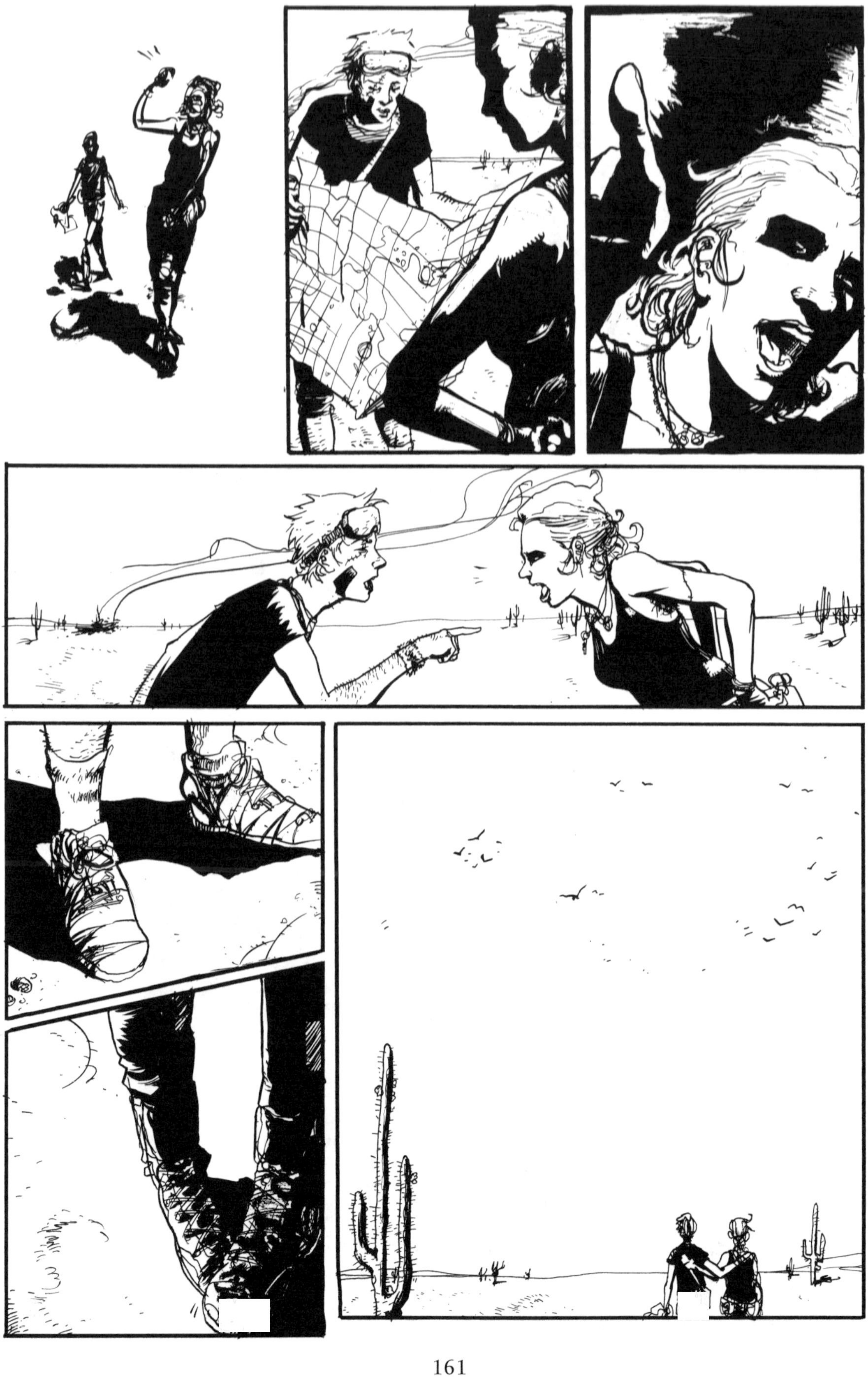

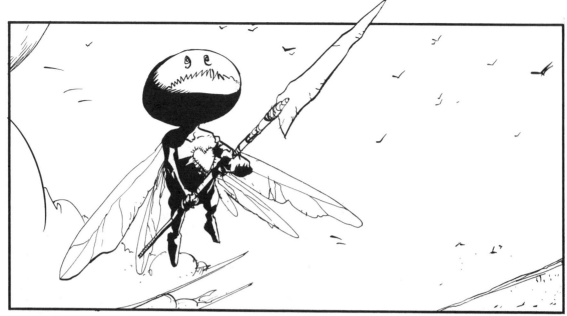

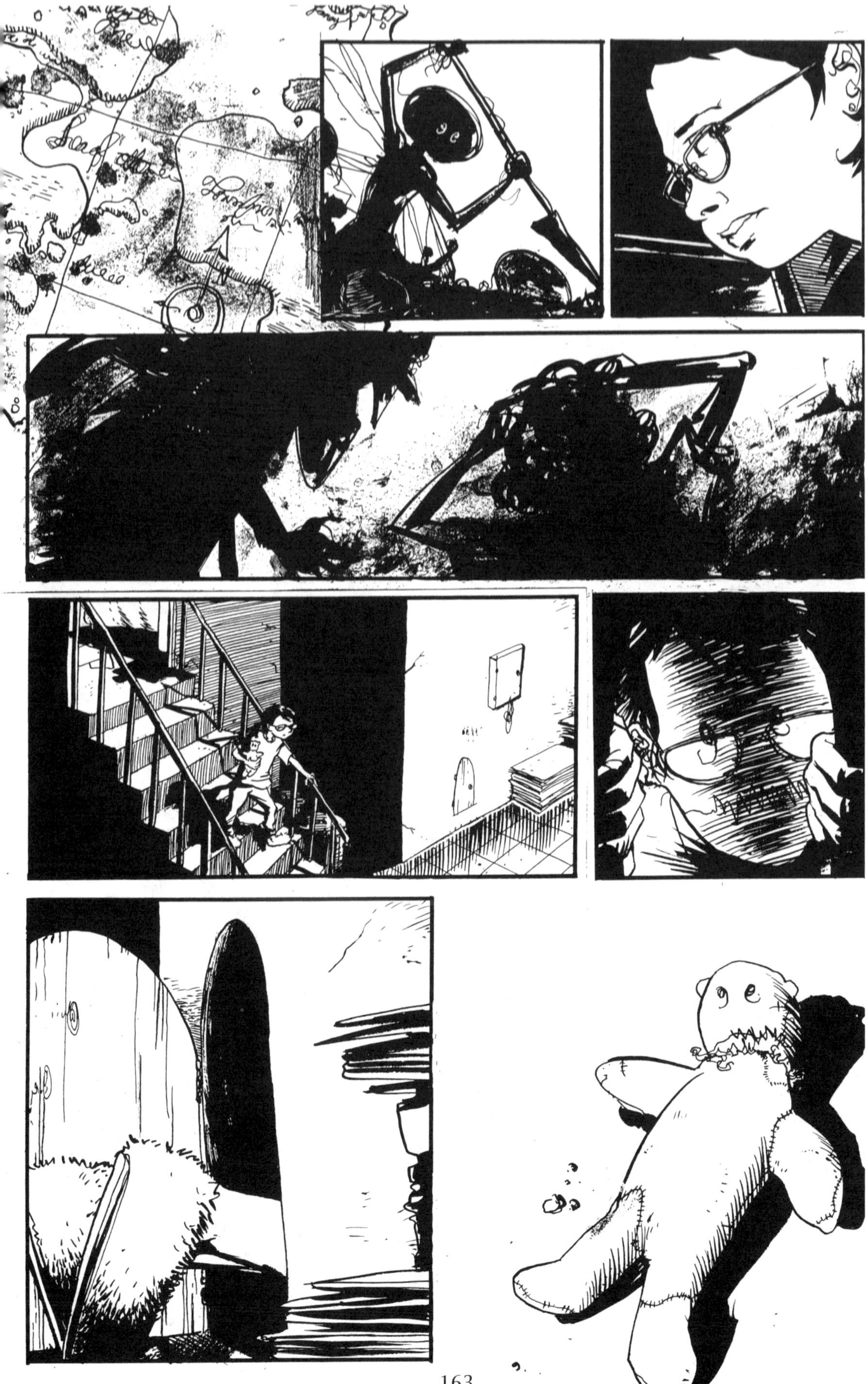

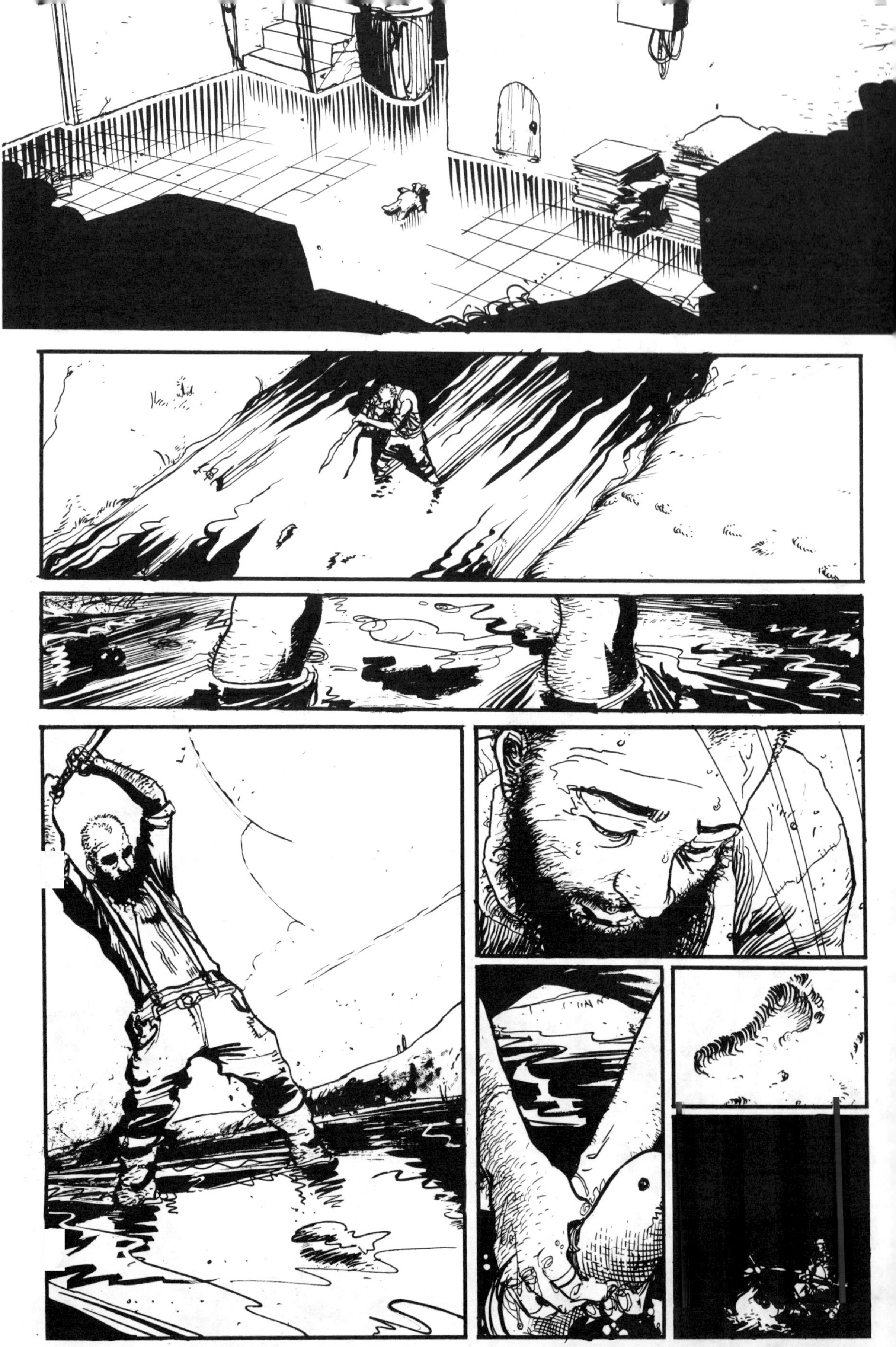

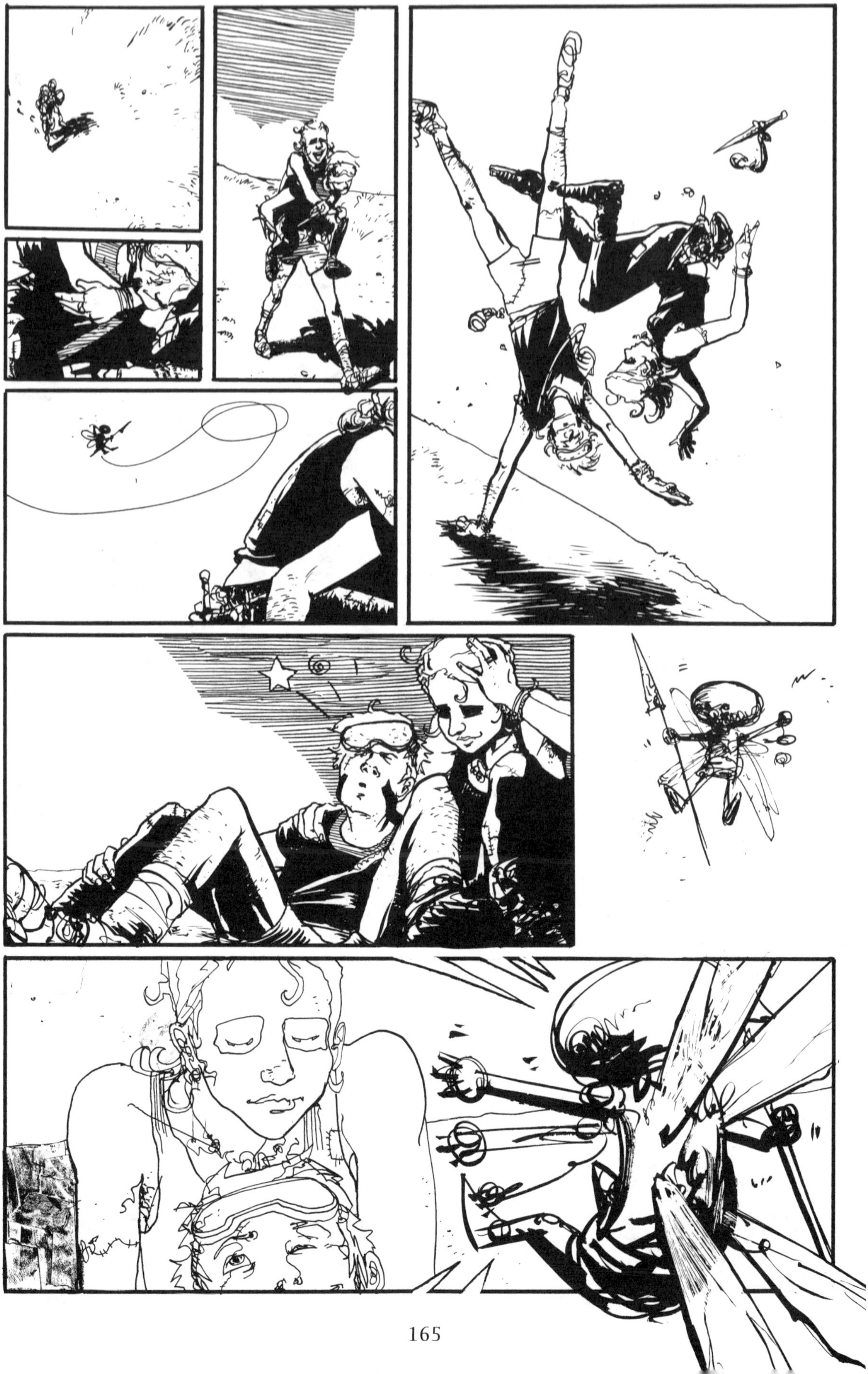

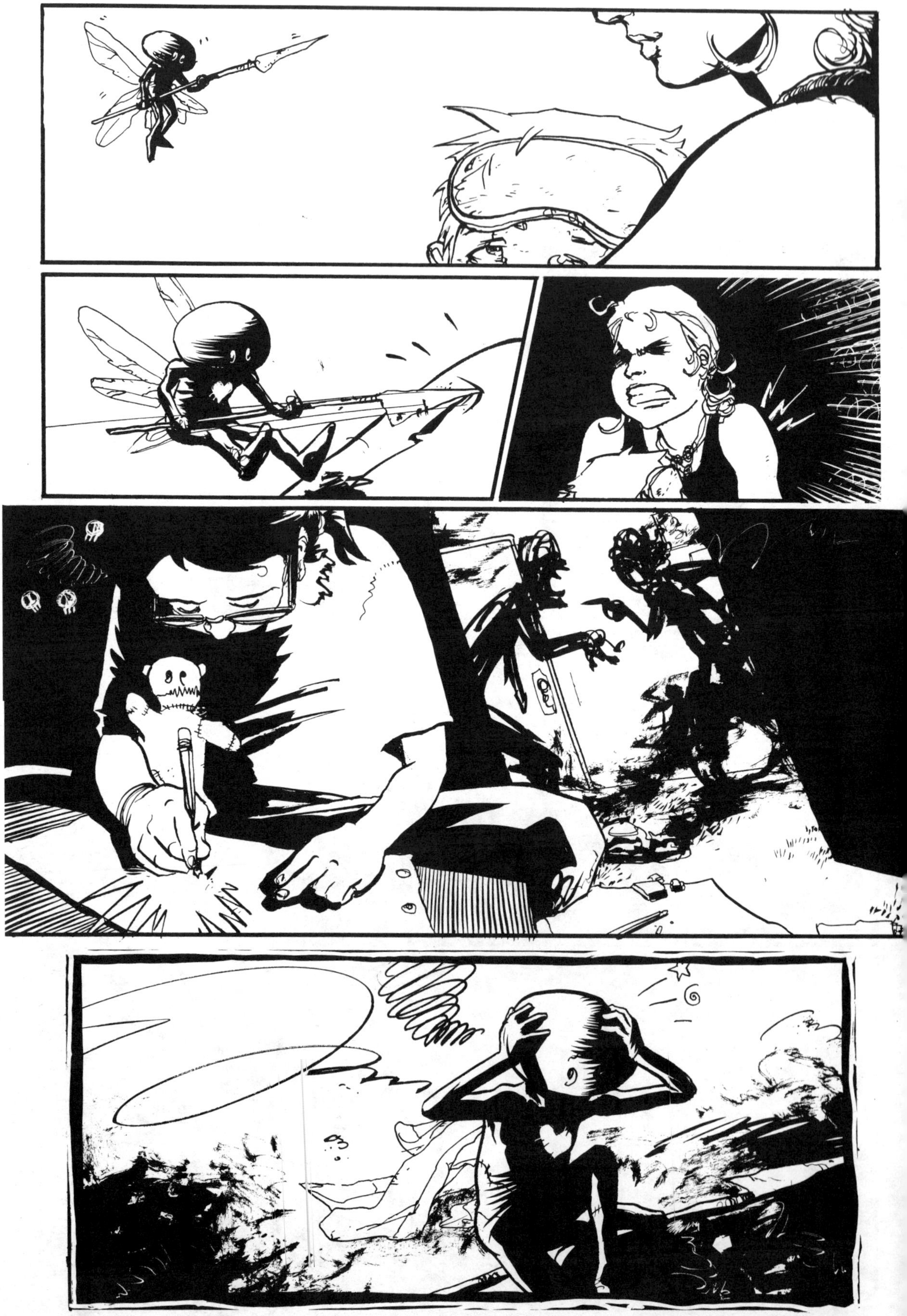

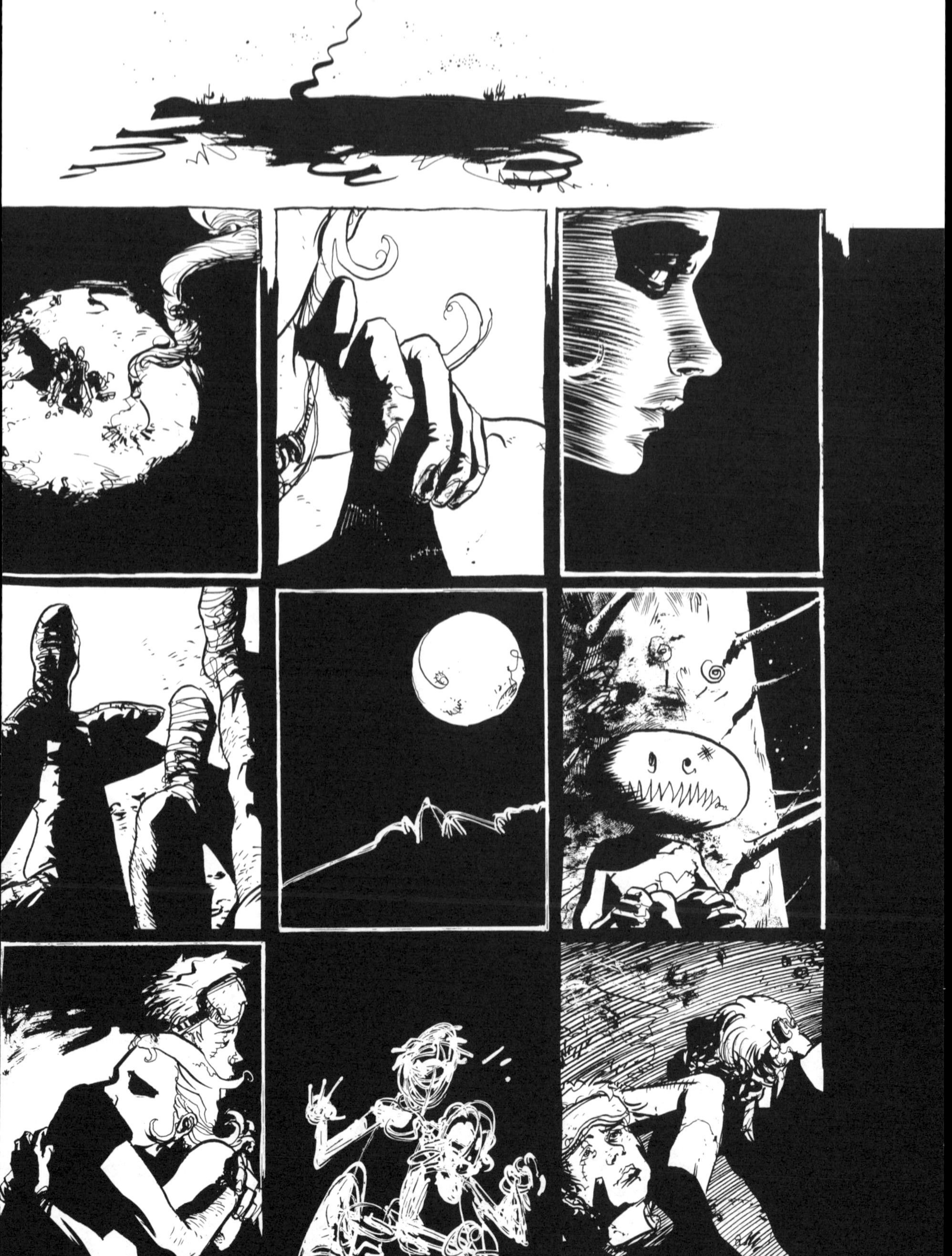

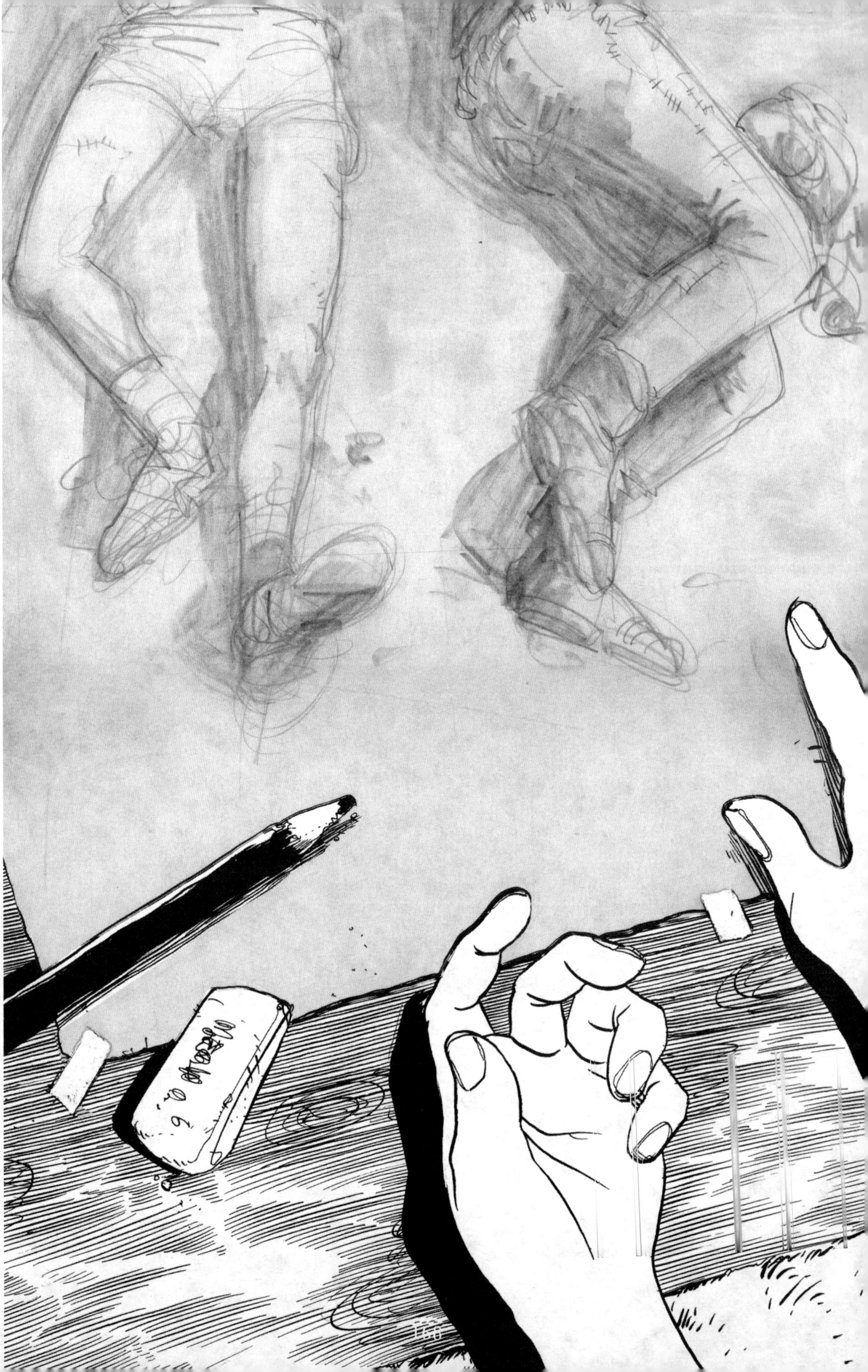

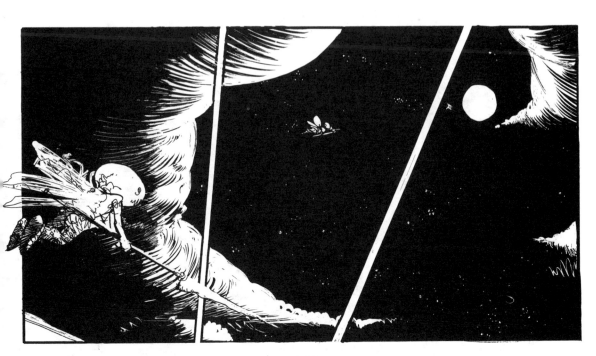

most of
all i want
too live
in a cloud
and have
stars
for friends
and see
endless
blue
skies
every
day when
i
wake
from
dreams
i count
my
fingers
continue /

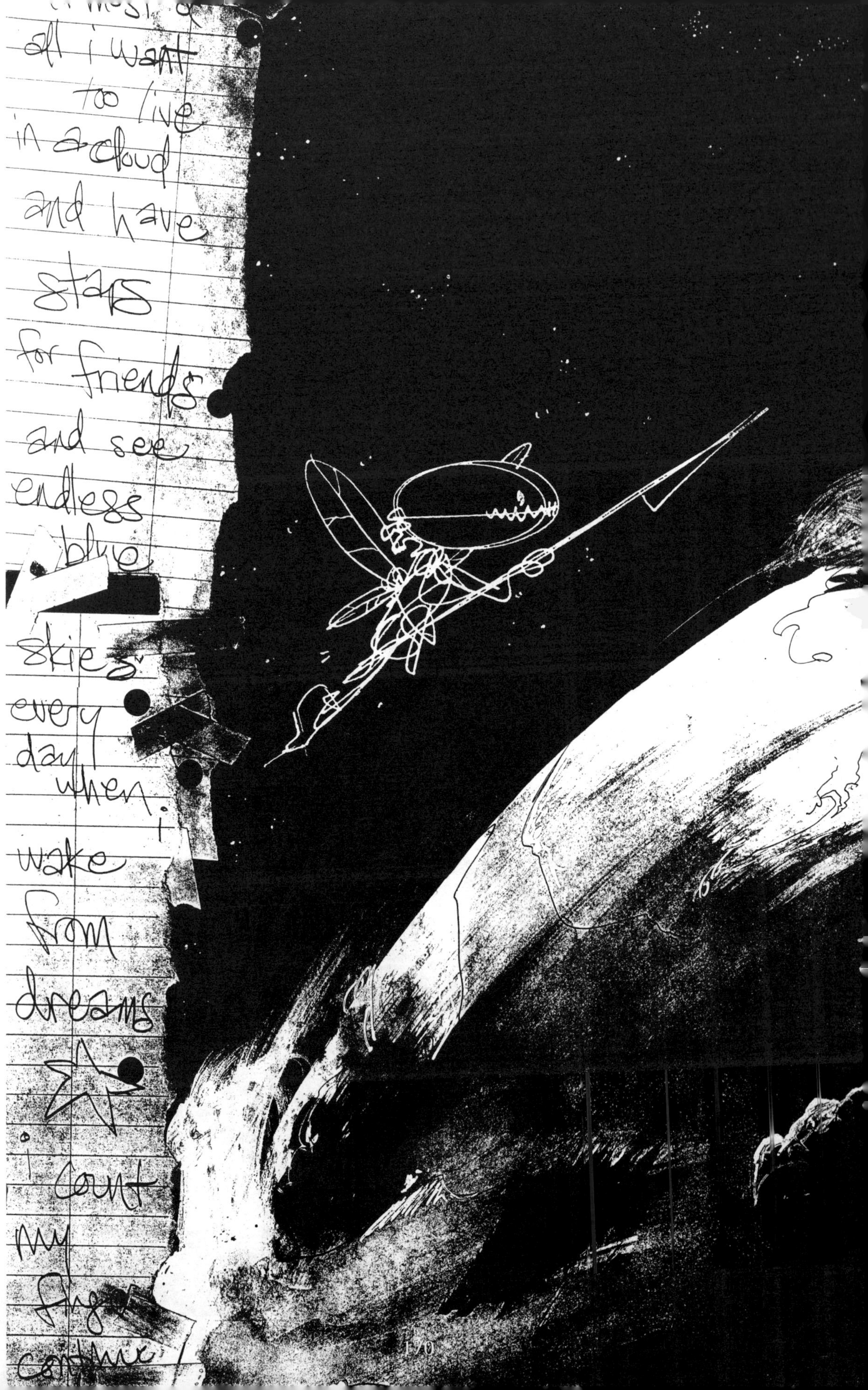

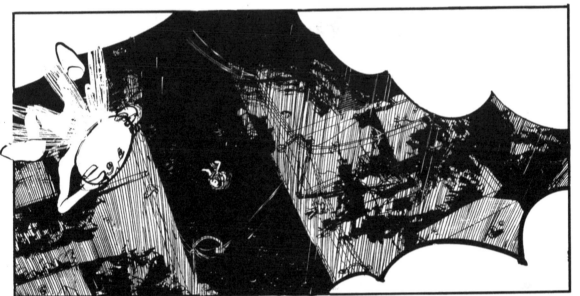

ended now!

CORE   BULLET   BOMB

7:14:

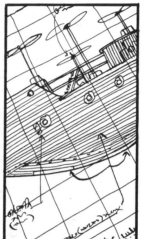

i saw it in a book. all she needs is to fall into deep sleep in the roots of a cowslip and none of those noises can trouble her ever again...

172

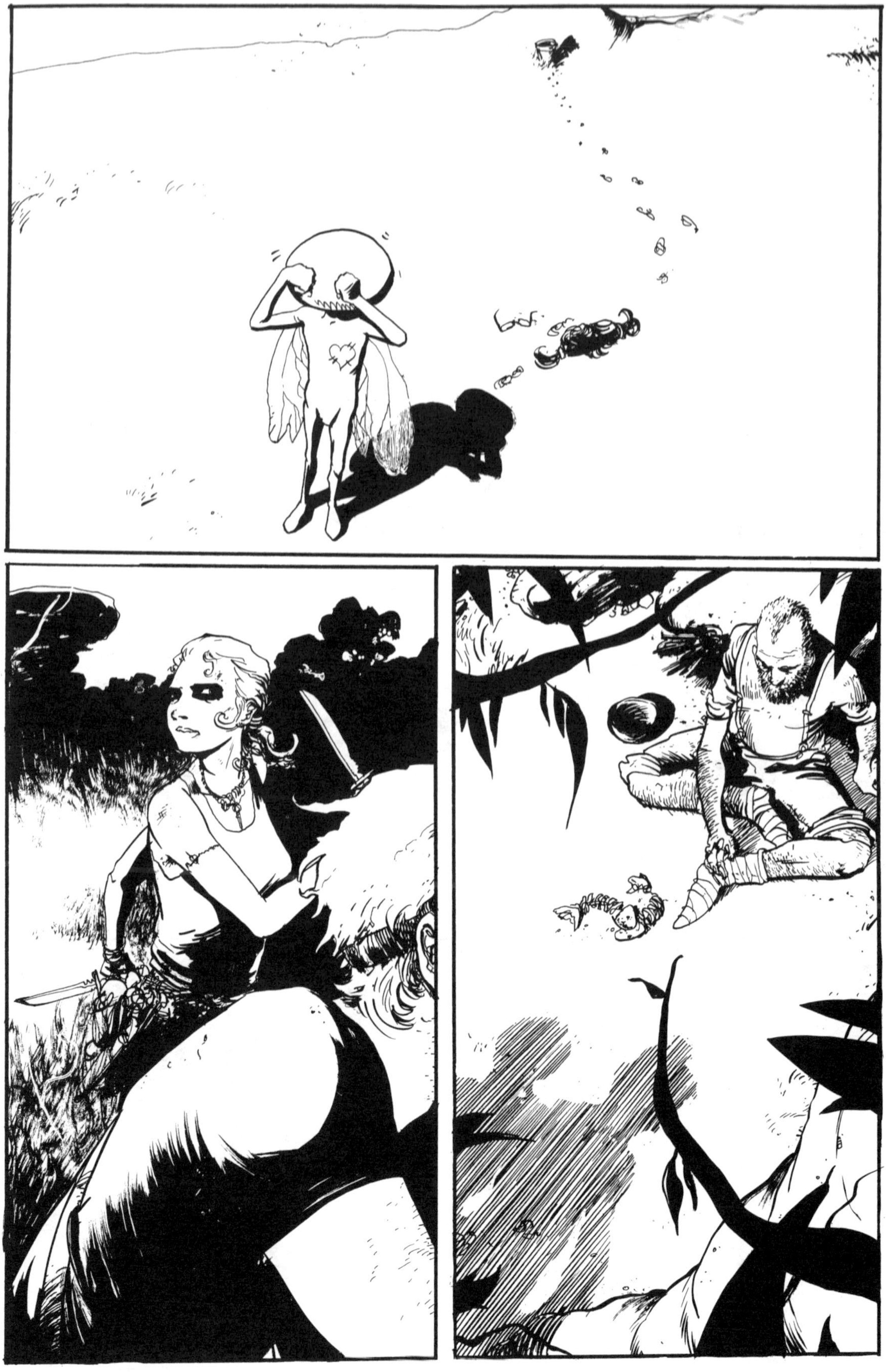

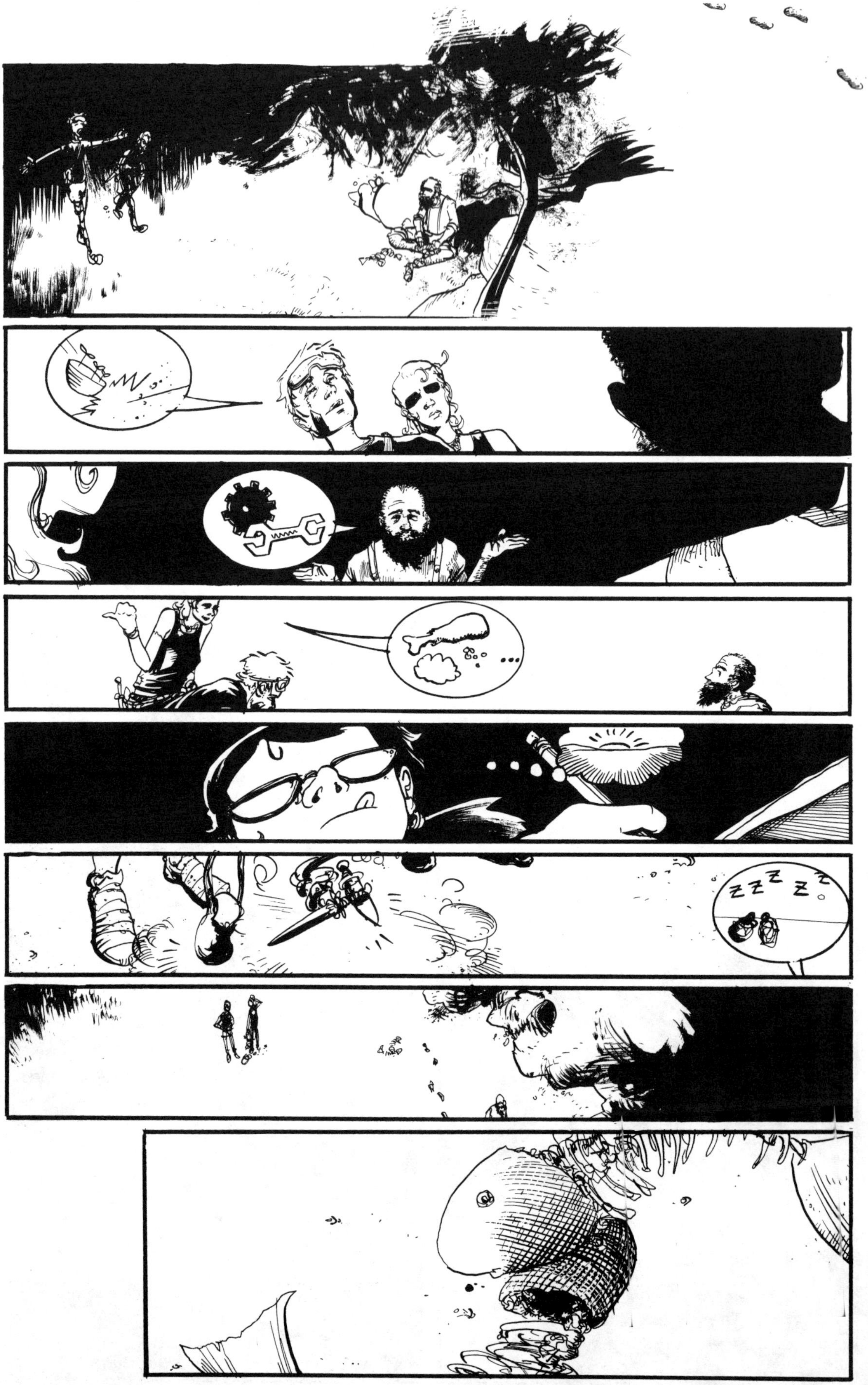
Z Z Z Z Z

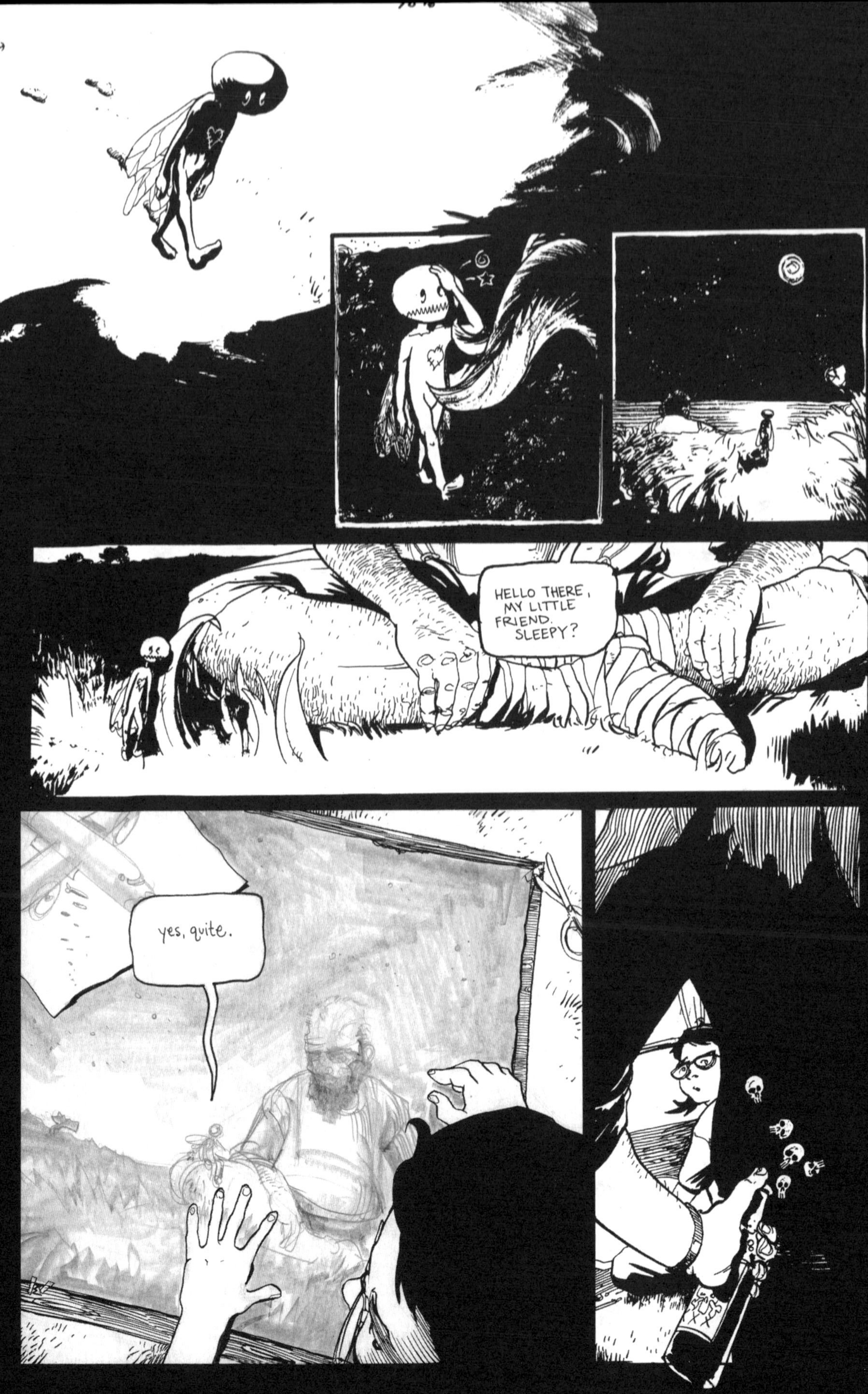
HELLO THERE, MY LITTLE FRIEND. SLEEPY?
yes, quite.

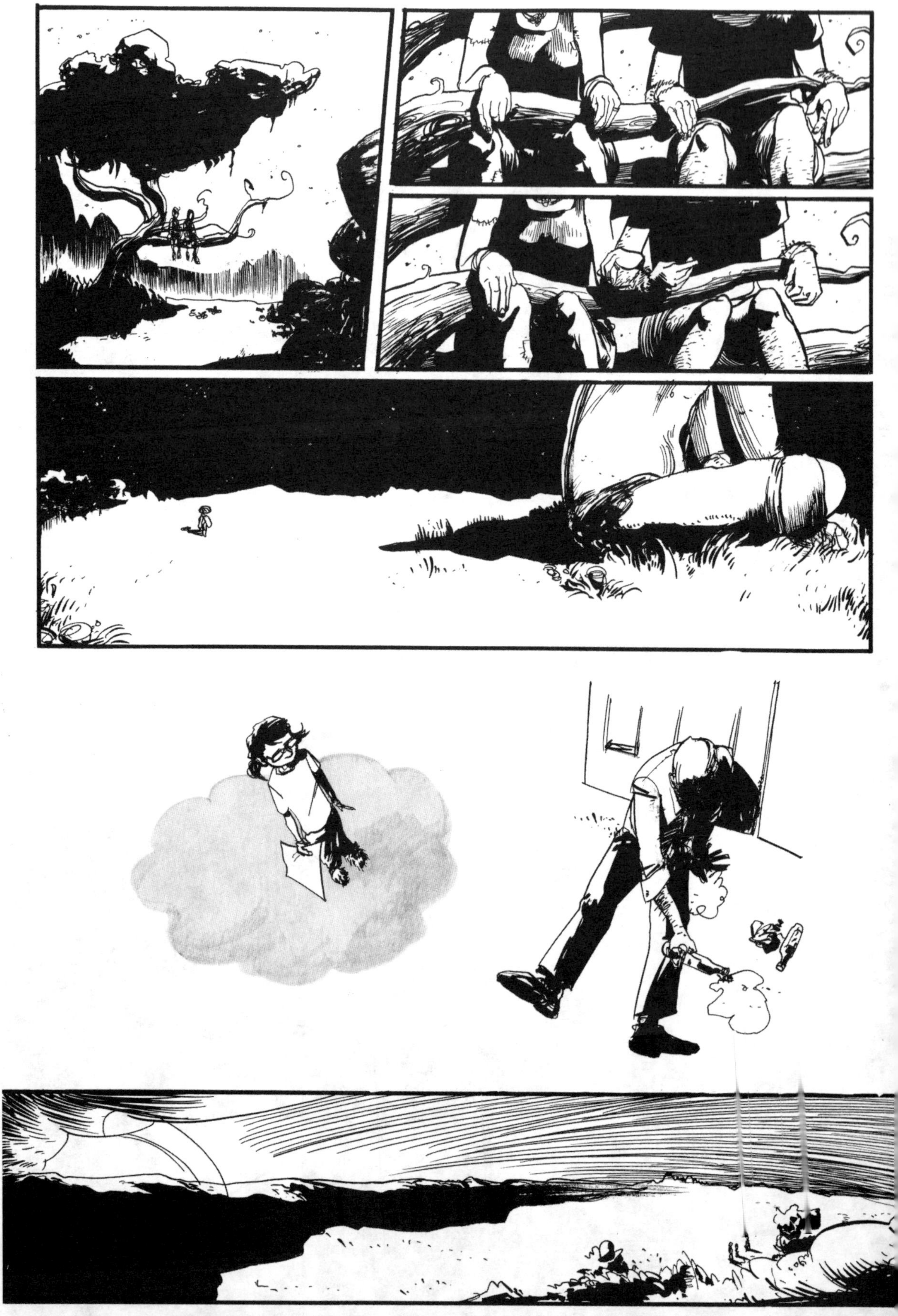

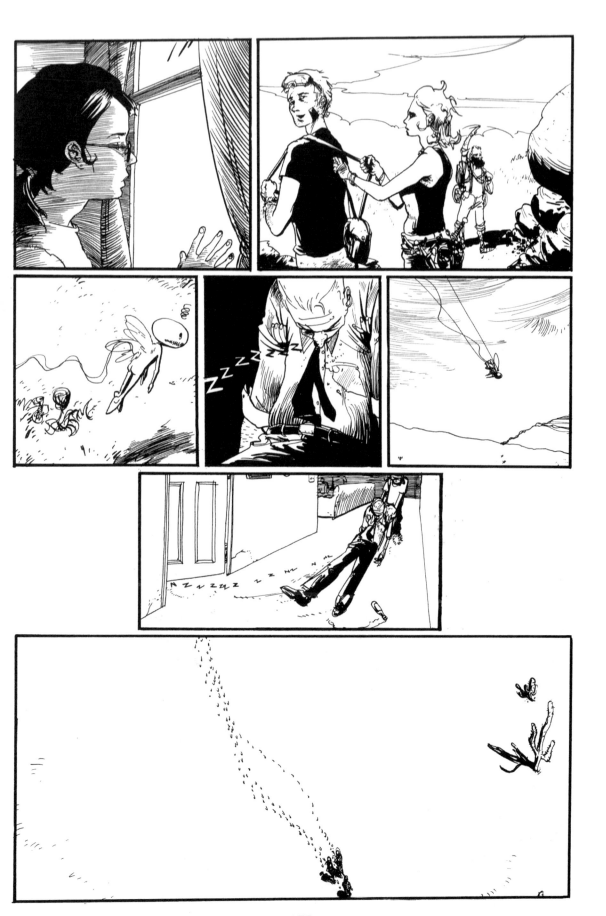

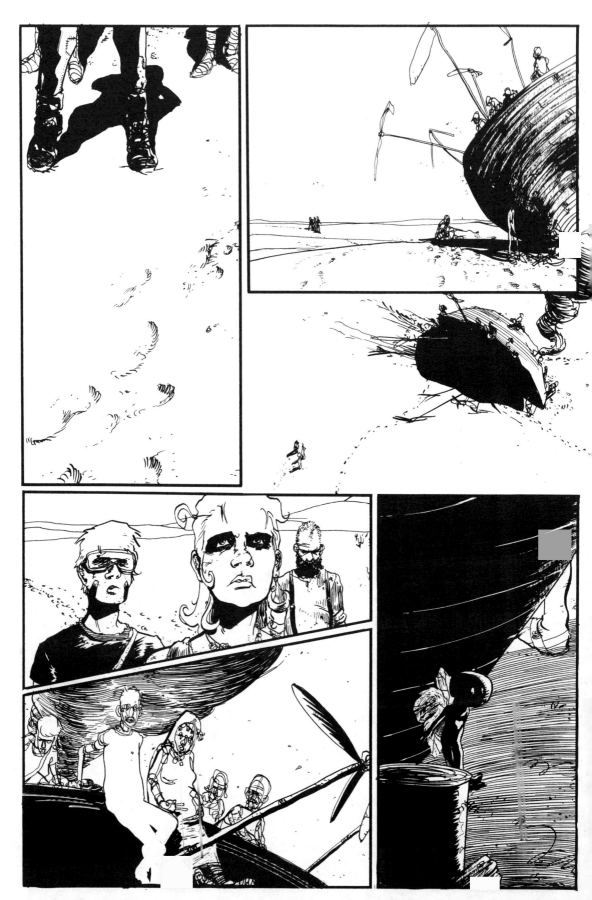

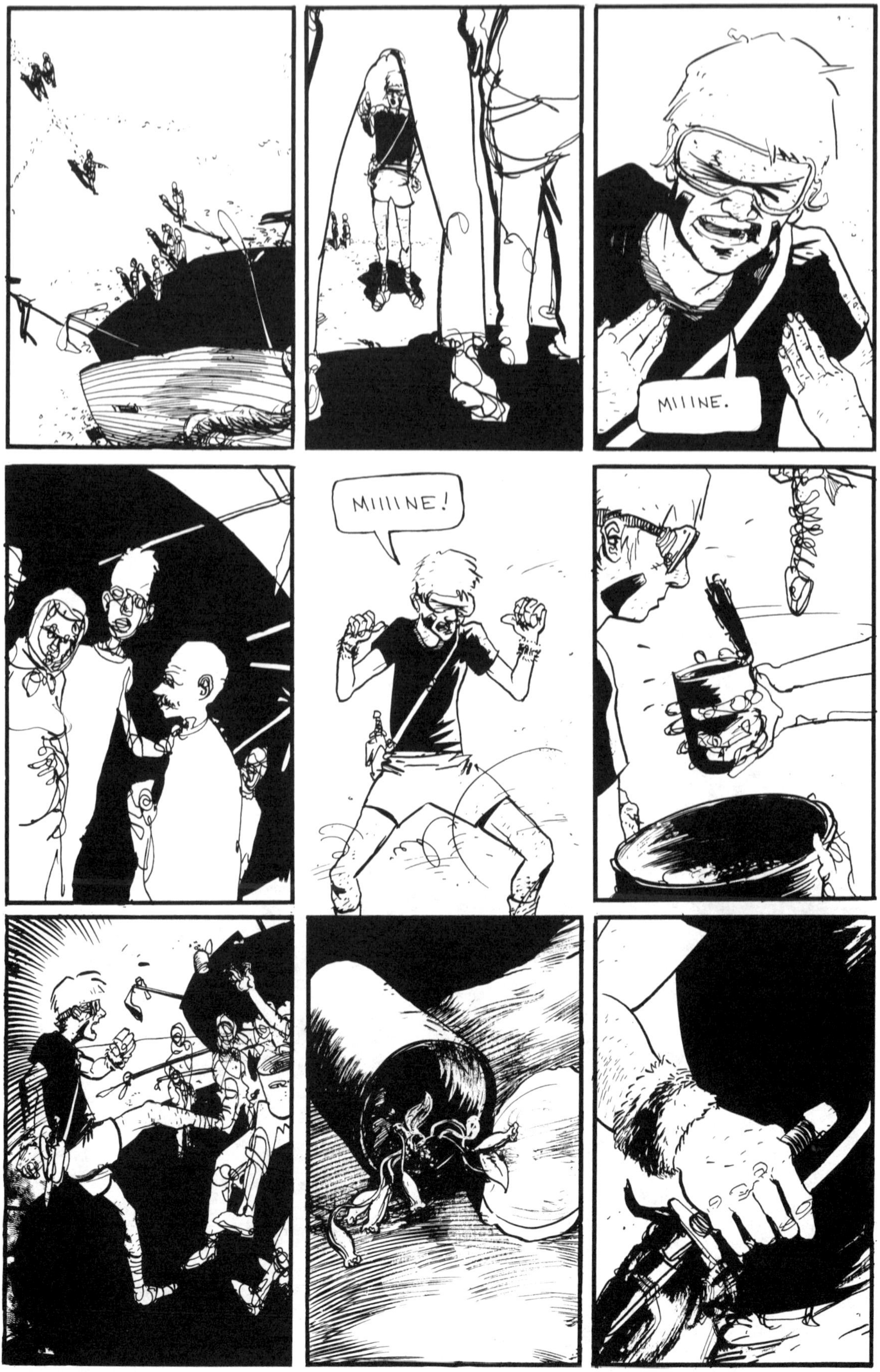
MIIINE.
MIIIINE!

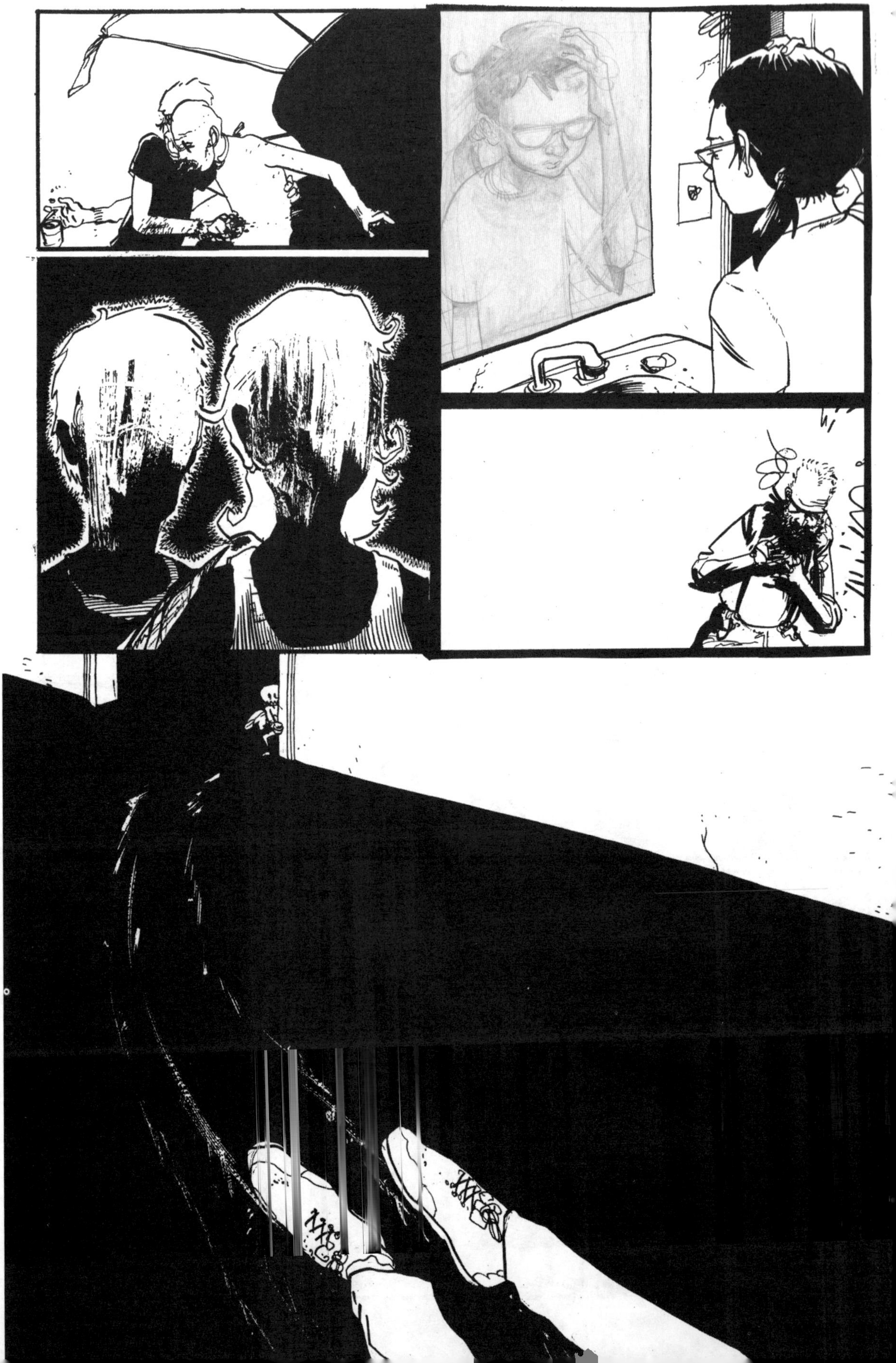

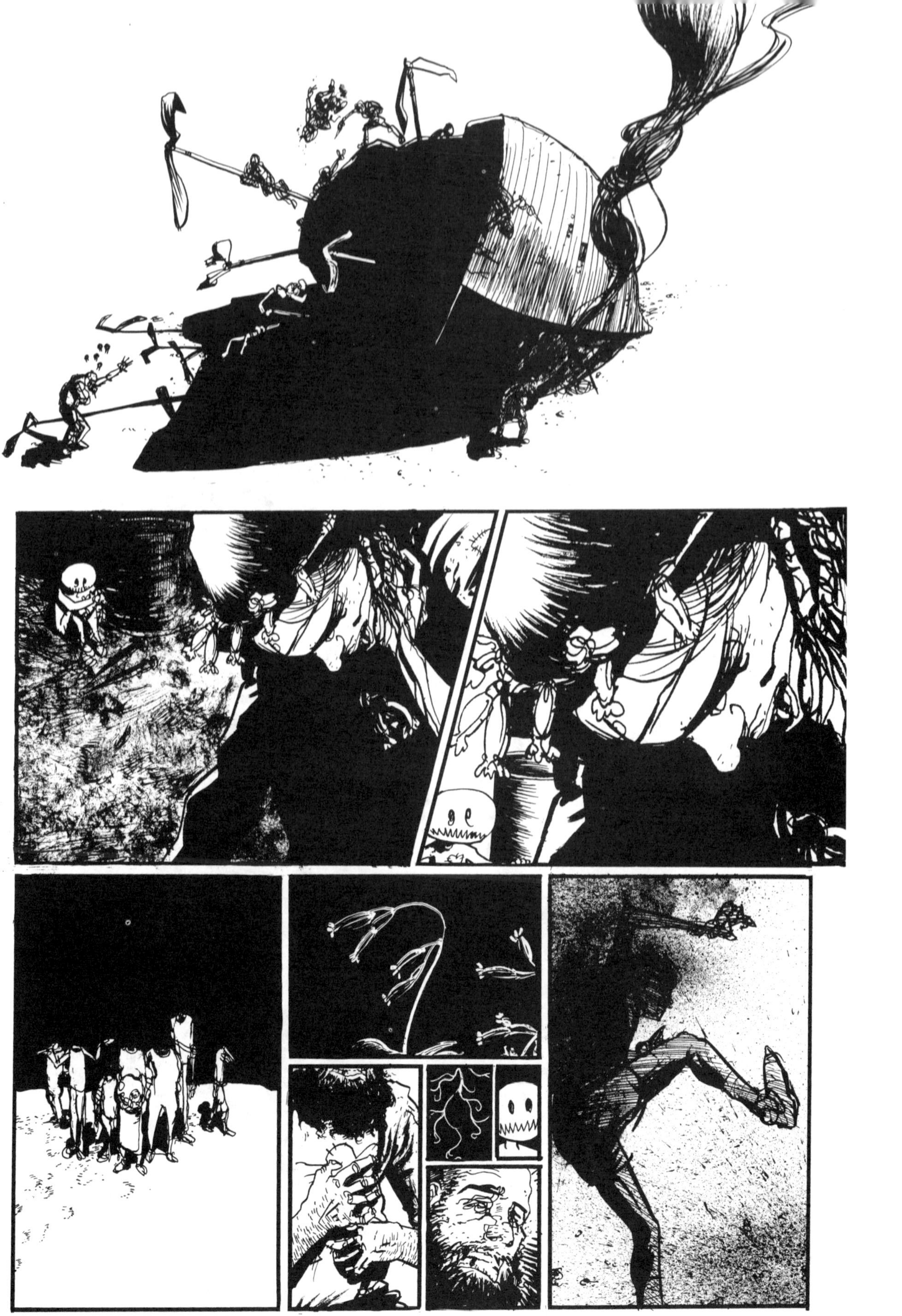

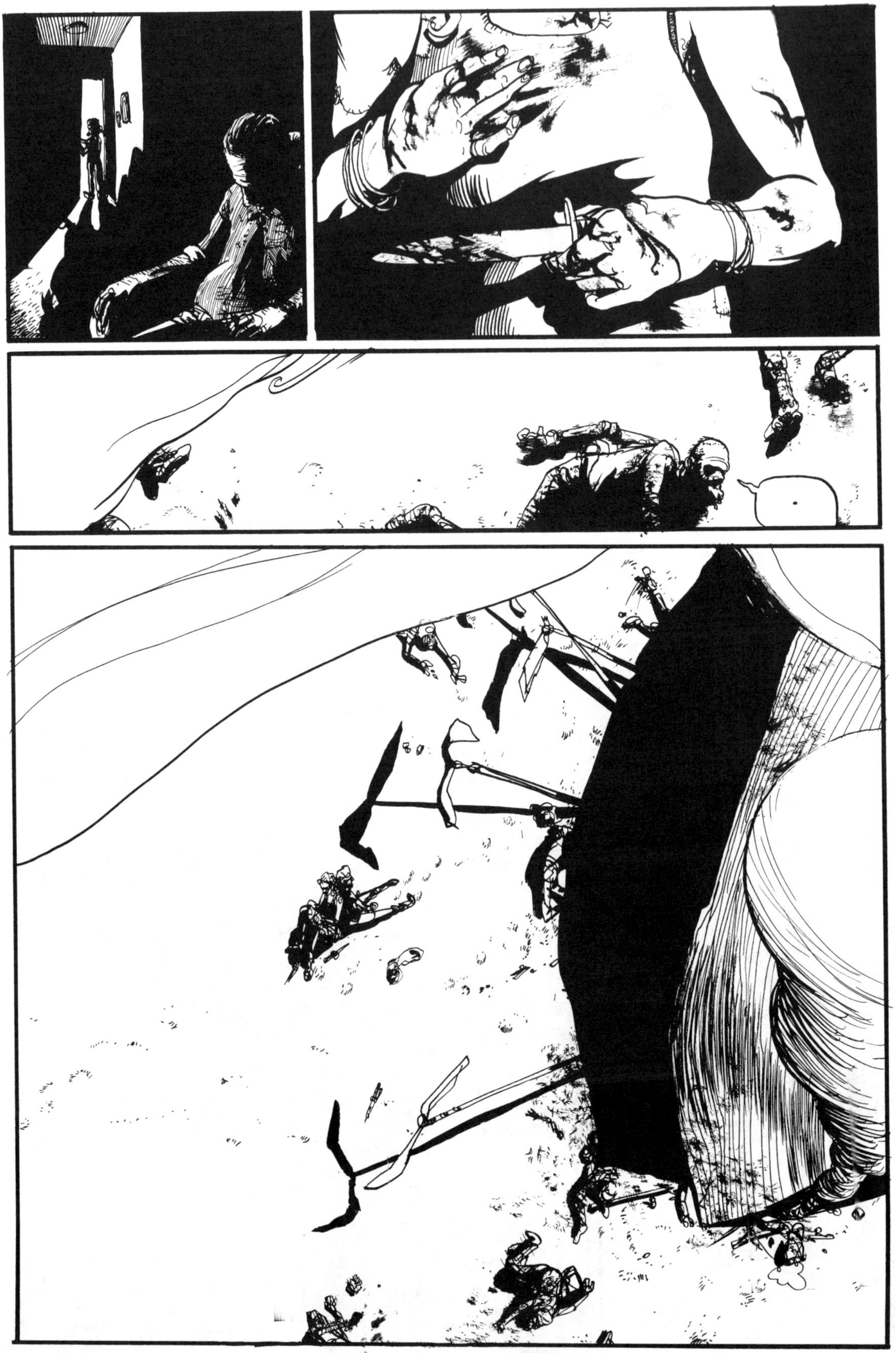

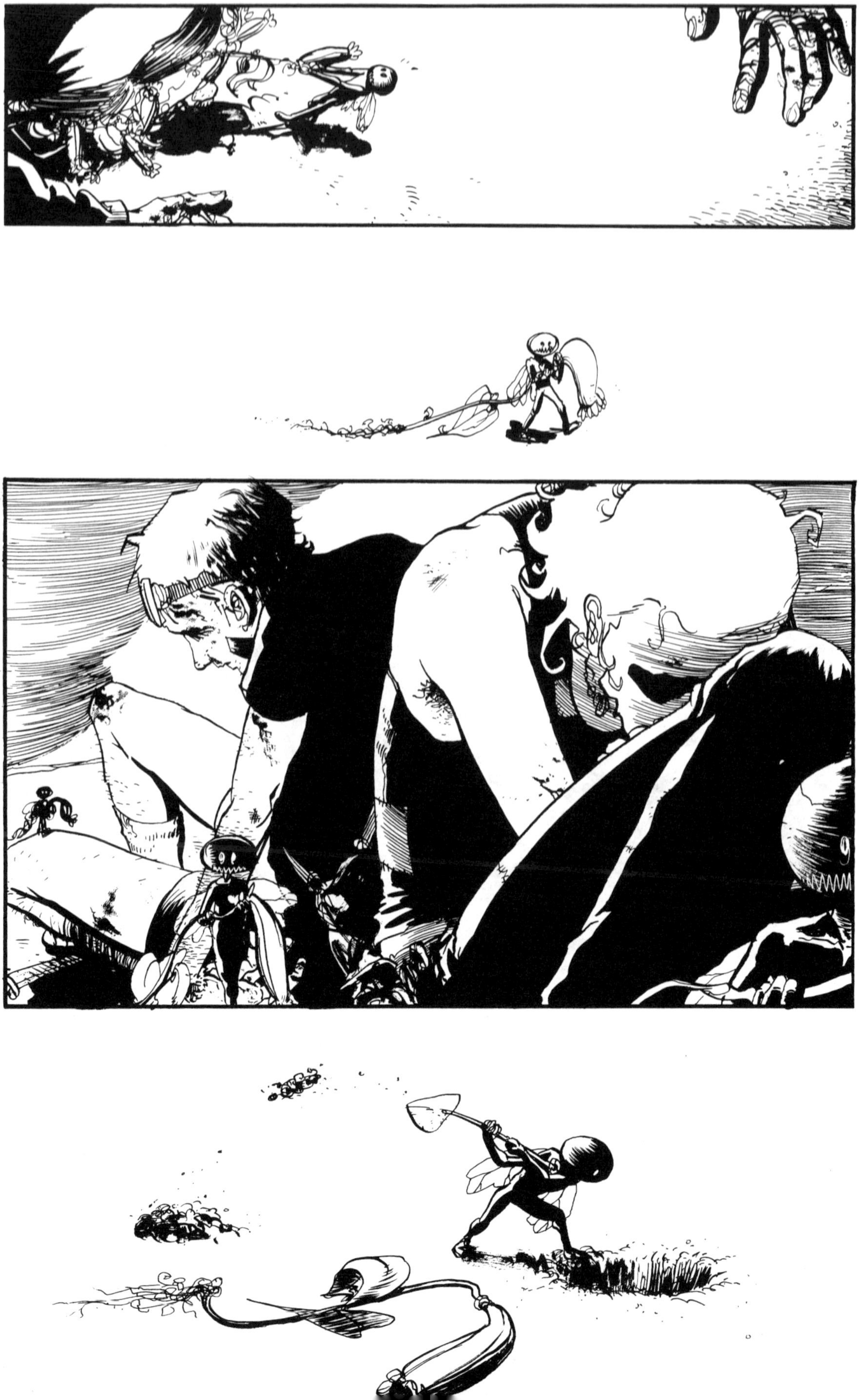

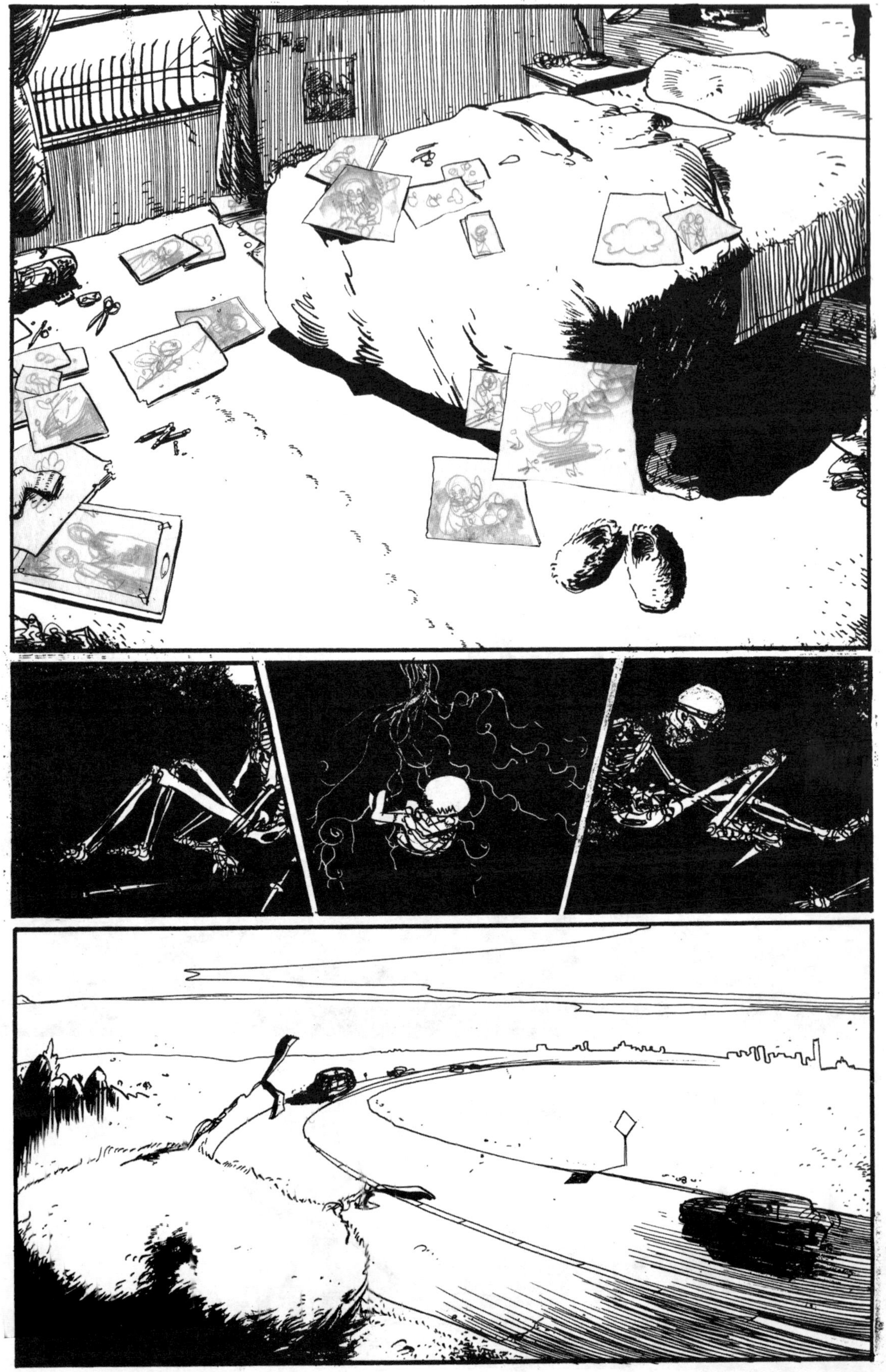

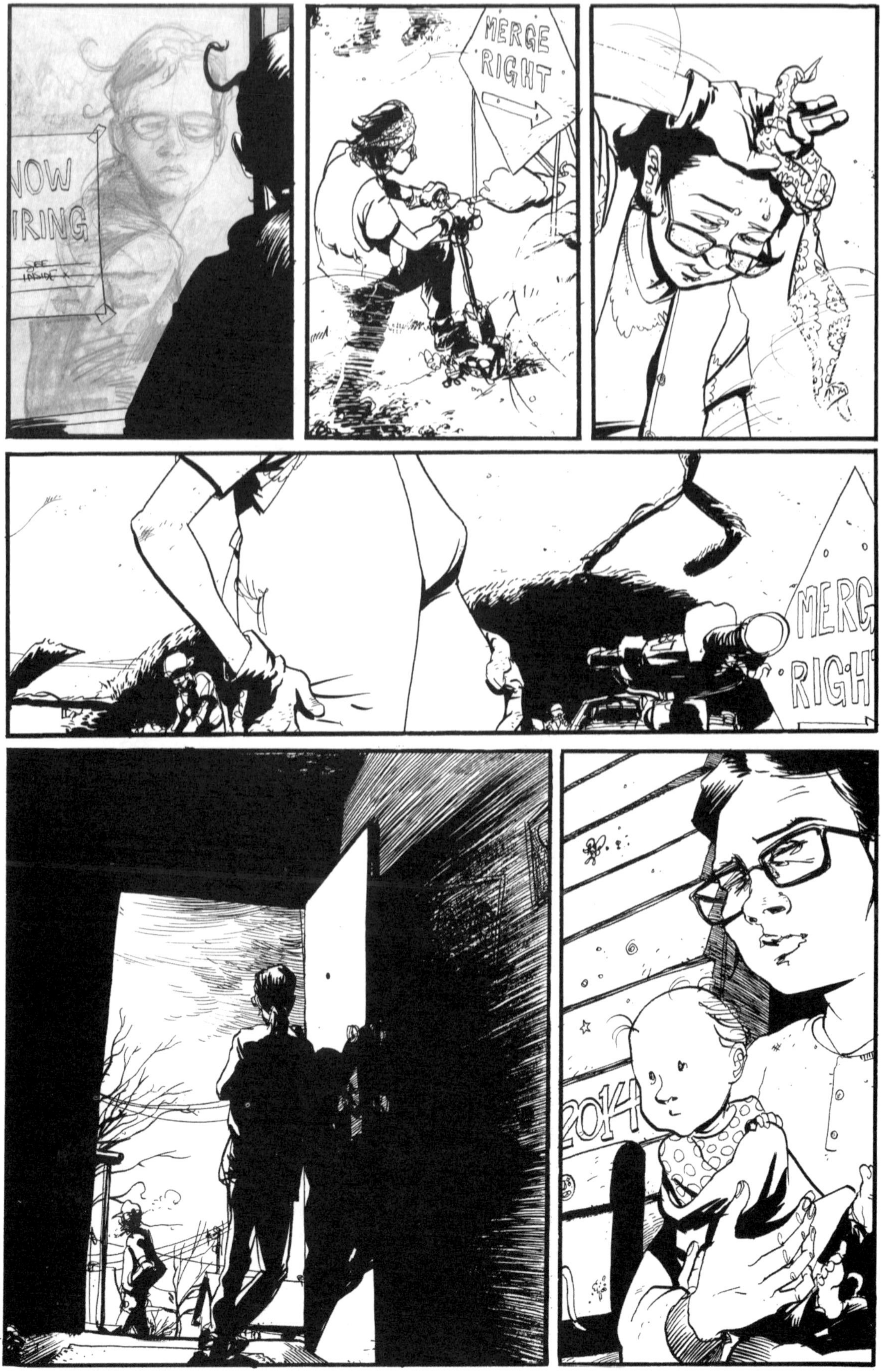
NOW
SEE INSIDE
MERGE RIGHT
2014

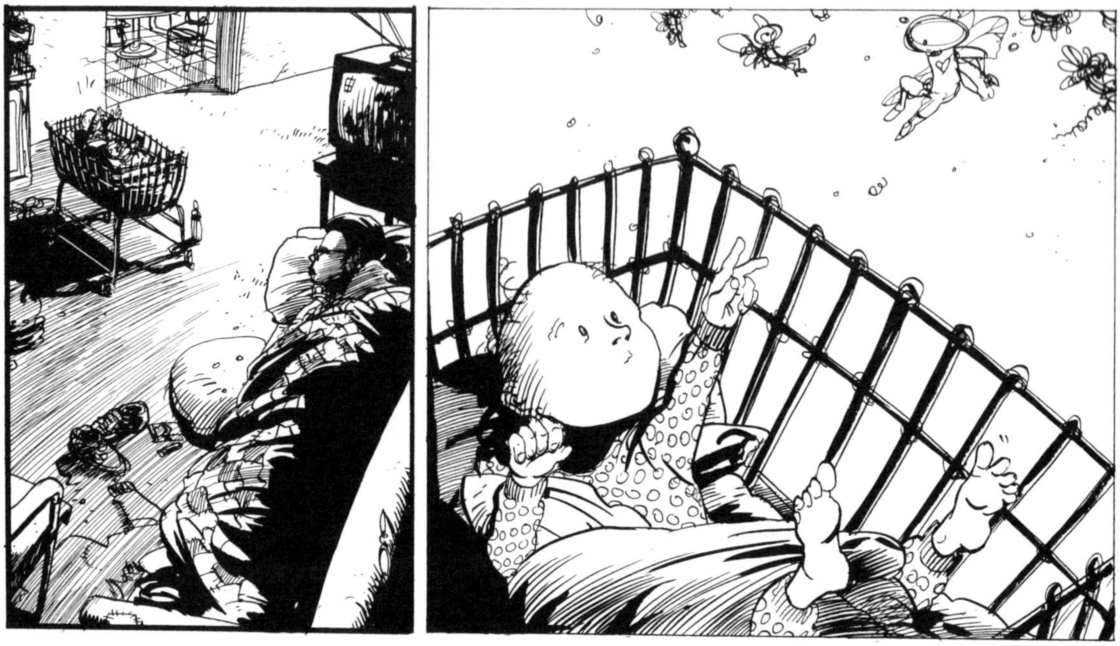

* something happened or happens just as it always does, and always will, just as freeways will always just be skeletons of the old storytellers, our lives laid across their tracks. sometimes we can't help but to feel small and i guess we're just terrified of disappearing after it all. it still keeps me up late, staring at the patterns on the ceiling, knowing that when all the songs have been sung it'll still never be quite enough. so when will we rise? when the words overcome us? when conflict becomes inspiration beyond us? our pockets are starved as the sky drops and we live on in dreams but that's the part of the story we cross out with a little grown-up smile or a roll of the eyes.
so when will we rise?
from now till we win
or until it's over..?

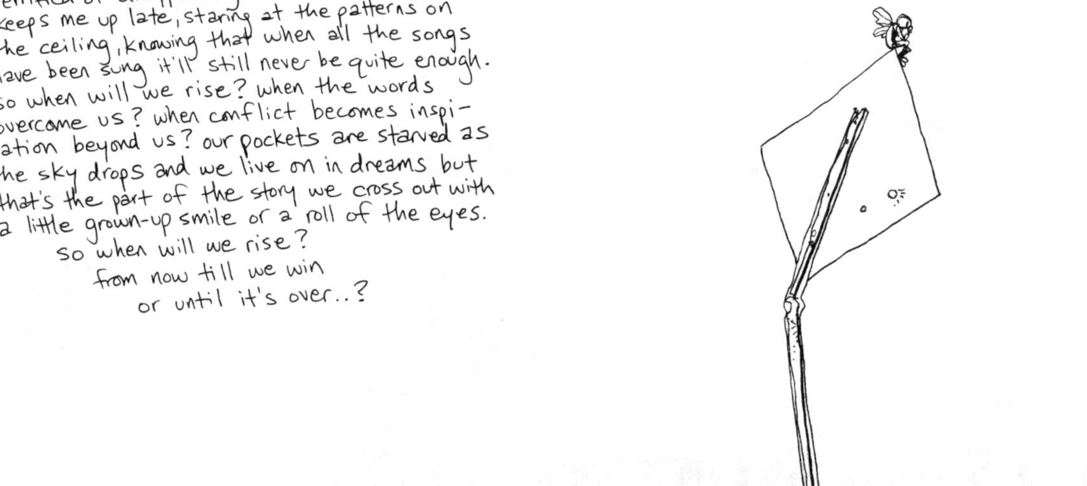

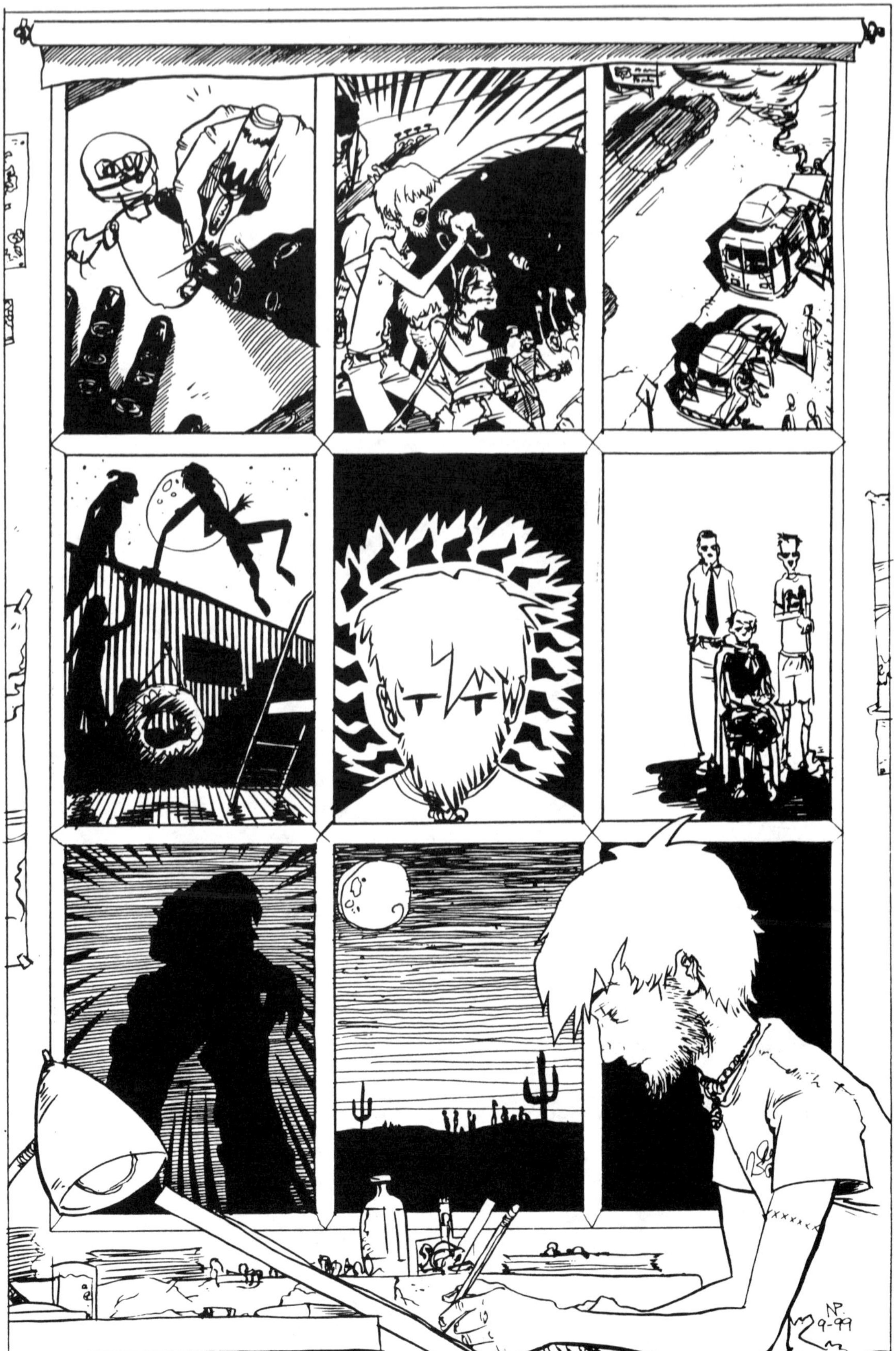
N.P.
9-99

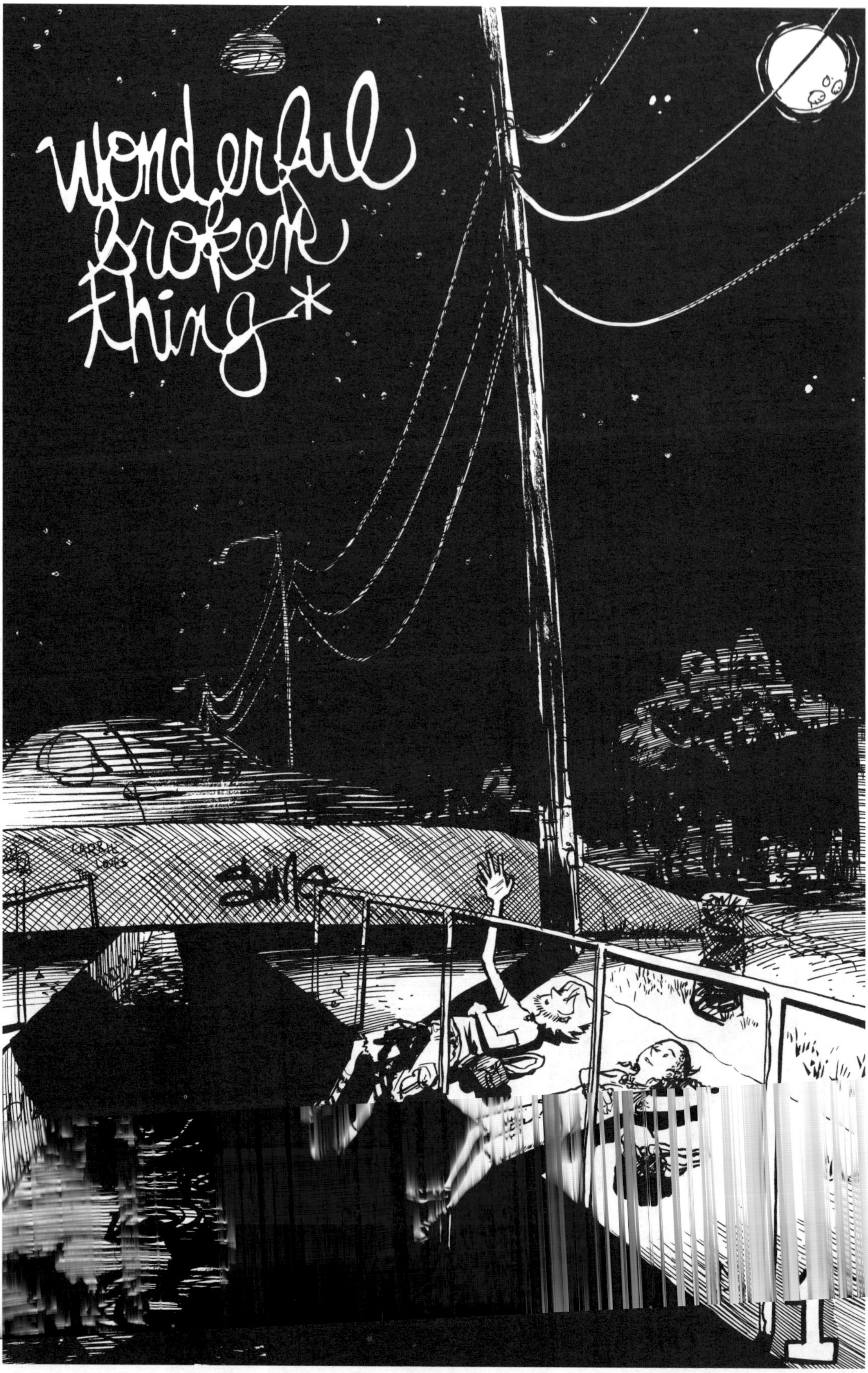
wonderful broken thing*

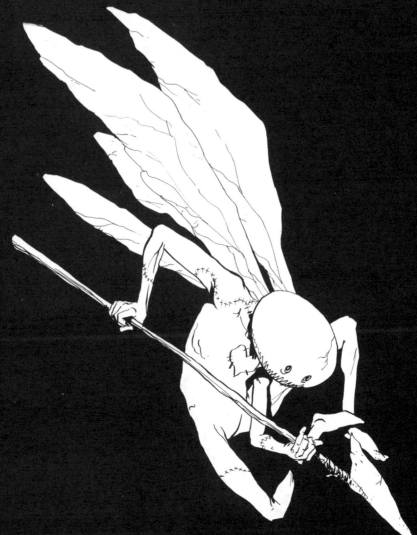

2

$2.95 in comic shops
$2.50 from the kids

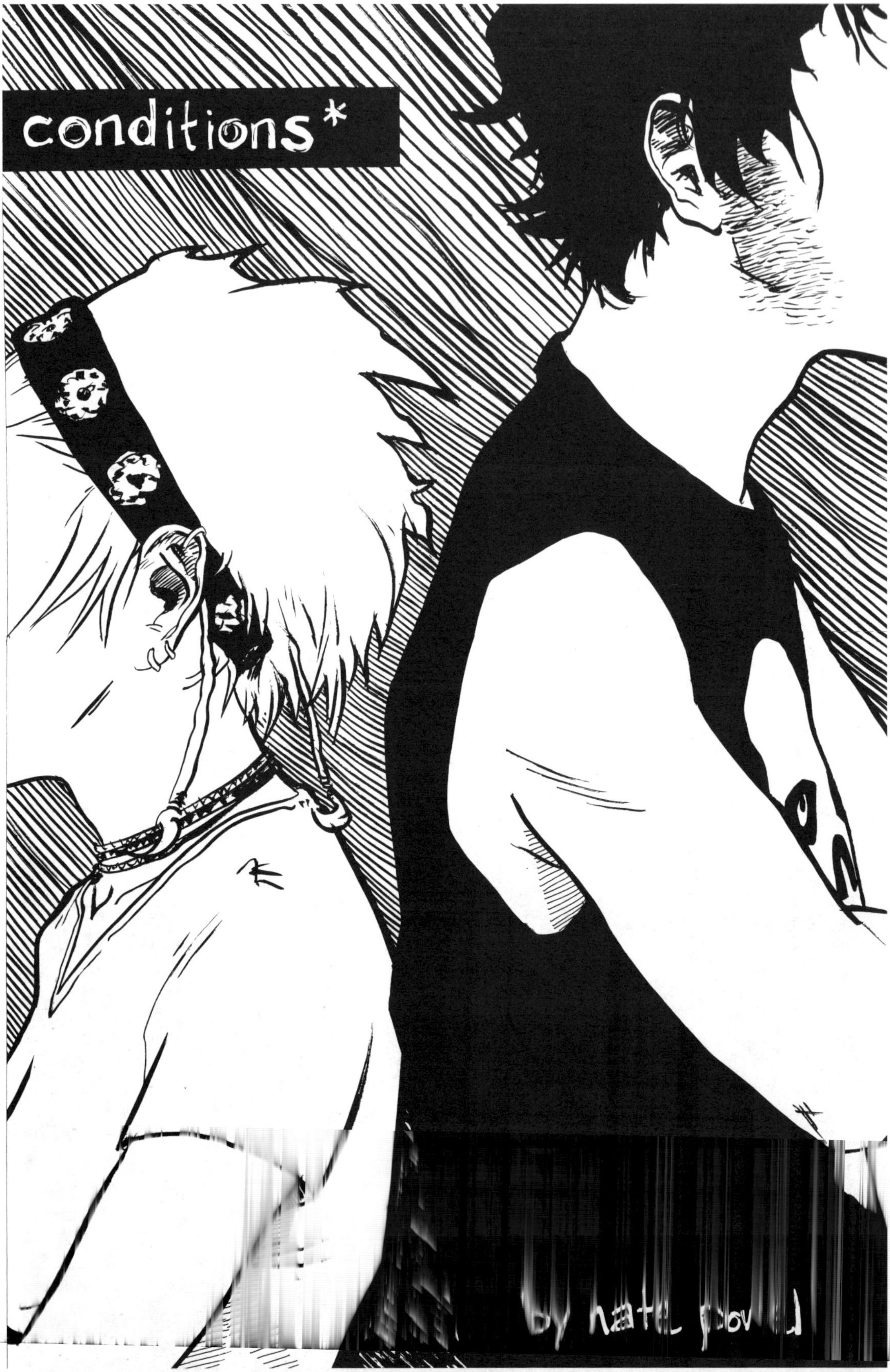
conditions*

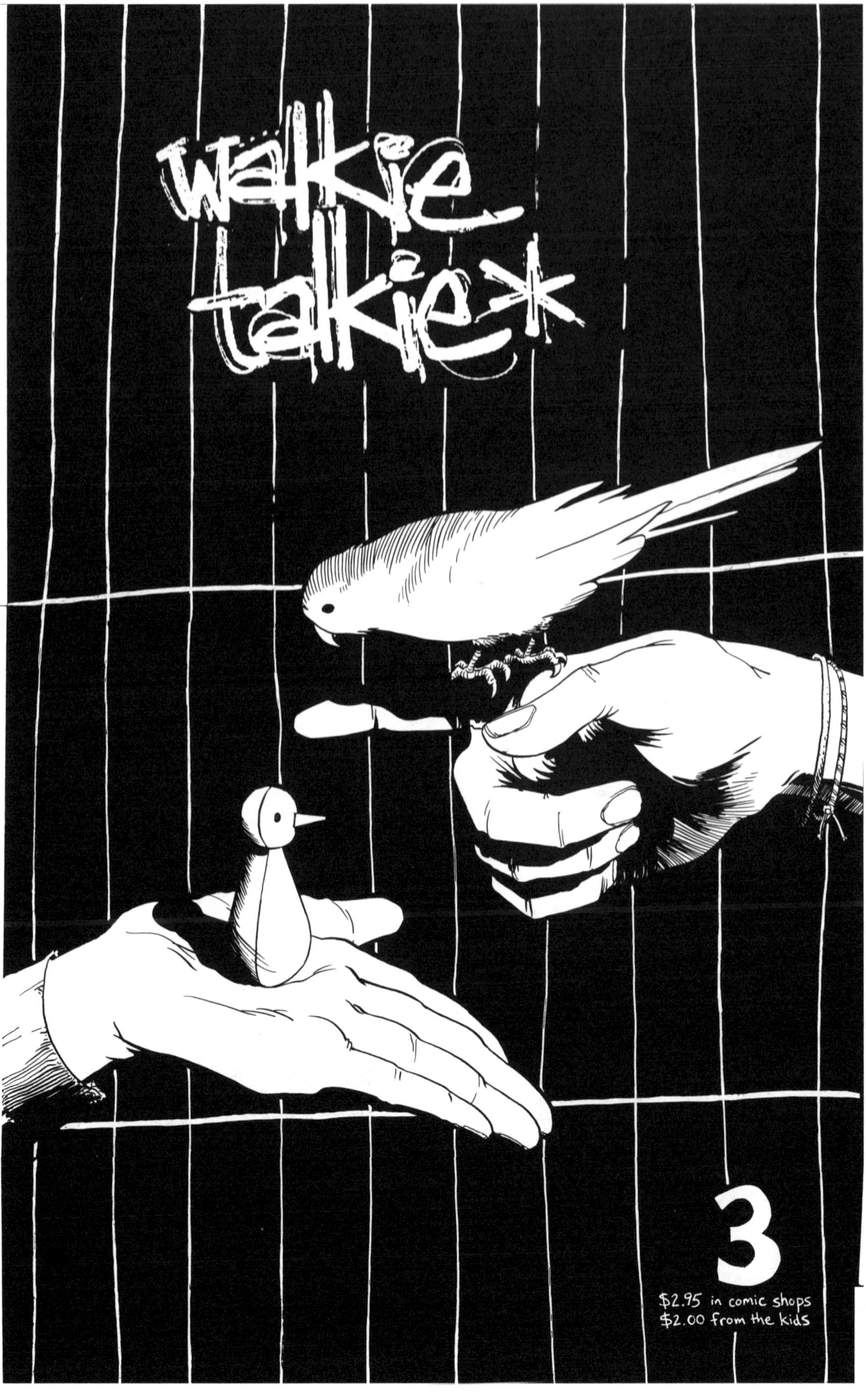
walkie talkie*
3
$2.95 in comic shops
$2.00 from the kids

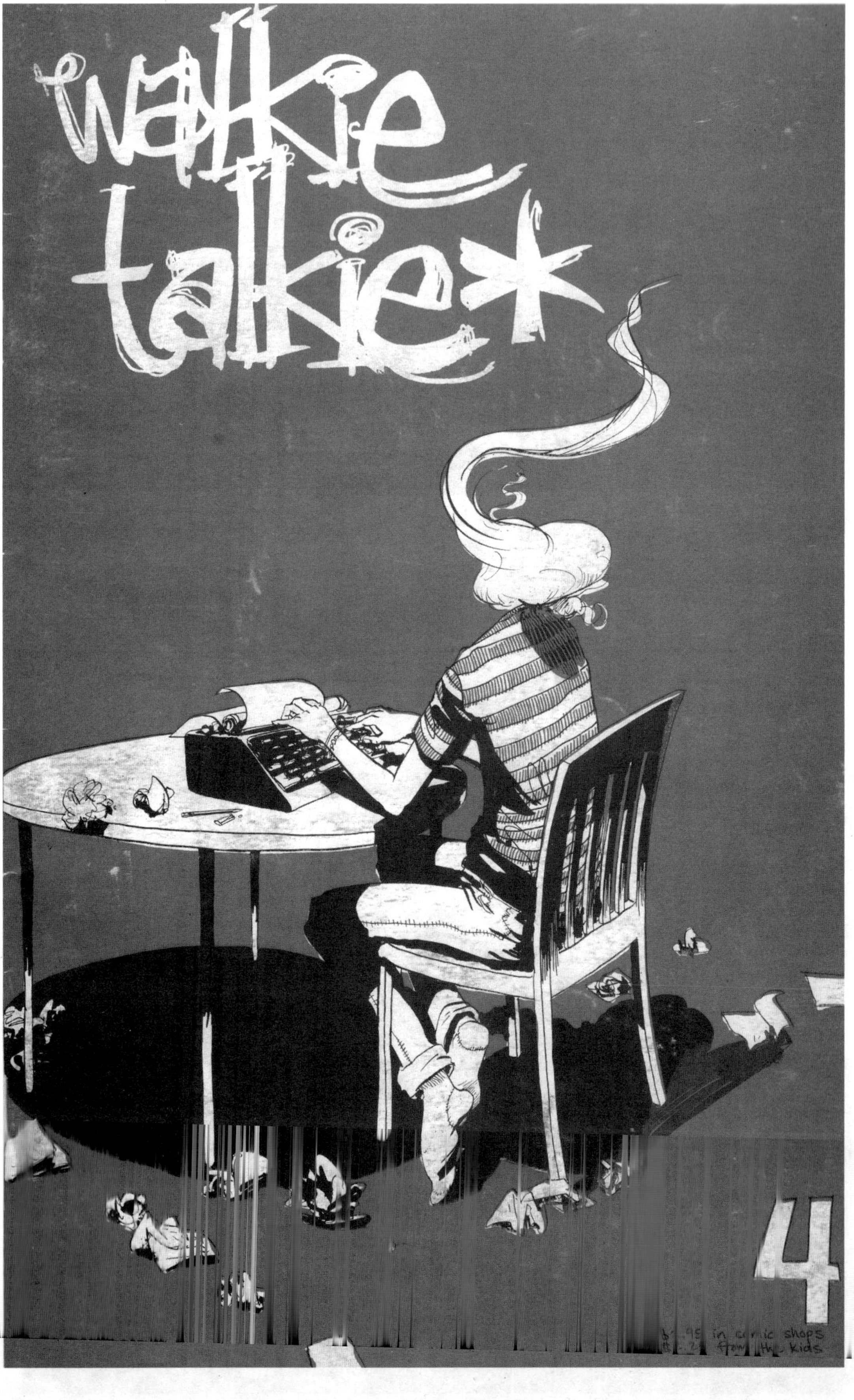
walkie talkie*
4
in comic shops
from the kids